BRITAIN'S LIBERAL EMPIRE 1897–1921

Also by Max Beloff

DREAM OF COMMONWEALTH, 1921–42 (Volume 2 of IMPERIAL SUNSET) (*in preparation*)

PUBLIC ORDER AND POPULAR DISTURBANCES, 1660–1714

THE FOREIGN POLICY OF SOVIET RUSSIA (2 volumes)

THOMAS JEFFERSON AND AMERICAN DEMOCRACY

SOVIET POLICY IN THE FAR EAST, 1944–51

THE AGE OF ABSOLUTISM, 1660–1815

FOREIGN POLICY AND THE DEMOCRATIC PROCESS

EUROPE AND THE EUROPEANS

THE GREAT POWERS

THE AMERICAN FEDERAL GOVERNMENT

NEW DIMENSIONS IN FOREIGN POLICY

THE UNITED STATES AND THE UNITY OF EUROPE

THE BALANCE OF POWER

THE FUTURE OF BRITISH FOREIGN POLICY

THE INTELLECTUAL IN POLITICS

THE GOVERNMENT OF THE UNITED KINGDOM (with G. R. Peele)

WARS AND WELFARE, 1914–1945

Edited by Max Beloff

THE FEDERALIST

MANKIND AND HIS STORY

THE DEBATE ON THE AMERICAN REVOLUTION

ON THE TRACK OF TYRANNY

L'EUROPE DU XIXe ET XXe SIECLE

AMERICAN POLITICAL INSTITUTIONS IN THE 1970s (with V. Vale)

BRITAIN'S LIBERAL EMPIRE
1897–1921

Volume 1 of IMPERIAL SUNSET

MAX BELOFF

Emeritus Professor of Government and Public Administration
University of Oxford

Second Edition

MACMILLAN
PRESS

First edition (Methuen) 1969
Second edition (Macmillan) 1987

Published by
THE MACMILLAN PRESS LTD
Houndmills, Basingstoke, Hampshire RG21 2XS
and London
Companies and representatives
throughout the world

Printed in Hong Kong

British Library Cataloguing in Publication Data
Beloff, Max
Imperial sunset. —2nd ed
Vol. 1: Britain's liberal empire 1897–1921
1. Great Britain—Colonies—History
2. Great Britain—Foreign relations
—20th century
I. Title
325'.32'0941   DA16

ISBN 0–333–44490–6
ISBN 0–333–44491–4 Pbk

for Michael and Jeremy

CONTENTS

vii

CONTENTS

PREFACE TO THE SECOND EDITION

When the first edition of this book was published in 1969 I had hoped that a sequel would follow very rapidly. For a variety of reasons my work on this project was interrupted. I now hope if all goes well to produce the second volume of 'Imperial Sunset' for publication in 1988. Meanwhile the republication of the first volume gives me an opportunity to look at the period that has elapsed since 1969 and to see what additional insights it provides in respect of the problems I undertook to investigate.

Such insights derive from two sources. There has been a large volume of historical scholarship devoted to all aspects of the imperial history of the period with which I was dealing, making use in large part of materials that became available subsequently to the works upon which I myself had to rely. In the second place there have been the events in the ongoing history of Britain's relations with the rest of the Commonwealth and with the rest of the world that cannot but affect one's judgement of their antecedents.

One reviewer of the first edition complained that I had made too much of the debate over Britain's possible entry into the European Communities which had become 'an intellectual and political bore', and felt that the knowledge that the EEC represented one of the 'author's ultimate guidelines' cast 'its own shadow' across the book as a whole.[1] On that score, I feel time has justified my original conception. Britain has become a member of the European Communities and with every year that passes, this fact becomes of increasing significance in its economic and political aspects and in its impact upon Britain's domestic affairs. On the other hand, the Commonwealth has clearly been downgraded in the list of Britain's priorities and with important divergencies of opinion developing among its member governments and with Britain occupying a less central role in the affairs of many member countries, even its perpetuation has been called into question. It seems more than ever reasonable to look at the development from British Empire into British Commonwealth and (latterly) from British Commonwealth into Commonwealth as a reaction not only to internal developments

ix

within the British system but also to the changing balances in economic and military power to which Britain's rulers were responding. In respect of that approach I see no need to change the framing of my original inquiry.

Domestic as well as international developments have also inevitably produced a new perspective upon the earlier period. A whole school of historical interpretation has grown up, of which Mr Correlli Barnett was the pioneer which sees in the decline of British power the consequence of an inadequate attention to industrial development, and the Empire-Commonwealth as, if anything, a burden rather than an asset to the home country.[2] Or again, the growing salience of race-relations as an issue of internal British politics has produced an examination of earlier British attitudes on questions of race and an effort to link the ideologies and practices of Empire and Commonwealth to changing conceptions of race.[3] These in turn are shown to have rested in large part upon developments in the natural and human sciences and particularly in anthropology which to some extent bridges that divide. The impact of such ideas as well as of changes in the religious outlook draws attention to the role of universities and in particular of Oxford as the main source in the pre-1914 period of the Empire's administrators and a principal source of its missionaries and teachers.[4]

The way in which one looks at these and other aspects of the imperial decline will indeed in part be a question of generations. A schoolboy growing up as I did, with much of the map coloured red and with memories of several visits to the British Empire Exhibition at Wembley at the age of twelve, must see things differently from the way in which they are seen by those whose most impressionable years fell during the height of the period of 'decolonisation' after the second world war.[5] And for today's youngsters Britain is no more than an offshore island with a cluster of tiny dependencies showing their peaks above the enveloping ocean like signposts to a lost continent.[6]

Geographical perspective may also give important differences of emphasis. It is not surprising that the author of important books offering a very critical handling of British imperialism should have spent much of his teaching career outside Britain.[7] Others, particularly the non-British and particularly perhaps Americans with their inbuilt anti-imperial bias, may see the British imperial retreat as only part of the general abandonment by European nations from the attempt to control the destinies of other continents, and argue that in the national histories of the peoples concerned, the period of empire may well come to be looked at as a mere passing interruption to their own indigenous development.[8]

With an abundance of new materials and of new perspectives, it is not surprising that most writers have concentrated on illuminating parts of the story through individual monographs rather than attempting a no doubt premature synthesis.[9] Had he not died all too early it is probable that the major contribution to a general view of the subject would have been made by John Gallagher. His Ford Lectures suggest that he would have followed up the thesis present in his earlier work that the Empire should not be seen as a separate aspect of the British presence but as an integral part of a larger world system.[10] With that in mind the importance of naval power upon which that system rested has received renewed emphasis.[11] A Canadian historian has seen the Empire as having been made possible only by Britain's maritime predominance in the first three quarters of the nineteenth century and has having been doomed once that predominance was challenged.[12] Yet to illustrate how far we are from an agreed version of what caused the ultimate weakening, another Canadian historian, a disciple of Mackinder rather than Mahan, argues that it was Britain's land empire in India that was the principal element in Britain's strength and its protection the key to the understanding of British diplomacy.[13]

John Gallagher was also a major influence in another development of the historiography of the latter years of Empire by directing attention to the fact that while the impulses to Empire–whether economic or strategic–may indeed come from the centre, their working-out on the ground depends upon an ability to identify those classes, elites and personalities through whom they can work–no Empire without collaborators! The natural impact of such a perspective is to give more weight to the contribution of the periphery and to see the imperial experience as a joint one, between coloniser and colonised.

Its most impressive fruits can be seen in the products of the Cambridge school of historians of India,[14] but studies of other parts of the dependent Empire have also profited from this approach.[15] It has also been increasingly the case that such history is written in, and by citizens of, the now independent countries that made up the Empire in the period covered by this volume; and their contributions are inevitably affected both by their varied commitments to their own national perceptions of their past and by the domestic imperatives of the present. The literature of Empire is thus both much larger and more difficult to grasp as a whole than when this book was first envisaged.

The strength of British political biography was of great assistance in focusing on the decisions that had to be made by government in the years dealt with in this volume. Only two major biographies of British statesmen have been added to the list since it was completed–Martin Gilbert's continuation of Randolph Churchill's life of Winston Churchill and the invaluable companion volumes of documents; and Stephen Roskill's magisterial biography of Maurice Hankey, the only major civil servant of the period to emerge from the obscurity with which Whitehall usually manages to envelop its denizens.[1b] But the publication of the second volume of the political biography of William Morris Hughes has enabled the influence of the leading Australian statesman of the time to be tackled alongside that of Laurier, Borden and Smuts.[17] While Curzon has yet to find a fully adequate biographer, there is much to be gleaned about India in his time and about India's own overseas Empire in the Persian Gulf from the letters of his wife, a book of quite unusual quality.[18]

One figure of the period who has had much biographical attention who was only marginal to imperial affairs but whose career and writings are reflective of much that went on was the economist John Maynard Keynes.[19] And the vicissitudes of socialist and particularly Fabian opinion where Empire was concerned are illuminated by the mass of material now published on Sydney and Beatrice Webb.[20] Unfortunately the consistent interest of Ramsay MacDonald in imperial and colonial affairs–he was to be the only Prime Minister until Churchill with serious first-hand knowledge of the Empire–has not much attracted the interest of his most recent biographer.[21]

Sydney Webb was himself to be, as was MacDonald, much concerned with a critical stage in the history of the British mandate in Palestine. Most of the history indeed of Britain's short-lived Middle Eastern Empire does fall beyond the scope of the present volume but it does deal with the wartime negotiations with the Allies and the Arabs and with the Balfour Declaration on Palestine as well as with the negotiation of the mandates themselves and the decisions made in 1921 about the handling of this new area of British responsibility. It is therefore worth noting that on all these topics there has been a good deal of research subsequent to the completion of this book which although it does not call into question the general account and interpretation of these events would now enable more definition to be given to the picture presented.[22]

New materials and more refined scholarship, however, remain subordinate to the changes brought about by new perspectives arising from the possibility of putting the British experience into a wider context. For the rulers of the British Empire in the period covered by this volume, what they had to guide them was partly the experience of the Empire's own past, notably the lessons to be learned from the loss of the American colonies which had already played their part in the evolution of the old Dominions. Perhaps more significant was the fact that their education had, except for the younger ones who had been exposed to the new vogue for modern history, been heavily biased towards the classics. It was the Greek city states and their colonies, the Athenian Empire and above all the Roman example of imperialism with which they were familiar, or believed themselves to be, which provided many of the vital categories into which they organised their subsequent experience.[23]

We can now derive some illumination from the parallel and experience of the French Empire different in its more assimilationist philosophy and to a major extent in the manner of its winding up as well as in its legacy both at home and overseas.[24] But an even greater impact upon our thinking must have been made by the experience of the two 'super-powers' whose world systems have superseded those of the west European imperial powers. To look at the Soviet Union as a multi-national empire is in itself illuminating, but it is derived from a different order of experience from that of the European powers whose expansion was overseas. More significant has been the still not fully chronicled and relatively recent establishment of Soviet influence in parts of the Caribbean, Central America and Africa. How much more effective one must ask is Marxism as a binding link than the liberal doctrines which were all that Britain had on offer? John Gallagher's belief that the imperialist prefers influence to formal rule would certainly be confirmed by Soviet experience. A classic case would appear to be that now provided by Afghanistan, a country whose political orientation was contested between Russia and Britain from early in the nineteenth century to the demise of the British Raj in India. The spectacle that we have seen of Soviet influence needing to be upheld by military force and indeed confirmed by military campaigns on some scale does point to one case at least where Marxism has not provided the cement needed to permit influence to be as useful as sovereignty.

Much more importance is rightly attached to the experience of the United States since its participation in the second world war enabled it to expand its influence world-wide, partly as a matter of national policy and partly, as in the history of other Empires, through a series of accidents.

It was the essence of the United States' case against the British Empire as developed in particular from the 1930s onwards that its existence was an affront to the two principles that should govern international life —self-determination in politics and non-discrimination in matters of trade. In the period that followed the defeat of the Nazis and the Japanese, and even before the struggle was decided, these principles produced intermittent pressures upon the United States' own allies–the French, the Dutch and the British. But when the Americans were confronted with the practices of Soviet anti-imperialist rhetoric and found that in order to resist them the United States required, or believed itself to require, a political and military presence in various parts of the world, they discovered that the absence of any doctrine as to how to behave in such circumstances and of any but the most limited experience of ruling outside their own borders made it difficult to establish to their own satisfaction the principles of a new Pax Americana. It was thus fated to reproduce the experience of the often reluctant imperialists of an earlier period without the self-confidence that had assisted the British and French pro-consuls or their masters at home. Furthermore because of the nature of the American political system and the diffusion of power within it, as well as the more overt nature of pressures upon government, even of a purely economic kind, the study of this American experience may assist in framing new questions in respect of our materials for the study of the British Empire's high tide.[25]

Meanwhile however we must expect that at least in this country, Imperial history like the rest of British history will be viewed essentially through the 'whig' interpretation, that is to say as a progress from less to more enlightenment and from central authority to wider liberty, that is to say from Empire to Commonwealth even as now defined and as now behaving. Thus the most learned of living British imperial historians, when republishing in 1982 his major work of synthesis, reprinted without reservation the preface to the original edition dated 1968. The Commonwealth, he wrote, 'was the heir of Empire, and imperial influences bore closely upon its earlier growth, but it developed a life and made a contribution to political thought and relations, not only distinct from those of Empire, but in many respects historically opposed to them.'[26] This contribution seemed valuable, no doubt during the period when the word was coming into fashion before 1921 and for subsequent decades when it was still proper to talk about the British Commonwealth. It is certainly harder to argue that this has been the case since it became just *the* Commonwealth after 1949. It may be possible to agree that it had its uses during the period of transition to independence on the part of formerly subject peoples but even the enthusiast for the association could by 1981 suggest that the Commonwealth might have thereby lost its raison d'être, even if he could add speculatively that perhaps it still had 'other causes to advance'. Where I would disagree is that to take these matters into account is to be 'subject to the tyranny of the contemporary'.[27] One must do one's best not to attribute to men in the past ideas which they did not have and knowledge of the future which is denied to all of us. What I believe was intended by the generations whose work I am attempting to analyse and explain, was a transformation of the Liberal Empire which is the subject of the present volume to a situation in which a combination of autonomy and a perception of the need for co-operation at the centre would enable even countries which could not be regarded as mere offshoots of Britain but as having their own individual personalities to be part of the new system, the British Commonwealth. It is even clearer now than when I began working on this topic over twenty years ago that this belief was an illusion, if an honourable one. Hence the title for the next volume, 'Dream of Commonwealth, 1921–1942'.

PREFACE

NOTES

[1] Review by 'T. R. R.' in *Journal of Commonwealth Studies* (March, 1971) 'T. R. R.' was Trevor Reese, the historian of the Royal Commonwealth Society.

[2] Correlli Barnett, *The Collapse of British Power* (London, 1972).

[3] See Paul B. Rich, *Race and Empire in British Politics* (Cambridge, 1972). On another significant aspect of racial policies in this period, see K. Ballhatchet, *Race, Sex and Class under the Raj: Imperial Attitudes and Policies and their Critics, 1793–1905* (London, 1980). Greater attention to the sexual aspects of racial policies also underlies the two articles by Ronald Hyam 'Empire and Sexual Opportunity' (*Journal of Imperial and Commonwealth History* (XIV. No. 2. January 1986) and 'Concubinage and the Colonial Service' ibid. (XIV. No. 3. May 1986), and the article by Gregory Martin 'The influence of Racial Attitudes on British policy towards India during the first World War' ibid. (XIV. No. 2. Jan. 1986).

[4] See Richard Symonds, *Oxford and Empire–the last lost cause?* (London, 1986).

[5] On the Exhibition and other aspects of the conscious dissemination of the imperial message, see John M. Mackenzie, *Propaganda and Empire: the Manipulation of British Public Opinion, 1880–1960* (Manchester, 1984).

[6] A highly suggestive study of these relics of Empire is that by Simon Winchester, *Outposts* (London, 1985).

[7] See D. A. Low, *Lion Rampant, Essays in the Study of British Imperialism* (London, 1972); *The Contraction of England* (an inaugural lecture) (Cambridge, 1984).

[8] Raymond F. Betts, *Uncertain Dimensions: Western Overseas Empires in the Twentieth Century* (London, 1985).

[9] A good example is H. C. G. Matthews, *The Liberal Imperialists* (London, 1973).

[10] 'What I am contending is that the 'empire' as a set of colonies and other dependencies, was just the tip of the iceberg that made up the British world system as a whole, a system of influence as well as power, which indeed preferred to work through informal methods of influence where possible, and through formal methods of rule only when necessary'. John Gallagher, *The Decline, Revival and Fall of the British Empire* (Cambridge, 1982) p. 75.

[11] See Paul M. Kennedy, *The Rise and Fall of British Naval Mastery* (London, 1976). The completion of Arthur Marder's history of the Royal Navy in this period has been invaluable to subsequent historians. Arthur J. Marder, *From the Dreadnought to Scapa Flow* (5 vols London, 1961–1970).

[12] See the paper 'The End of the Pax Britannica and the Origins of the Royal Canadian Navy: Shifting Strategic Demands of an Empire at Sea', presented by Prof. P. M. Gough to the 'Navy in the Modern World', Conference at Halifax, Nova Scotia in October 1985.

[13] 'Starting in 1798, upon French occupation of Egypt, the existence of Britain as a great power depended upon the maintenace of an Asiatic balance of power equivalent to that in Europe which European states had, during the eighteenth century, gradually accepted as the best guarantee of the existence of all of them.' Edward Ingram, *Commitment to Empire; Prophecies of the Great Game in Asia, 1797–1800* (Oxford, 1981). On the major instrument of British power in this area, the Indian Army see Stephen P. Cohen, *The Indian Army; its contribution to the development of a Nation* (Berkeley, California and London, 1971) and Philip Mason, *A Matter of Honour: an account of the Indian Army, its officers and men* (London, 1974).

[14] There is a good summary of the new literature on modern Indian history and a guide to recent work in Judith M. Brown, *Modern India, the Origins of an Asian Democracy* (Delhi and Oxford, 1985).

[15] See e.g. Monica Wilson and Leonard Thompson eds. *The Oxford History of South Africa*, Vol. II. 1970–1966. (Oxford, 1971) and Roland Oliver and G. N. Sanderson eds. *The Cambridge History of Africa* Vol. 6. c1870–c1905. (Cambridge, 1985) Vol. 7. c1905–1940. (Cambridge, 1986).

[16] Martin Gilbert, *Winston S. Churchill* Vol. III. (London, 1971; *Companion* (2 vols. London, 1972); Vol. IV. (London, 1975); *Companion* (3 vols. London, 1977); Stephen Roskill, *Hankey: Man of Secrets* (3 vols. London, 1970–1974).

[17] L. F. Fitzhardinge, *The Little Digger, 1914–1952: A Political Biography of Willam Morris Hughes* Vol. 2. (London, 1979). A new biography of Jan Smuts does not supersede that by Sir Keith

Hancock and concentrates very much on Smuts' role within South Africa, but does explain some aspects of Smuts' complex personality: Keith Ingham, *Jan Christian Smuts, The Conscience of a South African* (London, 1986).

[18] John Bradley ed. *Lady Curzon's India: Letters of a Vicereine* (London, 1985).
[19] See in particular Robert Skidelsky, *John Maynard Keynes. Vol. 1. Hopes Betrayed, 1883–1920* (London, 1983). Keynes's own writings for this period will be found in the first seventeen volumes of *The Collected Writings of John Maynard Keynes* published at Cambridge under the editorship of Professor Austin Robinson and Donald Moggridge from 1971 onwards.
[20] See Norman Mackenzie. ed. *The Letters of Sydney and Beatrice Webb* (3 vols. Cambridge, 1978); Norman and Jeanne Mackenzie eds. *The Diary of Beatrice Webb* (4 vols. London, 1982–1985).
[21] David Marquand, *Ramsay MacDonald* (London, 1977).
[22] See in particular, Isaiah Friedman, *The Question of Palestine, 1914–1918: British–Jewish–Arab Relations* (London, 1973); Elie Kedourie, *In the Anglo-Arab Labyrinth: The McMahon–Husayn Correspondence and its Interpretations, 1914–1939* (Cambridge, 1976) and A. S. Klieman, *Foundations of British Policy in the Arab World: The Cairo Conference of 1921* (Baltimore and London, 1970). See also the second volume of David Vital's history of Zionism: *Zionism: The Formative Years* (Oxford, 1982). A third volume covering the Balfour Declaration and the Peace Conference is to be published in 1987.
[23] See Richard Symonds, *Oxford and Empire.*
[24] See for instance, Raoul Girardet, *L'Idée Coloniale en France, 1971–1962* (Paris, 1972).
[25] For one interpretation of this aspect of the matter, see D. Cameron Watt, *Succeeding John Bull: America in Britain's Place, 1900–1975* (Cambridge, 1984). See also, Lord Beloff, 'The End of the British Empire and the Assumption of World-Wide Commitments by the United States', in Hedley Bull and W. Roger Louis eds. *The 'Special Relationship'; Anglo-American Relations since 1945* (Oxford, 1986). See also Phillip Darby *Three Faces of Imperialism: British and American Approaches to Asia and Africa 1870–1970* (London and New Haven 1987).
[26] Nicholas Mansergh, *The Commonwealth Experience* (2nd ed. 2 vols. London, 1982) Vol. I. p. ix.
[27] ibid. Vol. II. pp. 253–4.

SOURCES
AND
ACKNOWLEDGEMENTS

In public archives a number of collections of papers were examined and I am grateful to the Librarians and Keepers of these archives for their assistance. The Balfour Papers, Spender Papers, Cecil of Chelwood Papers, Sydenham Papers, Hutton Papers, Arnold-Forster Papers and Viscount Gladstone Papers were consulted in the British Museum. The Keeper of Western Manuscripts gave permission for writings by Lord Balfour and J. A. Spender to be quoted. The Austen Chamberlain Papers were examined in the University of Birmingham Library and extracts from the papers are reproduced by permission of the Librarian.

The Papers of the 11th Marquess of Lothian were consulted in the Scottish Record Office in Edinburgh, and are quoted by kind permission of the 12th Marquess.

In the Bodleian Library, Oxford, I was able to examine the Asquith Papers (by permission of Mr Mark Bonham Carter), the Bryce Papers, the Gilbert Murray Papers and the Hammond Papers. I must express my thanks to the Warden and Fellows of New College, Oxford, who gave permission for me to see and quote from the Milner Papers which are now deposited in the Bodleian Library. Where possible, references to the Milner Papers bear Bodleian shelfmarks in addition to those of New College.

Extracts from Crown-copyright records in the Public Record Office appear by permission of the Controller of Her Majesty's Stationery Office.

The following collections of papers in private hands have been used and I must express my thanks to their owners for allowing me to consult and quote from them: the papers of the late Lord Brand, by permission of Lady Ford; the papers of John Simon, 1st Viscount Simon, by permission of the 2nd Viscount Simon; the papers of Edward Grigg, 1st Viscount Altrincham, by permission of Mr John Grigg.

I have had only very limited access to the Round Table archives, but am grateful to Mr Dermot Morrah for his help in this connection, and also to Professor Carroll Quigley of Georgetown University for allowing me to see some of his notes on the Round Table.

Mr Edmund Ions of the University of York allowed me to use some of his transcriptions from the papers of Lord Bryce, and Mr G. Cook of Brasenose College showed me certain extracts from the papers of Sir Arthur Steel-Maitland. I am most grateful to the following for allowing me to quote from material of which they own the copyright: the 4th Viscount Esher for extracts from the *Journals and Letters of Reginald, Viscount Esher*, ed. M. V. Brett, and also from two unpublished letters written by the 1st Viscount; Miss Margery Bryce for extracts from the correspondence of Lord Bryce; Mr Randolph Churchill for extracts from the Chartwell Trust Papers and from unpublished letters by Winston Churchill in other collections of papers; Mr Julian Amery for a quotation from a letter written by his father in the Milner Papers; Professor Arnold Toynbee for quotations from letters written by Professor Gilbert Murray; Professor A. K. Lambton and Mr Francis Noel-Baker, for material from the Cecil of Chelwood Papers.

The Controller of Her Majesty's Stationery Office gave permission for material from the 1st Series of *Documents on British Foreign Policy, 1919–39 (D.B.F.P.)* to be reproduced.

I must finally offer my apologies to any owner of copyright material published or unpublished not mentioned in this note. I have been unable to trace the heirs or executors of the authors of some letters which I have used, and hope that they will accept this general acknowledgement.

I have not provided a bibliography of printed works, since this would be appropriate only to a work which claimed to be exhaustive. The full title of all books cited in the text is given on the first occasion the book is referred to and also the name of the publisher where passages are quoted. Unless otherwise stated the place of publication is London.

I was privileged to read in manuscript the draft of a work to be entitled *Retreat from Empire* by the late John Connell. Had he lived to complete the work it would have covered some of the same ground in a magisterial fashion, though from a very different point of view from mine. His early death was a major loss to British historical scholarship, as well as to his many friends. Other friends with whom I have been privileged to discuss some aspects of this study are Mr F. H. Hinsley of St John's College, Cambridge, Professor Robert Rhodes James of the University of Sussex, and Mr E. T. Williams, Warden of Rhodes House, Oxford.

Chapter 1

INTRODUCTION

The Choice of Europe

On 31 July 1961 Harold Macmillan, prime minister of the United
Kingdom of Great Britain and Northern Ireland, announced in the
House of Commons that it was the intention of his government to make
a formal application under article 237 of the treaty of Rome for
membership of the European Economic Community, better known in
ordinary English parlance as the Common Market.[1] The issue, as
Macmillan explained to the House, had political as well as economic
overtones as, although the treaty dealt with economic questions,
it had an 'important political objective' – the promotion of 'unity
and stability in Europe' which in turn was an essential factor in
'the struggle for freedom and progress throughout the world'. At the
same time he added a warning: if a closer relationship between the
United Kingdom and the countries of the E.E.C. 'were to disrupt the
long-standing and historic ties between the United Kingdom and the
other nations of the Commonwealth the loss would be greater than
the gain'. Commonwealth governments had been consulted before the
decision to undertake negotiations was reached, and would be consulted again before the House of Commons was asked to approve the
agreement which it was hoped would be reached with the E.E.C.

It cannot be said that the British position thus outlined was free of
ambiguities; indeed, some would trace the ultimate breakdown of these
negotiations eighteen months later to the failure to resolve them.[2] On
the face of it, it would appear that Macmillan was restating a familiar
British position, namely that no involvement in European affairs was
tolerable that did not carry with it the assent of the Commonwealth.
In other words, Britain's relations with what had once been the British
Empire were more important to her than those with her European

---

[1] H.C. *Deb*, vol. 645, cols 928–31. The treaty of Rome was concluded on 25 March 1957. For
British attitudes during the period when it was under negotiation and during the early stages
of the Community, see Max Beloff, *New Dimensions in Foreign Policy* (1961).
[2] On the negotiations and their failure, see Nora Beloff, *The General Says No* (1963).

1

neighbours. What was not clear, and what only the future could reveal, was whether statements of this kind represented a genuine commitment on the part of the British government or whether they indicated a now merely formal adherence to traditional views that no longer exercised real influence on the course of policy itself.

Perhaps one clue might have been provided by Macmillan himself when he spoke to the parliament of South Africa on 3 February 1960 on how, since the end of the second world war, the 'processes which gave birth to the nation states of Europe' had been repeated all over the world: 'Fifteen years ago this movement spread through Asia. . . . Today the same thing is happening in Africa. . . . The wind of change is blowing through this continent and, whether we like it or not, this growth of national consciousness is a political fact.'[1] It is true that Macmillan did not admit that the retreat from Empire that was Europe's response to the new nationalisms and in which Britain fully shared was necessarily a set-back for Britain and the Commonwealth. On the contrary: 'what Governments and Parliaments in the United Kingdom have done since the war in according independence to India, Pakistan, Ceylon, Malaya, and Ghana, and what they will do for Nigeria and other countries now nearing independence, all this, though we take full and sole responsibility for it, we do in the belief that this is the only way to establish the future of the Commonwealth and of the Free World on sound foundations'. Clearly, however, although Macmillan might hope that to meet the aspirations of the new nationalisms rapidly was the only way of keeping them out of the communist camp, the ties that Britain herself would be likely to retain with this class of her former dependencies would be substantially different from those that had prevailed in the case of the 'old dominions'.[2] It might reasonably be guessed that for a British government in 1961, an automatic priority given to the Commonwealth over 'Europe' was more likely to be based upon sentiment than upon a close assessment of comparative advantages from the point of view of the interests – political and economic – of the British themselves.

[1] Extracts from a speech by Harold Macmillan to the South African parliament, 3 February 1960. R.I.I.A., Documents, 1960, pp. 344–8.
[2] Macmillan failed to convince his South African audience; and the acceleration of independence for Britain's colonial territories in Africa and its effect upon the composition of the Commonwealth provided the background for South Africa's decision to withdraw its application to remain a member of the Commonwealth after it became a Republic. See the statement of the South African prime minister, H. Verwoerd, 15 March 1961, R.I.I.A., Documents, 1961, pp. 701–2.

What is curious in retrospect is that the third element in any balance sheet of Britain's external policies was not mentioned at all in Macmillan's announcement of his government's intention to seek membership of the European Economic Community; nor did it figure noticeably in the debate upon it on 2 and 3 August. That third element was, of course, the special relationship with the United States.[1] And this is the more surprising in that it was, more than anything, the French suspicions of the extent and influence of Anglo-American intimacy that was to bring about the collapse of the negotiations themselves.[2] The history both of the preceding decades and of subsequent years show indeed how unrealistic was any attempt to describe any two of these factors in British thought and policy without the third.

In this respect, words used by Winston Churchill in 1948 had represented a widely shared attitude: 'As I look upon the future of our country in the changing scene of human destiny I feel the existence of three great circles among the free nations and democracies . . . the British Commonwealth and Empire with all that comprises . . . the English-speaking world in which we, Canada, and the other British Dominions play so important a part . . . and finally . . . United Europe.'[3] Britain standing at 'the very point of junction between' the three circles had the 'opportunity of joining them altogether'. Time had shown and was to show that this formulation, while still not inappropriate during and immediately after the war, had been and would be increasingly called into question. Even before the decline of Britain's relative power and authority that had already set in, the formula provided an unclear guide to many policy decisions. But only by the beginning of the 1960s did the application to join the E.E.C. suggest that a fundamental choice would need to be made. As late as 26 November 1956 when the House of Commons debated the proposed free-trade area between the O.E.E.C. on the one hand and Britain and other west European countries on the other, Macmillan, then chancellor of the exchequer, had 'opened the debate for the govern-

[1] See for an outline treatment of this theme, Max Beloff, 'The Special Relationship: An Anglo-American Myth', in M. Gilbert (ed.), *A Century of Conflict* (1966).
[2] For the attitude of the American government towards British relations with the European organizations, see Max Beloff, *The United States and the Unity of Europe* (London and Washington, 1963).
[3] Winston S. Churchill, speech at the 69th annual conference of the National Union of Conservative and Unionist Associations, October 1948. Quoted by Kenneth N. Waltz, *Foreign Policy and Democratic Politics* (Boston, Little Brown, 1967), p. 226.

ment by making the customary reference to the three worlds of which Britain is conceived to be a part'.[1]

Now in 1961, despite Macmillan's reassuring words to the Commonwealth, a choice appeared to be in the making, and that choice appeared to be 'Europe'. But even so, one had to be cautious. If one assumed both that the intentions of the government were genuine, and that those who framed them were fully acquainted with the new European institutions and the spirit that guided them, it was impossible to believe that membership was compatible with the Commonwealth ties in the form in which they then existed. But it was still possible to profess the contrary. Duncan Sandys, secretary of state for Commonwealth Relations and a notable 'European' of the early post-war years, said in concluding the debate for the government: 'I believe that my European friends will not misunderstand me if I say that if I were forced to make this cruel choice I would unquestionably choose the Commonwealth. Happily, we are not confronted with this dilemma.'[2] And on the whole the debate in Britain, both during the negotiations and after their breakdown, was largely between those who believed a dilemma did exist and were prepared to come down on the Commonwealth side and against 'entry into Europe', and those who argued that this was not so and that it was possible to go into Europe and still preserve the essential advantages of the Commonwealth relationship. A minority no doubt favoured the European cause whatever the ultimate effects upon the Commonwealth, or believed that there was in fact no option and that Macmillan's decision had been a genuine acceptance of the European option however impolitic it was to say so; but this point of view was rarely pressed in public.

Six years after Macmillan's announcement, when a labour government set out on the same road that a conservative government had trodden before it, the issue was as uncertain as ever.[3] Indeed, neither of the other two choices was as yet altogether excluded from people's minds. Some still argued that a revived and renewed Commonwealth

---

[1] Ibid., p. 232.
[2] H.C. *Deb*, vol. 645, col. 1775, 3 August 1961.
[3] On 2 May 1967 the prime minister, Harold Wilson, announced in the House of Commons that the government had on that day decided to 'make an application under article 237 of the treaty of Rome for membership of the European Economic Community and parallel applications for membership of the European Coal and Steel Community and Euratom'. The Euratom treaty had been concluded at the same time as the treaty setting up the E.E.C. The European Coal and Steel Community had come into existence in 1952. Britain had had an agreement of association with it since 1955.

might even at this late hour provide a more appropriate framework for British policy. Others – less articulate in stating their preferences – would have preferred some North Atlantic arrangement which would have consolidated and registered the degree of British dependence upon the United States which already appeared to be a fact.

But the present study is not concerned with the future, nor even with the lessons of the years that immediately followed Macmillan's momentous declaration of 1961. We are concerned with the antecedents not of the declaration itself but of the state of mind which by 1961 made it possible for a conservative government to contemplate a set of economic arrangements for Britain inspired by the ideal of a united Europe – an ideal that went far beyond the economic, and looked to nothing less than a sacrifice of national sovereignty in important areas of national policy. To trace the evolution of British ideas on this topic it is necessary to go back at least to a stage when such a sacrifice would have been regarded as wholly outside the range of possibility, when Britain was the centre of a world empire apparently fully able to look after itself.

In the 1890s the atmosphere was not of that settled calm with which it was credited by later and even more anxious generations. However confident the mass of the population may have felt in the durability of Britain's world role, those who ruled in Britain knew full well the kind of dangers the country faced and the need to take steps to meet them. There is little evidence of complacency at the top. The rise of Britain to the position she then occupied, as told by the historians of the era, was bound to call attention to the precariousness of some of the supports upon which British power rested. It would need a profound belief in providence to make one refrain from wondering why a group of foggy islands off Europe's north-western shores, populated beyond the means of subsistence that the islands could provide, endowed with no great natural assets outside the coalfields, should have become both the centre of a world empire and a possible arbiter of European rivalries. It might seem that so artificial a superiority was certain to prove as transient as the hegemonies that it had replaced, although those in whose hands power lay were for the most part undaunted by the new challenges to Britain's position that they sensed. They believed that measures could be devised to meet them; and they believed that they had the right to take such measures. They took it for granted that the international world was one of competing powers and that their duty was to make the most of whatever assets were available to them.

5

The Reversal of Fortunes

As we know, they were doomed to be disappointed. The fabric of imperial power, though it largely survived the first world war, disappeared with quite startling rapidity in the aftermath of the second. Winston Churchill, already a subaltern serving in India in the year of Victoria's Diamond Jubilee, 1897, was to survive to vote in the division on 3 August 1961 in favour of the motion approving Britain's application to join the E.E.C. The decline and fall of the British Empire had been consummated within a single active lifetime.

It would, of course, be possible to account for this reversal of fortunes in a number of different though complementary ways. One could dwell upon the scientific and technical developments that made a community of no more than fifty million people inadequate for sustaining the industrial and armed panoply of a great power; and this consideration may have been foremost in the minds of those who sought 'entry into Europe' as the solution of Britain's problems in the second half of the twentieth century. One could point to the invention of the aircraft and of other new weapons and means of communication, that were to put an end to the long superiority of naval over land-based power just at the time when the theoretical basis of sea-power was finding its most notable expositors. One could examine or speculate upon the demographic, economic, and moral impact of Britain's heavy involvement in two major wars separated by a mere twenty years' interval of uneasy peace.

Alternatively, if one holds the view that it was the possession of an overseas empire that gave Britain her pre-eminence in world politics at the end of the nineteenth century, one would have to look more specifically at the reasons for her abandoning it. One could argue that the fate of the other empires that had existed alongside her own demonstrates that it was the spread of European education, European technology, and European ideas to non-European peoples that made it ultimately impossible to perpetuate a dominion over palm and pine. One could say that a change of attitude about the profitability of empire lay behind the readiness of the possessing classes to accept its liquidation.[1] One could argue that a welfare democracy of the kind into which Britain was evolving internally during the period of imperial decline might on occasion produce bouts of genuine patriotism and even of

[1] On this aspect of the matter, see John Strachey, *The End of Empire* (1959).

6

jingoism but would turn away from the more enduring and harassing burdens of empire.[1] For some generations the state and the great commercial interests operating overseas found no difficulty in attracting men of superabundant energy and talent to careers involving danger and discomfort; maybe there is evidence that the retreat from empire paralleled a decline in the attractiveness of such a way of life. It is possible that greater opportunities for individuals at home are inimical to the maintenance of external responsibilities. Or one could point to the connection that seems to exist between the decline of British power in the world, and the eclipse of those political and economic doctrines which had been the characteristic contribution of Britain to the nineteenth-century world.

The difficulty about accepting these approaches to the subject, whether by themselves or in various possible combinations, is that though they can be made to account for the basic changes that have taken place they throw little light on the actual decisions of policy that were made from time to time, or on the minds of those who made them. For some historians these exclusions are perfectly acceptable. We have been told by the president of the Historical Association that we should act on Kierkegaard's view of history when he said that history has to do with results and that motives and intentions are the business of ethics, because 'the results, the consequences of actions are there to be seen; the causes, the motives, are hidden in men's minds, and only God can disentangle them'.[2] But to write history of this kind would not help much in illuminating either the choices that lie before us, or the way in which we should deal with them.

No doubt much of human history consists in the more or less gracious acceptance of the ineluctable; but even the degree of grace is a matter of some interest. Why were British governmental institutions and even the party system so little affected by the retreat from empire when the collapse of almost all other imperial systems has entailed the most profound repercussions upon the domestic polity? But one can go farther than that. Political communities do in fact behave as though there are important choices to be made; their institutions are designed to produce and elevate the men who are to guide them in their choices; and these men will further their claims to leadership by espousing different and

[1] For stimulating if sometimes perverse treatment of British ideas of empire in the period, see A. P. Thornton, *The Imperial Idea and its Enemies* (1959).
[2] Geoffrey Barraclough, *History and the Common Man* (1967), being the presidential address to the Diamond Jubilee conference of the Historical Association at London, 12–16 April 1966.

rival solutions of the problems that they believe are before the nation. Therefore so far from it being a kind of subjectivist aberration, the attempt to understand how individuals and groups in the past interpreted the present and forecast the future is an essential part of the historian's task.[1]

In the case of the contemporary British debate about the future position of this country in the world, there is the additional advantage that derives from the continuity of institutions and of personnel. There has been no radical break of the kind that gives an air of unreality to so much discussion of Russian foreign policy, where one has to take into account the almost total replacement of one governing *élite* and its institutions by another. No doubt the British *élite* has evolved over the period,[2] but there has been no abrupt transformation. The permanent hierarchies, civil and military, have a continuous history, and in political life one parliament succeeds another with a carry-over of membership sufficient to make the process of change a continuous one. Careers in public life have been long enough for individuals to take part in more than one phase of the process with which we are concerned. Groups united by similar philosophies or attitudes may endure long enough to have to reformulate their policies to meet new circumstances.[3] The debate set off by Macmillan's announcement in 1961 was new in the nature of the precise decision that had to be taken; its component parts were familiar from the past.

In the widest sense the terms of the debate have to be traced well beyond any arbitrary starting-point in the 1890s to span a whole tract of English history from the reign of the first Elizabeth to the reign of the second. Elizabeth Tudor was the first English monarch since Henry II to reign over no foot of continental European soil, and the last to be spared the burden of transoceanic possessions. It would not need too much ingenuity also to regard her reign as the one which saw the full fruition of a culture markedly national in form and content, and markedly different, whether we take its religious or its secular aspects, from that of even its closest European neighbours. Despite

[1] Historians tend to underrate the importance of forecasting or prevision in the demands made upon statesmanship. There can be no healthy policy that is not based upon some conception of what the future will be like. See, on this subject, Bertrand de Jouvenel, *The Art of Conjecture* (1967).
[2] A beginning with studies of this kind has been made in W. L. Guttsman, *The British Political Elite* (1964).
[3] One group, the 'little Englanders' and their successors, has been the subject of an illuminating study by A. J. P. Taylor, *The Troublemakers* (1957).

8

English participation in the main movements in European history in subsequent centuries – the scientific revolution, the enlightenment, romanticism – foreign observers have felt that there was something about England that set her off from the rest of Europe.

For this feeling – which persists – many reasons could be adduced, but the one that now concerns us is that which springs from a tension not unknown in other European countries at different times but present in Britain to a unique degree – the tension between trade, migration, and political rule in distant continents on the one hand, and her position as an inevitable participant in the economic and political affairs of Europe on the other. Whether the two roles fortified each other or whether on the contrary they implied alternative commitments of the country's resources was always an open question and one that was often debated. The 'little Englanders', the 'imperialists', and even the 'good Europeans' of twentieth-century Britain can all claim a respectable ancestry.

Nevertheless, the terms of the debate were not the same in the period of overseas expansion as they became in the age of imperial decline. The arguments over Britain's relationship to the new European communities revealed a stock of ideas and attitudes that were essentially the product of an experience that began in the last decade of the reign of Queen Victoria. It was in the 1890s that the new challenges to Britain's world position first became fully apparent, and that alternative responses to them were first canvassed; whether to enter into a permanent agreement with one or more of the other great powers; or to remain independent of foreign alliances but to reinforce Britain's own position by a more calculated and systematic exploitation of the potential economic and military resources of the Empire – itself an idea that had exercised some attraction in British political circles since the 1870s; or finally, whether to seek, through some new combination of the English-speaking nations, to involve on Britain's side the vast and growing resources of the United States.

Such a systematic exposition of alternative courses of action does injustice to the complex realities of the situation. These broad currents of opinion were not wholly independent of each other and often co-existed in single minds. Their full implications often passed unperceived. Were there imperial reasons as well as those arising from the need to safeguard the security of the home islands that made it essential for Britain to pursue in an active fashion the maintenance of the balance

9

of power in Europe? Were Britain's overseas possessions a source of strength – capable of supplying in time of need both men and money for the purposes of imperial defence? Or were imperial commitments an added burden on the nation's resources, weakening Britain's position in relation to graver problems nearer home?

The answer to questions of this kind would vitally affect not only British imperial and foreign policy but also the raising and disposition of Britain's own armed forces. It was complicated by the fact, not always fully appreciated in popular discussion, that the Empire itself consisted of at least three very different components. The colonies of white settlement were already endowed with internal autonomy, and increasingly conscious, even in external affairs, of national interests and objectives of their own not necessarily identical with those of the mother-country. The Indian Empire was already feeling the stirrings of modern political nationalism. The tropical colonies suffered from neglect because it was assumed that they would remain indefinitely in a situation of total dependence, and that their resources would therefore always be available. Even this division was imperfect; Britain was just in the process of acquiring territories in east and central Africa whose place in this scheme was to be a matter of debate for the whole of the rest of the period.

What the protagonists of the principal alternative views on national policy had in common was their conviction that Britain should remain in the new circumstances a great world power, and that her imperial inheritance was an integral part of this position. The differences were those of method not of purpose. But there was a school of thought hostile to the whole idea of a positive world policy. They believed that Britain's prosperity was a function of her success as a manufacturing and commercial country, and that imperial possessions contributed nothing to this role. On the contrary, they involved Britain in problems of defence from which she would otherwise be free, in view of what they believed to be the invulnerability of the home islands themselves. To rule an empire was not compatible with the habits and outlook of a modern democracy. And this view shaded into a more or less outright pacifism which was – though scarcely until after the first war – to have some effect in shaping the national attitude, if not national policies.

A further complication was introduced by the change, at the turn of the century, in the dominating characteristics of the country's internal political life – the movement away from a limited conception of the state's functions towards a greater measure of collectivism. Hitherto, it had been in the name of economy and lower taxation that opposition had been offered to military or naval expenditure and to policies that seemed likely to call for their expansion. Now, expenditure for defence had to compete with other ways of spending money more congenial to democratic electorates. And this consideration might well affect foreign policy too; since in some circumstances an alliance might be thought of as a substitute for extra expenditure on armaments.[1]

Persons and Influences

Most of the men who held power in this period, whether as an outcome of the political process, or through their roles in the permanent civil and military apparatus of the state, or as manipulators of opinion – press lords and publicists – or as the heads of great commercial enterprises, either belonged to one of these identifiable schools of thought or were influenced by it. But neither interests nor ideas can be viewed as abstractions; in most cases a multiplicity of influences affected the making of individual decisions, and one must not expect consistency of belief or action over the whole of a man's career or feel certain that his opinions on one issue enable one to predict how he will react to another.

A definition of those who held power in Britain during this period should be a wide one. To pretend that a permanent secretary or a chief of the Imperial General Staff were mere executants of ministerial policy, or ambassadors purely mouthpieces of the foreign secretary of the day, would be to take the letter of the constitution for the reality. Indeed, with the growing complexities of public business, and the increased importance of technological factors, the drift was probably towards a greater role for the expert. But one must not think that the politicians did not count; it is essential to remember that the system of cabinet government which prevailed in Britain throughout these decades was largely a system of party government, with important modifications only in time of war.

It might seem then at first sight that the parties would be the vehicles through which the broad currents of feeling and opinion would most obviously make themselves felt. But this is true only up to a point. For one thing parties are not 'given' to the same extent as the more

---

[1] As one recent historian puts it succinctly: 'Old Age Pensions were financed by the *Entente Cordiale*'. George Monger, *The End of Isolation* (London, Nelson, 1963), p. 313.

formal elements of the political system. They are themselves the creation of changing circumstances. Taken together, the years under consideration saw among other things the rise of the labour party and its
substitution for the liberal party as the alternative party of government. But it was by no means clear at the successive stages through
which this process went, what the outcome would be; and the possibility
of some major new combination of the Centre was a live one from 1910
to the mid-1930s. Not only was there a shifting pattern of political
groups behind the monolithic appearance which the parties en-
deavoured to impose upon the electorate, but there were also the careers
of remarkable individuals who found the constraints of party difficult
to endure: Joseph Chamberlain, Lloyd George, Winston Churchill,
Ramsay MacDonald.

These figures (and lesser ones also) gathered round themselves
associates or disciples whose influence can be traced at the time or
subsequently. To trace groupings of this informal but powerful kind is
an essential part of relating ideas to practice. A further point which is
too often overlooked is the passage of time between the enunciation of a
doctrine and its efficacy in action. On the whole, statesmen, like other
busy men, have little time for general reading or reflection; to understand the workings of their minds it may be more important to know
what books were in circulation, or what ideas were being instilled at the
universities during their student years, than to know what were the
prevailing intellectual doctrines at the time when they actually came
into power.

It is equally true that the nature of a man's early experience of the
real world is likely to be a formative influence of even greater potency.
The South African war, the first world war, the great depression,
Munich, the battle of Britain – these are, as it were, the points of reference to which so many individuals recurred when asked to meet new
problems or new crises. For this reason, alone, biography would be an
essential component of a study of this kind. But it does not stand alone.
There is also to be considered the impact of those parts of the outer
world that Britain's leaders had seen for themselves.

Evidence abounds for the view that personal acquaintance with
another country or group of countries may powerfully affect political
judgement – favourably or unfavourably as the case may be. At some
time in the latter half of the nineteenth century it became possible for
an aspiring politician to contemplate a journey round the Empire, as

his predecessors when young might have made a grand tour of Europe. Personal contacts made on such journeys were often of lasting significance and can be traced through subsequent correspondence. More important still is the impact of passing an early part of one's active career in some position overseas. The fact that the young men of Milner's Kindergarten knew South Africa better than they did France or Germany helps to explain some of their later judgements of men and events.

Personal knowledge of European countries is often harder to document and outside the diplomatic corps it was probably not often so intimate. It is even harder to be certain of the linguistic accomplishments of public figures – it seems to have been a period of general decline in the importance attached, by cultivated society in England, to the knowledge of modern languages. Is it also true that a knowledge of English was thought less important on the continent than a century earlier? Such impressions may be misleading; what is clear is that the intellectual worlds of Europe and of Britain increasingly diverged in the twentieth century. The social sciences in particular – economics, politics, sociology – seems to have followed different courses. And although the reception into the English-speaking world of the 1930s of a rather high proportion of the refugee German and Austrian intelligentsia did something to acclimatize some continental ways of thought in Britain, this did not make a radical difference. The matter is not one of interest to intellectual historians alone, since it is important for understanding the failure of the new 'European' ideology to catch hold in wartime and post-war Britain as it did in so many quarters on the continent. Britain's refusal to take the leadership in the movement for a united Europe in the 1945–50 period cannot otherwise be fully understood.

A similar set of problems – other than the linguistic one – are equally important for the study of Anglo-American relations in the period. No other aspect of the subject has so suffered from over-simplification.

Finally, one has to ask what can be said about the effect on Britain's stance in external affairs of the changes in British society and of the arguments with which these changes were accompanied. It is absurd to rule out ideological factors in foreign policy or to regard them as being somehow illegitimate derogations from the national interest, as the national interest has always included a degree of concern with the triumph abroad of institutions or ideas cherished at home.

The period with which we are dealing was one in which the ideological factors in foreign policy were particularly strongly felt and debated. Before the first world war one important section of British opinion campaigned vigorously against an *entente* with the bloodstained tyranny of tsarist Russia. After the Russian revolution, and again after the setting up of the fascist and nazi régimes, the line of policy advocated for Britain was often justified by arguments derived from people's opinions as to the merits or demerits of the new systems. The Spanish civil war and the debate on it in Britain is shot through with ideological preferences, even though lip-service was often paid to 'strategic' and other respectable arguments.[1]

In the period after 1945 the same was true. An unwillingness to accept close relations with western Europe or the United States was often justified on 'socialist' grounds; enthusiasm for the granting of independence to Asian and African countries was often based upon assumptions that the new governments would be 'democratic' or 'socialist'. Even more important then, and earlier, were people's feelings about the way international relations in general should be organized and the institutions that seemed to embody those aspirations – the League of Nations and the United Nations. Such allegiances must be regarded as a fact, and were more influential than some advocates of *realpolitik* would be prepared to admit.

The important thing is not to discuss such influences in the abstract but to estimate their consequences. Perhaps the most important single question here is whether such ideological commitments had the effect of blinding those who adhered to them to the realities of the situation. Was it the real soviet Russia, the real nazi Germany, the real United Nations that people were praising or denouncing, or were these imaginary projections with only the most tenuous connections with reality?

Summary of this Volume

If these are the bare elements of the problem, it is obvious that they are numerous enough to make the task of the interpreter of policy an exceedingly difficult one. To treat the whole subject at equal depth for the whole of the period would be a daunting task. The present attempt

[1] See K. W. Watkins, *Britain Divided: the effect of the Spanish Civil war on British political opinion* (1963).

is more modest. Attention will be concentrated upon those aspects of the preceding decades that appear most relevant in respect of the debate over 'Europe' and 'Commonwealth' as it developed in the late 1950s and early 1960s. Instead of trying to cover even these aspects in equal depth, a choice will be made of those issues of policy that seem, whether because of their nature, or because of the materials to hand, most clearly to illustrate the main currents of opinion affecting the decisions that were made. Other writers would doubtless have made different choices and have treated them in a different way; but in an inquiry of this kind directed to a period so little removed from us in time, there is bound to be a strong element of the personal. For this reason, this book despite its length is properly to be classed as an essay rather than as a history.

Nevertheless it is convenient to divide the subject into broad chronological strata. This first volume, which takes the story to 1921 when the British Empire reached its maximum territorial extent, begins with a description of the position in 1897. Britain's rulers were conscious both of the loss of Britain's early lead in industrial strength, and of her consequent economic and political weakness in a world of competing great powers. The jealousies of foreign countries were largely directed against the Empire which was believed to be the source of Britain's strength. In fact, the position was much more complex. While Britain's responsibilities for defending the whole system were undoubted, there were considerable constraints upon the use of its resources for this purpose. The principal one was the increasingly autonomous outlook of the self-governing dominions.

The imperialists of the 1890s saw the remedy in the development of federal institutions, strengthened by preferential economic ties and possibly by the enlistment of the United States in some form of Anglo-Saxon combination. The formula did not prove anywhere an acceptable one, and was anyhow difficult to harmonize with the strongly paternalist tendencies in British opinion on India, and the more specifically economic approach to the tropical colonies.

The Boer War both encouraged belief in imperial solidarity through the presence of dominion contingents on the British side, and exposed the country's military weakness. It thus provoked a major effort at internal reform and helped in the reorientation of external policy. The setting up of the committee of Imperial Defence provided machinery for the consideration of important issues of policy, where necessary conjointly with the dominions. On the naval side, the preoccupation with the German threat led to a concentration of British sea-power in home waters and a policy predicated upon American benevolence. The weakening of Britain's relative strength in the Pacific was compensated for by the conclusion of the Anglo-Japanese alliance. Diplomacy lent itself to liquidating the sources of friction with France, and later with Russia. To do this was to accept the priority of maintaining Britain's position in Europe, and contrasted with policies essentially dominated by concern for India.

The whole effort depended, however, upon Britain's own strength. The imperialist cause was weakened by the divisions over tariff reform in Britain, and the machinery of the colonial conferences was inadequate for the purpose of securing a common approach to the Empire's problems. The degree to which the different component parts of the Empire saw their problems separately was underestimated by a ruling class largely out of touch with their needs and problems.

The coming of the liberal government of 1905 and the election of 1906 saw a large-scale change in the composition of the principal groups concerned with the making and execution of external policy. But despite the vigour of ideological controversy, the main lines of defence and foreign policy continued unchanged. Further attempts were made to bring the dominions into common defence arrangements and to give their leaders a greater awareness of the dangers threatening the Empire, and the army was reshaped to make intervention in Europe possible. The liberals also looked beyond the relationships with the dominions to two other important aspects of policy. By some advance towards the creation of representative institutions in India they raised the question of whether the ideas upon which the political advance of the dominions had rested, and which were now applied to South Africa also, could be adapted to suit the nationalisms of countries of wholly non-European stock and separate civilizations. In their tentative efforts in this direction they came up against the opposition of the existing dominions. The other issue was Ireland, where the question of home rule became alive once more after the elections of 1910 and the Parliament Act of 1911. Could some form of devolution both ensure the loyalty of Ireland in case of war, and prevent agitation about Ireland from weakening the British cause in the dominions and – even more important – in the United States? With the growing possibility of war with Germany, the position of the United States seemed increasingly crucial; and policy with respect to Canada, Japan, and Latin America had to be looked at in the light of this fact.

The war came at a time of considerable perplexity and turmoil in both internal and imperial affairs, and yet arose out of European issues. The survival of the liberal empire clearly depended upon victory; yet it was uncertain how its institutions could be adapted to make victory more certain.

The treatment of the war in the light of this question concentrates therefore not only on the military contributions of the Empire, and the institutions culminating in the Imperial War Conference and Imperial War Cabinet, which were devised for its strengthening and control, but also on the impact of dominion policy-makers upon the conduct of the war and the definition of war aims.

The course of the war itself and the commitment of the professional military to a western front strategy limited the role of statesmanship. In the first half of the war, the problems presented by the neutrality of the United States and its threatened intervention to promote a compromise peace were all-important. In the latter half of the war, with American collaboration assured, British attention turned to the new threat to the Empire presented by militant Russian communism. Both the Indian and the Irish questions took on a new urgency. War aims began to be defined in terms of the desirability of securing a situation in Europe that would free Britain from the need actively to intervene to preserve the balance, and of making gains outside Europe that would prevent any renewal of the threat to the Empire and its communications, either by a revived Germany or by a Russia, perhaps under German influence. A minority already saw the possibility that only a strong Germany could provide the necessary balance to Russia and looked beyond immediate hostilities to the possibilities of future co-operation with her. These various designs for the future depended upon estimates of what the United States' position would be, how far it would be prepared to co-operate in maintaining a settlement, and how far it would push its hostility to imperialism and its demand for freedom of the seas.

The principal problems of the peace conference had, therefore, all been foreshadowed before hostilities ceased, but were complicated by the pressure of public opinion at once for a severe peace and for a run-down of British strength. The dominions were concerned with their own immediate interests rather than with the future of the imperial system, and determined to avoid a renewal of a situation in which Britain's European policies could involve them in war. The territorial settlement was the product not of planned expansion but of the impossibility of restoring the defeated empires, including the Turkish Empire, and of the unwillingness to see soviet influence extend more widely than need be.[1]

Peace-making was in any event only one aspect of the British government's preoccupations. The wartime machinery for framing imperial policy was shown to have no peacetime future, but the influence of the dominions was not thereby diminished. On the contrary, it helped to fortify American pressure against the renewal of the Anglo-Japanese alliance, and was an obstacle to Britain's incurring new European commitments. The weakening of Britain's material position and the blow to British morale resulting from wartime losses increased British reluctance to take up the challenge of the United States, and British policy moved towards an acceptance of American naval parity and a subordination of British to American views on the Pacific.

The forcible suppression of Irish nationalism proved unacceptable to British opinion, and Ireland was allowed to mask secession from the Empire by accepting dominion status. Imperialist feeling proved too strong for the same solution to be contemplated in India's case; and the concessions made to Indian nationalism were inadequate to stifle its opposition.

In 1921, where we break off our account, the basic elements in the latter decline and disruption of the Empire could be perceived, despite its recent territorial expansion, particularly in the Middle East. The war had given a major impulse to anti-imperial feeling and weakened the self-confidence of the ruling *élites*. The country's economic plight was interpreted by capital and labour alike as calling for a minimum of public expenditure and consequently for major economies in defence. The desire to limit defence expenditure was a dominant factor in foreign policy, and helped to give emphasis to the conciliatory as opposed to the collective security aspects of the League of Nations.

[1] Professor Arno J. Mayer's book on the peace conference, *Politics and Diplomacy of Peacemaking* (London, Weidenfeld & Nicolson, 1968) was published too late to use in writing the relevant chapter in this volume. While his analysis is a useful corrective against underestimating the importance of the Russian and communist questions at Paris, his thesis that the dominant motive in allied (including British) policy was the strengthening of the existing ruling classes against the socialist challenge seems to me a dangerous over-simplification.

The realism of the pre-1914 debates over external policy gave way to the self-delusion typical of the inter-war decades.

In the Empire itself, reliance upon consultation and unspoken understandings made possible another generation of co-operation within limits with the old dominions but provided no basis for reshaping the rest of the system. British opinion was little concerned with the Empire and its problems except from narrowly business points of view. Liberal-minded men gloried in the presence of the ex-Boer Generals Smuts and Hertzog in the Empire's counsels, and did not face the fact that the price involved accepting increasing racial discrimination in South Africa; the time-scale for the development of Indian and other Asian nationalisms was wrongly estimated; the possibility of political unrest as a factor in tropical Africa wholly neglected.

Britain in 1921 still possessed an empire – though the ambiguous word commonwealth was much in vogue – but the British were not an imperially minded people; they lacked both a theory of empire and the will to engender and implement one. The quarter century between the colonial conference of 1897 and the imperial conference of 1921 when thus examined through the eyes of the British *élite* and its leaders is, then, a crowded and complex period which historical scholarship is by no means yet capable of bringing into perspective. The remaining chapters of this volume follow certain lines of inquiry into the composition and outlook of that *élite* and the nature of its institutions, and investigate the impact upon them of changes in other parts of the Empire, of the European convulsion and the rise of the United States, and of their own exposure to the deadly test of total war.

Chapter 2

DIAMOND JUBILEE

Threats to the Empire

The sixtieth anniversary of the accession of Queen Victoria was celebrated on Sunday, 20 June 1897, by special services at places of worship
throughout her dominions. Two days later the Queen drove in state for
three hours through the streets of her capital and was rapturously received by her loyal subjects. To spare the energies of the ageing
sovereign no foreign monarchs were invited to share the celebrations.
It was a family and a domestic occasion. But family was widely interpreted, and among those taking part were the prime ministers of all the
self-governing colonies – all fifteen of them were sworn of the Privy
Council at a ceremony at Windsor on 7 July – and colonial as well as
Indian troops.

'Although your Majesty's Home Troops were far the finest,' wrote
the Duke of Argyll, her son-in-law, to the Queen, 'we were much interested in the Colonials. Their uniform is dull-coloured. But we could not
help remembering that no sovereign since the fall of Rome could muster
subjects from so many and such distant countries all over the world.'[1]
In a memorandum for the Queen describing the occasion, Mandell
Creighton, Bishop of London and biographer of Queen Elizabeth I,
wrote: 'The occasion expanded into a significant manifestation of imperial greatness, and of a fundamental unity of purpose, which came
as a revelation to England and the Colonies alike, and awakened the
respectful wonder of all Europe.'[2]

These sentiments were in fact widely held and not in Britain alone.
It must have been at about this time that a Cape Breton poet wrote:

> Here's to Queen Victoria
> Dressed in all her regalia

[1] G. E. Buckle (ed.), *The Letters of Queen Victoria*, series 3, vol. III (1930), p. 181. George
Douglas Campbell (1823–1900), eighth Duke of Argyll, had been a prominent whig
statesman.
[2] Ibid., p. 190.

With one foot in Canada
And the other in Australia.[1]

The assumption was that the Empire represented in so tangible a fashion in the Jubilee celebrations was not only, as Creighton had pointed out, unmatched in history but also, as earlier empires had been, a single force in world politics. If the 'respectful wonder of Europe' noted by Creighton were to fail to balance the hostility of the principal governments of Europe which was also a fact of the times, it was still unnecessary to fear for the outcome. With imperial support, Britain could yet defy the world.

Such optimism was not universally shared even at this proud moment in the nation's history. Rudyard Kipling, whose *Recessional* is the main literary monument of the Jubilee, clearly felt that the mood of self-praise was hubristic and that sterner virtues would be needed if the country's world position was to be held.[2]

It has been said by another major poet that *Recessional* 'is one of the poems in which something breaks through from a deeper level than that of the mind of the conscious observer of political and social affairs – something which has the true prophetic inspiration'.[3] But it is also true that this vein of self-criticism can elsewhere in Kipling's poetry of this period sometimes have 'less the effect of sounding a clarion call at us than of blowing our own collective trumpet'.[4] Nevertheless, Kipling was primarily concerned to emphasize the constructive aspects of imperialism and if 'he never doubted the validity of western civilization' and 'never lapsed into sentiment over the supposed virtues of savages', it was 'the spread of law, literacy, communications, useful arts that he applauded, not the enlargement of frontiers'.[5] Nor was he alone in this in his generation; it was these aspects of their work and

[1] Quoted by F. R. Scott in P.-A. Crépeau and C. B. Macpherson (eds), *The Future of Canadian Federalism* (University of Toronto Press, 1965), p. 182.
[2] *Recessional*, although dated 22 June, was not published in *The Times* until 17 July. On 22 June itself *The Times* published an ode by Sir Lewis Morris (1833–1907) a less memorable poet; four lines – the whole ode takes up almost a column – will give the drift:

> Mother of freemen! over all the Earth
> Thy Empire-children come to birth
> Vast continents are thine, or sprung from thee
> Brave island-fortress of the storm-vexed sea.

[3] T. S. Eliot, 'Rudyard Kipling', in *A Choice of Kipling's Verse*, ed. T. S. Eliot (London, Faber 1941), p. 16.
[4] J. I. M. Stewart, *Eight Modern Writers* (Oxford, Clarendon Press, 1963), p. 286.
[5] Charles Carrington, *Rudyard Kipling* (London, Macmillan, 1955), p. 274.

B

outlook that brought Kipling close to Cecil Rhodes and Alfred Milner, two of the three men with whom he dined in April 1897 at the Atheneum to celebrate his election to the club.[1]

An element of prophecy may be found in Kipling's perception that the kind of strength that made it possible for the area of civilization to be extended – whether manifest in the soldier or the civilian administrator or technician – would be sapped by an excessive indulgence in the merely verbal, in the proclamation of imposing principles unaccompanied by the will to make the effort needed if they were to triumph.

From this point of view the most prophetic poem of all had been published three years earlier than *Recessional* in *The Jungle Book*: 'The Road Song of the Bandar-Log':

> Here we sit in a branchy row,
> Thinking of beautiful things we know;
> Dreaming of deeds that we mean to do,
> All complete in a minute or two –
> Something noble and grand and good,
> Won by merely wishing we could.[2]

For those entrusted with the responsibility of government any doubts that may have been felt were not due to the insights of poets but to an appraisal of the international scene itself. For them Britain was a power already on the defensive; the anxieties felt about Britain's position were not wholly new. The self-confidence of the mid-Victorians can be exaggerated in retrospect. The war of 1870 had seen a major change brought about in the European balance of power without Britain having a say in what was done. Although Britain in 1878 played some part in checking the southern thrust of imperial Russia and came well out of the subsequent contest for territory and influence in Africa and the Far East, the fundamental constituents of the balance of power appeared nevertheless to be altering to her disadvantage. The militarization of the principal continental powers by measures of conscription of increasing thoroughness was reaching the point where the British army, designed and maintained on lines dictated by its extra-European com-

---

[1] The fourth at dinner was C. F. Moberly Bell, manager of *The Times* from 1890 to 1908, through whom many of Kipling's poems of this period found their way into the columns of the paper. Ibid., p. 251, where Bell is wrongly described as editor.
[2] *A Choice of Kipling's Verse*, p. 262.

mitments, could scarcely be reckoned an important factor in the consideration of European statesmen. The British democracy, like its aristocratic leaders, appeared to be bemused by its addiction to competitive sport – Kipling's 'muddied oafs' and 'flannelled fools'.[1] In continental Europe its place was taken by military manoeuvres.

All then depended upon sea-power; protection from invasion, the safe-guarding of the trade-routes, and the ability to defend overseas possessions. But the superiority at sea that Britain appeared to possess in the second half of the century was not something that could be relied upon as though it were a gift of nature. It depended upon a variety of technological and diplomatic factors and could at times be challenged by a new rival, or by a combination of rivals; 'it was not Bismarck alone who was perturbed by the spectre of hostile coalitions'.[2] The French challenge that had so perturbed Palmerston in the early 1860s was not renewed; but the 1890s saw the rise of two new naval powers, the United States and imperial Germany.[3]

The challenge was all the more serious in that naval power was historically closely connected with pre-eminence in the industrial field, and here the relative decline of Britain was unmistakable. Indeed, the ability of the newer industrial giants to overtake her was not due only to their advantages in territory and population but also to the fact that, coming late into the race, they were not burdened with obsolete capital equipment or with obsolescent ideas and practices. Concern with the neglect of technology and the low esteem accorded to the technologist in British education and British society, which were to be a commonplace of social criticism for the next half century, was already vocal even if this criticism was not then or later as well-founded as is sometimes believed. During this period Britain produced the dreadnought, the tank, radar, and the jet engine, and played a leading role in the development of nuclear science; she can hardly be described as a lag-

---

[1] 'The Islanders' the poem in which Kipling upbraided his fellow-countrymen for their neglect of soldierly qualities and of military preparedness was written in 1902 by which time the Boer war had pointed the moral.

[2] Lord Strang, *Britain in World Affairs* (1961), p. 222. William Strang (b. 1893) entered the foreign service in 1919 and was permanent secretary at the Foreign Office from 1949 to 1953. His writings form a rare and useful exception to the absence of serious studies of British external policy and the machinery for its formulation and execution from the point of view of the professional diplomat.

[3] It is not without interest that the most serious studies of the naval aspect of British policy from the latter part of the nineteenth century to the end of the first world war should be by an American historian, A. J. Marder. For the naval problems of the 1890s, see his *British Naval Policy, 1880–1905* (London, Putnam, n.d. ? 1940).

gard in the application of science to war; but the conception of a nation led by aristocratic amateurs survived.

On the continent, however, whatever might be thought of the capacities of Britain in respect of land armaments, it was not contempt but envy that the country evoked; and the envy could easily turn into hatred. Historians, British and foreign, concur in noting the existence of these widespread feelings of hostility towards Britain, and there was clear evidence of it in the general sympathy expressed for the Boers both at the time of the Jameson raid and during the South African war itself.[1] The reasons for these feelings differed from country to country. In France there was the sense of historical injustice; so much of Britain's overseas empire had been built on the ruins of France's own imperial past and these historical memories were envenomed by more recent events in Africa. The Fashoda confrontation in 1898–9 was to reveal the full depths of these feelings. For Britain a presence on the upper Nile seemed a perfectly reasonable outcome of the responsibilities that had been assumed in Egypt – responsibilities exercised it was believed both on behalf of the civilized world and on behalf of the Egyptians. But to the French this self-assurance seemed like a provocation.

In the Russian case hostility was increased by the ideological gulf between the principal exponent of western liberalism and the citadel of autocracy. Although in Russia there was a minority of constitutionalists who saw the British system as one worthy of admiration and emulation, much of the opposition was composed of varying brands of socialists for whom Britain was the epitome of ruthless capitalism and imperialist oppression.

But ideology was only ancillary to the opposition between Britain and Russia arising out of points of friction in so many parts of the globe. Wherever Russian expansion reached, or wherever Russian influence in a neighbouring country appeared to be growing, the British would be found opposing it; at the Straits; in Persia; on the north-west frontier of India, and in China. Once again there seemed to be an element of artificiality about Britain's position. The Russians must have regarded their presence on the Pamirs as natural enough with all the land behind them securely controlled and in the process of colonization by Russian settlers;

[1] The parliamentary investigation into the Jameson raid was in progress at the time of the Jubilee celebrations (having held its first public session on 16 February), and the select committee's report was actually published on 13 July. See Elizabeth Pakenham (Countess of Longford), *Jameson's Raid* (1960), pp. 259–332.

but what were the British doing there, ruling over a totally different civilization and thousands of miles from home?[1]

In Germany it was the future rather than the past which provoked the anti-British sentiments that were increasingly vocal. Germany had not, in its own view, come well out of the partition of Africa; its ventures in China and the Pacific were unsympathetically regarded; it felt itself to be a world power, but did not possess the outward show of one, a fleet and important colonial possessions. It could deal with the former deficiency and was beginning to do so;[2] but as far as colonies were concerned, there were no more vacant spaces on the globe. Only a massive redistribution of territory following upon a major war could satisfy its needs.

The matter was not one of distant lands only. The most extraordinary situation that Britain had come to occupy was that which it enjoyed in the Mediterranean, where it had begun to exercise naval power as early as the mid-seventeenth century. Tangier and Minorca had passed into the limbo of lost possessions, but Gibraltar, Malta, Cyprus, and, to all intents and purposes, Alexandria as well, were now available to assist in the deployment of British strength. It took a keen eye to perceive that what appeared to the British to be the necessary adjuncts of a wholly defensive strategy were standing incitements to others.

After calling at Gibraltar on his way to India in 1886, Lord Rosebery wrote: 'We have held it for two centuries and the power of man has vainly tried to wrench it from us. It should be the symbol of England. Till I saw Gibraltar I never fully realized why we are so hated in Europe.'[3]

[1] The point was made forcibly in G. N. (Lord) Curzon's, *Russia in Central Asia* (1889), a description of his journey in the previous year along the new Trans-Caspian railway.

[2] The need for a powerful fleet if Germany was to claim her due position in the world had been strongly pressed in German naval circles since 1892 and the German Emperor had been converted to this view through his realization of Germany's inability to translate into action his sympathy with the Boers, and because of his belief that without a great fleet, Germany's colonial possessions would be at the mercy of Britain in any future conflict. The propagandists for a large navy deliberately fomented anti-British feeling. The naval race began with the enactment of the first German Navy Law at the end of March 1898. J. Steinberg, *Yesterday's Deterrent* (London, Macdonald, 1965). E. L. Woodward, *Great Britain and the German Navy* (1935).

[3] Lord Crewe, *Lord Rosebery* (London, John Murray, 1931), vol. 1, p. 283. It is not surprising that it was the Mediterranean agreements of 1887 that gave the first sign that Britain might have to fortify her own position by agreements with other powers with similar interests. It is true that they were made in a situation of temporary weakness and would probably not have been made later when the naval situation had been re-established. See Strang, op. cit., pp. 221–2.

Defence and Imperial Unity: Ireland

Although the possibility of invasion by a hostile coalition that had wrested command of the narrow seas from the British fleet could never be wholly absent from the minds of those responsible for British defence, it was not in the forefront of their preoccupations. What they did fear, however, was that Britain's overseas possessions might become targets for the cupidity of foreign powers, both for their own sakes and because of their contribution to Britain's power, particularly in respect of naval bases and coaling stations.

While some degree of responsibility for local defence had been handed over to the colonies of white settlement in the middle of the nineteenth century, and India was largely defended by an army raised in India, the defence needs of the Empire were an obvious and direct drain upon the exchequer. Some thought that this was unnecessary, and that Britain could remove the main source of friction if she refrained from trying to add to her colonial possessions.[1] It was also possible to take the other view, that Britain's own security depended not merely on home defence but also on the command of the sea-routes, and that this command in turn depended upon the imperial network. Enlightened self-interest therefore spoke in favour of an active policy of colonial defence. Where the two sides could find common ground was in the view that the benefits arising from Britain's defence obligations were at least reciprocal, and that it was therefore the duty of colonies now growing in population and wealth to contribute to the security of the system as a whole. This was not, of course, a new theme in the history of the British or other Empires. It had received classic treatment in the debates that followed the Seven Years war and culminated in the American revolution; and the omens from that experience were not encouraging.

While relations between the centre and the periphery in matters of defence are clearly a general problem of empire, the form they took in the British case was obviously affected by the existence both in the mother-country and the colonies of representative institutions. If the

[1] Recent research has tended to minimize the distance between the imperialist and anti-imperialist schools of this period and to prefer the terms 'forward school' and 'consolidationist': 'Certainly there were no voices among the prominent Radicals and Little Englanders prepared to advocate the liquidation of the Empire; their concern was rather to prevent its further extension in the form of subject tropical dependencies.' Eric Stokes, 'Milnerism', *The Historical Journal* (Cambridge), vol. V, 1962, p. 47. But one should not overdo this revisionism. If colonies were burdens rather than assets and likely sources of international conflict, then this must apply as much to older colonies as to new ones.

colonies were to share the burdens of defence, equity suggested that they partake in the making of foreign policies out of which the need for military action might grow. But it was difficult to do this without taking an intimate part in the governmental arrangements of the metropolis, and to this there were technical objections – more cogent in the eighteenth century than after the invention of the steamship and the telegraph. But the technical difficulties were less important than the political question of combining such participation with the autonomy at home that all these governments now craved. In this sense the Empire faced the same problem that sooner or later afflicts all alliances – namely that dangers and burdens are of necessity uneven, that burden-sharing is a useful myth rather than an exact guide to action, and that there is no half-way house between being part of a political community and being outside it. Only within a political community will inequality of burdens be accepted. What was still unclear at the time of the Diamond Jubilee and of the second colonial conference for which it provided the excuse and the setting, was whether the Empire was a political community or not. Fifty years were to elapse before a definite negative could be given to this question.

In 1897 it was still possible to be optimistic about receiving a positive response to this question from Australian colonies – soon themselves to accept federation in a single political community[1] – from New Zealand, and from the English-speaking elements in Canada, the Cape, and Natal. But there was much more doubt where empire was clearly the result of conquest and attempted assimilation – for instance, on Britain's doorstep in Ireland. It is tempting to narrow one's field of vision and to treat Ireland and the Irish question as a domestic British matter for which there is respectable precedent. It was the essential core of the unionists' case that the act of union with Ireland was as irrevocable as the act of union with Scotland, that the United Kingdom was not only one in constitutional law but one in national sentiment; and even the home rulers were prepared to accept governmental institutions making allowances for the separate personality of the smaller island, but not total separation. Once again foreigners perhaps saw more clearly. For them, Ireland was an imperial possession which Britain was determined to retain for familiar imperial reasons.

---

[1] The act of parliament creating the Commonwealth of Australia was signed by the Queen on 9 July 1900. The federation of the Australian colonies had been advocated for nearly two decades and the constitution itself drawn up at a convention in 1897–8.

It is true that occasionally the relevance of the Irish issue to the general problems of the Empire was stressed by a unionist spokesman. In a speech on 8 December 1888 Austen Chamberlain declared that the principles advocated by the followers of Parnell would spread to all British possessions and would undermine the ties of affection and respect binding the colonies to the mother-country. Above all, there was the need to consider the effect of giving in to Irish lawlessness on the Indian Empire.[1] And the conduct of some Irish members of parliament at the time seemed to suggest that they were not oblivious of the connection between their own claims and the anti-imperialist cause in general. They spoke of themselves as the natural representatives and spokesmen of the unrepresented nationalities of the Empire and rather paradoxically in favour of the rights of the Bantu of South Africa as well as of the right of the Transvaal Boers to self-government. With regard to India it was even suggested that the Irish find seats for some Indians so as to give India a direct voice at Westminster.[2] Meanwhile, Irish members themselves could voice appropriate sentiments: 'Parliamentary agitation,' said one of them in the House of Commons in 1884, 'would not be very effective until the Irish people, crushed down under their present tyranny affected a coalition with the oppressed natives of India and other British dependencies, and all regarded England as the common enemy.'[3]

It is not surprising that language of this kind caused alarm in Britain, particularly among those who doubted the tenacity of imperial sentiment among the voters. In 1887, the liberal unionist, Leonard Courtney, wrote to a friend in India: 'I see the contagion of Home Rule is extending to India as we know it must. How you on the spot must groan over such premature encouragement to foolhardiness. I don't fancy this trouble will become serious in our time; but the working man voter

---

[1] C. Petrie, *Life and Letters of Sir Austen Chamberlain* (London, Cassell, 1939), vol. 1, p. 36. Not all imperialist opinion accepted the existence of this connection. Cecil Rhodes much scandalized the unionists by making a gift to the home rulers of £10,000 in 1887 in view of Parnell's willingness to provide for the retention of some Irish members at Westminster in a future Home Rule bill – a device that Rhodes thought might pave the way for colonial representation in the future. See J. C. Lockhart and C. M. Woodhouse, *Rhodes* (1963), pp. 168–9.

[2] M. Cumpston, 'The Discussion of Imperial Problems in the British Parliament, 1880–1885', *T.R.H.S.* (1963), p. 39.

[3] F. H. O'Donnell, quoted by Cumpston, loc. cit. It has been pointed out that since the Irish question with its interminably divisive effects on British domestic politics was an unpopular subject in parliament at this time, the Indians did not gain much from this association. See M. Cumpston, 'Some Early Indian Nationalists and Their Allies in the British Parliament, 1851–1906', *E.H.R.*, vol. LXXVI (1961), p. 286.

would think no more of giving up India than of giving up Ireland, not caring to inquire seriously what would be the fate of either when abandoned.'[1]

It was not only in India that the echoes of Irish nationalism were felt. It struck an answering chord in the growing national sentiment of the colonies of settlement, and even where this was not a dominant factor, colonial politicians like their United States counterparts were not above encouraging platonic expressions of sympathy with Irish aspirations in the hope of getting or retaining Irish votes. These factors explain the resolutions favouring home rule passed in the Canadian and Australian parliaments.[2]

But this reaction was not universal. The English historian, Goldwin Smith, who after settling in Canada in 1871 had become an important exponent of Canadian nationalism, argued strongly against home rule and accepted the chairmanship of an anti-home rule association in Toronto; his argument being that the disruption of an existing union could not lead to the creation of a wider one.[3] Some of the problems that home rule raised were to reproduce themselves in the context of growing colonial autonomy – for instance, the question of a contribution to the general needs of imperial defence. Under the first Home Rule bill, for example, Ireland would have paid some 40 per cent of her tax revenue to meet imperial costs settled by a parliament in which she would not be represented.[4]

Leaving aside the material interests of certain of the landowning class, the principal objection to home rule was strategic. Ireland differed from the rest of the Empire primarily in its proximity to the main British Island. If one believed that a hostile power might wish to invade England – and from the early 1890s a major war was widely held to be more than likely in the near future – then it seemed clear that Ireland must be held.[5] The memories of the threat from the French at the time

[1] Quoted by Stokes, loc. cit.
[2] In an undated letter to Bryce probably written late in 1907 or early in 1908, Goldwin Smith wrote that the Canadian parliament had 'thrice passed votes in favour of Home Rule without any regard to British interests merely to cultivate the Irish vote'. Bryce Papers, Bodleian Library, English Correspondence, vol. 17.
[3] *Correspondence of Goldwin Smith*, ed. A. Hamilton (London, 1913), p. 447. See also, Elizabeth Wallace, *Goldwin Smith: Victorian Liberal* (Toronto, 1957), p. 92. Goldwin Smith was not unwilling to consider an eventual union between Canada and the United States.
[4] Donald C. Gordon, *The Dominion Partnership in Imperial Defence, 1870–1914* (Baltimore, Johns Hopkins, 1965), p. 76.
[5] It may be an exaggeration, however, to say that 'after about 1893 war was universally regarded, in England at least, as fairly imminent, inevitable and not undesirable' (Marder,

of the 1798 rebellion were still alive. The Home Rule bills, it is true, had excluded both foreign policy and defence from the scope of the proposed Irish legislature, but could one be certain that the movement towards national self-determination would stop at this point? The history of nationalism in continental Europe suggested the contrary.

It is also true that so long as the union persisted Ireland was not a particular military danger. In 1905 the secretary to the committee of Imperial Defence noted questions about Ireland, as a preliminary to a paper by the General Staff on the role of Ireland in a possible war, for he doubted whether the matter had ever properly been thought out. At the time the likelihood of a rising in Ireland in conjunction with a raid from outside seemed remote, and such a raid would probably be received unenthusiastically; the communications of the invading force would be cut while the troops in Ireland could easily be reinforced.[1]

A direct military threat was not very strongly felt until the Easter rising of 1916, but meanwhile the diplomatic awkwardness of Irish dissidence, given the growing importance attached to relations with the United States, became an increasing source of anxiety. When after the general elections of 1910 home rule once more became a live issue, the elimination of this possible source of friction with the United States was regarded in some quarters as highly relevant. The influential editor of the *Observer*, J. L. Garvin, wrote in a letter intended for Balfour's eye:

> What we need is better relations with America. The new alliance between the Irish and German vote in the United States is a more important thing than almost anybody here seems to realize. It is one of the greatest dangers that ever threatened the Empire. Yet if some form of home rule made the relations of England and Ireland better and the relations of the Empire and the United States better also, the Irish at home would not only stand by us to a man against Germany but would be foremost in our fighting line.[2]

---

op. cit., p. 20). If this had been the case the advocates of 'preparedness' would have had an easier time.

[1] Sir George Clarke to Balfour, 5 August 1905. Balfour Papers, B.M. Add. 49702.

[2] J. L. Garvin to Balfour's secretary, J. S. Sandars, 27 January 1910. Balfour Papers, B.M. Add. 49795.

Costs and Complications in Ruling India

India, like Ireland, divided British opinion, but in a different way. Whereas Britain had once felt her position in India was destined to be transitory, few could now see how it would end and most people in Britain were reconciled to its indefinite continuation. Some might rejoice in this fact, others regret it, arguing that so long as Britain was committed to the defence of a long land frontier in India, it would involve the country in permanent hostility towards India's neighbours, notably Russia, and that this would limit Britain's freedom of action elsewhere in the world. It was a denial of the salutary principle that Britain should have no permanent commitments.[1]

It is true that in the 1880s there had been a brief revival of the pre-Mutiny view that 'the purpose of the British in India was to prepare India for their departure' and that this would be done by a very gradual transfer of authority to the 'growing class of educated Indians'.[2] But after the return of the conservatives to power in 1888 a period of caution ensued. Neither Lansdowne, viceroy from 1888 to 1893, nor his successor Elgin made much of a personal mark on India and policy was largely determined by the government at home.[3] In the Indian case one finds at its extreme the inherent problem of the Empire – what did Britain derive from it and how great were its costs?

The question of the profitability of empire, in the narrow economic sense, in the specific case of India is something that can be argued at length; certainly at the turn of the century and for some time afterwards it would have been difficult to gainsay its importance. Immediately before the first world war India was Britain's best customer and accounted for something like a tenth of her foreign trade.[4] But there could be a legitimate doubt as to the extent to which this commerce

[1] See Thornton, *The Imperial Idea and its Enemies*, p. 41.
[2] S. Gopal, *British Policy in India, 1858–1905* (Cambridge University Press, 1965), p. 176.
[3] Henry Petty-Fitzmaurice (1845–1927), fifth Marquess of Lansdowne, viceroy from 1888 to 1893) had previously served as governor-general of Canada (1883–8). He was to be secretary for war from 1895 to 1900 and foreign secretary from November 1900 to December 1905. Victor Alexander Bruce (1849–1917), ninth Earl of Elgin, was appointed viceroy by Rosebery in 1893 and held the office until 1898. An Indian historian remarks that Elgin 'had been convinced that he lacked the ability that would justify the appointment' which was his first in national politics. 'History,' the same authority comments, 'has provided us with no reason to differ from his estimate of himself.' Gopal, op. cit., p. 180. Elgin was to be colonial secretary from 1905 to 1908 – a Campbell-Bannerman appointment not renewed by Asquith.
[4] E. Monroe, *Britain's Moment in the Middle East* (1963), p. 11. It has been argued that India financed two-fifths of Britain's balance of payments deficit. E. J. Hobsbawm, *Industry and Empire* (1968), p. 123.

31

was dependent upon the retention of political power by Britain. On the whole, British governments did not by now use their power to increase British exports to the subcontinent.[1] When they did so the result was greatly to strengthen Indian discontent, as in the tariff legislation of 1896 forced upon a reluctant viceroy by the home government. In the views of many Englishmen this was only to be expected.[2] It could certainly be argued that India, though important, was not vital to Britain either from the trading point of view or for the opportunities of investment that it provided.[3] Considerable sectors of British society depended, however, upon posts in the civil and military hierarchies of the Indian Empire. It has even been argued that the individuals who sought careers in India (and who often died there, as the memorial tablets in the old churches of Calcutta and Madras and in many an English parish church so abundantly testify) were a net loss to the home country.[4] But it is possible to argue (as with posts in Africa and Malaya later on) that the energies thus rendered fruitful would have found no legitimate outlet at home, and that overseas empire may thus have been Britain's substitute for domestic fascism. There is also a far less hypothetical point, namely that of the effect on the British public mind of the presence in society of quite large numbers of influential persons whose active life had been spent largely in India, and who carried over from that experience a bias perceptible in their reaction to many major issues of foreign policy or defence. One is so used to coming across an ex-colonel of the Indian army as a stock figure in a play or light novel that it is odd how one forgets that there should have been this element in the population ubiquitous enough for it to be recognized at once by the ordinary playgoer or reader. Other imperial powers had their counterparts – but not on the same scale.

At the turn of the century most of the major political figures in Britain, including Lord Salisbury (who had done a spell at the India Office in 1866–7), agreed that the justification of Britain's continued presence in India must be derived from the benefits that British rule could bring to the Indian people, rather than from what the British themselves might obtain in the shape of material rewards.[5] If there were satisfactions to be won, they were to be sought in the non-material sphere: as one viceroy put it, in the fact that British gentlemen were

[1] M. and T. Zinkin, *Britain and India* (1964), pp. 62–3.
[2] Gopal, op. cit., pp. 212–14.   [3] Zinkin, op. cit., p. 61.
[4] Ibid., p. 66.   [5] Gopal, op. cit., p. 65.

engaged 'in the magnificent work of governing an inferior race'.[1] Devotion to the welfare of the Indian masses did not, of course, imply any belief that the régime rested on consent; indeed, after the Mutiny this would have been hard to maintain.

'The government of India,' wrote Sir James Fitzjames Stephen in 1883, 'is essentially an absolute government, founded not on consent, but on conquest . . . it represents a belligerent civilization.' And again: 'The government which now exists has not been chosen by the people. It is not, and if it is to exist at all, it cannot look upon itself as being the representative of the general wishes and average way of thinking of the bulk of the population which it governs.' And for Stephen (though not for all other Englishmen) this 'essentially European' government was both legitimate and destined to be durable. The reason was that the welfare of the Indian people which Stephen accepted as being the government's justification for its existence could only be promoted 'by the introduction of the essential parts of European civilization into a country, densely peopled, grossly ignorant, steeped in idolatrous superstition, unenergetic, fatalistic, and indifferent to most of what we regard as the evils of life, and preferring the repose of submitting to them to the trouble of encountering and trying to remove them'.

Sentiments such as these, widely held no doubt but rarely so effectively expressed, have usually been looked at from the point of view of the growth of the Indian nationalist movement. It triumphed largely because it acquired the sympathies of precisely those people in Britain whom Stephen was attacking, those who believed in 'The Doctrine of the Divine Right of Representative Institutions, or the Sovereignty of the People', or who held that the use of absolute power could 'never be justified except as a temporary expedient used for the purpose of superseding itself and as a means of educating those whom it affected into a fitness for parliamentary institutions'.[2]

If one's focus is on India this emphasis is reasonable enough. But focussing on Britain the result was different in two ways. In the first place, in any absolute government, the role of the army must in the end be decisive. Historically whigs objected to a standing army in time of peace because it could lead directly to the establishment of a despotism, and Britain had devised safeguards to render standing forces ultimately

---

[1] Lord Mayo (viceroy, 1869–72), quoted by Gopal, op. cit., p. 121.
[2] Quoted in C. H. Philips (ed.), *The Evolution of India and Pakistan 1858–1947* (Select Documents) (London, Oxford University Press, 1962), pp. 56–60. Stephen was the law member of the Supreme Council during Mayo's viceroyalty.

dependent upon parliament and not on the executive. India had no parliament, and to the problems of internal security were added those of possible foreign invasion, and of uncertain and turbulent frontiers. It is thus not surprising that 'approximately half the British army was stationed in India' in addition to the Indian army itself, which was British officered except at the most junior level, in total about a quarter of a million men, and backed by huge reserves of potential manpower.[1] In spite of these forces, considerable danger still existed. A Russian attack, so Salisbury pointed out in a letter to the governor of Bombay in 1900, would not even need to aim at conquest; the 'spasm of sedition' which an attack would arouse would suffice to enable Russia to 'shatter our government and reduce India to anarchy'.[2]

In the second place, the government of India was exercised in a way which set it off from the rest of the British constitutional system, except for those colonies which had no important local representative institutions and were still ruled by the Colonial Office. Under the British constitutional system, based upon the twin principles of parliamentary sovereignty and ministerial responsibility, those affected by any action of government could challenge it through their elected representatives. In the case of India, the secretary of state participated in the general responsibility to parliament of the cabinet to which he belonged, but he was neither in theory nor in practice responsible to parliament for the day-to-day administration of the Indian Empire. Ever since the act of 1858 the secretary of state had been required to act in consultation with a body known as the Council of India. Since the further legislation of 1869, this body had been wholly composed of governmental nominees, principally appointed from among those with long experience of Indian administration. The extent to which there was an actual constitutional restraint on the secretary of state, notably in respect of expenditure had been uncertain at first; in general, the tendency was to underline the secretary's authority lest the supremacy of the cabinet itself be challenged.[3]

But the ambiguity stood. In describing the system as it existed

[1] Monroe, op. cit., p. 11.
[2] Lord Salisbury to Sir Henry Stafford Northcote, 8 June 1900. Quoted by J. A. S. Grenville, *Lord Salisbury and Foreign Policy, the close of the nineteenth century* (London, Athlone Press, 1964), pp. 295–6. cf. D. R. Gillard, 'Salisbury and the Indian Defence problem', in K. Bourne and D. C. Watt (ed.), *Studies in International History* (London, Longmans, 1967).
[3] For a description of the British arrangements for handling Indian affairs at this time, see ch. XI, 'The Home Government 1858–1918', by Sir H. Verney Lovett, in H. H. Dodwell (ed.), *The Cambridge History of India* (Cambridge University Press, 1932), vol. VI.

during the first world war, the Mesopotamia commission of 1917 reported:

> The Government and Administration of India are vested in the Secretary of State for India in Council and in the Governor-General of India in Council and the former body dominates the latter. The powers of the Secretary of State for India are immense, greatly exceeding those exercised by an ordinary Secretary of State. So far as finance and expenditure are concerned, the Council stands to the Secretary of State for India in much the same relation as that in which Parliament stands to the other Secretaries of State.[1]

Different secretaries attached varied degrees of importance to co-operation with the Council. This is of some importance for the history of policy towards India, as the influence of the Council tended to be conservative. But in respect of the British government itself it was the immense scope of the powers of the secretary of state himself that were the anomaly. The existence of the Council did provide some excuse for parliament's failure to interest itself in Indian affairs. This was particularly notable in the period 1880–1905, although even then there was some expression of interest, not only by Irish members. An Indian was returned for an English constituency (as a liberal) in 1892 and in the following year an Indian parliamentary committee was set up on a non-party basis; it had 154 members in the first session in which it operated and 200 by 1905. But the importance of India was not matched by the time and attention devoted to it by parliament.[2]

In these circumstances the primary responsibility for defending the interests of India fell upon the government of India and in particular upon the viceroy. How far this might carry him in opposition to the home government would vary; in the end, as the Mesopotamia commission pointed out, it was the secretary of state whose will must prevail. It was almost inevitable that the government of India's views should differ from those entertained at home. Its first responsibility was to the defence and security of India, and it naturally regarded these

[1] *Report of the Mesopotamia Commission* (Cd. 8610), p. 101, in C. H. Philips, op. cit., p. 24. The Mesopotamia commission was set up to investigate the handling of the Mesopotamia expedition by the government of India after the disaster of Kut-el-Amara in 1916. It brought to light the importance of private correspondence between the secretary of state and the viceroy as the means by which the Council of India had been kept out of important aspects of India policy for some time past.
[2] M. Cumpston, in *E.H.R.*, loc. cit.

35

as the first claim on British resources and as the prior consideration in the formation of British policy. A viceroy of powerful character and with an important political base at home, as Curzon was shortly to demonstrate, was not without means of making his opinions felt.

But there were obstacles in the way of governing for India's exclusive good. In the first place, although India was not a colony of settlement, the opinions and prejudices of British residents there could not be ignored. Salisbury compared unfavourably the treatment meted out to the native races of India by the race-conscious British with the methods of the Russians,[1] pointing out that it was impossible to minister to the martial pride of the Indians by obtaining 'some proportion of military honours and grades for the native princes' despite the fact that this move had the backing of the Queen.[2]

There were also the pressure groups at home whose angle might be self-interested, as in the case of the cotton lobby, or inspired by what those on the spot thought was a dangerous and ignorant idealism often tinged with party zeal. This tended to imbue those who had to deal with Indian affairs at the top with the kind of impatience with parliamentary democracy to which Kipling gave voice. 'One of the many unrecognized advantages which we derive from the possession of India,' wrote one viceroy, 'is a field of administration which furnishes us with the practical confutation of a great many liberal fallacies.'[3]

The problem was thus to combine within a single system of government both an empire dedicated to the ideas of representative government and to a high measure of autonomy for its member nations, and an empire to which most responsible persons believed these principles to be inapplicable; either because they were unsuited to peoples of another and very different civilization or because they would, if introduced, lead to the complete severance of ties with the imperial metropolis. It was more than merely an English domestic problem, since the question of how to care for Indian interests was to prove one of the most difficult of those involved in any scheme of imperial representation at the centre.

The colonial conference of 1887, the first product of the movement towards some imperial system of this kind, did not include any repre-

---

[1] Salisbury to Northcote, 8 June 1900. Quoted in Grenville, op. cit., pp. 295–6.
[2] Grenville, loc. cit.
[3] Lord Lytton to the Earl of Cranbrook, 30 April 1878. Quoted in S. R. Mehrotra, *India and the Commonwealth, 1885–1929* (London, Allen & Unwin, 1965), p. 126. The whole problem of the role of India in the imperial structure is much illuminated in this work.

sentative of the Indian Empire; and the same was true of the 1892 and 1897 conferences, membership of which was limited to the colonial secretary and the prime ministers of the self-governing colonies. The first hint of representation for India came with the conference of 1907 when a member of the Indian Council, Sir J. L. Mackay, was described as present 'on behalf of the India Office'.[1] The early nationalist movement in India did not itself accept the principle of differentiation. Its leaders professed loyalty to the Crown, and sought to make a future self-governing India a full partner in Britain's imperial tasks.[2] As late as 1907 it was possible for the Congress leader G. K. Gokhale (1866–1915) to say: 'I want India to take her proper place among the great nations of the world,'politically, industrially, in religion, in literature, in science and in arts. I want all this and I feel at the same time that the whole of this aspiration can, in its essence and in reality, be realized within the Empire.'[3]

Political events in India were to turn nationalist aspirations in a different direction, and the responsibility of representing India's interests at the centre of imperial affairs continued to rest with the government of India which in the last resort was inseparable from the government of the United Kingdom. Nevertheless, the government of India wielded a certain influence. It was responsible for the protection of imperial interests in the Persian Gulf and southern Arabia;[4] the British presence in the Far East had come about through a process of expansion dictated largely by Indian interests. Britain without India would not have been the world power that at the time of the Diamond Jubilee she seemed to be. At that time it could well be argued that she had as much right as Austria-Hungary to be styled a dual monarchy or dual empire. Nor, but for the existence of the Indian Empire, would Britain have been drawn into the most recent of her other imperial extensions – the East African territories.[5]

[1] J. L. Mackay (1852–1932), first Earl of Inchcape, banker and shipowner, was a member of the secretary of state's council from 1897 to 1911. See generally J. E. Tyler, 'The Development of the Imperial Conference, 1887–1914', which is chapter XI of E. A. Benians, Sir James Butler, and C. E. Carrington (eds), *The Cambridge History of the British Empire*, vol. III. (Cambridge University Press, 1959).   [2] Mehrotra, op. cit., p. 21.
[3] Speech at Allahabad, 4 February 1907. Quoted from Philips, op. cit., p. 163.
[4] Indian army troops had been used in the Ethiopian campaign of 1868. From 1869 on the Indian government paid a subsidy towards the maintenance of a British naval force in the Arabian Gulf as well as in the Bay of Bengal.
[5] 'At the first level of analysis the decisive motive behind late Victorian strategy in Africa was to protect the all-important stakes in India and the East.' Ronald Robinson, John Gallagher, and Alice Denny, *Africa and the Victorians* (London, Macmillan, 1961), p. 464.

The East African extension of British power, including the occupation of the Sudan after Kitchener's victory at Omdurman in 1898, was in itself an outcome of the position that Britain had created for herself in Egypt by the events of 1882; and that, in turn, is to be explained largely in the light of the route to India.

It is true that the occupation of Egypt was intended to be temporary, that the idea was to restore financial stability and the capacity for autonomous rule. But for those entrusted with the task, notably Lord Cromer who, as British agent and consul-general, was the effective ruler of the country from 1883 until his retirement in 1907, the improvement of the administration and the welfare of the people came to have priority over political evolution.[1] Service with Cromer in Egypt was second only to service in India as a school of imperial paternalism and it is not without significance that Milner, who was to be the most powerful exponent of this aspect of the imperial creed, should first have made his mark in Cromer's service.[2]

Service in Egypt or India produced a strong cast of mind. It could be combined in home affairs with strong conservatism and with resistance to the further encroachment of democracy; but this was not universally true. A young army officer in India so radical in his views on home politics that he declared himself ready to enter parliament as a liberal but for the obstacle of home rule, could nevertheless describe the external aspect of his policies as follows:

2. Imperialism abroad.

East of Suez Democratic reins are impossible. India must be governed on old principles. The colonies must be federated and a system of Imperial Defence arranged. Also we must combine for Tariff & Commerce.

3. European Politics.

Non Intervention. Keep absolutely unembroiled – Isolated if you like.

[1] Sir Evelyn Baring (created first Earl of Cromer in 1901) was born in 1841 and entered the army in 1858. From 1872 to 1876, he was private secretary to the viceroy of India, the Earl of Northbrook. He had taken part in running the finances of Egypt between 1877 and 1879 and was made financial member of the viceroy's council in 1880 (d. 1917). For a general account of Britain's role in Egypt, see John Marlowe, *Anglo-Egyptian Relations 1800–1953* (1954).

[2] Alfred Milner (1854–1925), raised to the peerage as Lord Milner in 1901, was under-secretary for finance in Egypt 1889–92. From 1892 to 1897, when he went to South Africa as High Commissioner, he was in England as chairman of the Board of Inland Revenue. Milner's appeal in England was handicapped by his having been born in Germany, though of British parentage, and speaking English with a strong German accent.

4. Defence.

The colonies must contribute and hence a council must be formed.
A mighty navy must keep the seas. The army may be reduced to a
training depot for India with one army corps for petty expeditions.[1]

The New Imperialism and Cecil Rhodes

But a full imperial programme of this kind required the evaluation of
other factors, many of which rested upon assumptions about the conduct of foreign powers and of colonial statesmen that were to prove ill-
founded. The failure to apprehend the difference in atmosphere
between Britain and the self-governing colonies was to be the most important, if least appreciated, weakness of the imperialist school in
Britain, and some of the adherents of the school never fully grasped this
point. Thus, looking back to this period in memoirs published in 1953,
Leo Amery could still argue that the correct response to the new challenge to Britain's power in the 1890s would have been a common
scheme of imperial defence. It should have been based upon the expansion of imperial economic power and the defeat of this conception
was due simply to the strength of the free trade interest in Britain itself.[2]
The imperial outlook of the 1890s was always the view from Whitehall
and Westminster.

The new British imperialism of the period hoped to reshape relations
with the self-governing colonies, as well as augment the strength of the
Empire by a better use of the resources of the more recently acquired
tropical territories. This marked a change from the assumptions of the
mid-Victorian period, when the ultimate dissolution of the entire imperial structure had been so generally taken for granted.[3] It is, perhaps,
because the adherents of the imperial idea were forced to reverse this

[1] Winston S. Churchill (aet. 22) to Lady Randolph Churchill, Bangalore, 6 April 1897.
Randolph S. Churchill, *Winston S. Churchill* (London, 1967), Companion Volume 1, part 2,
p. 751. In an earlier letter, Churchill strongly criticized a recent speech by Lansdowne suggesting an increase in the army. 'If the navy were kept up to the proper strength an army
would not be needed for defence: for offence an army corps or perhaps two would adequately
carry out such enterprises in foreign countries – out of Europe – as might be expedient.'
Winston S. Churchill to Lady Randolph Churchill, Bangalore, 8 December 1896. Ibid.,
p. 709.
[2] L. S. Amery, *My Political Life* (1953), pp. 87–8.
[3] See C. A. Bodelsen, *Studies in Mid-Victorian Imperialism* (Copenhagen, 1924).

once powerful tide of opinion that their writings and speeches took on such a strongly ideological flavour.[1]

A partial reversal of opinion had actually begun in the late 1860s, and by the early 1880s parliament had accepted generally the fact of empire, and the view that self-government rather than separation was the proper destination of the colonies of white settlement. In the case of tropical dependencies strong emphasis was laid (as with India) on the civilizing mission of Europe; and Gladstone did not limit this to British influence, approving on these grounds the acquisition by Germany of African colonies despite opposition expressions of uneasiness.[2]

His vision of a common European responsibility in the backward areas of the world did not survive into the harsher and more competitive climate of the 1890s. The new situation was expounded by his successor as liberal prime minister, Lord Rosebery, in a speech before the Royal Colonial Institute in March 1893:

> It is said that our Empire is already large enough and does not need extension. That would be true enough if the world were elastic but unfortunately it is not elastic, and we are engaged at the present moment, in the language of mining, in 'pegging out claims for the future'. We have to consider not what we want now but what we shall want in the future. We have to consider what countries must be developed either by ourselves or by some other nation, and we have to remember that it is part of our responsibility and heritage to take care that the world, so far as it can be moulded by us, shall receive an English-speaking complexion, and not that of other nations . . . we have to look forward beyond the chatter of platforms and the passions of party to the future of the race, of which we are at present the trustees, and we should in my opinion grossly fail in the task that has been laid upon us did we shrink from responsibilities and decline to take our share in a partition of the world which we have not forced on but which has been forced on us.[3]

It was also possible to take a strongly imperialist view about existing British possessions and the need to safeguard them and exploit their

---

[1] On the development of the imperial idea in the 1880s and 1890s, see Thornton, op. cit., ch. 2.
[2] Cumpston, in *T.R.H.S.* (1963), loc. cit.
[3] Quoted by B. Semmel in *Imperialism and Social Reform: English Social-Imperial Thought 1895–1914* (London, Allen & Unwin, 1960), pp. 54–5.

potential, and yet to express reservations about unlimited expansionism:

> With all my strong and ever-increasing jingoism I have no sympathy
> with the lust for unlimited empires. Our danger is that one great
> section of opinion is for claiming everything, while another large
> school is for sticking to nothing that involves any sacrifice or even
> discomfort, and British policy halts between the two opinions. The
> true Jingo is for limited expansion but unlimited tenacity. [1]

In his influential Cambridge lectures, published in 1883 as *The Expansion of England*, the historian Sir John Seeley had pointed out that the European powers generally were likely to be eclipsed by the new giants, the United States and Russia. Britain had defeated its continental rivals in the competition for empire because of its greater freedom from European commitments; it was now in a position to transform its colonial empire into a 'Greater Britain' and join Russia and America as a great world power.

Closest in his views to Seeley was the radical politician and former liberal minister, Sir Charles Dilke. [2] Dilke who had seen at first hand much more of the overseas world than other British statesmen of the time wrote a number of works on the imperial theme and on defence questions between 1880 and 1890. His collaborator, the military historian Spenser Wilkinson, argued that he was the real founder of modern British imperialism since he was the first writer to call attention to the historical significance of the cohesion of the British peoples and fully to understand the link between this fact and the problems of defence. [3] Nevertheless, Dilke's position differed in two respects from that of many writers of the imperialist school. He was not an isolationist in regard to Europe, believing that a Europe in which Britain played no part would be too heavily weighted against the forces of freedom; in the 1880s this made him an advocate of renewing with France the liberal entente of

---

[1] Milner to Lord Goschen, 22 June 1890. Quoted in J. E. Wrench, *Alfred, Lord Milner* (London, Eyre & Spottiswoode, 1958), p. 104.
[2] Sir Charles Wentworth Dilke (1843–1911) (second baronet) had been under-secretary at the Foreign Office 1880–2 and a member of Gladstone's cabinet as president of the Local Government Board from 1882 to 1885. He had voted for the Home Rule Bill of 1886. Following upon divorce proceedings in 1885–6 he was out of public life for some years returning as liberal M.P. for the Forest of Dean in 1892, a seat he retained until his death. His principal work, *Problems of Greater Britain*, appeared in 1890. See Roy Jenkins, *Sir Charles Dilke: A Victorian Tragedy* (London, Collins, 1958).
[3] Spenser Wilkinson, *Thirty-Five Years 1874–1909* (1933), pp. 127, 132.

earlier in the century. He was also critical of the federation movement which was active in the 1880s, no doubt because he perceived the extent to which such ideas were unpopular in the self-governing colonies themselves.[1]

In a way, however, it was not any of those who devoted themselves to a formal investigation of the imperial problem who best symbolized the imperial spirit but rather Cecil Rhodes, the entrepreneur and colonial statesman whose involvement in the Jameson Raid affair was one of the issues before the select committee which inquired into the raid. Rhodes himself was not at any time, despite his sympathies for it, directly involved in the movement for imperial unity; his own activities were confined to South Africa and to its northward extension into the territory that still in part bears his name.[2] 'His was not,' as has been pointed out, 'the Imperialism of direct domination, but that Colonial Imperialism, based on a confident local nationalism, which he shared with John A. Macdonald in Canada, and with men like Alfred Deakin in Australia or Seddon in New Zealand.'[3] Nevertheless Rhodes's local nationalism was combined with a belief in the destinies of the British race in which he echoed the sentiments of Rosebery and Chamberlain; and as with the latter this could even spill over into a generalized view of a teutonic racial superiority.

The development of these views can be traced in the series of wills which Rhodes made.[4] The first of these, drawn up in 1877 at the early age of twenty-four, provided that his property should go to the secretary of state for the colonies and the attorney-general for Griqualand West and be used by them to found a secret society with the following objectives:

[1] J. E. Tyler, *The Struggle for Imperial Unity* (1938), pp. 77–8. The imperial federation movement did not run very deep. 'Man's thoughts in those days did not, in the constitutional field, go beyond some vague idea of federation. Even that was limited to the then governing or self-governing white communities of the empire. The future emergence of the dependent Empire into the higher status of equal free partnership if not rejected altogether, was at any rate relegated to a dim and remote future. Still less was there any positive conception of the relation of imperial unity to an evolving external world.' Amery, op. cit., vol. I, p. 15.
[2] Cecil John Rhodes (1853–1902) secured the chartering of the British South Africa Company for the settlement of what came to be Rhodesia in 1889. From July 1890 to January 1896 he was prime minister of Cape Colony.
[3] Amery, op. cit., vol. 1, p. 182. Sir John Macdonald (1815–91), the maker of the Canadian confederation, was prime minister of Canada from 1867 to 1873 and 1878 to 1891; Alfred Deakin (1856–1919) was prime minister of Australia from September 1903 to April 1904, June 1905 to November 1908, and June 1909 to November 1910; Sir Richard Seddon (1845–1906) was prime minister of New Zealand from 1893 to 1906.
[4] For the history of Rhodes's wills, see Frank Aydelotte, *The American Rhodes Scholarships* (Princeton University Press, 1946), ch. 1.

(1) to perfect the system of colonization by British subjects of suitable lands in Africa, the Near East, South America, and the islands and coasts of the Pacific;

(2) the ultimate recovery of the United States as a free member of a Federated Empire;

(3) the inauguration of a system of colonial representation in the Imperial Parliament to consolidate the Empire.

The general aim, as Rhodes described it was to form a new world power great enough to render future wars unnecessary and to promote the best interests of humanity at large. His second and third wills were along the same lines. In the fourth will, Rhodes looked beyond the extension of the British Empire to world government and questioned the idea of a secret society as a suitable instrument of his purpose. His new plan for a university at Cape Town was dedicated to preparing men for the task of putting his ideals into practice and this scheme was adumbrated in his fifth will. The sixth will in 1893 embodied a transition from a purely South African scheme to one providing for the foundation of scholarships at his own university, Oxford, for South African, Australian, Canadian, and New Zealand scholars. His last will in 1899 extended the scheme to the United States and Germany and laid down the criteria for the choice of scholars.

When the will was published and put into effect it was naturally regarded as presumptuous by anti-imperialists. 'I cannot help,' wrote Goldwin Smith, 'deploring the adoption of Oxford as a pedestal for a trophy of Cecil Rhodes.'[1] But over half a century later it became evident that of all the legacies of the period of imperial enthusiasm, the Rhodes scholarships looked like being the most enduring and not the least influential. In the old dominions, and in the United States, former Rhodes scholars formed a conspicuous element in the political and administrative élite; and the decision to extend the scheme to the newer members of the Commonwealth after 1947, while one that could be held to be scarcely in accordance with some of Rhodes' sentiments on race, was also likely to be of some importance for their future relationship with the rest of the Commonwealth. The very success of the scheme,

[1] Goldwin Smith to Bryce, 4 January 1903. Bryce Papers, English Correspondence, vol. 16 James Bryce (1838–1922) (first viscount Bryce, 1914) had published *The American Commonwealth* in 1888. He had held office under Gladstone and Rosebery and was to be chief secretary for Ireland from December 1905 to January 1907. He served as ambassador to Washington from February 1907 to April 1913.

combined with Rhodes' early enthusiasm for secret societies, provided material for those in other countries who were always prone to see the British Empire itself in conspiratorial terms.[1]

The afterthought which led Rhodes to add the United States to the list of countries whose young men were eligible for his Oxford scholarships points to the ambiguity and hesitations about the role that the United States should play in the new era of British imperial policy. The sudden enthusiasm for active co-operation on both sides of the Atlantic (which so surprisingly followed the Venezuela crisis of 1895-6 when the two countries were closer to war with each other than at any time since 1862, if not 1815), was partly the product of external events and of the scant sympathy elsewhere than in Britain for the Americans in their war with Spain. In part it also reflected internal developments, notably the feeling of the dominant classes on the eastern seaboard of the United States that their position was being undermined by the new political weight of more recent non-British immigrant groups.[2] Between this self-conscious element in American society and the British upper classes (also feeling the pressure of insurgent democracy, though in different ways) there developed a number of new links in business and politics. These were strengthened by the availability of American brides with dowries that could help to make up for the adverse effect on England's landed fortunes of the imports of grain from America's own prairies. In the words of an American sociologist: 'A British American, White Anglo-Saxon Protestant (WASP) establishment, consolidated through family alliances between Mayfair and Murray Hill involving millions of dollars authoritatively ran the world as their ancestors had done since Queen Elizabeth's time.'[3] This is, of course, not strictly speaking true. They did not run the world; though some of them might have liked to. Indeed, Chamberlain's famous speeches adumbrating the possibility of an Anglo-American alliance in 1898-9 represented a very temporary phase in the relations between the two countries.[4]

[1] An American writer contrasts Rhodes the 'vulgar megalomaniac' with Cromer 'the educated man of sacrifice and duty'. Does this mean more than that the Barings had money and that Rhodes needed to make it? See H. Arendt, *The Burden of Our Time* (London, Secker & Warburg, 1951), p. 212.
[2] Gilbert (ed.), *A Century of Conflict*, p. 157.
[3] E. Digby Baltzell, *The Protestant Establishment* (London, Secker & Warburg, 1965), p. 11. The 'Wasp' element was not always insisted upon; Curzon's father-in-law – the future viceroy was married in Washington in 1895 – was Levi Zeigler Leiter, not a very 'Waspish' name.
[4] See 'America and the British Foreign Policy-Making *Élite*, from Joseph Chamberlain to

It has usually and rightly been assumed that the principal reasons for the failure of this idea of an Anglo-American combination at the time were to be found on the American side. Isolationism remained for another generation and more the guiding principle of American external policy, and there seemed few advantages to be gained from stepping in to uphold a balance of power that Britain unaided could no longer maintain. The more prudent British statesmen like Arthur Balfour, however strong their belief in the desirability, and indeed inevitability, of close Anglo-American relations, were careful to moderate the tone of their speeches on this theme.[1]

The feeling that the two great co-heirs of Anglo-Saxon freedom and civilization have a common mission [wrote Balfour to the American ambassador a few years later] has more quickly developed on this side of the Atlantic than on the other – at least among the general mass of the population, and . . . there is therefore some danger lest phrases which are suitable enough in Great Britain may seem excessive in America, and may excite, not sympathy, but surprise and ridicule.[2]

In addition, not all those who cherished the imperial vision believed that the task of overseas rule could usefully be shared with the United States. It is true that it was being debated whether the United States, following its defeat of Spain, should remain to rule the Philippines. Kipling's poem 'The White Man's Burden' provided a slogan for annexation; indeed, his first action on completing the poem was to send it to Theodore Roosevelt, the newly elected vice-president of the United States.[3] But Kipling himself was somewhat ambivalent in his attitude to the United States after his period of residence there, feeling

---

Anthony Eden, 1895–1956', in Donald Watt, *Personalities and Policies* (London, Longmans, 1965).

[1] Balfour, whose previous offices had included a notable tenure of the Irish secretaryship from 1897 to 1891, was at the time of the Diamond Jubilee, first lord of the treasury and leader of the House of Commons. He succeeded his uncle Salisbury as prime minister in July 1902 and held office till December 1905. Although himself a bachelor, he profited by the change in English upper-class life in the last two decades of the nineteenth century which was in part due to the influx of talented American women impatient of the formal stuffiness of the masculine dominated society that they found. On this and in particular on the 'Souls', the clique to which Balfour belonged, and on its influence on the whole imperialist tone, see Kenneth Young, *Arthur James Balfour* (London, Bell, 1963), pp. 141–5.

[2] Balfour to Joseph Choate, 1 July 1905. Balfour Papers, B.M. Add. 49742.

[3] Carrington, *Rudyard Kipling*, pp. 276–8. On Roosevelt's ambivalent attitude to the British Empire, see 'Theodore Roosevelt and the British Empire', in Max Beloff, *The Great Powers* (London, Allen & Unwin, 1958).

that many Americans lacked the proper deference due to a more mature civilization.[1]

And there were other doubters as well: the young Winston Churchill, whose mother was notable among the American brides of a slightly earlier generation, wrote to her from India with an adult scepticism.

> As a representative of both countries – the idea of an Anglo-American rapprochement is very pleasant. One of the principles of my politics will always be to promote a good understanding between the English speaking communities. At the same time alliances are useless. When countries were ruled by individuals, these had their personal honour involved in their public pledges. Nowadays a democracy is protected from the obligation by a pleasing vagueness. So many people bear the responsibility that the weight is insignificant. As long as the interests of two nations coincide as far as they coincide – they are and will be allies. But when they diverge they will cease to be allies.[2]

Shortly afterwards he returned to the theme in relation to Chamberlain's speech of 13 May warning the European powers that war, terrible as it was, would not be too high a price to pay for an Anglo-American alliance:

> The idea of an Anglo-Saxon alliance may delight or alarm Editors, jingos and idiots of various countries. It will not trouble diplomats who know that no alliance is possible until community of interest is established. Is it likely that the cute Uncle Sam will pick our Asiatic, African and European chestnuts out of the fire for us?[3]

Over forty years later it was to be a principal objective of Churchillian diplomacy to persuade the Americans to do just that; his earlier scepticism proved justified on the whole.

---

[1] Stewart, *Eight Modern Writers*, p. 50.
[2] Winston S. Churchill to Lady Randolph Churchill, 22 May 1898. Randolph S. Churchill, op. cit., Companion Volume 1, Part 2, p. 937.
[3] Winston S. Churchill to Lady Randolph Churchill, June 1898. Ibid., p. 947. For Chamberlain's pronouncements on Anglo-American relations at this time, see J. L. Garvin, *Life of Joseph Chamberlain* (London, Macmillan, 1934), vol. 3, pp. 296–306. Chamberlain himself married, as his third wife, the daughter of the secretary for war in Cleveland's first administration.

Chamberlain and Salisbury

Chamberlain, who had shown little interest in foreign affairs before 1897, did not long remain on the American tack. His prime concern during the remainder of his active political life was to develop the unity and resources of the Empire and to do this by economic means. Stated in general terms, this policy had an obvious appeal;[1] but it was defended with arguments which often irritated its opponents by a cavalier ignoring of facts, such as the greater importance of foreign as compared with imperial trade.[2]

The vision of an empire linked together by ties of trade, which was to force Chamberlain into taking up the cause of protection at home, tended to focus upon the older self-governing colonies and on the newly acquired tropical territories in Africa and Asia. These most nearly corresponded to the idea of undeveloped estates;[3] but little that was positive was done to provide capital for them.[4] As well as the general domestic aversion to a return to protection without which no preferential system could be built, important interests were quick to take fright at such notions. The Lancashire textile industry had found new and expanding markets, not only in India but also in China and the Near East and clung to the traditional view that its prosperity was bound up with the free import of cheap food and raw materials.[5] Domestic opposition, however, was more immediately obvious than that of the champions of preferential tariffs in the self-governing colonies. They were prepared to temper the impact of their tariff autonomy on British trade by giving British products a preferential position, despite Britain's difficulty in reciprocating, but the intention was merely to prefer the British pro-

[1] The economist, W. A. S. Hewins, who provided much of the intellectual material for the protectionist or 'tariff reform' campaign, wrote in his memoirs: 'The new Imperial policy of Chamberlain made an immense appeal to the working classes of the country. It was not they who were his opponents. Those who were against him were the vested interests, the lower middle classes and the academic world.' Hewins, *Apologia of an Imperialist* (London, Constable, 1929), vol. 1, p. 284.
[2] Thornton, op. cit., pp. 99–100. On the other hand, it is true that the decade of the nineties saw an increased proportion of British trade carried on within the Empire. Semmel, op. cit., p. 149.
[3] 'Since 1884 Britain had assumed responsibility for the Niger Coast, Somaliland, for portions of Malaya and New Guinea, for Bechuanaland, Zululand, for regions in East Africa and beyond the Limpopo River, for Upper Burma and Zanzibar.' R. Koebner and H. D. Schmidt, *Imperialism* (Cambridge University Press, 1964), p. 196.
[4] S. B. Saul, 'The Economic Significance of Constructive Imperialism', *Journal of Economic History*, vol. XVII (1957).
[5] Semmel, op. cit., p. 147.

47

duct against the foreign.[1] The ultimate objective was to create domestic industries, after which British industries would no longer be favoured. Ideas of imperial unity in economic matters implied the specialization of function; but this was incompatible with the development of self-sufficient national communities on a par with Britain itself. By 1897 conflict over this was already in the air.

The arguments of the Chamberlain school were not relevant to the very different problems created by the existence of the Indian Empire, and Chamberlain himself never showed much interest in this aspect of the imperial system. If there had been any follow-up to a suggestion made in 1898 that Chamberlain should himself be named viceroy he might no doubt have shown equal interest in its specific problems.[2] As it was, he neither visited India nor spoke about it, to the annoyance of Curzon and the school that regarded India as the keystone of the entire imperial structure.[3] His lack of interest may be the reason why he was prepared, early in 1902 after the breakdown of his overtures for an American or German alliance, to advocate a policy for Britain 'of a splendid isolation, surrounded by our kinsfolk.'[4]

The economic and the ideological aspects of Chamberlain's imperialism are closely mingled. Two informal empires of trade and investment had come into being in the nineteenth century, where British interests

---

[1] The enactment of the Canadian tariff of 1897 with its preferential provisions was greeted by Kipling with verses in which the message is clear even if the metaphor is strained:

> A Nation spoke to a Nation,
>   A Queen sent word to a throne:
> 'Daughter am I in my mother's house,
>   But mistress in my own.
> The gates are mine to open,
>   As the gates are mine to close,
> And I set my house in order'
>   Said our Lady of the Snows.

Eliot (ed.), *A Choice of Kipling's Verse*, p. 100. Is there any other poem written to a tariff?
[2] The idea of making Chamberlain viceroy was proposed to Balfour in a letter from St John Loe Strachey, on 12 April 1898 (Balfour Papers, B.M. Add. 49797). Strachey was the very influential editor of the *Spectator* from 1898 to 1925 and father of the future labour minister, John Strachey (1901–63), author *inter alia* of *The End of Empire*.
[3] 'I often wonder,' wrote Curzon to Northbrook in 1903, 'what would have become of him and us, if he had ever visited India. He would have become the greatest Indian Imperialist of the time. The colonies would have been dwarfed and forgotten; and the pivot of Empire would have been Calcutta. Not having enjoyed this good fortune, we are now forgotten, and the Empire is to be bound together (or as we are told, if the prescription is not taken, destroyed) without apparent reference to the requirements of its largest and most powerful unit,' Mehrotra, op. cit., pp. 243–4.
[4] Grenville, op. cit., p. 366.

might call for protection by British power.[1] One was in Latin America, where the increasing challenge of the United States (despite Salisbury's brave words about the Monroe Doctrine during the Venezuela crisis) was hardly contested. During the Venezuela blockade in 1902–3, Britain at first participated alongside Germany and then backed down in the face of American pressure, thus showing that she would not be a party to any European attempt to dispute the *de facto* responsibility of the United States for the behaviour of Latin American governments.[2]

The other, more contentious, area was China where, after the country was opened up to foreign commerce in the middle of the century, Britain had secured a larger share of the country's trade than any other power. Britain supplied the powerful director of the Chinese maritime customs as well as the chief engineer of China's northern railways. But this virtual monopoly was now being challenged both by the other maritime powers and by Russia's overland pressure.[3] Despite the prominent role of China in Britain's diplomacy after 1898 there may have been some failure fully to realize what was at stake:

> It is difficult for us today [wrote Amery fifty years later] to realize the position we held in China at the close of the last century, and still more to realize how we then envisaged the future. For some fifty years we had been active in opening up an empire hitherto sealed off from the outer world . . . No one was clamouring to see Queen Victoria Empress of China as well as Empress of India. But no one at the time of her Diamond Jubilee would have dismissed the idea as inconceivable.[4]

While it is true that Chamberlain did not ignore the importance of China, he tended to think of the question as one of trade and its pro-

[1] 'Never had the flow of British capital to Latin America been so great as in the decade of the eighties, and never had European economic penetration, led by Britain, been so extensive.' R. A. Humphreys, 'Anglo-American Rivalries and the Venezuela Crisis of 1895'. *T.R.H.S.*, 5th ser., vol. 17 (1967), p. 146. On the limitations of this protection, see D. C. M. Platt, *Finance, Trade and Politics in British Foreign Policy 1815–1914* (Oxford, Clarendon Press, 1968), part III, ch. 6.
[2] By the 1960s the British government was actively concerned about the decline of British commerce and influence in Latin America and was trying, through the active encouragement of 'Latin American studies' at the universities, to focus attention on its affairs once more. But any British student who went out to most of these countries must have been impressed by the abundant evidence of the achievements of British enterprise and technology now largely abandoned to other hands, and by the relics of British settlement and of the educational and cultural institutions that went with it. 'Informal empire' leaves its mark as well.
[3] Grenville, op. cit., pp. 131–2.
[4] Amery, op. cit., pp. 144–5.

tection, and to think that it was possible to ignore more general considerations of politics and great power diplomacy.[1]

Lord Salisbury who was, despite Chamberlain's flamboyance, the dominant British statesman of the 1890s, brought a different kind of intellect and temperament to bear on the problems of Britain's position. During his administrations vast new territories were added to the Empire, and he accepted the defence of the Empire as the most important task of British statesmanship. But although he regarded it as inevitable that the great powers should assume a preponderating influence over the less developed parts of the world, whether as colonies or as areas in which commerce could be furthered without the burdens of direct imperial rule, he did not seek the extension of empire for its own sake and was more influenced by considerations of power, prestige, and strategy than by economic arguments.[2]

He was conscious of the limited extent of British power and of the obstacles to the long-range planning of foreign policy implicit in Britain's domestic political arrangements. He preferred – as his China policy showed – to keep the 'open door' for British trade without the new military and political commitments that direct annexations of territory would involve. In dealing with Britain's rivals he was concerned rather to promote conciliation than, like Chamberlain, to exploit the tensions between them.[3] A war between major powers, whatever its origin, would be dangerous to the thin crust of civilization; this was implicit in his conservative and sceptical outlook on politics. It is hard in retrospect to say he was wrong.

A feeling for the organic aspects of human society and for the limitations upon human contrivance made him perhaps less enthusiastic to strengthen the bonds of empire by paper constitutions that did not arise directly from the deeper urges and purposes of its peoples. In a speech shortly before his retirement, he defined his own stand as follows:

> There are very important men, men of great interest and authority, who think the moment has come for some legislative action on our part which should federate the Colonies. I exhort them before they do so, carefully to consider what steps they are going to take and what results they may expect from them. We have no power by

[1] Grenville, op. cit., p. 156.
[2] Ibid., pp. 19, 135.
[3] Ibid., pp. 315, 436–7.

legislation to affect the flow of opinion and of affection which has so largely risen between the mother country and her daughter states . . . The tendency of human beings, and of statesmen – who are human beings – is to anticipate all such matters, and to think that because their own wretched lives are confined to some sixty or seventy years, therefore it is open to them to force an anticipation of the results which the natural play of forces and affections and the alteration of the judgement and the mutual feelings of the various peoples in the world will bring before us.[1]

As a short-term diagnosis, Salisbury's could not be bettered. In two world wars the rallying of the overseas peoples of British stock, and of many of their non-English-speaking fellow-citizens, to Britain's support seemed a full justification both of Salisbury's position, and of the idea of the Commonwealth that Balfour developed out of it. It may be that an opportunity was missed to provide an institutional structure to strengthen the sense of common identity now breaking down, as the role of the Crown began to seem less adequate with the general decline in respect for the hereditary and prescriptive aspects of the British system.

The Generation in Power

Important, however, as were the opinions of the leading ministers, particularly on questions in which parliament showed only a spasmodic interest, it is equally important to gauge the attitudes of others who were collectively involved in the principal decisions. To these decisions they might contribute either through active support or criticism or simply by putting up enough opposition to theoretically available alternatives to exclude them in practice. Although foreign observers perceived a formidable unity in the British governmental machine in its conduct of external affairs, closer investigation shows many divisions and uncertainties.[2] It is difficult, however, to go deeply into the opinions dividing the British policy-making *élite* in the eighteen-nineties and subsequent decades, because of the unevenness of the biographical data upon which such studies must rest. Much is known about statesmen and soldiers, less about diplomats, and very little indeed about civil

[1] Salisbury speech to the Primrose League, 7 May 1902. Quoted in Kenneth Young, *Arthur James Balfour* (London, Bell, 1963), p. 193.
[2] For a famous description by an envious admirer of the ability of the British governmental system to put up an unbreakable front, see Charles de Gaulle, *Mémoires de Guerre* (Paris, Plon, 1954), vol. 1, pp. 138–40.

servants. The documentation of journalists and publicists is also very uneven, and only now beginning to be properly explored.[1] In 1897 a socially narrower *élite* existed than later on, since the country was ruled by 'the last government in the western world to possess all the attributes of aristocracy'.[2]

Nevertheless one common element does link men of any particular period, and that is the factor of time itself. Basic experience is determined by the date of birth, so that one can talk in terms of a political generation of fifteen or twenty years; though clearly there must be a certain arbitrariness in choosing initial dates.

It can be assumed that few men exercise an important influence on public affairs before the age of thirty; in the professions of war and diplomacy, promotion comes more slowly, and this was still truer in the nineteenth century before the coming of the concept of early and compulsory retirement. The generation that dominated Britain at the time of the Diamond Jubilee was composed of men who had been born before the repeal of the corn laws in 1846 and who had known at first hand the relative peace and security of the mid-Victorian years; 'the Age of Equipoise' as one recent student of those times has styled it.[3]

It is striking that this generation does not entirely reflect the idea of British 'isolation' that is traditionally associated with the policies of Salisbury.[4] None of Victoria's servants could equal her own intimacy of European connections through ties of family,[5] and few the breadth of travel of her heir;[6] although one must add that they knew more about Europe than they did about Ireland, the self-governing colonies, or the United States.[7]

[1] We know that the *History of the Times*, of which volumes 3 and 4 published in 1947–52 cover the period 1884–1948, is by no means complete and that the archives have more to reveal. A. M. Gollin, *The Observer and J. L. Garvin* (Oxford University Press, 1960) is a pioneer work which suggests what might still be done in this field.
[2] Barbara W. Tuchman, *The Proud Tower* (London, Hamish Hamilton, 1966), p. 3.
[3] W. L. Burn, *The Age of Equipoise* (1964).
[4] On this subject, see C. H. D. Howard, *Splendid Isolation* (New York, 1967).
[5] See the genealogical table appended to Elizabeth Longford, *Queen Victoria* (1964).
[6] Edward, Prince of Wales, the future Edward VII (b. 1841), had visited Canada and the United States in 1860, Palestine and the Near East in 1862, India in 1875, Ireland in 1868 and 1885, and had travelled much in Europe. See Philip Magnus, *King Edward the Seventh* (1964).
[7] General Sir Edward Hutton wrote to Lord Minto that he was horrified at the king's ignorance of the self-governing colonies. Hutton to Minto, 10 January 1902. Hutton Papers, B.M. Add. 50081. Sir Edward Hutton (1848–1923) had seen service in many parts of the world before becoming general in command of the Canadian militia, a post he held from 1898 to

The range of Salisbury and Chamberlain, the two most powerful members of the government, has been indicated already. The widest experience was that of Lansdowne; secretary of state for war until he succeeded Salisbury at the Foreign Office in November 1900, who had already been both governor-general of Canada and viceroy of India; nevertheless, for him Europe was by no means a *terra incognita*. He spoke fluent French (his mother's native tongue) and was thus perhaps to be regarded as a personally predestined instrument of the coming *entente*.[1] The first lord of the admiralty, G. J. Goschen, provided something of a German balance to Lansdowne's French orientation. Of German origin, and educated partly in Germany, he naturally spoke the language. His world (unlike that of his aristocratic colleagues) was that of business and finance. Private business had taken him to South America and official financial assignments to Turkey and Egypt.[2] Finally among the senior ministers concerned with external affairs, there was the secretary of state for India, Lord George Hamilton, whose political career had been mainly concerned with Indian and Admiralty matters.[3]

The front opposition bench in 1897 was largely occupied by younger men, but the four seniors in age possessed a wide range of knowledge. The liberal leader in the Commons, Sir William Harcourt, had always been mainly concerned with domestic and Irish affairs, although he was also a considerable authority on matters of public international law. His opposition to imperialist tendencies was thus based upon general principles rather than on any first-hand acquaintance with the particular issues involved. Sir Henry Campbell-Bannerman, who succeeded him as leader in 1899, had had ministerial experience at the Admiralty, the War Office, and the India Office, had travelled a good deal in Europe, and spoke good French and some German. John Morley, a former chief secretary for Ireland, was not a cosmopolitan figure despite his studies in French intellectual history; he had, however, visited the United States in 1867 and was to do so again in 1904. James Bryce, whose previous ministerial posts had included a spell as under-

---

1900. After service in South Africa he was from 1901 to 1904 the commander of the Australian militia. Gilbert Elliot (1847–1914) (fourth earl of Minto from 1891) was governor-general of Canada from 1898 to 1904 and viceroy of India, 1905–10.

[1] See Lord Newton, *Lord Lansdowne* (1929).

[2] G. J. Goschen (1831–1907) was created a viscount on his retirement in 1900. Milner had served Goschen as private secretary from 1884 to 1885 while the latter was chancellor of the exchequer.

[3] Lord George Hamilton (1845–1927) held the India Office from 1895 until October 1903.

secretary of state at the Foreign Office, had since the publication of his *American Commonwealth* in 1888 been a recognized authority on American affairs. He was by far the most widely travelled man to hold high office in the period.

With ministers of long and often wide experience, the day of the dominant civil servant had not yet dawned although the Foreign Office was about to undergo a major change: 'while Salisbury's Foreign Office can still be discussed in Palmerstonian terms, Grey's resembled its modern-day counterpart. After 1906, men who had been clerks began acting as true advisers.'[1] The key figure was the permanent under-secretary; the post was held from 1894 to 1906 by Sir Thomas Sanderson who had entered the office as a junior clerk in 1859. Sanderson 'thought of himself as the chief of a department whose job was to carry out the instructions of his minister . . . [he] did not consider it his function to give advice or make suggestions to Lord Salisbury except on the rare occasions when the latter solicited his views'.[2] There was real expertise available, however, from the senior clerks who were heads of departments, as they frequently held such a post for from eight to ten years in contrast to the more rapid shifting of positions which became typical of later times.

At the Colonial Office Sir Edward Wingfield, who became permanent under-secretary in 1897, had entered the office in 1878 after a career at the Bar; his successor (in 1900) Sir M. F. Ommaney was a former soldier who had been crown agent for the colonies since 1877.

During Chamberlain's tenure of the colonial secretaryship the problems of the colonial service were systematically examined for the first time. The service had hitherto been dominated by patronage, and most appointments overseas were made by the secretary of state on the basis of personal recommendations. Experienced officials could be unemployed for long periods, and they even found it difficult to collect the pensions to which they were entitled. Salaries on the spot were paid by colonial governments out of local revenues and differed considerably as between one colony and another: 'Standards in a word were absent at both the London and the colonial ends. The duties, contracts, and quality of officials presented such a confused picture world-wide that

[1] Zara Steiner, 'The Last Years of the Old Foreign Office 1898–1905', *The Historical Journal*, vol. VI (1963), p. 59.
[2] Ibid., p. 63.

imperial unity appears to have depended on little more than common nationality.'[1]

To Chamberlain recruitment by examination, as for the Indian Civil Service, offered the best model for improvements; but it was felt that the unpopularity of the West African service because of the climate would reduce the number of candidates, and hamper the growth of a unified service. As a result, the I.C.S. like the principal services in Britain itself – including of course the Colonial Office – relied upon competitive examination, but entrance to the colonial service continued to the end to be based upon direct interview, coupled increasingly with the development of systematic contacts with Oxford and Cambridge and with headmasters of schools.

Clearly the kind of recruits obtained by the colonial services were different from those attracted by the intellectual prestige of the administrative class at home or the I.C.S., and so largely of course were the tasks they were called upon to perform.[2] In particular, at a time when Indian developments clearly foreshadowed the possibility of self-government, the development of ideas of indirect rule and the general belief in the durability of colonial rule in Africa helped to differentiate these two contrasting worlds, and to divide those elements in British society with interests in one or the other.[3]

At the India Office the position of permanent under-secretary had been held since 1883 by Sir Arthur Godley, who had been one of Gladstone's secretaries, and was to remain in this position until 1909.[4] Neither he nor Sir D. Harrel, who held the same position at the Irish Office from 1893 to 1902, appear to have made any important contribution to policy.[5]

[1] Robert Heussler, *Yesterday's Rulers, The Making of the British Colonial Service* (Syracuse University Press; London, Oxford University Press, 1963), pp. 7–8.
[2] Richard Symonds, *The British and Their Successors* (1966), pp. 126–7. In the inter-war period recruitment for Ceylon, Malaya, and Hong Kong was removed from the I.C.S. orbit and brought under the same colonial office machinery as dealt with Africa.
[3] Curiously enough the general volume of the *Cambridge History of the British Empire* for this period has no chapter dealing with services in the field, as though policy was self executing; there is, however, a chapter on the Colonial Office; R. B. Pugh, 'The Colonial Office, 1801–1925', *C.H.B.E.*, vol. III, ch. XIX.
[4] Godley (1847–1932) was created Lord Kilbracken on his retirement. At the India Office he lasted through nine secretaryships of state and six viceroyalties, but he does not rate a mention in the relevant volume of the *Cambridge History of India*.
[5] On the other hand his successor, Sir Anthony Macdonnell (1844–1925) (created a baron in 1908), who held the post from 1902 to 1908 was a highly controversial figure. He brought to the office twenty-five years of experience in India, yet another example of the persistent interaction between Irish and Indian affairs. Himself an Irish Catholic, he was known as the

More important than most of the departmental heads of the period were probably two royal servants: Sir Arthur Bigge was private secretary to the queen from 1895 until her death, and then to George V as Prince of Wales and as King from 1901, until his own death in 1931; his senior, Sir Francis Knollys, born in the year of Queen Victoria's accession, was from 1870 private secretary to Edward VII as Prince of Wales and as King, and joint private secretary to George V in 1910–11. This long continuity in the key position at court may have played a significant part in the role of the Crown in the period.[1]

Although the permanent officials of the Foreign Office were not yet important figures in the making of policy, the part played by the senior diplomats of this generation is undeniable. Indeed, the feeling that ambassadors at major posts were more important than the permanent secretary continued even after the latter began, as he did from Lansdowne's time, to exercise more of a role in the formation of policy. Thus when it was suggested to King Edward in 1909 that the then permanent secretary, Hardinge, would be a suitable viceroy of India and when the king declared his preference for having Hardinge in London, the prime minister remarked, so Hardinge tells us, that it was unlikely that he, a former ambassador, would be content to remain indefinitely at the head of the Foreign Office and that he would 'have a good claim to the embassy at Paris whenever that post should fall vacant'.[2] This was the last great age of the resident ambassador; an age when it was still appreciated that intimate knowledge of the governing class of the country to which he was posted could only come from long residence. The decline in the average tenure of top positions, which was a continuous one from the first world war onwards, may account for the later set-backs of British diplomacy and the occasions upon which develop-

---

'Bengal tiger' in India, whereas in Ireland he was largely sympathetic to the nationalist cause.

[1] Bigge, born in 1849, after service in the Zulu war of 1878–9, had entered the royal service as groom-in-waiting in 1880. He was raised to the peerage as Baron Stamfordham in 1911. Knollys' first position at court had been as gentleman usher in 1868. He was created Viscount Knollys in 1911.

[2] Lord Hardinge of Penshurst, *My Indian Years, 1910–1916* (London, John Murray, 1948), p. 2. Sir Charles Hardinge, 1858–1944, after a career in the diplomatic service became an assistant under-secretary in the Foreign Office in 1903. From April 1904 to February 1906 he was ambassador at St Petersburg. He was to be permanent secretary at the Foreign Office rom 1906 to 1910 and again from 1916 to 1920. From 1910 to 1916 he was viceroy of India. His last post was that of ambassador to Paris, November 1920 to December 1922. (He was created Baron Hardinge in 1910.)

ments abroad seem to have come as a surprise to the British government.[1]

Sir Horace Rumbold, ambassador at Vienna from 1895 to 1900, had begun his career as an attaché at Turin in 1849 and had served in many capitals in Europe as well as at Washington, Santiago, and Buenos Aires. Part of his education had taken place in Paris; he had connections among the French aristocracy and had married the daughter of an American diplomat.[2] Sir Edmund Monson, ambassador at Paris from 1896 to 1904, had seen varied service in Europe and South America. Sir Frank Lascelles, ambassador at Berlin from 1895 to 1908, had served at Washington and in Egypt and Persia as well as at a number of European capitals. Sir Charles Scott, who was at Copenhagen in 1897, was to be transferred in 1898 to the embassy at St Petersburg and to remain there until 1904; his earlier experience had included Mexico. Sir Francis Plunkett at Brussels (who was to be at Vienna from 1900 till 1905) had twice served in Japan and was another member of the service with an American wife. Sir Edwin Egerton, whose tenure of the legation at Athens lasted from 1892 to 1904 and who was to follow this with the Rome embassy from 1905 to 1908, varied the marriage pattern by marrying a Russian. His previous postings included Cairo and Constantinople as well as Buenos Aires. More unusual was the case of Sir Philip Currie (Constantinople 1893–8 and Rome 1898–1903) since he had spent much of his previous career in the Foreign Office itself and had indeed preceded Sanderson as permanent undersecretary.

Thus Europe and the Middle East provided the principal background for most senior diplomats, though Britain's informal empire in Latin America was well represented, and the Far East not wholly omitted.

---

[1] This theme will have to be taken up again in later pages. But there is no doubt of the importance attached in pre-1914 Britain to accurate and specialized knowledge where foreign affairs were concerned. It was also true of the more serious press. The years of the great ambassadors were also the years of the great foreign correspondents, particularly where *The Times* was concerned. The current view in Fleet Street that any reputable journalist can report any country's affairs at the briefest notice and with minimum preparation suggests that amateurism may not be a cause of Britain's decline so much as a consequence of it.

[2] Sir Horace Rumbold (eighth baronet) was born at Calcutta in 1829 and died in 1913. His son Sir Horace Rumbold (ninth baronet) was born at St Petersburg in 1869 and had an equally varied and distinguished career as a diplomat, ending with a five-year tenure of the Berlin embassy – 1928–33 (d. 1941). His son, Sir Anthony Rumbold, was a prominent member of the foreign service after the second world war. Three generations of ambassadors is unique, at least in this period, but a serious study of the foreign service might reveal the extent to which family connections were important in deciding upon it as a career.

But direct knowledge of the United States was still uncommon, and even more rare was any first-hand acquaintance with the countries of the Empire now beginning to voice demands for some share in the formulation of imperial policy.

A key post, particularly in view of Canada's important and complex relations with the United States, was that of minister (from 1893, ambassador) at Washington. The post was held from 1889 to 1902, through the whole period of crisis and subsequent rapprochement between Britain and the United States, by Sir Julian (from 1899 Baron) Pauncefote. His career breaks the usual pattern in that after an education partly acquired abroad, he had gone to the Bar and then occupied government legal posts in Hong Kong and the Caribbean, finally entering the Colonial Office in 1874. Two years later he had transferred to the Foreign Office where he had been permanent under-secretary from 1882 until his departure for the United States.

One diplomat born as far back as 1844 had not yet reached the summit of his career in 1897. This was Sir Francis Bertie, the assistant under-secretary from 1894 to 1903. He then spent two years at the Rome embassy, and this in turn was followed by a very long tenure of the embassy at Paris from January 1905 to April 1918.[1]

In the Far East, which was the main focus of international rivalries in the late eighteen-nineties, Britain's representatives were of rather a different stamp. Sir Claude Maxwell Macdonald had had military experience in Africa before being posted as minister to Peking in 1896 where he was in virtual command of the besieged legations during the Boxer rising of 1900. After the relief of Peking he was transferred to Tokyo and remained there first as minister, and from 1905, as ambassador until his retirement in 1912. In moving to Tokyo Macdonald exchanged posts with another remarkable figure, Sir Ernest Satow, who had started his career in the consular service in Japan in 1862. He had held posts in Siam, Uruguay, and Morocco before returning to Japan as

---

[1] Sir Francis Bertie (created Viscount Bertie on his retirement) was thus sixty when he entered on his eleven-year mission to Paris – an age at which he would now be compulsorily retired. In view of the improvements in medical science it is curious that modern practice is to curtail the period of professional activity in government service – it being curtailed at the other end likewise by the prolongation of the period of formal education. It is also noteworthy that the politicians who ultimately make these decisions should have exempted themselves from the principle. In 1897 Bertie headed the African and Far Eastern departments. Unlike his chief, Sanderson 'he was inclined to express his opinions freely and offer advice even when it was not sought' (Steiner, loc. cit., p. 67). His importance under Lansdowne was to be considerable. (Bertie died in 1919.)

minister in 1895. His final posting as minister in Peking lasted from 1900 to 1906.[1]

If the bias of the Foreign Office was still European, the careers of the soldiers and sailors reflected the long period of European peace. The commander-in-chief Lord Wolseley had served in the Crimea as had the future first sea lords Admirals Sir John Fisher (1904–10 and 1914–15) and Sir Arthur Wilson (1910–11); their predecessor Admiral Lord Walter Kerr (1899–1904) had fought in the Baltic campaign of 1854–5. But otherwise the dominant experience was that gained in India and Egypt – especially of course among the soldiers – though Admiral Kerr had commanded a naval brigade at the relief of Lucknow. Some had seen active service in China or South Africa; General Sir Neville Lyttleton who was to be chief of the general staff in 1904–8 had served in Canada at the time of the Fenian troubles; Admiral Wilson had been an instructor to the Japanese navy in the 1860s.[2] So it was understandable that to the armed services the defence of the Indian Empire should seem a more realistic and urgent problem for study than warfare on the European mainland, where, except for the distant shores of the Black Sea, no British soldier had fought since Waterloo. And many servants of the queen, so often sons of men who had themselves served overseas, had been born far from the home islands – Lord Roberts in India, Admiral Fisher in Ceylon.[3]

The generation in power at the time of the Diamond Jubilee and their immediate successors were to bring about important changes in the machinery of government and in the organization and recruitment of the services. But they relied largely upon their own ability to see where the weaknesses were to be found, and where changes needed to be made; they did not expect either in the reorganization of the institutional structure or in the shaping of policy to get much guidance from parliament or the electorate. A certain conscious distrust of

[1] Sir Ernest Mason Satow (1843–1929) was also a prolific writer on historical and diplomatic subjects. In writing of him in the *D.N.B.*, the historian Harold Temperley remarked that Satow was 'the only Englishman who hitherto has represented this country in both China and Japan and spoken the language of each'.

[2] On Britain's share in the modernization of the Japanese navy, see Ian H. Nish, *The Anglo-Japanese Alliance* (London, Athlone Press, 1966), p. 8. The big Japanese expansion programme after 1895 was largely carried through in British shipyards. Ibid., p. 36.

[3] Field-Marshal Frederick Roberts (1832–1914) (created in 1901 first Earl Roberts of Kandahar, Pretoria, and Waterford – the names are significant) was the most popular soldier of the period. At the time he was commanding the forces in Ireland. From 1899 to 1900 he was commander-in-chief in South Africa. In 1900 he succeeded Wolseley as commander-in-chief, holding this post until it was abolished as part of the army reforms of 1904.

democracy and its operations in these fields was prevalent among the ruling *élite*. How many in their hearts would have agreed with Lord Esher when he wrote 'the English people, led by a foolish half-informed press, are children in foreign politics. They have always been so . . .'?[1]

Pressures for Reform

Parliament's interest in such matters was intermittent; foreign affairs were generally regarded as an Executive responsibility and except when passions were aroused by the intrusion of what seemed to be a direct moral issue, as in Gladstone's campaign over the Bulgarian atrocities, or by pressure on the public purse, there was general acquiescence in the situation. Any attempt to make parliament a more important factor came from the radical side in politics, from those who were opposed to the continuous extension of British territory and British responsibilities that seemed to be the outcome of liberal and conservative policies alike.[2] The radicals' mistrust of British foreign policy was also stimulated by the belief that the diplomatic service which had largely escaped the mid-nineteenth century reforms in the civil service was still an aristocratic preserve.[3] A qualifying examination had been introduced for candidates in 1856, though after the 1870s university graduates were exempted from most of the papers. In 1880 the examination became competitive, but only those who had received a nomination from the secretary of state were entitled to sit for it; and candidates were still required to possess an independent income (the more necessary in

[1] Lord Esher to Maurice V. Brett, 8 April 1903. M. V. Brett (ed.), *Journals and Letters of Reginald Viscount Esher* (London, Ivor Nicholson & Watson, 1934), vol. 1, p. 397. Reginald B. Brett (1852–1930) who succeeded as second Viscount Esher in 1899 is a conspicuous example of the extent to which in a still largely aristocratic setting, an individual with good connections could exercise influence quite apart from any positions held by him. Esher who had been a liberal M.P. from 1880 to 1885 was secretary of the Office of Works from 1895 to 1902, and in that capacity the principal organiser of the Diamond Jubilee celebrations. In 1899 he refused the offer of the permanent under-secretaryship at the Colonial Office, and in 1900 the same post at the War Office. He was deeply involved, however, from 1902 to 1904 in the army reforms and the creation of the committee of Imperial Defence. On close terms with both Queen Victoria and her successor, he was the natural recipient of many confidences particularly on questions on the borderline of politics and service affairs.
[2] See Peter G. Richards, *Parliament and Foreign Affairs* (1967), pp. 20–3.
[3] Of the senior diplomats referred to above, Monson, Plunkett, and Currie were educated at Eton, and the output of distinguished members of the service from this single school was to continue at a remarkably high level throughout. Between 1908 and 1913, nine of the sixteen successful candidates for the Foreign Office itself came from Eton (Steiner, loc. cit., p. 89), so there was at least one important personal link between those in the office and those in the field.

that the first two years' service was unpaid). The notion that the result was 'a service staffed with wealthy young aristocrats with a reputation for good manners, a dilettantish attitude and a questionable ability to represent British interests',[1] seems difficult to square with the hard and detailed work put into the many important negotiations in which Britain was involved in the pre-1914 era. The diplomatic service was only part of the administration of foreign affairs at this time. The Foreign Office was separate from it, and there were no fewer than five distinct consular services, namely the general service, the Levant service, and the China, Japan, and Siam consular services, for membership of which an arduous linguistic apprenticeship was required.[2]

Pressures for reform additional to those exerted by the radicals arose from the heightened degree of nationalist and imperial sentiment in the 1890s and from its stimulus by the new popular press. These pressures could to some extent be manipulated when it was desirable to change course, and resulted in an all-round defiance of foreign powers when they clashed with British interests rather than for particular policies. The substitution of Germany for France, and even Russia, as a target for patriotic suspicions was to be almost as rapid a process as the making of the *ententes* themselves. But what statesmen of the old school most feared was that the new popular passions could be stimulated by propaganda from service quarters into demanding greater armaments than the economic wisdom of the time believed compatible with the country's solvency.

The view that the outlay on the services, as well as other forms of government spending (including colonial grants and subsidies), were more than the country could afford, dictated the memorandum sent to Salisbury in September 1901 by his chancellor of the exchequer. It advocated important economies, while admitting that 'such a policy would doubtless excite the wrath of the Navy League', the 'Service Members', and the *Daily Mail*.[3] Salisbury's reply showed his own sar-

[1] Donald C. Bishop, *The Administration of British Foreign Relations* (Syracuse University Press, 1961), p. 206.
[2] Lord Strang, *The Diplomatic Career* (1962), p. 34.
[3] Lady Victoria Hicks Beach, *Life of Sir Michael Hicks Beach* (London, Macmillan, 1932), p. 152. Sir Michael Hicks Beach (1837–1916) (Viscount St Aldwyn 1906, Earl St Aldwyn 1915) was chancellor of the exchequer from June 1895 to July 1902. The Navy League was established in 1895, see Marder, op. cit., pp. 49–54. The House of Commons of 1895 had eighty-one members with a service background, the great majority of them on the government side. Soldiers far outnumbered sailors. J. A. Thomas, *The House of Commons 1832–1901* (Cardiff, 1939), pp. 14–17. The *Daily Mail* had been founded in 1896 and reached the unprecedented circulation of over half a million three years later. It was a maxim with Alfred

donic awareness of the difficulty: 'after the beginning of the year, when I saw how blindly the heads of our defensive departments surrendered themselves to the fatal guidance of their professional advisers, I realized that we were in the face of a Jingo hurricane, and were driving for it under bare poles'.[1]

In the government's view it was essential, at a time when the ground seemed so treacherous to have a free hand both to plan for a distribution of available resources and for negotiation with foreign powers and the self-governing colonies. It seemed less possible to rely on the electorate and its representatives now that the franchise had been enlarged; less effort was made than in the middle of the nineteenth century to influence opinion, for instance, by the publication of extensive blue-books or diplomatic documents.[2] An incautious reference in parliament could produce difficulties for the government, and there was an added complication in the fact that the foreign secretary was in the House of Lords and that questions on Foreign Office business were normally handled by a junior minister. In 1899 there was a government ruling that the under-secretary of state for foreign affairs would not answer supplementary questions. When this ruling was challenged in an adjournment debate on 18 February 1901, Balfour referred to occasions when the press had been asked to alter answers given to supplementary questions 'lest they should produce some unfortunate impressions in the Chancelleries of other powers'. Every dispatch and telegram sent abroad was carefully drafted and perhaps submitted to the cabinet . . . 'and yet', he went on 'you ask the Under-Secretary for Foreign Affairs, or the Secretary if he be in this House, to say on the spur of the moment, without notice, without previous consideration that which in its effects may be as dangerous as any formal communication by telegram or despatch'.[3]

Balfour's reference to the secretary of state suggests that it was not merely the possible lack of information available to a non-cabinet member that he had in mind. Indeed, his cousin, Lord Hugh Cecil, in supporting the government referred to the limitation on the discussion of delicate questions of foreign affairs as similar to regulations

Harmsworth (the future Lord Northcliffe) that its readers liked a 'good hate'. R. C. K. Ensor, *England 1870–1914* (Oxford, Clarendon Press, 1936), pp. 312–15.
[1] Salisbury to Hicks Beach, 14 September 1901. Hicks Beach, op. cit., vol. 2, p. 153.
[2] Richards, op. cit., p. 83.
[3] H.C. *Deb.*, 4th series, vol. 89, col. 333.

prohibiting the lighting of matches in the British Museum or Bodleian Library.[1] This particular restriction was not of the first importance and was lifted when Sir Henry Campbell-Bannerman, who had attacked it in the debate, became prime minister with Sir Edward Grey as his foreign secretary, the first member of the House of Commons to hold the office since 1868.[2] But the general reticence about publicity in matters of external affairs was and remained characteristic of British government.[3]

Fissures Within the Empire

Because external affairs were thought to be so essentially executive in their nature and so unsuitable for handling through the ordinary processes of parliamentary government, the difficulties of co-operation with the self-governing colonies were often underestimated. Their governments might wish to draw closer to Britain as dangers to their own interests developed; Canadian enthusiasm for the imperial tie was largely determined by the degree of political and economic pressure exercised from time to time by the United States.[4] At other times these needs were offset by their fear of involvement in European affairs.[5] In general, however, they denied that their own institutions and their own political habits should be modified by needs arising from the new context of international affairs and from Britain's needs in particular.[6] Answering an English writer who had expressed the hope that Lord Minto, the newly appointed governor-general, might give Canada strong government the principal Canadian liberal newspaper wrote:

India requires a strong government, Canada most emphatically does not require strong government, except such as is given by representa-

[1] The government secured the rejection of the motion by 249 votes to 204 despite some dissent on their own side.
[2] Sir Edward Grey (1862–1933) (created Viscount Grey of Fallodon in 1916) had himself been parliamentary under-secretary for foreign affairs in 1892–5; he was to be foreign secretary from December 1905 to December 1916.
[3] Nish shows how gingerly the British government went about the task of making known the Anglo-Japanese alliance in 1902. Op. cit., pp. 218–24.
[4] See N. Penlington, *Canada and Imperialism 1896–9* (University of Toronto Press, 1965).
[5] For the particular attitudes of the different colonies, see J. E. Tyler, *The Struggle for Imperial Unity* (1938).
[6] Britain was, of course, powerless to deal with domestic legislation in the self-governing colonies where this impinged upon foreign policy except through persuasion which might not be effective. A notable example was restriction of immigration by race at a time when Britain was seeking closer relations with Japan. Nish, op. cit., p. 77.

tives of the Canadian people elected at the polls. And our conception of the growth of the empire is not that Canada should become more like India, but that India should become more like Canada; the ideal being not a group of dependencies governed from one central point, but a league of self-governing communities.[1]

It seemed to many colonial leaders that this concept was one which British statesmen, looking at the system from a central point of view and further removed from the grassroots of politics, had much difficulty in grasping. A young Canadian civil servant on a visit to Britain wrote in his diary on 3 April 1908:

> There is in England a real governing class, in the sense that it seeks to control and guide the national interests both in England and in the dominions beyond. The English mind has been so long trained in this way of looking at the world that I can see wherein it will be many years before it will ever come fully to appreciate what self-government means.[2]

By this time, however, experience in negotiation had shown the limitations of British action in making the imperial vision effective; notably in the most important sphere of all, defence; for each of the self-governing colonies had a different outlook arising from its own geographical situation and past history. In Australia and New Zealand the compelling factor was geographical isolation and a sense of insecurity that seemed to increase rather than decrease with the technical innovations, such as faster shipping routes and the submarine cable, that should have brought them closer to the centre of the Empire. In fact, however, the same technical innovations that gave greater mobility to the British fleets also made the peril from Japan seem far less remote.

Isolation and insecurity were heightened by fragmentation – the Australian colonies were not federated until 1901 and their populations

[1] *The Globe* (Toronto) 19 December 1898, quoted by Penlington, op. cit., p. 141 fn. At this time the position of the governor-general was still ambiguous: 'in most internal matters the governor-general acted as a constitutional monarch, but on many external matters, he was acting on his own discretion as a representative of Britain's external policies'. But this made difficulties where Canada had external policies that might be distinct from Britain's. In this case imperial and Canadian questions could hardly be kept apart. Ibid., pp. 141–2.

[2] Quoted from Mackenzie King's diary in R. M. Dawson, *William Lyon Mackenzie King, Vol. 1, 1874–1923* (London, Methuen, 1959), p. 168. The name dominions for the self-governing colonies came into use in 1907.

were concentrated on the coastal strips of the east, south-east and south-west. Neither Australia nor New Zealand had an effective hinterland to which they could retreat if beleaguered by an enemy.[1]

Unlike Canada and South Africa, white society in Australia and New Zealand was homogeneous and no large segments, hostile in principle to the advantages of strong ties with Britain, existed in either country. The Australians were therefore prepared to accept the need for British protection and to contribute to the maintenance of British ships in their waters so long as these could not be moved without their consent. If there was some degree of misunderstanding over the original agreement of 1887, in that the British held that the Australians were contributing to the imperial navy while the Australians were emphatic that they were paying for their own defence, there was not the feeling as yet that the ends of British and Australian policy could differ. But there were possible differences over means.

The Canadian situation and attitude were very different. Geography and economics as well as past experience forced the Canadians to consider the only possible threat to them as being that from the United States. But as a Canadian military historian has pointed out, this threat was either 'incredible' or 'irresistible'.[2] Nor clearly could the British navy do much about it. On practical grounds the Canadians were therefore less interested in imperial naval than in military co-operation, and there was the political complication that any party wishing to unite English-speaking and French-speaking Canadians could only do so by emphasizing Canadian nationhood at the expense of the British connection.

In these circumstances Canadians felt that their best interests would be served by allocating resources to building another transcontinental railway rather than to building up their naval or military power.[3] Although Canadian statesmen were ready to defend Canada, they were not prepared to give important help out of their own resources, believing that Britain would continue to have the means for defence owing to the obligations imposed upon her by the existence of the dependent empire.

In all three cases, imperial considerations only affected the issue

[1] For New Zealand, see B. K. Gordon, *New Zealand becomes a Pacific Power* (University of Chicago, 1960), chs. 1, 2.
[2] R. A. Preston, *Canada and 'Imperial Defence'* (Durham, N.C., Duke University Press, 1967), p. 187.
[3] Ibid., p. 186.

when it was convenient for the colony concerned, or indeed for Britain, that it should do so in the light of local political considerations. In New Zealand, and to a lesser extent in Australia, imperial sentiment was part of the internal political balance and this helped to keep it alive.

The 1897 colonial conference was primarily concerned with naval affairs, and considerable pressure was exercised by the Colonial Office to get the Australian colonies to waive their veto over the movement of ships out of Australian waters which the Admiralty believed to be inimical to the full efficiency of Britain's naval dispositions taken as a whole. But it became clear that such a veto was a precondition of the financial contribution and it was dropped.[1]

The position of Cape Colony and Natal, faced by the hostility of the two Boer republics, with their European sympathizers was naturally different, and the Cape Colony government offered a cruiser to the navy without any strings attached; though the ship was never forthcoming and the offer was eventually commuted for an annual subsidy of £30,000.[2] The Canadian premier Laurier refused to make any naval contribution, arguing that whatever the Australians might say they were contributing to general imperial defence and that to act similarly would not be in Canada's interests.[3]

Proposals for co-operation over land forces were better received, as the allocation of responsibility and resources was easier to assess. In Australia and New Zealand British command of local forces to act for local defence roused no conflict between colonial and imperial interests. In Canada, also, a militia force improved with British help could be justified to the electorate and provide a valuable source of party patronage;[4] and for this reason the Canadians were prepared to put up with a series of tactless and politically naïve G.O.C.s. In 1897 Laurier approved a scheme for the interchange of military units within the Empire, and in the following years such ideas were pursued further. But Chamberlain himself had to admit that the colonies could only be persuaded, not coerced into co-operation.[5]

To some people, wide implications existed even in the modest steps that were actually taken. Arnold-Forster wrote to Hutton, for instance:

[1] Donald C. Gordon, *The Dominion Partnership in Imperial Defence, 1870–1914* (Baltimore, John Hopkins Press, 1965), pp. 134–5.
[2] Ibid., pp. 135–6.　　　　　　　　　　　　　　　　　　[3] Ibid., p. 135.
[4] Preston, op. cit., pp. 155–259 *passim*.
[5] Interview with Hutton, August 1898. Hutton Papers, B.M. Add. 50078.

To my mind there will never be true and effective co-operation until the colonies share the burdens of the Empire in peacetime as well as in wartime. Why should not India, Singapore, Gibraltar, Wei-hai-wei, and other common possessions of the Empire be defended by all those who are, so to speak, their joint owners? However, alas, we are far enough from either consummation at present.[1]

In fact, this consummation was to remain an idea without serious political content. The Boer war gave the impression of the Empire fighting in a common cause, but the reality was different. Above all, Laurier's support for sending Canadians to fight in South Africa, however presented, split his own administration and led to attacks from French-Canadian nationalists in Quebec.[2] His policy was an uneasy compromise between all the pressures playing upon him.[3]

The main importance of the Boer war was its effect on Britain's own thinking, but the changes made in British defence had their imperial context as well. The setting up of the British Army Council inspired the creation of the Canadian Militia Council and of the Australia and New Zealand Defence Councils, and this meant the end of the system of British officers holding supreme commands in the self-governing colonies, thus eliminating one important source of friction.[4]

The colonial conference of 1902 dealt with two major matters in the defence field, the old question of naval subsidies and a New Zealand proposal for a unified militia force. Again the Colonial Office pressed for an end to the Australian veto on the removal of ships and again it was unsuccessful. Instead, the Australians secured two concessions: an increase in the number and size of the ships on the station, and the retention of the principle of a proportionate sharing of the cost between the United Kingdom and Australian governments. Australian and New Zealand sailors manned some of the ships, thus establishing the principle that this part of the navy had a specifically Australasian character.

The New Zealand scheme was a particular brain-child of the Prime

[1] Arnold-Forster to Hutton, 26 April 1898. Hutton Papers, B.M. Add. 50078. Wei-hai-wei was demanded on lease from China in March 1898 as a counter to Russia's demand for Port Arthur. It proved useless as a naval base but was only returned to China in 1930, twenty-five years after Russia lost Port Arthur.
[2] Henri Bourassa who led the Quebec dissidence helped in Laurier's overthrow in 1911 in conjunction with the Ontario conservatives.
[3] Joseph Schull, *Laurier, the First Canadian* (Toronto, 1965), p. 391.
[4] *C.H.B.E.*, vol. III, pp. 368–9.

Minister, Seddon, who envisaged the creation in each self-governing colony of a militia force, armed and equipped for overseas service in the general imperial interest. The Cape and Natal supported the proposal but both Canada and Australia were hostile. Laurier reiterated Canada's willingness to stand by the Empire in case of need; but was emphatic that each case must be considered on its merits.[1] Hutton, writing from Australia, was afraid that Seddon's idea strongly backed by the secretary of state for war, St John Brodrick, had led to a 'totally erroneous conception of Australian feeling towards the question of Imperial Defence' among certain members of the War Office. 'Australians,' he went on, 'are peculiarly sensitive of any interference with what they consider to be their constitutional rights, and the proposal that a Militia Reserve should be created in Australia which would be subject to the control and orders of the War Office for service on a National Emergency is peculiarly one which is bound to create universal dissatisfaction.'[2] A month later he was writing that the proposal had done immense harm in Australia and had made his hopes 'for a sound military and political system of defence in Australia immeasurably harder to carry into effect.'[3]

The most therefore that could be done was to concentrate on measures of co-ordination between imperial and colonial forces; and this was made even harder by the unwillingness of many British soldiers and officials to take sufficiently seriously the specific outlook and needs of the colonies. Thus when it was suggested in 1903 that Frederick Borden, the Canadian defence minister, should go to England to discuss the Canadian militia and its problems, the governor-general was worried because he felt that there was no one with whom he could usefully consult. 'British officials,' he wrote, 'appear to me to be absolutely out of touch with colonial military sentiment or possibilities . . . I don't see how I can feel justified in saving Imperial military control if there is no intelligent attempt from the old country to assist in doing so.'[4] In fact, however, the Canadian wish to have a Canadian rather than a British officer in command, which was the principal question at issue, was not one which the British government felt it could gainsay:

Whatever may be the idea from the military point of view, we can,

[1] D. C. Gordon, op. cit., pp. 158–66.
[2] Hutton to Brodrick, 30 January 1902. Hutton Papers, B.M. Add. 50085.
[3] Hutton to Minto, 24 August 1902. Hutton Papers, B.M. Add. 50081.
[4] Minto to Hutton, 3 May 1903. Ibid.

as a matter of fact, only make those arrangements with which the Government of Canada fully agrees. I should therefore not oppose the Bill giving the Dominion Government the *Right* to appoint a Canadian officer to command the Militia.[1]

The questions of military organization have been taken beyond the scope of the present chapter; but they provide some of the most obvious illustrations of the extent to which the apparent solidarity of the Empire at the time of the Diamond Jubilee masked the growth of societies which were very different from the society of Britain itself, and governed by different notions as to their place in the world. Statesmen who tried to create institutions expressing common purposes or even to facilitate the mobilization of the Empire's power whenever its very existence and that of its component parts might be challenged were building upon shifting sands. It was possible to discount the solidarity of the British system of power too rapidly altogether; and the Germans were twice to make this same mistake, but the centrifugal tendencies were there already.

If the Britain of the Diamond Jubilee had been more democratic, or if the self-governing colonies had been less so; if the British had found it easier to make genuine partners of the politically conscious Indian *élite*; no doubt things would have been very different. Attempts to bridge the psychological gaps were not lacking over the next few decades; but the Empire was so diverse and the environment and upbringing of its leaders so different from country to country that the problems of co-operation were not much less than those that existed between Britain and certain foreign countries. Indeed, in some respects the task of foreign negotiation was easier; the world of European diplomacy was still a fairly homogeneous one. The decisive factor was Britain's own strength whether measured in material terms, in the resolution of her people, or the quality of her leadership. At the time of the Diamond Jubilee, they were about to be put to their first stern test for over eighty years.

[1] Note of talk with Borden. Arnold-Forster Papers, Diary, vol. 1, 1903.

Chapter 3

THE WEARY TITAN

The Turning-point

The period from 1898 to 1907 is generally, and rightly, regarded as a turning-point in the history of Britain's relations with foreign powers.[1] It saw the conclusion of the Anglo-Japanese alliance – the first such formal undertaking towards another great power of the new era. It also saw the making of the *ententes* with France and Russia which, although formally consisting only of agreements on matters external to Europe in dispute between the parties, was to prove in effect a commitment to the support of the Franco-Russian alliance against Germany and Austria.[2] Although some historians have held that the Anglo-Japanese alliance was an outcome of rivalries in Europe, its most

[1] The works by Grenville and Monger already referred to have made full use of the material now available on the diplomatic history of these crucial years and largely supplanted earlier treatments of the subject.

[2] It has been pointed out that the agreements with France on 8 April 1904, and with Russia on 31 August 1907, as well as the Anglo-French agreement of 1912, did not commit Britain to fight in Europe, and that the formal position remained as it had been in January 1902 when the Intelligence Division of the War Office drew up a memorandum on Britain's treaty obligations, showing that these were limited to a commitment in certain circumstances to go to the assistance of Belgium, Holland, Norway, Sweden, and Portugal. Since the obligation towards Norway and Sweden was a joint one with France, in the event of a Russian attack, it was not likely to materialize. Salisbury's comment that too much should not be made of such documents, and that 'our treaty obligations will follow our national inclinations and will not precede them', was largely justified in the sequel despite the significance of the Belgian guarantee in 1914. See V. Cromwell, 'European Treaty Obligations in March 1902', *Historical Journal*, vol. VI (1963), pp. 272-9. The ancient treaties with Portugal acquired a new importance with the use of Portuguese African ports by the Transvaal to import arms during the crisis of 1899. As a result of the negotiations of that summer a new agreement was reached by which in return for a pledge not to let arms pass into the Transvaal if war came, Britain renewed her 1661 commitment to the defence of Portugal and her colonies. The likely hostility of Portuguese opinion to this agreement compelled the British government to agree to it remaining secret. In 1898 there had been a secret agreement with Germany about an ultimate partition of the Portuguese colonial empire should Portugal fail to keep her hold on her overseas possessions. This agreement was also part of the attempt to create a favourable international environment within which to deal with the South African question. Grenville, op. cit., ch. VIII and pp. 260-3. It is ironical indeed, in the light of these facts, to reflect that whereas neither Britain nor Germany retains any colonial possessions in Africa, the Portuguese colonies remain intact.

recent historian has pointed out that 'Britain entered into the alliance largely by reason of her eastern rather than her European interests'.[1] The second version of the alliance in 1905 with its extension to cover India, supports this thesis.

During the Russo-Japanese war itself Britain was concerned with the imperial aspects of Russia's defeat, not with the effect upon Europe of a much weakened Russia, and therefore turned a deaf ear to French appeals for mediation to terminate the war before Russia was driven to the point of collapse. Britain, it was felt, could better deal with the German naval challenge once her problems in the Far East had been resolved by a Russian retreat. It has been suggested that a primary concern over Europe came only with the summer of 1905, and with the realization then that a conflict deriving from imperial issues might well be fought out on European battlefields.[2]

There is therefore some ambiguity about the intentions of the *ententes* with France and Russia. It was essential to clear up differences with these two powers because of the failure to reach agreement with Germany, and the consequent conviction that Germany was determined to challenge Britain on the seas and in the colonial sphere. It is also, however, true that those most favourable to the new course in the Foreign Office, such as Bertie, Hardinge, and Eyre Crowe, were much more concerned about the balance of power in Europe than about direct rivalry overseas.[3] Thus, when in 1907 Eyre Crowe produced his celebrated memorandum on British policy with its indictment of German policies, Sanderson (then in retirement) found Germany's methods indefensible but could excuse her because she had come late into the colonial field and was doing no more than emulating powers such as Britain itself who had made their bid earlier. Britain should only commit herself against Germany when her own vital interests were directly affected.[4] 'Sanderson's voice,' it has been remarked, 'came from a past when colonial disputes still determined the more fluid relationships

---

[1] Nish, op. cit., p. 231.
[2] Monger, *The End of Isolation*, pp. 184–5, 194–207.
[3] Eyre Crowe (1804–1925) (knighted, 1911) had entered the Foreign Office in 1885 and was a senior clerk by 1906. He became an assistant under-secretary in 1912 and was permanent under-secretary from November 1920 to April 1925. He was the son of a British diplomat, the first commercial attaché ever appointed in the service with the whole of Europe as his sphere. He had a German wife and spoke English, German, and French with equal fluency; also some Italian. Francis Oppenheimer, *Stranger Within* (London, Faber, 1965), p. 208.
[4] G. P. Gooch and H. V. Temperley, *British Documents on the Origins of the War*, vol. III (1928), Appendices A and B.

between the great powers. Hardinge and Bertie thought in terms of the continent of Europe and the balance of power.'[1]

While different people may have emphasized different aspects because of the particular bent of their own experience, it is obvious that it was a single problem that needed resolution. Britain was involved in overseas policies that could not be abandoned without loss of standing and economic setbacks that might have their political repercussions; conversely, her ability to defend her overseas interests might be seriously or even totally reduced if the European continent were dominated by a single combination, especially if it threatened her own shores.[2] Thus home defence – including the question of whether the navy alone was sufficient to guarantee the inviolability of Britain's shores, and if so the implication of this for the disposition of naval forces – was directly relevant to imperial strategy, and to the role of the self-governing colonies. So too the role of the army, which ever since the time of Cardwell's reforms had been organized with the primary purpose of providing for garrisons overseas, now had to be scanned again in the light of the new European situation.[3] The changing political perspective thus fortified the painful experience of the South African war that the efficiency of the army could not be taken for granted, and required serious thought about its future.

Those most closely in touch with European developments, and who understood the new conditions brought about by the existence of the continental mass armies, quickly grasped the new requirements arising if Britain were forced to take part in continental alignments. During the Moroccan crisis of April–May 1905 the government generally believed that if Britain went to France's aid victory would be certain. The French army would hold the Germans; the German navy would

[1] Steiner, loc. cit., p. 79. Monger argues that not until the Algeciras conference (January–March 1906) did the maintenance of the French *entente* as such assume priority in British policy. Op. cit., pp. 268, 280.
[2] There had been some suggestion that Russia would come to the aid of France if Britain pressed home too far her advantage after Fashoda. The South African war again provided an occasion for Franco-Russian discussions about possible action against Britain, and there were talks between the two general staffs in July 1900 and February 1901. The possibility was mooted of joint Franco-Russian naval action in the Mediterranean, the Indian Ocean, and the Pacific. But it was made clear that the Russians would not contemplate an invasion of India until the completion of the Tashkent–Orenburg railway. H. Seton-Watson, *The Russian Empire, 1801–1917* (1967), pp. 577–8. The railway was, in fact, completed only in 1906, by which time the diplomatic situation had been transformed. On the international diplomacy of the period generally, see A. J. P. Taylor, *The Struggle for Mastery in Europe, 1848–1918* (Oxford, Clarendon Press, 1954).
[3] Edward Cardwell (created viscount in 1874) was secretary of state for war, 1868–74.

risk a fleet action in which it would be beaten, and a force landed in Schleswig-Holstein would complete Germany's discomfiture. Austen Chamberlain, chancellor of the exchequer, the only British statesmen with a first-hand knowledge of both France and Germany, was less optimistic:

> England [he wrote] can no longer give a European ally money, or find soldiers on the continent. A continental ally wants help in men, and that help at once. If we had 250,000 men or 300,000 men fully trained and able to move at short notice, an open alliance with us would be an absolute protection and a sure guarantee of peace . . . But France might well hesitate to proclaim, as it were offensively, a solidarity with us, and bring upon herself a war, in which assuming that we supported her, we could not effectively restore the balance in point of numbers, already weighed down by an excess of 200,000 men on the German side.[1]

To some extent, of course, changes in British policy were the ineluctable consequences of the rise and fall of other powers. Britain's Mediterranean position had classically rested upon the support to the Ottoman Empire, whose continued decline made such reliance inadequate. The view has been taken that Britain in fact had lost control of the Mediterranean by 1894, since she could not match the combined strengths of the Russian and French fleets.[2] Between 1895 and 1897 a realignment took place and Britain ceased to make the defence of the Straits a cardinal element in her strategy. One consequence was the increasing authority of Germany at Constantinople.[3] It was the move southwards of the fulcrum of British power in the Mediterranean that gave Egypt its strategic importance, and made control of the Nile valley and the Suez Canal rather than of the Straits the thing that

[1] Sir Charles Petrie, *Life and Letters of Sir Austen Chamberlain* (London, Cassell, 1939), vol. 1, pp. 133–4. Petrie does not indicate the nature of the document quoted, nor its precise date. Austen Chamberlain (1863–1937) (knighted, 1925) had studied both in Berlin and Paris and received from these experiences a distinct and permanent pro-French bias. He was chancellor of the exchequer from October 1903 until December 1905 having held lesser offices since 1895. He was to hold a variety of posts in different governments between 1915 and 1931.
[2] Monger, op. cit., p. 2.
[3] The German concession for the Baghdad railway awarded in 1903 with its implied bypassing of Suez and with its ultimate threat to the British (and Indian) interests in the head of the Persian Gulf was symbolic of the new relationship. It is true that in 1914 Britain (like France) reached an agreement with the Germans which suggested a preference for a German as opposed to a Russian presence in Turkey. Even after the *entente* the Russian danger was never overlooked. Taylor, *The Struggle for Mastery in Europe*, pp. 518–19.

mattered most.[1] Naval opinion, in particular Fisher, did not, however, abandon its view of the importance of the Mediterranean. In a private letter on 2 August 1900 he deplored the fact that Corfu had ever been handed over to Greece. 'It's a most splendid place for the Fleet and of enormous importance in case of war. The epitaph of England will be: "What was won by the sword was given up by the pen." '[2]

In a letter to the first lord of the admiralty on 1 December 1900 Fisher wrote: 'The Mediterranean is of necessity the vital point of a naval war and you can no more change this than you can change the position of Mount Vesuvius, because geographical conditions, Sebastopol and Toulon and the Eastern question will compel the battle of Armageddon to be fought in the Mediterranean.'[3] He wanted the fleet there strengthened and made ready for instant war. In 1901 the Channel fleet was made an integral part of the Mediterranean fleet and thus available for joint operations.[4] Even when the French and Russian dangers were eliminated by the *ententes*, the government, and still more its naval advisers, were reluctant to accept the idea that Britain might need permanently to share its authority in the Mediterranean. There was thus an interval between the acceptance of co-operation with the French on land and a naval agreement, but in the end there was no escaping the limitations on British power. To meet the new dangers, Britain would in the end 'be constrained to adopt a course till then avoided – partition of Middle East interests with rivals'.[5]

Britain now had to face one general issue, namely whether her constitutional structure, based upon the supremacy of parliament, was able to make formal alliances which could pledge her to particular action in circumstances which could not be foreseen and which might occur when another government had replaced the one in power. Salisbury had taken the negative view on this point very strongly indeed. In 1896 he had rejected a proposal to renew the Mediterranean agreements and defend Constantinople in the event of a Russian attack, and in the same year he instructed the ambassador to Berlin to explain that

[1] Grenville, op. cit., pp. 94–97. See the discussion of British interests in the Straits and in Egypt and the Canal in the Memorandum by the Director of Military Intelligence, 13 October 1896, printed in Marder, *British Naval Policy*, Appendix III.
[2] Fisher to Lady Fisher, 2 August 1900. Marder, *Fear God and Dread Nought* (London, Cape, 1952), vol. 1, p. 159. Corfu, a British protectorate since 1815, had been given to Greece in 1863.   [3] Fisher to Selborne, 1 December 1900. Ibid., p. 168.
[4] Ibid., pp. 152, 175.
[5] Monroe, *Britain's Moment in the Middle East*, p. 19.

Britain could not join the Triple Alliance – Germany, Austria, Italy – because of her wish to refrain from any engagement to go to war in any contingency whatever: 'That is the attitude prescribed to us on the one hand by our popular constitution which will not acknowledge the obligations of an engagement made in former years – on the other by our insular position which makes the burdensome conditions of an alliance unnecessary for our safety.' In 1901 he argued with his colleagues against a German alliance on the grounds, among others, that it would be unpopular, and that if a government declared war for an object unwelcome to public opinion the government would be turned out.[1] As we have seen, the Japanese treaty was to surmount this constitutional barrier, though not without a warning from Salisbury; but no other engagements of a precise kind were entered into before the war of 1914. The Constitution was always there to deter those who urged Britain into more definite commitments.

The Boer War and Imperial Cohesion

The main reason why Britain had to consider modifying her traditional position arose from her final assertion of paramountcy in Southern Africa – the Boer war. The origins of the war are still a matter of controversy, as they have been ever since its outbreak.[2] On the whole, opinion now minimizes the grievances of the non-Boer inhabitants of the Transvaal and the interests of the mining companies, and stresses the determination of Milner and Chamberlain to assume political control of the Transvaal, so as to prevent trouble elsewhere in South Africa and demonstrate the solidity and strength of the Empire. It was, of course, assumed too readily that the use of force would settle the matter quickly in Britain's favour. The early military reverses encouraged a continental league against Britain, and revealed the wide spread of animosity against her in Europe. The superior naval strength that Britain could still deploy and the unwillingness of Germany to challenge it prevented such a league materializing, as Russia and France would not move without German support and might not have been willing to act even with it.[3] Later on in the conflict, when important British forces were locked up in South Africa, it could be argued

<hr />

[1] Grenville, op. cit., pp. 52, 155, 353–4.
[2] For two recent treatments by South African historians, see J. S. Marais, *The Fall of Kruger's Republic* (London, 1961), and G. H. Le May, *British Supremacy in South Africa, 1899–1907* (London, 1965).   [3] Grenville, op. cit., p. 290.

that Britain's power elsewhere in the world could not be exerted without a reliable alliance.[1]

United States opinion showed from the beginning much sympathy for the Boers on anti-imperialist grounds. This grew as resistance was prolonged and was fully exploited by the Irish and other anti-British elements in American opinion, but although these opinions were powerfully represented in Congress, President McKinley's administration was determined not to allow any friction arising from the war to affect the good understanding with Britain that had developed during the Spanish–American conflict.[2] His secretary of state and other like-minded protagonists of America's own imperial mission were firmly on Britain's side, and there was thus no response to German and Russian efforts to get the United States to take the lead in imposing mediation upon the belligerents.

Theodore Roosevelt, though not unmoved by Boer gallantry, was convinced that for the sake of the general balance of power in the world Britain must remain supreme south of the Zambesi; and he apparently believed that if a European coalition did threaten the existence of the Empire the United States should be prepared to intervene on Britain's side. But the need seriously to consider this possibility did not arise, and Roosevelt as president maintained his predecessor's policy of neutrality.[3] Where he erred was in assuming that the analogy of the United States would hold good, that Boer and Briton would be fused into a single people with the British strain the dominant one.[4]

The position taken up by the United States made it possible for Canada to take her own line about the war. Canadian opinion was divided, with French Canada (as might be expected) very disinclined to co-operate in subduing another minority people within the Empire. The British government would have preferred a financial contribution but Laurier made it clear that this was not the kind of crisis which would be felt to justify such a measure.[5] Volunteers for the armed forces would not have been hard to get; but Chamberlain did not feel that this would fulfil the need to demonstrate imperial solidarity.[6] In the end regular contingents were forthcoming.

[1] Lord George Hamilton to Curzon, 15 March 1901. Monger, op. cit., p. 13.
[2] See John H. Ferguson, *American Diplomacy and the Boer War* (Philadelphia, 1939).
[3] Roosevelt became president (on McKinley's assassination) on 14 September 1901.
[4] See 'Theodore Roosevelt and the British Empire', in Max Beloff, *The Great Powers* (1958).
[5] Laurier to Minto, 30 July 1899. From a copy in the Hutton Papers, B.M. Add. MSS. 50079.
[6] 'We do not intend.' wrote Chamberlain to Minto, on 7 October 1899, 'to accept any offer from volunteers. We do not want the men, and the whole point of the offer would be lost

Even so, those who thought in imperial terms were worried about the spirit that had been revealed in some Canadian quarters. Writing to the governor-general, General Hutton referred to an interview he had had with the Canadian defence minister, Frederick Borden, after the 'Black Week' of British disasters in December, 1899. ' "General," he snarled at me across his table, "I ask myself this question. Is it worth Canada's while to remain part of an Empire which can suffer disasters such as those of Methuen, Gatacre and Buller?" ' This outburst was regarded by Hutton as 'a true indication of the attitude which Canadians represented by Laurier and his supporters would take up in the event of our arms, military or naval, receiving a serious check in any of those numerous incidents of war which the obligations of Empire enjoin'.[1]

In the end Canada sent 8,300 men, Australia 10,000, and New Zealand 6,500. With contingents from smaller colonies the imperial contribution was about 30,000 compared with 366,000 from Britain itself and 52,000 men raised in South Africa.[2]

This was sufficient to make the optimists feel that the Empire's cohesion had been decisively demonstrated. As early as October 1899 Chamberlain was writing: 'I am sure that the action of Canada and of all the other Colonies will have a lasting impression in this country and will tend more than anything else to draw the Empire closer together.'[3]

Chamberlain's son Austen, then civil lord of the admiralty, put the same view forward in his election address in September 1900:

> This war will always be memorable as the first instance in our history of the active co-operation of all the great self-governing colonies with the Mother Country in a common struggle in defence of British rights and British honour. The Empire hitherto little more than an aspiration, has thus become a reality, and a great step forward has been made towards that closer union upon which are founded our best hopes for the future of the British race.[4]

---

unless it were endorsed by the government of the colony and applied to an organized body of the Colonial Forces.' Garvin, *Joseph Chamberlain*, vol. 3, pp. 531–2.

[1] Hutton to Minto, 10 January 1902. B.M. Add. 50081. (Sir) Frederick Borden was minister of militia and defence throughout the premiership of Sir Wilfred Laurier which lasted from July 1896 to October 1911.

[2] *Cambridge History of the British Empire*, vol. VIII; *South Africa* (Cambridge, 1963), p. 619. Gordon, op. cit., pp. 138–43.

[3] Garvin, op. cit., vol. 3, p. 533.   [4] Petrie, op. cit., p. 89.

What had to be weighed, however, was the reaction towards this participation in the colonies themselves. Mackenzie King, who was in England when the war broke out, was so fired by the rallying of the Empire to the common cause that he even talked in terms of imperial federation.[1] But the strains that participation brought to light within Canada made it evident that involvement in any imperial war was bound to be a threat to national unity. King, whose whole political career was to be concerned with the preservation of Canadian nationhood, may well have been influenced by this experience as well as by the conscription crisis of the first world war to pursue a policy of extreme disengagement where imperial commitments were concerned.

In Britain itself there was much emphasis on the precedent created for imperial co-operation in future wars. 'The leaders of the Dominion armies in the First World War,' it was later pointed out, 'were almost all men who had volunteered for South Africa and who were inspired in equal measure by national pride and the sense of imperial partnership.'[2]

The external consequences of the war were, however, much less significant than its effect on the British public mind. Whatever the historian may now see as being the primary cause of the conflict, to many people at the time the case against Britain seemed an overwhelming one. Here was a great empire fighting to destroy the independence of two small pastoral republics for the sake of the profits of mine-owners and financiers.[3] The war offered a clear illustration of the basic Hobson–Lenin theory of imperialism, and even those whose analysis was by no means Marxian could equally well criticize and even oppose the war on old-fashioned radical grounds.[4]

The war produced, or perhaps exaggerated, lines of division within the liberal opposition that were never to be healed altogether, and which

[1] Dawson, *Mackenzie King*, p. 90.
[2] Amery, op. cit., vol. 1, p. 158.
[3] The fact that a number of the capitalists involved were 'international' (i.e. Jewish) gave a somewhat anti-semitic tone to some aspects of pro-Boer radical propaganda; but the anti-semitism of the left, partly no doubt because of the fact that some of its main protagonists were Roman Catholics, had no future in Britain compared to what it was to enjoy on the continent. On the anti-semitic aspect of J. A. Hobson's indictment of imperialism, see R. Koebner and H. D. Schmidt, *Imperialism* (Cambridge, 1964), pp. 250–3.
[4] The war, wrote Goldwin Smith to Bryce on 3 December 1899, was 'not necessary for any purpose but those of Chamberlain and Cecil Rhodes. It will make England deservedly detested. I am not sure that she had done anything morally much worse for herself since Joan of Arc than she does in crushing that little Commonwealth.' Bryce Papers, English Correspondence, vol. 16. On the general subject of anti-imperialism, see also Bernard Porter, *Critics of Empire* (London, Macmillan, 1968).

help to explain the secessions from the liberal party which assisted the labour party to supplant it after 1918. To have been right about the Boer war was essential to the credentials of a true radical. In all this, there was of course a great measure of self-deception. In their sense of outrage at what seemed a wanton assault on the liberties of a free people, British radicals did not look too closely at the nature of Boer society or Boer unwillingness to accept British rule. That the funda-mental clash in South Africa was between white and native was more obvious to those who had to deal with policy there than to their liberal critics.

> The Anglo-Dutch friction [wrote Milner] is bad enough. But it is child's play compared with the antagonism of the White and Black. That the white man must rule is clear – but *How*? There is a point where my views and those of most Englishmen differ radically from those of most Colonists. And this, and not the Dutch business, is the subject with respect to which I foresee the greatest difficulty.[1]

Liberals were slow to appreciate the full force of this argument. The reconciliation of Boer and Briton by restoring self-government to the Transvaal and the Orange Free State, and the creation of the South African Union, were regarded as major triumphs for the liberal as opposed to the imperialist handling of overseas problems. Yet the nature of the bargain implied that the 'native question' should be decided locally and not at Westminster. It was only afterwards that radical protest in Britain took up the cause of the disfranchised African majority; and respect for the Boers was replaced by a savage contempt. It was the spiritual descendants of the pro-Boers who were responsible for forcing South Africa out of the Commonwealth in 1961.

The principal effect of the war itself was to accelerate the process of re-examining Britain's military establishment and the means through which it could best be planned and administered.[2] Boer successes pointed the need to investigate the make-up and efficiency of the army; the obvious part that the navy had played, even without being

[1] Sir Alfred Milner to the Rev. M. G. Glazebrook from Cape Town, 29 September 1897, in A. E. Wrench, *Alfred, Lord Milner* (London, Eyre & Spottiswoode, 1958), p. 182.
[2] The origins of the Committee of Imperial Defence and its role in pre-1914 Britain have been the subject of much study. See N. H. Gibbs, *The Origins of Imperial Defence* (Oxford, 1955); John Ehrman, *Cabinet Government and War, 1898–1940* (Cambridge, 1958); F. A. Johnson, *Defence by Committee* (New York, 1960). See also W. C. B. Tunstall, 'Imperial Defence, 1897–1914', chapter XV of *C.H.B.E.*, vol. III, and Denis Judd, *Balfour and the British Empire* (London, Macmillan, 1968).

engaged, to prevent external intervention gave to the problem of re-taining the command of the seas a new urgency. There was much con-cern for the scale of military expenditure and a strong desire for economy.[1] Finally there was an obvious need both for consistency and continuity of policy at home and for some method of dovetailing the defence plans of the Empire with those of the home government.

Not only the self-governing colonies but India also was involved. The first British troops landed in South Africa came from India and but for the efficiency with which they were collected and sent, Natal might have been lost during the first month of the war. Even so, there was a good deal of friction over the allocation of the cost of the Indian effort.[2] What was gratifying was that no ill-effects on India's own defence were felt as a result of the war, though knowledge of India's vulnerability influenced the conduct of British diplomacy. Arguing for a temporary reduction of troops in India, the secretary of state for war was able to say in a memorandum for the cabinet in November 1905: 'During the war in South Africa the Army in India was short of establishment to the extent of 11,000 men and no evil consequences resulted.' By 1905 the international situation was much more favourable and the sea was open in case India ever required reinforcement.[3]

The Creation of the C.I.D.

These questions of home and imperial defence were not thought to be suitable for handling by the British cabinet in the ordinary way of business – it being remembered that the cabinet of the time was simply a gathering of the ministers with no secretariat and no agenda or record-keeping or follow-through organization. The lessons of the war and previous experience with committees investigating specialized

[1] It has been reckoned that in the last quarter of the nineteenth century, Britain spent be-tween 2 and $2\frac{1}{2}$ per cent of G.N.P. on defence – India at that time paying for its own defence. The figure rose to $6\frac{1}{2}$ per cent during the Boer war but fell to between 3 and $3\frac{1}{2}$ per cent during the period 1904–14. In the late 1920s the figure actually fell below 2 per cent, but rearmament in the 1930s pushed it up to 5 per cent in 1938. These estimates were given by Sir Richard Clarke at a seminar in All Souls College, Oxford, on 12 October 1964. To go back to the position at the time of the Boer war it has been reckoned that between 1895 and 1902, British defence spending increased at a greater rate than that of any other major power except Russia. Monger, op. cit., p. 8.

[2] Grenville, op. cit., p. 268.

[3] Memorandum by H. O. Arnold-Forster, Arnold-Forster Papers, B.M. Add. 50352. Arnold-Forster (1855–1909) was secretary of state for war from October 1903 to December 1905. He succeeded St John Brodrick (1856–1942) (ninth Viscount Midleton 1907, first Earl Midleton 1920) who had held the office since November 1900.

aspects of defence gave rise to a new piece of machinery, the committee of Imperial Defence which came into being in stages. The
Defence committee of the cabinet which had existed since 1895 was
placed on a permanent footing in December 1902. Its chairman was
the lord president of the Council, the Duke of Devonshire, who had been
chairman of the old Defence committee: but in October 1903, when he
resigned on the tariff issue, the prime minister himself took over. The
other members who were to form the permanent nucleus of the committee were to be the first lord of the admiralty, the first sea lord and the
director of naval intelligence; the secretary of state for war, the commander-in-chief and the director of military intelligence. It was intended
that others should attend when invited. The main innovation was the
combination of political heads of departments and service chiefs in a
single body, although it was emphasized that constitutionally there
had been no change as the body was advisory only and in no way
affected the full responsibility of the cabinet. A minor point, though it
was significant for the future, was the introduction of a Foreign Office
clerk to keep minutes.[1]

On 5 March 1904 Balfour moved in the House of Commons a resolution which ran: 'That in the opinion of the House, the growing needs
of the Empire require the establishment of the Committee of Defence
upon a permanent footing.'[2] This was decisive in incorporating the
committee into the standing machinery of British government, and its
formal birth may be dated to the Treasury minute of 4 May 1904
which set up its secretariat. The prime minister retained full power to
summon whoever he wished to the committee, and fairly regular
attenders, in addition to the core taken over from the 'transitional'
committee, were the secretaries of state for foreign affairs, India, and
the colonies, and the chancellor of the exchequer. In addition from 1905
Lord Esher, the report of whose committee on the War Office had been
a crucial factor in the creation of the committee, was made a permanent
member although he held no other governmental appointment. The
original intention was to provide for continuity when the liberals
took over the government, as was clearly about to happen.[3]

[1] The clerk was William Tyrrell (1866–1947) (knighted 1913, baron 1929), who had been
Sanderson's private secretary and was to be private secretary to Sir Edward Grey from 1907
to 1915. After holding other foreign office posts he became permanent under-secretary from
1925 to 1928 and ambassador to Paris, 1928–1934.
[2] See Monger, op. cit., p. 228 fn.
[3] There is a suggestion in the Esher papers that the original idea came from the king and that
he would have wished both Esher and Milner to become members. Esher, *Journals and Letters*,

It has generally been agreed that the C.I.D., particularly through the operations of its various technical sub-committees (the whole tightly knit together by the secretariat), performed to the full the specifically military aspect of its tasks which were largely concerned with the 'infrastructure' of defence.[1] It achieved a smooth transition from peace to war in 1914, in striking contrast with past experience, and it was not to blame for the fact that, as the struggle wore on, it became something quite different from what had originally been anticipated by both military and naval planners.

Originally the C.I.D. was intended to cover a wide canvas which was to include basic strategy, particularly in the imperial context. Some felt that here too considerable success was achieved; an undated note by the committee's first secretary, Sir George Clarke, points out that before the committee was established there had been no direct link between ministers and naval and military experts, or between the different departments involved in defence:

There was no proper record of the progress of Imperial questions, and none could be compiled without laborious reading through Departmental papers. It was no one's duty to look ahead and to foresee Imperial questions which might arise at any time. The grave defects of our system of government may be expressed in a single sentence: 'questions of Imperial Defence were never properly focused'.

Although at the time of writing only one colonial representative, Sir Frederick Borden, had ever been present, 'the Colonies' (he wrote) 'accepted the conclusions of the Committee more readily than they would those of the War Office or Admiralty'.[2]

---

vol. 2 (1934), p. 114. In any event, Esher's close connection with the court would have provided a possible additional reason for his membership. Esher's membership was, of course, an additional source of concern for radical opinion which was very worried about the possible by-passing of the cabinet despite Balfour's assurances. This suspicion was alive among the more radical members of the new cabinet itself. See Monger, op. cit., pp. 285 fn., 309 fn.

[1] One area which was recommended to the C.I.D. for advance preparation was the financial which Sir Francis Oppenheimer, the vigorous commercial attaché in Germany, called to the attention of the Foreign Office on the basis of his observation of the detailed plans being made in Germany for the handling of banking questions in time of emergency. 'After more than a year of persistent inquiries about what was being done in the matter,' he writes, 'I learned that the subject had been found too complicated. It had been decided to drop it. And so my warning was brushed aside on the very ground that justified it. When war came, we suffered all the consequences that ought to have been forestalled.' Oppenheimer, op. cit., p. 218.

[2] Sydenham Papers, B.M. Add. 50836. Sir George Clarke (1848–1933) (created Baron Sydenham in 1919), a soldier by profession, had been secretary of the Colonial Defence com-

One merit of the flexibility of the committee's membership was, indeed, that colonial representatives could be present on an equal footing with the United Kingdom ministers. Borden's presence at the 'transitional' stage of the committee in 1903 was made much of by Balfour who told the king that although it appeared that 'this particular gentleman' was 'of rather inferior quality', and that it would be necessary to be careful what was said before him, a new precedent 'of great imperial significance had been set up' – the committee had the potentiality to become an 'Imperial Council'.[1]

Although Balfour was being pretentious in talking of an 'Imperial Council' and although Clarke with his Australian experience should have known better than to assume that any alterations in the United Kingdom governmental machine could prevent the dominions making their own defence arrangements, the system had great practical utility at a time when common purposes and interests undoubtedly existed. The C.I.D. also provided useful machinery for associating dominion governments with imperial actions as a result of the development of the colonial conferences.[2] The 1897 conference had called for periodic conferences on matters of common interest and the next such gathering was in 1902 at the time of the coronation of Edward VII. It was again restricted to the prime ministers of the self-governing colonies, and was presided over by Chamberlain as colonial secretary. The discussions were partly held in private and it is clear that Chamberlain still regarded the main subject-matter as being 'the policy of the Empire', and hoped to transform it into a body with policy-making powers:

The weary Titan [Chamberlain told the Prime Ministers] staggers under the too vast orb of its fate. We have borne the burden for many years. We think it is time our children should assist us to support it, and whenever you make the request to us, be very sure we shall hasten gladly to call you to our Councils . . . I have always felt myself that the most practical form, in which we could achieve our

mittee from 1885 to 1892 and governor of Victoria from 1901 to 1904. He was a member of Esher's War Office Reconstruction committee and secretary of the C.I.D. from the establishment of that office. He was retired from the office in 1907 owing to his opposition to Fisher's dreadnought programme and was made governor of Bombay, a post which he held till 1913. In later life he developed extreme right-wing opinions and a devotion to the 'Baconian' theory of Shakespeare. See his writings, *My Working Life* (1927), and *Studies of an Imperialist* (1928).
[1] Young, *Balfour*, pp. 224–5.
[2] See J. E. Tyler, 'Development of the Imperial Conference, 1887–1914', ch. XI of *C.H.B.E.*, vol. III.

object, would be the establishment ... of a real Council of the Empire to which all questions of Imperial interest might be referred ... the Council might in the first instance be merely an advisory council ... But, although that would be a preliminary step, it is clear that the object would not be completely secured until there had been conferred upon such a Council executive functions, and perhaps also legislative power ...

But such language was very remote from the feelings of his auditors, and in the words of Chamberlain's biographer: 'in 1897, the idea of a Council of Empire had provoked long discussions. This time it was not even criticized; it was ignored.'[1]

It was agreed that colonial conferences should meet regularly at least every four years, and become events in their own right and not merely part of a royal occasion. The next conference was therefore due in 1906 and in a dispatch in April 1905, Chamberlain's successor at the Colonial Office, Alfred Lyttelton put forward new proposals which again echoed the 'Imperial Council' idea.[2] The colonial conference would be restyled 'Imperial Council' and exist as a commission representing all the states concerned, in session in London and aided by a secretariat. It might deal with civil matters affecting the whole Empire as the C.I.D. dealt with military ones. In this form the colonies obtained no share in the formulation of either foreign or strategic policy. Although the first reaction of some of the colonies was favourable, Canadian opposition caused a substantial watering down of the idea when it was discussed at the conference of 1907.[3]

Reshaping Naval Policy

The reshaping of naval policy was the first and most important task before Britain's defence planners. Anxiety about the naval position antedated the Boer war, and protection against invasion became first priority for naval planners. In the summer of 1893 Spenser Wilkinson wrote a letter to *The Times* arguing that Britain could only be secure if

[1] Julian Amery, *Life of Joseph Chamberlain*, vol. IV (1951), pp. 421–2.
[2] Circular Despatch of 20 April 1905 (printed in Cd. 2785). There is a draft dated 7 December 1905 in the Balfour Papers, B.M. Add. 49698. Alfred Lyttelton (1857–1913) a barrister, entered parliament in 1895. He was secretary of state for the colonies, October 1903 to December 1905.
[3] Owing to internal political difficulties in both Australia and New Zealand the conference due to be held in 1906 did not take place until April–May 1907.

she had a navy 'invincible against any combination'. Unwillingness to rely upon allies to make up the balance of naval power characterized naval thinking right down to the outbreak of war. Wilkinson went on to argue that such a navy would give control of the seas as a whole, and that to abandon control would mean the annihilation of the British Empire and of the British Isles themselves: 'I assert therefore, that we cannot please ourselves whether we keep or neglect the Empire. We are compelled to choose between two extremes. England must either become the dependency of another Power holding the mastery of the seas or she must herself command the sea and lead the world.'[1]

Admiral Fisher went even further in his belief in the concentration of naval strength and that the dispersal of small squadrons of second-rate ships too weak to fight and too slow to run away did not add to Britain's real strength at sea.[2] As late as 1900, for nearly two-thirds of every year there was no organized naval force in home waters, as the Channel fleet was away cruising in Spanish or Irish waters.[3] The Boer war emphasized the lesson of the priority of naval strength. In November 1903 Balfour reported on the possibility of a serious invasion with France as the presumed invader. While the soldiers, he found, argued that the navy offered no certain protection, the navy claimed that no one would take the risk and face the cost of an invasion unless the navy were driven out of home waters. It believed that this could be prevented even in unfavourable conditions.[4] In a memorandum for the cabinet in February 1904 Balfour drew the lessons of the immediate past:

> When a foreigner talks of war he always means a war in which the Army plays the first part; when an Englishman talks of war he

---

[1] Spenser Wilkinson, *Thirty-Five Years* (1933), pp. 186, 190. Besides his numerous writings on military policy and his personal correspondence with many leading figures, Spenser Wilkinson had an *entrée* to Foreign Office circles through his marriage to Eyre Crowe's sister.
[2] Fisher deplored the sending of navy men into the African bush, and on punitive expeditions on the east and west coasts of Africa, because of the parsimony of the War Office and want of foresight in preparing the proper men for the work on the old principle of applying to the admiralty to send ships. He urged 'the necessity for organizing a force of black troops for African and other tropical service in sufficient numbers to prevent the ever-recurring requests to the Admiralty to send ships and land men'. Fisher to Lord Spencer, 16 May 1901. Marder, *Fear God and Dread Nought*, vol. 1, p. 192.   [3] Ibid., p. 149.
[4] Balfour Papers, B.M. Add. 49700. Soon after his appointment to the War Office, Arnold-Forster noted that the commander-in-chief, Lord Roberts appeared to take the same view: 'He now inclines to the view that *invasion* on a large scale may not be anticipated. Putting himself in the position of a Commanding Officer of an invading force, he cannot perceive how the difficulties he would have could be overcome.' Diary entry, 27 October 1903. B. M. Arnold-Forster Papers, Diary, vol. 1.

always means a war in which the Navy takes, if not the most prominent, yet the most fundamental and important share in the military
operations, whether these be by sea or by land. Without the Navy
we should never have been allowed to fight out the South African
war to a successful conclusion; without the navy we should be incapable of fighting Russia in Central Asia.[1]

The Dogger Bank crisis in October 1904, when hostilities with Russia
and even with France seemed possible and when four battleships of the
Channel fleet had to be recalled instantly from Gibraltar and attached
to the Home fleet, showed that the dispositions of the navy did not
correspond to the theory of concentration.[2] Admiralty policy was
thereafter regulated accordingly (though the process was not complete
until 1909) and it was, of course, much influenced by the belief, from
1906 onwards, that the principal threat against which it was necessary
to stand on guard was Germany.[3] The upshot may conveniently be
stated in the words of a naval historian:

On the presumption that the building up of the German navy represented the real menace, the strategical disposition of British troops
and squadrons was reorganized to concentrate the main strength in
the North Sea and the Channel, instead of in the Mediterranean,
which had been for so long the main focus of British sea-power.
The new plan reduced the Mediterranean fleet from twelve battleships to eight and instituted a new Atlantic fleet of eight battleships
based on Gibraltar and available to reinforce either the Mediterranean fleet or the Channel fleet which was based on Dover and consisted of ten of the most modern battleships. Independent squadrons
of armoured cruisers, available to reinforce the main fleets when
required were allocated to the Atlantic, East Indies, Australia and
Pacific. Joint manoeuvres were held twice a year between the Atlantic
and Channel fleets. This interlocking policy served two purposes;
the rapid reinforcement of any fleet which might find itself in the

[1] Balfour Papers, B.M. Add. 49698.
[2] The Russian fleet on its way from the Baltic to fight the Japanese fired in a fog upon some
fishing vessels in the North Sea and produced some alarm as to the possibility of a clash;
the help given by the French to the Russian ships on their route to the Far East was also productive of friction with Britain, by now Japan's ally. Marder, *From the Dread Nought to Scapa
Flow* (London, Cape, 1961), vol. 1, pp. 41–2, 110.
[3] 'Our only potential foe now being Germany, the common-sense conclusion is that the outlying fleets no longer require to be maintained at the strength which was admittedly necessary
a year ago when France and Russia were our most probable opponents.' Admiralty memorandum, 'The Home Fleet', December 1906, quoted ibid., p. 71.

centre of war operations, and a considerable economy in the number of ships required to maintain British sea supremacy. It also made certain that the main concentration of sea-power was always within easy reach of the North Sea, though not so obviously as to cause legitimate alarm in Germany.[1]

The policy of concentration was fundamental to both inter-imperial and foreign relations from this time forward, and one of its earliest consequences was in relation to the United States. By the second Hay–Pauncefote treaty of 18 November 1901 Britain abandoned the rights to the share in the prospective isthmian canal that she had possessed under the old Clayton–Bulwer treaty of 1850. This treaty also, in the words of an American historian, 'symbolized the passing of British dominance and the advent of American hegemony in the Caribbean'.[2]

With this tacit admission of American supremacy in the western hemisphere and that British colonial and economic interests there depended upon American goodwill, the argument for maintaining the old West Indian and North American squadron disappeared and it was withdrawn. This was not an easy argument to express because although the experts appreciated the facts, the general public, then as later, overestimated British strength. In suggesting the line Balfour might take in the House of Commons on this issue, Clarke wrote: 'The important thing is to be strong in European waters while holding our squadrons ready to go elsewhere if required.' So much could be admitted publicly.

> What it is best not to say [he went on] is that we believe that the idea of opposing the navy of the U.S. in the Caribbean and the North Atlantic close to its bases must be abandoned. This has naturally altered some of the strategic aspects of this part of the world. In years not far distant we shall be quite unable to oppose the navy of Japan in its own waters. It is best to recognize facts but not always to proclaim them from the housetop.[3]

[1] P. K. Kemp, 'The Royal Navy', ch. XIII of S. Nowell-Smith (ed.), *Edwardian England*, (London, 1964), pp. 502–3.
[2] R. W. Leopold, *The Growth of American Foreign Policy* (New York, 1962), p. 226. The earlier version of the treaty had included a prohibition on fortification which Balfour was inclined to wish to see maintained when it ran up against trouble in Congress. See his correspondence with J. St Loe Strachey in March 1900 in which the latter suggests that the assumption should be no war with the United States. Balfour Papers, B.M. Add. 49797. The Boer war and Britain's sense of isolation contributed to the eventual acceptance of the new text more favourable to the American claims. Grenville, op. cit., pp. 376, 379–81, 385, 388–9.
[3] Clarke to Sandars, 31 March 1905. Balfour Papers, B.M. Add. 49701.

Although the way in which the major challenge of a hostile battle fleet should be met was quite clear, the future use of sea-power for interfering with an enemy's trade, which had played so notable a part in previous British wars, was still obscure, as technological change had to be taken into account. The development of the submarine and other torpedo-launching craft had helped to diminish the fear of invasion, but at the same time made close blockade impossible. In consequence, 'between 1904 and 1914 there was evolved the blockade strategy of the War, that of distant surveillance by the main fleet in well-defended bases'.[1] The question of commerce interception, with all the problems it raised of neutral rights, was not one which naval men alone could be left to solve. Britain had been unwilling to press her claims too far in the South African war in the face of German protest, though the degree of concessions made to the neutral position was apparently not made clear to the Admiralty.[2] Generally speaking the British interest was assumed to be on the neutral side. In any future war Britain might hope to remain outside, and would wish her commerce to be free of interference by the belligerents. Should she be at war herself, then the most important thing to aim at was maximum freedom for her own commerce; as compared with the days of sail, attacks on shipping were easier and defence more difficult. Finally, in the wars that others had fought since the 1860s, economic pressure had played a minor role.[3] The submarine was not viewed for its potential as a commerce raider, no doubt because the wholesale violation of the traditional norms of sea-warfare by a determined Germany was not envisaged. These facts may explain the long delay when war came in devising an answer to the submarine menace. It meant a renunciation of the classical doctrines of sea-power, through which Britain had risen to pre-eminence and which were as deeply rooted as the fatal doctrine of the 'breakthrough' which was responsible for the terrible and largely futile losses of the war on land.

Military Reorganization

Military reorganization was slower than naval; the 1890s had prompted much talk about reform but the forces opposed to change had been proved powerful. Apart from the changes in the War Office recom-

[1] Marder, *British Naval Policy*, p. 370.
[2] Selborne to Balfour, 29 August 1904. Balfour Papers, B.M. Add. 49708.
[3] Sir Herbert Richmond, *Statesmen and Sea Power* (Oxford, 1946), pp. 280–1.

mended by the Esher committee, the most important immediate reaction to the war was to imitate the navy in reducing the number and strength of overseas garrisons. On 29 August 1904 Arnold-Forster wrote to Esher about a recent visit to the continent:

> When I see the amount of energy, forethought, science, and skill which are devoted to military organization in France, and even in Switzerland, and when I compare it with the amateur way in which matters are transacted in this country my heart sinks. We are still labouring under the delusion that with our 'worst' we can successfully contend with their 'best'. Some day we shall have a rude awakening.

He went on to argue in favour of withdrawing as many troops as possible from the colonies – Egypt, Canada, the West Indies, and possibly Bermuda – as part of a general reorganization of the army.[1] This general approach had the support of Clarke, who pointed out that the defences of Halifax and Bermuda seemed to be based on a standard derived from the position at the time of the American Civil War,[2] but Clarke nevertheless objected to any suggestion of reductions in Egypt and, for the time being, at Singapore and Hong Kong likewise.[3]

The cabinet decided on 6 February 1905 to withdraw troops from the West Indies and Bermuda and reduce the establishment in the Mediterranean.[4] The needs of Egypt were to be met by withdrawing troops from Crete, where some had been stationed since the 1897 rebellion. It was agreed that the South African garrison should be maintained. Milner had strongly pressed for this as a permanent arrangement, South Africa would provide suitable opportunities for training; in July 1903 it had in fact been announced that 25,000 men would be kept there for that purpose. But the force was whittled away and little remained by the time the Union was set up in 1910.[5] Finally, Canada was to take over responsibility for the garrisons at Halifax and Esquimault.[6] These changes would be based on the assumption that Britain's needs could be met by an expeditionary force of 35,000 men.

[1] Copy in Arnold-Forster Papers, Diary, vol. 5, B.M. Add. 50339.
[2] Notes on discussion with Lord Kitchener on 8 July 1904 sent to Balfour on 9 July. Sydenham Papers, B.M. Add. 50836.
[3] Clarke to Sandars, 23 January 1905. Balfour Papers, B.M. Add. 46701. See also an unsigned paper of July 1904 dealing with the importance of the garrison in Egypt. Ibid., B.M. Add. 49698.
[4] Arnold-Forster Papers, Diary, vol. 10.   [5] Amery, op. cit., vol. 1, p. 203.
[6] On this, see Preston, op. cit., pp. 336–43.

No consideration was given to the far larger forces that would be needed if Britain took part in a continental war, though some people already believed that the method of expanding the forces in the event of war was more important than the organization of the regular army.[1] Preparations of this kind involved contemplating some form of national service, and the National Service League to advocate universal training and compulsory service was set up late in 1905 with Lord Roberts as its president, although it remained a minority movement.[2] One reason why there was little sympathy in official circles for the national service movement was that it seemed irrelevant to the needs of India. Balfour took the view that Indian defence remained Britain's first concern, and in a memorandum in December 1904 wrote that of the 209,000 soldiers needed by the Empire, 27,000 were wanted for home defence, 30,000 in the colonial garrisons, 52,000 for the Indian garrisons, and 100,000 for immediate readiness to reinforce India.[3] Despite the relief occasioned by the Russo-Japanese war, Indian needs were not overlooked at any time.

It would indeed have been difficult to do so during the viceroyalty of Curzon. Between 1898 and his departure in November 1905 Curzon was not only in charge of the government of India but in a position to express his long-held view that India was the key to Britain's entire world position.[4] While London was prepared to hold in check Curzon's propensity for forward policies in the Persian Gulf, Afghanistan, and Tibet, it did not challenge the importance of Indian defence as such.[5] The government might have tried to meet the burden of it by some greater measure of Indianization of the armed forces than any contemplated at the time, but against this there was the feeling that Britain's authority would be fatally weakened unless she made it clear she was holding India by virtue of her own strength.[6]

[1] Amery, op. cit., vol. 1, p. 213.
[2] Spenser Wilkinson attended the inaugural meeting but took no part in the League, believing that no British government would propose such a thing in peacetime nor would the country accept it. He noted that none of the people at the meeting had any real knowledge of the French or German systems or were able to make trustworthy comparisons between the Swiss system and the British militia and volunteers. Wilkinson, op. cit., p. 271.
[3] Monger, op. cit., pp. 95-6.
[4] 'India is not much thought of or understood at home. But it is out and away the biggest thing the English are doing anywhere in the world. If we lose it we shall drop straight away to a third-rate power.' Curzon to Balfour, 31 March 1901, Balfour Papers, B.M. Add. 49732.
[5] Michael Edwardes, *High Noon of Empire: India under Curzon* (1965), pp. 161-3.
[6] 'The day we cease to hold India by the strong hand and by virtue of being the better men, we shall be in danger of losing it altogether, and for this reason I look with some suspicion

Although Lord Kitchener, who went out to India as commander-in-chief in 1902, clashed with Curzon over their respective spheres of authority, he agreed with the viceroy on the importance he attached to Indian defence and in his determination to secure the resources needed for it.[1] When in 1904 Kitchener asked for reinforcements in connection with troubles with Afghanistan, Clarke wrote to Balfour: 'It must be for the Cabinet at home not for the Government of India to decide when the occasion arises whether it is desirable to commit our whole military resources to a campaign in India . . . it is as probable that the military forces of India will be required for service in other parts of the Empire as that they will have to be ranged on the North-West frontier.'[2] Even stronger were the objections to the apparent claims of Curzon for a high degree of autonomy over the organization of the Indian army, and foreign policy itself. 'India,' wrote Clarke, 'seems to be drifting into the position of an allied power making enormous contingent demands upon the predominant partner but unwilling to discuss matters of joint interest.'[3]

It is therefore easy to understand that historians of British policy should see Curzon's resignation in August 1905 as due primarily to disputes over foreign policy and Balfour's insistence on the authority of the home government, rather than to the disagreements with Kitchener which were its ostensible cause.[4] But although this was the version which the government itself preferred to make known, there is perhaps more to be said for the view of an Indian historian that it was in fact a mere personal conflict between Curzon and Kitchener 'not a conflict of implacable convictions but a clash of seismic wills on an issue

on any policy however good which tends to take the responsibility off our shoulders.' Arnold-Forster Papers, Diary, 25 May 1905, vol. 13.

[1] Lord Kitchener (1850–1916) had made his reputation in the Middle East and the Sudan. In 1899 he had been made chief of staff of the forces in South Africa and was commander-in-chief there from 1900 to 1902. He remained in India until 1909. From 1911 to 1914, he was agent and consul-general in Egypt and after the outbreak of war in 1914 he became secretary of state for war.

[2] Notes made on 22 November 1904. Sydenham Papers, B.M. Add. 50836.

[3] Memorandum, 'The Kabul Mission and its Results', 17 June 1905, sent by Clarke to Balfour. Balfour Papers, B.M. Add. 49701. There is an echo of this language in the letter sent by Balfour to Esher on 6 October 1906 concerning a demand by Kitchener for a definite pledge of reinforcements in the event of war with Russia: 'I decidedly disapprove of arguments based on "pledges" alleged to have passed between the Indian government and our own. India ought not to treat with us as if we were an allied but *foreign* power. We are engaged in a common work and we are the predominant partner.' Balfour Papers, B.M. Add. 49719. Esher's own attempt to put the matter in perspective is to be found in his letter to Kitchener of 4 October 1906, Esher, *Journals and Letters*, vol. 2, pp. 189–92.

[4] Monger, op. cit., p. 216.

of no serious consequence, and under the stress the illogical system of military administration in India broke'.[1]

The Tariff Reform Argument

The dissatisfaction widely expressed with the military's amateurism and reliance upon tradition was paralleled by disquiet over British industry and commerce's disregard of the no less serious and determined challenge of Britain's rivals, notably Germany. Although the promotion of British commerce by direct government action was thought by some representatives of the 'Old Diplomacy' to be outside their province and to some extent beneath them,[2] it cannot be said that British industrialists showed themselves ready to profit by whatever facilities were offered them.[3] British enterprise overseas was not a thing of the past, particularly where major engineering projects were concerned, such as the Aswan Dam in Egypt or the first oilfields concession in Persia in 1905 – so important for later naval history. But in those branches of industry in which scientific research and development was all-important Britain's failure to develop an adequate structure of scientific education and the general indifference of the governing *élite* to the problems were already having their effects. The dyestuffs industry was by 1900 dominated by Germany, despite the fact that the key invention in the synthetic field had been made by an Englishman.[4]

It was even more remarkable that so little attention was paid to the biological sciences with their intimate relationship to development in

[1] Gopal, *British Policy in India*, pp. 290–1. For an account of the Curzon–Kitchener quarrel from a point of view sympathetic to the latter, see Philip Magnus, *Kitchener, Portrait of an Imperialist* (London, John Murray, 1958), ch. 11.

[2] See on the whole subject of the role of economic questions in British foreign policy, D. C. M. Platt, *Finance, Trade and Politics in British Foreign Policy* (Oxford, Clarendon Press, 1968).

[3] The autobiography of Sir Francis Oppenheimer, *Stranger Within* (London, Faber, 1960), is particularly revealing in this respect. Oppenheimer, a baptized Jew, British-born and Balliol-educated, but of German descent, succeeded his father as honorary consul-general in Frankfurt in 1900 and was in January 1912, attached to the Berlin Embassy as commercial attaché for northern and central Europe. Despite the importance attached to his reports in both capacities on Germany's economy and its relation to her international ambitions, Oppenheimer's elevation from the consular service to the foreign service, the first of its kind, was clearly resented by important members of the Foreign Office, and notably by Hardinge. This later on rendered him very vulnerable to the attacks made on all those in the service during the war who had German names or connections. In Hardinge's case at least a trace of anti-semitism would seem to have crept in (p. 321). On the other hand, Oppenheimer's attempts to interest British manufacturers in new possibilities on the continent fell quite flat.

[4] One must not exaggerate the relative decline of British industry. In 1914, for instance, three-fifths of the world's ships were still being built in British yards. Nowell-Smith (ed.), *Edwardian England*, p. 116.

the tropics. 'Frenchmen, Italians, Germans, Americans, even Japanese are shooting ahead of us,' wrote an eminent scientist to the India Office in 1897 hoping to get great co-operation from it for Sir Ronald Ross in his epoch-making study of malaria.[1] In the social sciences also, where Britain had been a pioneer in the nineteenth century, the classical orthodoxies remained dominant and the large new fields for investigation demanded by the modern interventionist state and its new enterprises were little explored. The foundation of the London School of Economics in 1895 was intended to fill this gap though its subsequent development did not altogether coincide with the aims of its founders.[2]

These aspects of British life indicate why, in spite of notable achievements – for instance, in the naval race itself – Britain's continental rivals made light of her strength. Britain neither presented the picture of self-confident private enterprise that was turning the United States into the world's greatest industrial nation without the aid of a powerful state machine, nor approached the controlled urge to national power and expansion of imperial Germany. The emergence of 'tariff reform', or protection, as a strong divisive issue must therefore be regarded not merely as a continuation of the campaign for imperial preferences in order to hold the Empire together but also as a reply to the German and other challenges.[3] Other measures advocated were to abandon the criteria of the market-place and create, through tariffs, planned emigration policies, and other means, an economy directed as much by considerations of power as by those of private profit.

After the removal of Joseph Chamberlain himself from the arena Hewins, who was at this time closely in touch with Balfour, wrote to him on 18 February 1907:

> I should define the new policy as the deliberate adoption of the Empire, as distinguished from the United Kingdom, as the basis of public policy, and in particular, the substitution in our economic policy of Imperial interests for the interest of the consumer, those interests being measured not necessarily by the immediate or even the ultimate gain of a purely economic character arising from a

---

[1] A. R. Ubbelohde, 'Science', ch. 5 of Nowell-Smith (ed.), *Edwardian England*, pp. 232–3.
[2] Hewins, op. cit., p. 2. See Sir Sydney Caine, *History of the Foundation of the London School of Economics and Political Science* (1963).
[3] See G. S. Graham, 'Imperial Finance, Trade and Communications, 1895–1914', ch. XII of *C.H.B.E.*, vol. III.

particular line of policy, but by the greater political or social stability, or greater defensive power, of the Empire.[1]

The motives that brought Chamberlain into the fray included concern about the increased tax burden, and the desire to find new forms of indirect taxation out of which to finance some of the inescapable demands for welfare legislation which was itself thought of as a contribution to national strength. Imperial preference therefore became a scheme for 'tariff reform', which involved not only duties imposed on foodstuffs for the sake of helping the colonies and improving their markets for British manufactures but an all-round tariff on manufactures as well, with a view to safeguarding the home market.[2] Balfour, never fully converted to the taxing of food, regarded tariff reform largely as a means of giving Britain bargaining power in commercial negotiations with foreign countries. There were also those who thought that any shift towards protection would make Britain's military preparedness more vital than ever, as nothing else was so likely to precipitate a conflict with Germany.[3]

The opposition to protectionist measures was also many-sided. There were, of course, important economic interests involved. A contrast has been drawn between the 'neo-mercantilist imperialism' of Chamberlain, and the 'financial imperialism' that prospered under a system of free trade and which was politically represented by Rosebery and the liberal-imperialists. The tariff reformers were less concerned about profitability of investment than about the use of real resources, and were worried about growing unemployment in certain home industries. The British investor preferred the risks and high returns of foreign investment to imperial ventures;[4] conversely, emigration, which increased after the South African war following a decline in the 1890s, was much more Empire-directed.[5] The interests arrayed on the

[1] Quoted in Peter Fraser, *Joseph Chamberlain – Radicalism and Empire 1868–1914* (London, Cassell, 1966), p. 283. Chs X–XII give an account of the internal convulsions of the conservative party over protection between 1903 and 1911. Hewins resigned his position as director of the London School of Economics in 1903 in order to become economic adviser to the tariff reformers. His *Apologia of an Imperialist* gives an important account of the movement from the inside.
[2] Amery, op. cit., vol. 1, p. 264.
[3] Spenser Wilkinson, op. cit., p. 263.
[4] B. Semmel, *Imperialism and Social Reform* (London, Allen & Unwin, 1960), pp. 145, 147, 152.
[5] The proportion staying in the Empire increased from 28 per cent in the period 1891–1900 to 78½ per cent in 1902–12. De Witt Clinton Ellinwood, 'Lord Milner's Kindergarten, the British Round Table Group and the movement for Imperial Reform' (unpublished thesis, Washington University, 1962. Copy in Rhodes House Library, Oxford), p. 172.

side of free trade were of course powerfully supported by the economic orthodoxy of the day.[1] More important still were the misgivings expressed about the repercussions on British home politics of a shift to protection. Churchill spoke of the certainty that to tamper with free trade would mean setting up a complete protective system, 'involving commercial disaster and the "Americanization" of British politics'.[2]

Against this opposition the strongest argument was the imperial one, that the self-governing colonies were demanding preferential treatment which could not be granted so long as Britain rigidly adhered to free trade. Such considerations undoubtedly weighed heavily with Balfour:

> If, as seems certain [he wrote], Canada and the other Colonies are prepared to employ their tariffs in order to further an Imperial ideal, and if, as seems probable the rejection of their overtures will lead to their withdrawal, and we become worse off as an Empire than if those overtures had never been made, I should be sorry to think that I belong to a Government or party which hastily rejected them.[3]

The difficulty, he felt, was to be certain how far the new circumstances would carry the colonies towards a new system. The colonial conference of 1902 had suggested that there was no possibility of constructing a single empire free trading area; but he agreed with the protectionists that it was 'quite impracticable' to leave the colonial question exactly where it stood:

> The possibility of new commercial relations between Canada and the U.S.A.; the awakening of Australia to her increased need for the

[1] 'It has been as easy in my lifetime for a professed protectionist to be appointed to an economic chair in this country as for an earnest Protestant to be elevated to the Cardinalate', Amery, op. cit., vol. 1, p. 52.
[2] Churchill to Balfour, 25 May 1903. Balfour Papers, B.M. Add. 49694. Fraser interprets this as meaning that Churchill who left the party over the issue, like Hugh and Robert Cecil who stayed with it, was concerned lest the party should be made over by Chamberlain into a centralized and democratically run instrument instead of being controlled by the traditional upper-class leadership (op. cit., p. 271). This is perhaps less than the whole truth. What impressed foreign observers of the United States at this time of high protectionism was the extent to which the entire political system seemed geared to providing advantages for specific 'interests'; it was the period when the Senate was dominant and when the Senate was known as 'the millionaires' club'. It was corruption rather than excessive democracy which would have seemed to be the hallmark of Americanized politics.
[3] Balfour to Devonshire, 27 August 1903. Bernard Holland, *Life of the Duke of Devonshire* (London, Longmans, 1911), vol. 2, pp. 331–2. The eighth Duke of Devonshire (1833–1908), the most important of the liberal-unionist free-traders, was lord president of the council in the last Salisbury and the Balfour governments. (He resigned on the protection issue.)

protection of a powerful and therefore imperial fleet in the face of a victorious Japan; our ignorance as to how far the colonies are ready to make genuine gaps in their protective wall of tariffs for our benefit – an ignorance which paralyses effort on this side of the water in favour of close fiscal union – and tends to make Imperialists rely unduly on Protectionist support – all these considerations point to the extreme desirability of having a full and free discussion with our colonies on the present position and future organization of the Empire.[1]

In believing that the main import of preference related to the future political organization of the Empire, Balfour was accepting an argument that Hewins among others was advancing with some conviction:

The negotiation of a scheme of mutual preference would in the first place accustom Canada as well as other parts of the Empire to the settlement of foreign affairs in conjunction with the Mother Country and in the second place would gradually and inevitably lead to the evolving of some form of Imperial machinery to meet the immediate needs of inter-Imperial association.[2]

Not all versions of the political consequences of the Chamberlain programme were identical. For Richard Jebb, an independent-minded publicist with direct knowledge of the development of colonial nationalisms, it was a substitute for federation rather than a step towards it. 'It implies,' he wrote, 'the first substitution of alliance for federation, of the colonial ideal for the English ideal, as the guiding principle of closer coherence between the mother-country and the self-governing colonies.'[3] He later explained that 'the notion of alliance suggests that the central principle of Imperial Organization is to be sought in the system of consultation between the governments of the allied nations

[1] Balfour to Austen Chamberlain, 10 September 1904. Petrie, op. cit., vol. 1, pp. 148 ff. Colonial protective tariffs, even with preferential arrangements, were a source of anxiety for British manufacturers who hoped to find outlets there. The bulk of British exports still went to foreign countries but in recent years the imperial share had been on the increase. Semmel, op. cit., p. 149.

[2] Hewins to Balfour, 25 January 1907. Balfour Papers, B.M. Add. 49779. It is interesting that this view that preferential economic arrangements would inevitably have political consequences in the form of closer integration was precisely that of the later progenitors of the European common market, and in particular of Jean Monnet. The German *Zollverein* provided, of course, a common point of reference on both occasions.

[3] Quoted by J. D. B. Miller, *Richard Jebb and the Problems of Empire* (1956), p. 11. Richard Jebb (1874–1953) published his much discussed *Studies in Colonial Nationalism* in 1905. He became a member of the Compatriots. See infra p. 99.

by means of frequent conferences and permanent ambassadors'.[1] He was advocating that the colonial high commissioners in London be made members of their home governments and privy councillors and invited on occasion to attend meetings of the British cabinet which was likely to remain 'the predominant if not always the executive department in foreign affairs', so long as Britain provided 'most of the joint fighting power' and controlled the 'subject dependencies'.[2]

A rather similar suggestion in the form of an 'Imperial Committee of the Privy Council' had been put forward by the jurist Sir Frederick Pollock; but Jebb was wary of Pollock because the latter was a free-trader. Nevertheless, in a letter to the *Morning Post* on 14 March 1911, Pollock, along with Pember Reeves, Milner, A. V. Dicey, Alfred Marshall, and others, supported Jebb's suggestion about the use of the high commissioners as a link with their governments in matters of external policy.[3]

Colonial Views on Tariff Reform

The proposed imperial gathering to hammer out these questions which Balfour offered the protectionists was not possible in the lifetime of his government, for by the time of the 1907 colonial conference the liberals were in power and the issue so far as British politics was concerned mainly affected the internal affairs of the opposition. Meanwhile, colonial opinion varied greatly. Some gave colour to the Hewins view, as did the leader of the conservative opposition in Canada, Robert Borden, who was quoted by Chamberlain to Balfour as writing that much more than economics was involved and that even the 'continuance of Canada as a dependency of the Empire' might be in question.[4] Official statements and other utterances by colonial statesmen could

[1] Quoted, ibid., p. 15, from 'Notes on Imperial Organisation', a paper read to the Royal Colonial Institute on 13 November 1906.
[2] Quoted, loc. cit.
[3] Ibid., pp. 15–16. The tariff reformers' paper was from 1904 to 1911, the *Standard* which was bought by Sir Arthur Pearson to fill this role and placed under the editorship of H. A. Gwynne who had been a war correspondent in Africa, the Balkans and China and had directed Reuter's services in South Africa during the Boer war. In 1911 Gwynne resigned from the *Standard* and took over the editorship of the *Morning Post* which he retained until the paper was amalgamated with the *Daily Telegraph* in 1937. A close friend of Rhodes, Milner, Kipling, and Kitchener, as later of Carson and Haig, H. A. Gwynne (1865–1950) was the most prominent journalistic exponent for a generation of imperialist and extreme right-wing views.
[4] Young, op. cit., p. 221.

also be quoted to suggest the dangers of failing to meet the demand for preferential access:

> The rebuff and cold shoulder given to Mr Chamberlain's proposals in certain quarters [the prime minister of New Zealand had declared in 1903] lead to the inference that an uncertain trade done with small profits with alien nations is preferred to a continued commercial connection between the home country and the Colonies. The dismemberment of the Empire seems to be regarded with satisfaction by those from whom better things and greater consideration might have been expected.[1]

But New Zealand was then, as later, a special case in its dependence upon the United Kingdom market.

Elsewhere, a desire for preferential arrangements was only one point in a more general programme of economic advance some parts of which were regarded as even more important. The governor-general of Australia warned Balfour that public opinion there favoured raising the tariff wall higher against the foreigner rather than lowering it for the British manufacturer. Britain would have to give more than she received, though this might be worth doing for the sake of guiding emigration to British rather than foreign countries. 'The Chamberlainites,' he wrote, 'are wrong in making so much of the loyalty to the Empire cry. That does not enter in here. There is a strong feeling of devotion to the Throne, rather than to Great Britain, which is odd, since the King is personally unknown.' To Balfour's interest in how the growth of Japan as a great power would affect the Australian desire for imperial unity, Northcote referred to the Australians' curious indifference to the Russo-Japanese war and to the difficulty of making them think imperially. Australia would fight for Britain if necessary but where business was concerned they would deal with things on business principles.[2]

The Canadian position was more complicated. It was Canada that had successfully pressed Salisbury's government for an abrogation of Britain's commercial treaties with Germany and Belgium to enable the dominion to inaugurate a policy of preferences in the tariff of 1898;

[1] Sir Richard Seddon, telegram to *British Australasian*, quoted in a document on the preference situation of 12 February 1907, sent to Balfour at Lyttelton's suggestion. Balfour Papers, B.M. Add. 49779.
[2] Lord Northcote to Balfour, 21 August 1904; Balfour to Northcote, 20 October; Northcote to Balfour, 23 November. Balfour Papers, B.M. Add. 49647.

and, in addition to the preferential treatment of British goods, preferential agreements had been made with the other self-governing colonies, the West Indies and the Straits Settlements. But although both the main Canadian parties seemed at one on the policy, the counter-attraction of commercial arrangements with the United States remained very strong.[1]

In these circumstances the need to influence leading opinion in the colonies was almost as important as agitation at home. Edwardian England was particularly productive of small groups of people, uniting the political and intellectual worlds, and setting themselves to orient national policy in a particular direction. The first of these with an imperial flavour, the Coefficients, was founded by the Webbs in 1902 and included liberal-imperialists, socialists, and some conservatives as well as W. Pember Reeves, the agent-general of the New Zealand government, as a spokesman for colonial opinion.[2] But divisions over imperial preference split the group from very early on, and when Chamberlain made it a party issue in May 1903 agreement was rendered impossible.[3] Its successor the Compatriots was founded early in 1904 by Amery, who had been a member of the Coefficients, and some of his friends, who were afraid that otherwise the straight protectionist element in Chamberlain's campaign might overshadow the imperial aspect.[4] 'At present no doubt,' wrote Amery to Milner, 'we shall mainly think and worry about the economic side, but there are [sic] lots more in the background, from compulsory service and the demolition of the Treasury to the construction of an Imperial Council and the putting of the House of Commons in its proper place.'[5] Many of those associated with these groups had connections overseas, particularly in Canada, which were used to propagate their beliefs. But the other side was not idle. In 1903 two young liberal politicians, Edwin Montagu and Auberon Herbert, went on a visit to Canada with the blessings of

[1] Goldwin Smith in 1904–5 repeatedly warned Bryce that 'reciprocity' with the United States was gaining ground as an alternative and that if a good offer were made by the United States it would be accepted in the end. Bryce Papers, English Correspondence, vol. 17.
[2] On the Coefficients, see Semmel, op. cit., ch. III, 'A Party of National Efficiency.'
[3] Amery, op. cit., vol. 1, pp. 223–5.
[4] The founder members included important journalists and publicists – Hewins, Halford Mackinder, J. L. Garvin, H. A. Gwynne, F. S. Oliver, Leo Maxse, and John Buchan. Buchan did not remain with them long being, in Amery's view, always a free-trader at heart, 'an Imperialist of the Rosebery rather than the Chamberlain school'. Ibid., p. 266.
[5] Amery to Milner, 26 February 1904, in A. M. Gollin, *Proconsul in Politics* (London, Blond, 1964), p. 105. There was also a secret society known as the Confederacy dedicated to driving Free-Traders out of the conservative party. See Gollin, *Balfour's Burden* (1965), pp. 224–6.

the party leadership and on their return published a book, *Canada and the Empire* (with a preface by Rosebery), the theme of which was that Canada did not wish to see a preferential system set up.[1]

The Pressures on Imperial Strategy

The future of the Empire was not to be settled by political debate either in Britain itself or in the wider Imperial framework. Attitudes both at home and overseas were inevitably coloured by the changing international scene, and Balfour's instinct was right in pointing out that the rise of Japan was bound to affect Australia's outlook, just as Canada's position reflected the changing roles and policies of the United States, while all the self-governing colonies were affected by the increasing degree of British involvement in Europe.

At first sight it seems that the arguments against alliances of any permanent kind such as Salisbury had been putting forward would be equally applicable to an alliance with Japan. Indeed, he was to maintain as much: there was no justification 'for surrendering without reserve into the hands of another Power the right of deciding whether we shall or shall not stake the resources of the Empire on the issue of a mighty conflict'. Holding, with some exaggeration, that Japan was 'like ourselves' a parliamentary country, he argued that it was also liable to have its policy 'reversed by the issue of a night's division'.[2] Nevertheless it was clear that Britain could not both maintain her position in the Far East and meet the dangers nearer home without some reinforcement. It was the penalty for the extent of her interests and commitments. The choice of Japan as a partner in the Far East was due to a convergence of interests that did not exist in the case of other powers.[3] Britain's first hopes were placed in the United States, and approaches were made in March 1898 and January 1899 for co-operative action to maintain the principles of the 'Open Door' in China,

[1] S. D. Waley, *Edwin Montagu* (Bombay, Asia Publishing House, 1964), pp. 12–13. Edwin Montagu (1879–1924), M.P. 1906–22, held various junior offices between 1910 and 1914 including that of under-secretary at the India Office from 1910 to 1914. He entered the cabinet in January 1916 as chancellor of the Duchy of Lancaster, and was minister of munitions from July to December 1916. He was secretary of state for India, July 1917 to March 1922. Auberon Herbert (1876–1916) succeeded as Lord Lucas in 1905; under-secretary, War Office, 1908–11, Colonial Office, 1911–14; president of the Board of Agriculture, 1914–15.
[2] Memorandum, 7 January 1908, quoted Grenville, op. cit., p. 414.
[3] On the negotiation of the alliance and its early history, see Ian H. Nish, *The Anglo-Japanese Alliance, the Diplomacy of Two Island Empires, 1894–1907* (London, Athlone Press, 1966).

which meant in fact opposing Russia. The American 'Open Door' notes of 6 September 1899 and 3 July 1900 were an attempt to secure the adherence of the European powers to a policy which would have been acceptable to both Britain and the United States, but it was plain that no American force would be committed to upholding the principle, in view of the relatively small American interests involved. The Anglo-German agreement over China of 16 October 1900 was equally abortive though for a different reason. The Germans would not interpret it in an anti-Russian sense because, for them, China was a minor consideration compared with security in Europe and they were not prepared to take risks in a secondary theatre.[1]

Britain's weakness during the South African war was the deciding factor, and the crucial element in her calculations – as in Japan's – was the growth of Russian sea-power in the Far East as well as Russian expansion overland at China's expense. After some soundings on the possibility of an arrangement in which Germany also should participate, the Foreign Office became the centre of pressure for an agreement with Japan alone; its principal protagonist was Bertie, who headed the Asiatic department from 1898 to 1902.[2] An important consideration was that Japan believed itself capable of resisting Russian pressure alone provided France did not come to Russia's aid. From Britain's point of view, as the Admiralty made clear, the dangers of a naval war against a Franco-Russian combination would be minimized if an agreement could be reached with Japan.[3]

When the draft of the alliance was presented to the cabinet the essential element was that Britain should be neutral in a war between Japan and one power (i.e. Russia) but belligerent if Japan faced two hostile powers (i.e. Russia and France). The representatives of the War Office and India Office took the view that this was a one-sided arrangement and that Japan should undertake obligations for the defence of India as well.[4] But Britain did not press the point against Japanese objections. More serious was a Japanese demand that Britain should undertake fixed obligations in respect of her Far Eastern naval dispositions; and a rather watered-down guarantee of Britain's intentions to keep up her strength in these waters was included as a secret part of the final text signed on 30 January 1902.[5]

[1] Taylor, op. cit., pp. 392–5. [2] Nish, op. cit., pp. 113–14.
[3] See the discussion of the 'Selborne Memorandum' of 4 September 1901 in Nish, op. cit., pp. 174–7.
[4] Ibid., pp. 181–4. [5] Text of the alliance. Ibid., pp. 216–18.

There has been much argument among historians as to the extent to which the alliance signalized a definite repudiation of traditional policies and a major departure in foreign policy. The nature of the commitment would seem to support this view, but as it concerned a part of the world to which public opinion was not particularly sensitive it appeared to be purely a local arrangement and did not provoke a major debate.[1] The alliance played its part in circumscribing the repercussions of the Russo-Japanese war of 1904–5; and the Japanese victories together with Russia's internal upheaval seemed to have ended the threat it was designed to meet. Nevertheless the alliance was renewed in 1905 (two years before its date of expiry) in a revised and enlarged form, itself largely the product of consideration by the recently formed committee of Imperial Defence.[2]

A principal reason was the persistent fears of Russian pressure on India, exerted not so much in the hope of replacing Britain there, for India might be 'too big a mouthful to swallow', but because such pressure could always be used to make Britain subservient to Russia in Europe.[3] Indeed, in some circles the difficulties of defending Britain's position by military means in, for instance, Afghanistan, were considered so great as to make a diplomatic solution preferable and suggested the offer to Russia of an outlet for her energies in the Mediterranean itself.[4]

An alternative in the face of such arguments was the extension of the alliance to cover the maintenance of the *status quo* in the Far East, particularly Japan's position in Korea, and the defence of India. The C.I.D. talked in terms of a Japanese commitment to supply a large number of troops – 150,000 was the figure spoken of – for the defence of India itself should the need arise.[5] Since Kitchener, fearful of a conflict over Eastern Persia, was pressing for a heavy commitment of British troops, the appeal of this kind of proposal to the home government was obvious enough. What was not clear was whether the Indian government would welcome such a contribution of alien troops, nor does it appear that it was in fact consulted. The secretary of state for war, with military opinion behind him, also argued that any Japanese help must be additional to what Britain could spare for India, not a

[1] Nish, op. cit., pp. 242–4.   [2] Ibid., p. 248.
[3] Memorandum in the Balfour Papers, 21 December 1903. Balfour Papers, B.M. Add. 49728.
[4] Conversation between Arnold-Forster and Balfour, 28 April 1904. Arnold-Forster Papers, Diaries, 1903–8, vol. 3.
[5] Nish, op. cit., pp. 306–7.

substitute for it. Otherwise, as Balfour himself admitted, there would be a danger that some future Radical government would use the alliance as an excuse for cutting down on Britain's military effort.[1] The new treaty signed on 12 August 1905 did not, therefore, specify the nature of the military assistance to be granted to each other by the two powers, although the principle of its extension to India was duly accepted.[2]

Britain's naval situation now became one of considerable strength. The Russian fleet had been destroyed. The American fleet, second in strength to Japan's in the Pacific, was not regarded as potentially hostile. Japan could be left to guard the Far East while the concentration of British naval power in home waters was for the time being superior to any possible enemy combination.[3]

The military position was not so clear. In 1906 the C.I.D. decided that the idea of Japanese military assistance in India itself was not palatable, and it was also unacceptable to the civil authorities in India, although Kitchener himself was not averse to it. Although the idea was examined again in 1907, it became clear as a result of military and naval discussions with Japan that direct Japanese assistance in India was not likely to materialize. If it came to war, Japan would be left to hold Korea without British naval help and her help to India would consist of a diversionary attack on the Manchurian frontier.[4] But by this time both sets of proposals were becoming academic because, for reasons of general international policy, both Britain and Japan were busy seeking to settle their differences with Russia by diplomatic rather than military means. By 1909 it was Japan itself that began to look the real danger, and the British possessions in the Far East were held to be secure only so long as the alliance lasted.[5]

The conclusion and extension of the Anglo-Japanese alliance throws light not only on Britain's strategic priorities but also on relations with the self-governing colonies. The hostility of the Pacific colonies to Asian immigration (including Japanese immigration) was well known and much resented in Japan. The Australian state governments had passed exclusionist legislation in the 1890s, and this had been consolidated

[1] Ibid., pp. 318–19.
[2] The text is given, ibid., pp. 331–3.
[3] Ibid., p. 353. Already at the beginning of 1905 before the signature of the alliance, the British enjoyed 'a naval supremacy without parallel in their history'. Taylor, op. cit., p. 426.
[4] Nish, op. cit., pp. 353–8.
[5] Marder, *From the Dreadnought to Scapa Flow*, vol. 1 (1961), pp. 236–7.

after the formation of the Commonwealth. At that time the Anglo-Japanese alliance was in process of negotiation but the United Kingdom government did not inform the Australian government of the fact, nor did the Australians regard its conclusion as a reason for modifying their policy. In 1905 Clarke pointed out that there was some absurdity in an alliance with a country against whose citizens one's colonies were actively discriminating, but Balfour's reply was that immigration was not a subject upon which Britain either could or should coerce the colonies and the offending legislation was never vetoed.[1]

For those concerned with the central problem of imperial defence, Australian behaviour seemed irritatingly parochial and the Australians so dependent upon Britain that they could be spoken to firmly.[2] In any event, there could be no holding back from the alliance because of Australian objections: 'we cannot allow the trade halls of Melbourne and Sydney to influence our foreign policy.'[3] In the event they did not, nor did Britain on this issue influence Australia. It was Japan's willingness to overlook the slight, rather than any understanding between Britain and Australia, that made the treaty and its renewal possible. At the 1907 colonial conference the subject was not discussed.

The change in the direction of British concern from France and Russia to Germany in the last years of conservative rule was, as we have seen, primarily the consequence of the German naval challenge. As it was possible to define the issues of conflict between Britain and France with some accuracy, their settlement proved a matter well within the scope of diplomacy. Britain secured a formal abandonment of French claims to interfere with her control in Egypt; France was encouraged to seek a substitute in Morocco.[4] The transformation of the relationship into something much more far-reaching began when Germany tried to build up a continental coalition against Britain, first in 1904 by an attempted alliance with France, and then in 1905, after Russia's defeat, by attempting to force France into a dependence upon Germany which Russia would be forced to follow. It was the course of German diplomacy in 1904–5, including a renewed attempt at an agreement with

[1] I. A. Nish, 'Australia and the Anglo-Japanese Alliance', *Australian Journal of Politics and History*, 1963.
[2] Clarke to Balfour, 27 May 1905. Balfour Papers, B.M. Add. 49701.
[3] Clarke to Balfour, 14 October 1905. Balfour Papers, B.M. Add. 49702.
[4] There were also minor agreements about Newfoundland and its fisheries, Siam, and frontier questions in West Africa. Morocco was regarded as of naval importance to Britain because of its relationship to Gibraltar. Thus to accept French domination there implied that Germany rather than France was the important naval competitor. Grenville, op. cit., p. 432.

Russia as well,[1] that formed the background to Grey's handling of the European situation when he replaced Lansdowne at the Foreign Office in December 1905. If France were not supported over Morocco, or wherever else the German challenge might come, then the formation of a continental league would be inevitable.[2] The course of events in Europe thus fortified the growing mistrust of Germany, Britain's competitor on the world stage, to which public opinion was much more directly alive.

The change in 1905 can indeed be regarded as dramatic enough to justify the term 'a revolution in European affairs'.[3] In the early part of the year the British government was still concerned only with the relief to Britain's imperial anxieties afforded by Russian defeats. It refused French appeals to mediate in order to prevent Russia being so weakened as to make Germany supreme in Europe.[4] Only in the summer was the direct connection between the imperial and the European arena appreciated, and it was realized that the decisive event in Britain's imperial fortunes might be a war between France and Germany, fought out on European battlefields.[5] It was left to Grey and the liberals to reverse the priorities, for while Lansdowne had been worried about the naval effects of Germany getting a Moroccan port, Grey was principally affected by his desire to preserve the *entente* and would have been prepared to concede a port to Germany as part of a settlement.[6]

Naval opinion of British relations with France and Germany changed in 1901–2, at least as far as Fisher was concerned,[7] but there were reservations about the extent to which the new line should develop and it was clear that support for France might entail military rather than purely naval commitments. In August 1905 Clarke was suggesting to Balfour that the general staff should be required to draw up a paper on Belgian neutrality showing what advantages would accrue to France or Germany by invading that country and what resistance the Belgians could be expected to make.[8] There was as yet no direct con-

---

[1] The Kaiser pointed out to the Tsar the advantages to be gained from a military demonstration against India. See Lord Newton, *Lord Lansdowne* (1929), pp. 318–20.
[2] Taylor, op. cit., pp. 414–37.
[3] Taylor, op. cit., p. 427.
[4] Monger, op. cit., pp. 184–200.
[5] Ibid., pp. 206–7.   [6] Ibid., pp. 268–80.
[7] Marder, *Fear God and Dread Nought*, vol. 1, pp. 167–201, 218.
[8] Clarke to Balfour, 17 August 1905. Balfour Papers, B.M. Add. 49702. It was also assumed that Holland was in danger from Germany and that it was important to heal the breach with

tact with the French on the military level,[1] but on 31 January 1906 Grey took the crucial step, after consulting with the king and the prime minister, of authorizing contacts between the British and French general staffs.[2] By September Esher was writing, 'L'Allemagne c'est l'Ennemi,'[3] and Fisher, 'Germany is our only possible foe for years to come.'[4]

It was easier both to find grounds of agreement with the French and to sell an understanding with France to British opinion than to perform the same operation in regard to Russia. Tsardom, even tempered by revolution, was not easy to swallow. At the time of the Dogger Bank incident public feeling against the Russians had run very strongly indeed.[5] Furthermore, to the Indian government a rapprochement with Russia seemed utopian, and met with resistance from both Curzon and his successor Minto.[6]

During the last years of the conservative government relations with the United States were uneventful. The Hay–Pauncefote treaty had removed the major possible element of contention between the two countries. American suspicions of Japan were not yet aroused to the point of making the Anglo-Japanese alliance a source of division, and the idea of a German alliance, which was thought likely to cause complications with the Americans, had been abandoned.[7] Yet, despite President Roosevelt's expression of his desire that the two countries should remain closely in touch, Washington obviously felt that open indications of common accord should be avoided.[8] For this reason, though Balfour might muse on the desirability of forming an alliance with the United States for protecting the integrity of China, this did not represent any serious alternative to reliance on Japan.[9] And there was some feeling that the Americans were prone to pursue their policies without taking the British fully into their confidence.[10]

---

that country caused by the South African war. The king was urged to use his personal influence with the Dutch queen. Arnold Forster Papers, Diary, 1 October 1904, B.M. Add. 50340.

[1] Hargreaves, 'Origin of the Anglo-French Military Conversations in 1905', *History N.S.*, vol. XXXVI, 1951.   [2] Taylor, op. cit., p. 437.

[3] Esher to M. V. Brett, 6 September 1906, *Letters and Journals*, vol. 2, p. 183.

[4] Fisher to Tweedmouth, 26 September 1906. Marder, op. cit., vol. 2, p. 92.

[5] Monger, op. cit., pp. 169–72.

[6] Monger, op. cit., pp. 284–92. M. Edwardes, *High Noon of Empire* (1965), pp. 191–2.

[7] Monger, op. cit., p. 66.   [8] Ibid., p. 182.

[9] Balfour to Lansdowne, 11 February 1904. Balfour Papers, B.M. Add. 49728. Draft of letter from Balfour to Spring-Rice, 17 January 1905. Balfour Papers, B.M. Add. 49729.

[10] Lansdowne to Balfour, 18 January 1905. Balfour Papers, B.M. Add. 49729.

But the major obstacle to fuller accord still appeared to be the question of Canada's future. American hopes of ultimately absorbing the dominion were not regarded in Canada as abandoned. Imperial statesmen thought the influx of American capital into Canada was likely to encourage the idea of independence at the expense of the imperial connection.[1] The decision of the arbitration tribunal over the disputed border between Canada and Alaska in 1903 was regarded by the Canadians as a clear indication that Britain was prepared to sacrifice Canadian interests to the bettering of relations with the United States. The C.I.D. continued to occupy itself with the problem of the defence of Canada, but it was clear by now, as Balfour perceived, that all depended on the evolution of Canadian opinion itself and the direction taken by Canadian national sentiment. If Canadians preferred remaining within the Empire to becoming fully independent, it was hardly likely that the United States would forcibly challenge their decision.[2]

Looked at from the point of view of Britain as an imperial power, the most striking thing about the dramatic changes in foreign policy around the turn of the century was the extent to which the statesmen were prepared to act on their own judgement and to ignore counter-pressures whether from the self-governing colonies or the government of India. Despite the image of the 'Weary Titan', British manpower and the revenue from British taxation were the principal sources of the strength, particularly the naval strength, on which the imperial structure rested. In some respects the independence of the statesmen and their advisers were curtailed by the need to respect the prejudices of the electorate; but for most of them this was not a serious servitude. Policy was made within the narrow Whitehall–Westminster circuit and as a result of the information flowing into it from the external world. If the strains on the party and weaknesses in its posture made a further prolongation of conservative rule impossible, the machine seemed strong enough to stand up to new and inexperienced managers.

[1] Minto to Hutton, 16 July 1901.—Hutton Papers, B.M. Add. 50081.
[2] Balfour to Selborne, 1 January 1905. Balfour Papers, B.M. Add. 49708.

Chapter 4

THE EMPIRE AND THE ENTENTES

Policies and Politics in the Liberal Era

The advent of a liberal government in December 1905 and its confirmation in office by the spectacular electoral landslide of January 1906 did not, as we have seen, interrupt the transformation of Britain's diplomatic position inaugurated under the conservatives by the Anglo-Japanese alliance and the *entente* with France. Indeed, the latter was given a further impetus almost at once when, on 31 January 1906, the new foreign secretary, Grey, authorized staff talks between the two countries; and its efficacy in action was made manifest at the Algeciras conference which sat from January to March and which confirmed against German pressure the predominant position of France in Morocco. It is true that no new political commitment was entered into, but the very fact of staff talks – essential if Britain were effectively to come to the aid of France at the outset of a war which might be brief and decisive – was if anything more conclusive: 'once the British envisaged entering a continental war, however remotely, they were bound to treat the independence of France, not the future of Morocco, as the determining factor. The European Balance of Power, which had been ignored for forty years, again dominated British foreign policy; and henceforth every German move was interpreted as a bid for continental hegemony'.[1] The Anglo-Russian agreement of 31 August 1907 was much less a commitment to mutual support and much more a mere settlement of particular issues – Tibet and Persia – but given the Franco-Russian alliance it too pointed in the direction of further involvement.

In other respects also the continuity of national and imperial policy appeared to be unbroken. The committee of Imperial Defence continued its labours; the expansion of the navy and its redeployment for its new tasks continued; the reorganization of the army with a view to the possible need of an expeditionary force on the continent was to be

[1] Taylor, *The Struggle for Mastery in Europe*, p. 438.

108

the principal task of the new secretary of state for war, Haldane.[1] One should note that it took a decisive civilian intellect at the War Office to bring about a fundamental shift, whereas at the Admiralty it was the professionals – and notably Fisher himself, first sea lord until 1910 – who took the lead. The civilian first lords, until the advent of Winston Churchill in October 1911, played a role of much less significance. Nor indeed did Fisher hesitate to manipulate the strong current of public opinion that could be aroused in favour of a strong navy, notably in his relations with the leading journalist of the imperialist school, J. L. Garvin.[2]

But it would be a mistake to think that the shift in political control at Westminster made no difference. The imperialist vision – whether in the form of political federation or in that of economic union – had been repudiated by the electorate. Some of its advocates found themselves in a position of almost total alienation, not only from the government of the country but from the very institutions from which it derived its authority. This alienation was rendered all the more extreme by the dependence of the government upon Irish support after the general election of January 1910, and by the limitations upon the power of the House of Lords imposed by the parliament act of 1911 which made the eventual passage of a Home Rule Bill inevitable. The home rule crisis of 1914 drove some of the imperialists of the conservative party into actions that must be styled treasonable, and only the agreed freezing of the Irish situation on the outbreak of war prevented the conflict from coming to a head in actual violence.

It was not, of course, only on the issue of imperial unity that the political clashes between government and opposition reached peaks of antagonism unparalleled since the Reform Bill agitation of 1830–2. Indeed, apart from Ireland, the liberal-imperialists who held the key positions in external affairs under both Campbell-Bannerman and his successor in April 1908, H. H. Asquith, were doing little that could be regarded as a threat to the future of the Empire. Some, however, might feel that the degree of autonomy granted to South Africa in 1910,

[1] R. B. Haldane had been an M.P. since 1885; he was secretary of state for war from December 1905 to June 1912 and lord chancellor from then until the formation of the first coalition in May 1915 when he was sacrificed to the conservative endorsement of the allegations that he had German sympathies. He was again lord chancellor in the first labour government in 1924.
[2] Garvin originally an Irish Catholic Nationalist was editor of *The Observer* from January 1908 to February 1942. On his relations with Fisher, see A. M. Gollin, *The Observer and J. L. Garvin, 1908–1914* (1960).

modelled as it was on the situation in Canada, Australia, and New Zealand, posed a possible risk; and still more people viewed with apprehension the first timid moves towards representative institutions in India. What really stirred class feelings above all, however, was the challenge to the propertied classes inherent in the government's social and fiscal legislation – and still more in the language of its radical wing.

The liberal government represented a party that was itself a coalition between disparate elements. It was not so much that the old whig families still retained some hold, despite the large-scale secession from the party over home rule in 1886; it was that the non-whig element was made up of at least two strands. There were those who were primarily concerned to bring to the tasks of government the professional and business spirit of the upper middle class to which they belonged by birth and education; and there were also those whose experience was of a lower rung in the ladder of wealth and privilege. For the latter, the attack on privilege and the promotion of welfare measures were the principal tasks with which they now felt themselves to be confronted; and they inherited the old radical distrust of an activist foreign and imperial policy, believing it expensive for all and beneficial to the upper classes alone. And this radical element shaded off into the ranks of the government's allies on the left, the Irish, and the labour party – now for the first time a strong, if not yet a fully independent, parliamentary force.

Even so, the parliamentary and party framework did not contain the whole of the forces making for change in Britain. The labour party was only one aspect of a labour movement in which ideas of direct action for the amelioration of social conditions had a considerable hold – ideas which in the temper of the times could, and sometimes did, lead to violence. Violence was also involved in the struggle for female emancipation, centred around the symbol of the franchise.[1] If the ultimate catastrophe of the war came upon a government and people not fully aware of what was upon them, it may have been because the internal stresses monopolized the attention of all except the minority of individuals or groups primarily concerned with external affairs and defence.

[1] The significance of the degree of violence, actual or threatened, in the period was first called attention to by the historian, George Dangerfield, in his *The Strange Death of Liberal England*, published in 1935. But similar phenomena can, of course, be found in most if not all the major industrial countries at this time. For the background of the labour movement and its problems, see E. H. Phelps Brown, *The Growth of British Industrial Relations* (1959).

One must not assume, of course, that the political groupings of the time lend themselves to neat arrangement in a sort of spectrum. It was possible to combine an impatience with the waste of human resources involved in poverty and uncivilized living conditions at home with a rather robust if paternalist attitude towards empire. The Fabians of the Webb brand were very far from the out-and-out radical and pacifist stream with which they were ultimately to fuse in the labour party of the post-1918 era, and many of the more imperialist members of the conservative party were sympathetic to important aspects of the movement for social reform. Historians have perhaps too easily accepted the view that the attitudes of the politically active are determined, as is political allegiance more generally, by the ramifications of the class structure. Individual temperament may be too little regarded. It was not easy to see where the protagonists of a more active style of government fitted into the party structure of the 1906–14 period, but the theme is best explored not in any of the histories but in the key political novel of the period, H. G. Wells's *The New Machiavelli*, published in 1911.

New Personalities

The change in the party tenure of power did indeed coincide more or less with a shift in generation in the leadership of the country and the Empire. This brought to the centre of the stage a group of men differing to some extent from their predecessors in the variety of their social provenance, and to a much greater degree in their experience and political attitudes. There is no generation we need so much to understand; for the men who took charge of Britain's affairs, between the retirement of Salisbury and the fall of the Lloyd George coalition in 1922, were responsible both for the ordeal that Britain was forced to undergo in the great war – assuming this to have been avoidable – and for her share in the peace-making. For both their historical roles they have received rather little sympathy, and yet when one looks back at their achievements and personalities across the intervening years, one is impressed by the high seriousness and sense of responsibility they brought to their tasks, and by a certain intellectual energy and purposefulness which was largely lacking in their successors. This they perhaps owed in part to an unquestioned assurance – irrespective of party allegiance – in the importance of Britain's role in the world, and in the country's capacity to play it to the full.

The leading statesmen themselves, excluding only Winston Churchill (one could make the number a round dozen without stretching the point too much), were all born between 1847 and 1863, and all entered public life at a time when Bismarck dominated the European scene and when Britain's industrial and naval predominance was beginning to face the challenge of the new giants. In order of age they are, Rosebery (born in 1847), Balfour (b. 1848), Asquith (b. 1848), Milner (b. 1854), Haldane (b. 1856), Bonar Law (b. 1858), Curzon (b. 1859), Rufus Isaacs (first Marquess of Reading, b. 1860), Grey (b. 1862), and finally, three men born in 1863, Austen Chamberlain, Arthur Henderson, and David Lloyd George. Rosebery, a precocious beginner and prime minister before he was fifty, was not in fact to hold office again, and was removed from his erstwhile colleagues (and virtually from active politics) by his distaste for some of their doings. Nevertheless, during the early years of the period the possibility of his return to the fray was something that had to be borne in mind by the makers of political combinations at a time when both main parties were undergoing major strains. He was still a public figure whose views commanded a hearing.[1]

All the rest were still active in the politics of the 1920s, and Henderson, as well as (briefly) both Reading and Chamberlain, held office in the 1930s. Lloyd George himself never returned to power after his fall in 1922, but for almost another two decades his very existence was a threat to the men in office and much of the domestic politics of the period was concerned with keeping him out lest he disturb their comfortable and disastrous routines. Alone among this group, he survived to see the second world war and could, had he wished, have served under Churchill. But it is essentially the first world war, both in its diplomatic and imperial aspects, that was the major scene of the group's activities.

A few points of particular relevance should be emphasized. They were, as has been said of the *élite* of this period as a whole, socially more heterogeneous than their predecessors. To four members of the old governing class – Rosebery (Eton and Christ Church), Balfour (Eton and Trinity, Cambridge), Curzon (Eton and Balliol), Grey (Winchester and Balliol) – may be added, as assimilated to this milieu despite his bourgeois parentage, Austen Chamberlain (Rugby and Trinity, Cambridge). Haldane, though he made his way to politics through

[1] On Rosebery, see the sympathetic study by Robert Rhodes James, *Rosebery* (1965).

earning distinction at the Bar, was the head of an ancient, rich, and important Scottish family. But alongside them are three examples of the careers in public life open to those of middle-class parentage and upbringing for whom professional distinction or administrative skill could open all doors, Asquith, Milner, and after a more bizarre beginning, Reading. The fact that both Asquith and Milner were Balliol men reminds one that, despite popular legend at home and abroad, it was the university rather than the school that was often the decisive element in a man's career. Bonar Law, a Canadian-born Glasgow-educated businessman, brings in a still more unusual element. Finally, and more portentously, come the representatives of social strata hitherto wholly excluded from the world of high policy-making – the Welsh country solicitor David Lloyd George, and the trade-unionist and party official, Arthur Henderson.

The extent to which their earlier experience fitted them to understand the rapidly changing world in which Britain had now to struggle for its existence is not very clear. Balfour, Rosebery, and Curzon were much travelled aristocrats. Milner, with his part-German parentage and education; Haldane, the former student at Göttingen whose knowledge of German philosophy was to be counted against him in the wartime frenzy; and Chamberlain, who after studying in Paris had sat at Treitschke's feet at Berlin; were all in their different ways well equipped to measure the extent of the German threat to Britain's world leadership. By contrast Grey, the member of the group whose concentration on foreign affairs was the most complete and long-lasting, was little familiar with Europe and spoke no foreign languages. His membership of a royal commission on the West Indies in 1897 was his nearest approach to the new world until he was sent on a special mission to the United States in 1919. Asquith's Europe amounted to no more than the Mediterranean playground that, with the growing ease of travel, was exerting its pull on the inhabitants of the cloudy northern islands. Lloyd George, by contrast, learned something of Germany when he went to study its social insurance system during the period when he was laying the foundations of the British welfare state; Henderson had his contacts in the international and trade-union movement. Where the problems of empire were concerned, Ireland for Balfour, South Africa for Milner, and India for Curzon, were in their different ways all deeply significant. The most obvious gap is the lack of first-hand experience of the United States, though both Balfour and

Rosebery had included it in their youthful travels. Balfour had a number of American correspondents, and both the first and the second Lady Curzon were Americans. But Grey, who attached great importance to Britain's relations with the United States, was still dependent for his knowledge of that country's role in world affairs either upon Britain's own representatives at Washington, or upon those of the United States in London (who were not always in the confidence of their governments), or finally upon the casual American visitors. These were increasing in numbers at this time, even if not all of them were as free as the ex-president, Theodore Roosevelt, in giving advice upon the conduct of the Empire's affairs.[1]

Political figures of the second rank of this generation who affected the conduct of external affairs included men as far apart in personality and politics as Ulster's champion Edward Carson, and Walter Long, both born in 1854 (Long was to be colonial secretary from 1916 to 1918) and Sidney Webb (b. 1859) and Philip Snowden (b. 1864). Webb, as Lord Passfield, was to be an exceedingly indifferent colonial secretary from 1929 to 1931, and Snowden's envenomed insularity was to help poison relations with France during the same administration.

Three men in this group may be dealt with at slightly greater length. Lord Derby (the 17th earl, 1865–1948), who had served as A.D.C. to his father when governor-general of Canada, and a private secretary to Lord Roberts during the South African war, was secretary of state for war from December 1916 to April 1918. He then succeeded Bertie as ambassador to France and remained there until November 1920. This breach, under the stress of war, with the tradition of reserving representative positions abroad for professional diplomats was continued in the person of his successor but one, Lord Crewe (1858–1945). He was Rosebery's son-in-law and biographer, whose earlier posts had included the lord lieutenancy of Ireland and the Colonial and India Offices, and his tenure of the Paris embassy lasted from 1922 to 1928 through a period of crucial importance in the relations of the two countries. Finally, one may note Robert Cecil (b. 1864), later Viscount Cecil of Chelwood, not so much for his important role in the war and, later, League of Nations diplomacy, but because he tried to bring problems of foreign affairs out of the closed circle of those in the know and into the arena of democratic debate. This tendency, much more

---

[1] For Roosevelt's public intervention at a crisis of Britain's relations with Egypt, see Max Beloff, 'Theodore Roosevelt and the British Empire', in *The Great Powers* (1959).

usually found among his juniors, probably arose from his work for the League of Nations Union and similar activities. The importance of this will concern us later; but it is worth noting that a 'League' attitude to foreign affairs did not prevent an instinctive preference for one foreign country against another. Cecil, for instance, tended towards an anti-French position, just as his principal collaborator in the League of Nations Union, the scholar Gilbert Murray, tended towards a pro-French position.

The civil servants of this vintage produced some powerful individuals with long tenure of the chief posts. At the Colonial Office, Sir Francis Hopwood (b. 1860, later Lord Southborough) was permanent under-secretary from 1907 to 1911, after varied service including missions to Canada and South Africa. He was succeeded by Sir John Anderson (b. 1858) who had been secretary to the colonial conferences of 1897 and 1902, and the principal British official in Malaya from 1904 to 1911. His successor, who held the post from 1916 to 1921, was Sir George Fiddes, whose early training included three years as Milner's secretary in South Africa. Sir Charles Lucas, historian of the Empire, became, in 1907 after thirty years in the office, the first head of the newly created dominions department. In 1909 Lucas went on a visit to Australia, New Zealand, and Fiji, being the first permanent official from the Office to be sent out directly by it to 'the Dominions which had suffered most from distance'.[1]

At the India Office, Arthur Godley (Lord Kilbracken) ended his long tenure in 1909. His successor, Sir Richmond Ritchie (1909–12), although born in India and the son of a member of the viceroy's council had served only in the office and never in India itself; but Sir Thomas Holderness (1912–19) and Sir Frederick Duke (1920–4) had both had ample Indian experience.

At this point one might mention the name of one imperial pro-consul, General Sir Richard Wingate (1861–1953) who after service in India, around the Red Sea and in the Nile valley became, from 1899 until 1916, Sirdar (commander-in-chief) of the Egyptian army and governor-general of the Sudan. From 1917 to 1919 he was high commissioner in Egypt. Two other men graduated from the armed services to the vital position of secretary of the committee of Imperial Defence, Sir George Clarke (Lord Sydenham) who held the post from

[1] See his report, Cd. 5100. Lucas, an imperialist of the Chamberlain school, retired in 1911 and devoted himself to writing.

1904 to 1907 (and whose later career has been mentioned already), and his successor Admiral Sir Charles Ottley (b. 1858), whose services as naval attaché had taken him to the United States, Japan, Italy, France, and Russia.

In dealing with the new and more active role of the Foreign Office itself under Lansdowne and Grey we have touched on the background and careers of Eyre Crowe and Hardinge. Another combination of Indian and diplomatic experience, though not at Hardinge's level, was provided by Sir Mortimer Durand. He had been born in India, and after a career there from 1873 to 1894 he then occupied diplomatic posts at Teheran, Madrid, and finally, Washington – where he served as ambassador from 1903 to 1907, though without great success. The Washington post was not easy to fill as Washington society was more 'political' in the narrow sense than was that of the great European capitals, permanent officials were less important, and the Americans themselves more suspicious of the attentions of foreign diplomats, especially if British. The most obvious and conventional appointment to the post in the period was that of Sir Cecil Spring-Rice (b. 1859), son-in-law of Sir Frank Lascelles. Spring-Rice had served in Washington as a junior in the 1890s and had retained many American friends and correspondents, but by 1913, when he took up the most of ambassador which he held until 1918, his friends of the Cabot Lodge–Theodore Roosevelt circle were out of power. With Wilson, Bryan, and Lansing successful contacts proved much harder to establish, nor did the neutrality of the United States with its overtones of moral superiority prove very acceptable to a patriotic Englishman whose mind was always, and naturally, dwelling on the holocausts in France and Flanders.[1] The same qualifications of wide general experience and previous knowledge of Washington explain the appointment to the embassy there from 1924 to 1930 of the last of this generation of diplomats to hold it, Sir Esmé Howard (later Lord Howard of Penrith). In between came two non-professionals, Lord Reading from 1918 to 1919, and the businessman turned wartime administrator, Sir Auckland Geddes (Lord Geddes). The alternation between the professional diplomat and the statesman or man of affairs, which began with the appointment of Bryce and has remained characteristic of Britain's handling of the Washington embassy down to the present day, is per-

---

[1] Stephen Gwynn in his *The Letters and Friendships of Sir Cecil Spring-Rice* (2 v. 1929) omitted some of the more critical passages from the ambassador's wartime letters home.

haps the best indication of the uncertainty that has prevailed as to whether Washington is a foreign capital like any other, or the second centre of an English-speaking world linked to London by ties much more significant than those of traditional diplomacy.

Of a rather different kind was the career of Sir Edgar Vincent (b. 1857) whose earlier years were largely spent in dealing with the financial problems of Egypt and Turkey, but who became, as Lord D'Abernon, Britain's ambassador to Berlin from 1920 to 1926. He was thus a principal instrument in the policy of reconciliation with Germany that led to the Locarno treaties of 1925.

More conventional careers were those of almost the last group of professional diplomats to wield power in their own right as the long-term tenants of important embassies. They included Sir Arthur Nicolson (Lord Carnock), ambassador at St Petersburg from 1905 to 1910, and then permanent under-secretary at the Foreign Office between Hardinge's two terms; Sir Rennell Rodd (Lord Rodd) who after much experience of the Near East held the Rome embassy from 1908 to 1919; Lord Goschen's younger brother, Sir William, Vienna 1905–8 and Berlin 1908–14; and finally Sir George Buchanan (b. 1854) who, as ambassador to St Petersburg from Nicolson's departure until 1918, saw the beginning of the collapse of the old European order.

On the service side, this is of course the generation that supplied most of the leading figures in the 1914–18 war. Of Kitchener (b. 1850) something has already been said; after succeeding Cromer in Egypt he was recalled in 1914 to be secretary of state for war, a post he retained until his death at sea *en route* for Russia in June 1916. He was the first British example since Wellington of the soldier-statesmen, which is perhaps the best single indication of the essentially civilian nature of Britain's imperial power. Of other soldiers, the list includes Sir John French and Sir William Robertson, both born in 1860, Sir Douglas (Earl) Haig (b. 1861), and Sir Henry Wilson (b. 1864); of sailors, Admirals Jackson (b. 1855), Jellicoe (b. 1859), and Wemyss (b. 1864). If one reflects that the only military operations of any scale in which British forces were involved, between their receiving their first commissions and 1914, were Kitchener's Nile campaign and the Boer war, it is not hard to understand their intellectual unpreparedness for the trench warfare and submarine menace that were to prove the characteristic features of the Great War.

In no other field did the environment change so rapidly and decisively, and in no other profession was the path to the top so severely governed by routine considerations of seniority. Indeed, the influence of this generation of service chiefs did not even end with the war itself; the Earl of Cavan, C.I.G.S. from 1922 to 1926, was born in 1865, Admiral Madden, Jellicoe's brother-in-law (first sea lord from 1927 to 1930) in 1859.

Finally, one must add that this generation also provided most of the political leaders in the dominions under whose aegis the new imperial relationship took shape. Robert Borden was born in 1854; of the Australians, Deakin was born in 1856 and Hughes in 1864; of the New Zealanders, both Massey and Ward were born in 1856; of the South Africans, Botha in 1862.

Moves for Change and Reform

In the period between 1906 and 1914 there was a perceptible gap between the preoccupations of most of those we have named and their associates of an older and younger generation, and those of the politicians and civil servants and publicists most closely involved in the social, political, and constitutional controversies of the period. From the point of view of the social reformer or opponent of privilege, all the talk of foreign threats to Britain's position was largely beside the point, and indeed represented a distraction from the task in hand as well as a competing demand on the nation's resources. It was possible then, as it was possible for the later school of 'revisionist' historians retrospectively, to deny the reality of the German threat and the need to face it by military or diplomatic means. Such a view is now scarcely tenable. It is clear that the German government, strongly impelled in this direction by the dominant forces in German society and strongly upheld by the representative figures of the German intellectual world, was embarked on a programme of building up German strength in Europe with the object of challenging Britain's world role. This must be accounted the major single cause for the transformation of Austria's Balkan difficulties into the seeds of a general war.[1] But for those who were not directly in contact with Europe and who were absorbed in the domestic struggle, there were plenty of excellent reasons for ignoring this fact. Once they became aware of it the change might be dramatic – as when

[1] See for a recent German study of this point, F. Fischer, *Germany's Aims in the First World War* (1967), a translation of his *Griff nach der Weltmacht* (1961).

Winston Churchill, in October 1911, exchanged the Home Office for his historic tenure of the Admiralty. Or an immediate crisis might temporarily turn a radical into a mouthpiece of resistance, as when Lloyd George made his famous Mansion House speech on 21 July 1911, at the time of the Agadir dispute.[1] But for the most part foreign and imperial affairs remained outside the ordinary man's immediate concern.

It is true that, by the theory of the constitution, nothing stopped parliament but its own indifference from probing more deeply into these mysteries. And occasionally some part of it was stirred to active concern by some particular aspect of British diplomacy. Usually, as might be expected in a democracy, it was questions of ideology rather than of national power that created the excitement, as in the case of the Labour and radical opposition to the Russian *entente* on the grounds of the oppressive nature of the Tsar's régime.[2] But there were few occasions before the final crisis of 1914 when it was the opinion of the House of Commons that counted in these things. As compared with the nineteenth century, blue books were fewer and less informative; Grey was never called upon to justify his policy in the way in which Palmerston had had to do in the Don Pacifico debate.[3] Nor is all this surprising when one remembers that the staff talks with the French, around which everything hinged, were undertaken without the rest of the cabinet knowing, after the prime minister and foreign secretary had consulted the king. To carry out the policy of preventing a continental coalition, by preventing either France or Russia from becoming subservient to Germany – a policy that involved a risk of war – could only be reconciled with preserving the unity of the government's majority by not making it more specific than necessary. Of course, this semi-secrecy was later to be a main argument against the 'old diplomacy' both in Britain and America, and was to figure largely in the mythology of the supporters of the League system. The question is whether, given the conviction of Grey and his immediate colleagues about the reality of

[1] On this episode, see Taylor, op. cit., pp. 467–73.
[2] Jewish circles were also active in criticizing close relations with Russia, thus enhancing the anti-semitism of the ultras like Leo Maxse. See Max Beloff, *Lucien Wolf and the Anglo-Russian Entente* (London, Jewish Historical Society of England, 1951). As with similar propaganda against the appeasement of Germany in the 1930s or of Russia again in 1944–5 (for the sake of the Poles), it made little difference. *Realpolitik* was not a German monopoly; the existence of parliament merely made it harder.
[3] On this subject generally, see Max Beloff, *Foreign Policy and the Diplomatic Process* (Baltimore, 1955).

the German threat and the danger of neglecting it, it was not their duty to pursue the policies that they did and to treat the parliamentary process as a means rather than as an end in itself.

Men who were chiefly concerned with preparedness, and for whom Parliament was primarily important as a source of funds, might even encourage illusions about the immediacy of the threat if that were the only method getting their way. Thus Esher rebuked Admiral Fisher for resisting the C.I.D.'s investigation into the possibility of Britain being invaded, which Fisher had regarded as a mere scare in view of Britain's naval strength and as a result of the C.I.D.'s desire to usurp the functions of the service chiefs: 'It is,' Esher reminded him, 'the discussions which keep alive popular fears and popular interest, upon which alone rest the Navy Estimates . . . An invasion scare is the mill of God which grinds you out a Navy of Dreadnoughts, and keeps the British people warlike in spirit.'[1] Haldane's army reforms and the minute preparations for an expeditionary force were less easy to dramatize, and the major shift in British thinking about the nature of a future war was not much canvassed in public debate. Yet it proceeded, and by the time of the Agadir crisis, had virtually taken place: 'the Admiralty was forced, for the first time to subordinate its own plans to the shipping of an expeditionary force to northern France. The decision to take part in a continental war was given practical shape.'[2]

The role of the C.I.D. was indeed primarily that of compelling the various elements in the machine to act together, and to ensure that the best use was made of the facilities for making war that existed, whether at home or overseas.[3] It was an element of professionalization in a largely amateur world, where tradition and habit still counted for a great deal.

The degree of professionalization that was attained depended on different factors in the different departments and services. Haldane had fought off the devotees of economy, as well as the forces of tradition, to remodel the regular forces and reorganize the volunteer effort in the territorials.[4] The idea of a naval staff proved even less acceptable than the army reforms. The resistance of the admirals was too much for

[1] Esher to Fisher, 1 October 1907. Esher, *Letters and Journals*, vol. II, p. 249. Cf. Marder, *Fear God and Dread Nought*, vol. 2, p. 144.
[2] Taylor, op. cit., p. 471.
[3] The principal first-hand account of the role of the C.I.D. before 1914 is that in Lord Hankey, *The Supreme Command, 1914–1918* (London, Allen & Unwin, 1961), vol. 1, part I.
[4] See Dudley Sommer, *Haldane of Cloan* (1960), chs. 10–15.

McKenna, and was the principal reason for his replacement by Churchill in 1911. Churchill managed to force the creation of a Naval War Staff despite professional objections to what was regarded as a land-based *élite*, but it was not an important instrument by 1914, and the main issue in naval strategy remained the responsibility of the first lord of the admiralty and the first sea lord – a conjunction which was to function badly in both peace and war.[1]

A similar spirit of reform overtook the Foreign Office under the aegis of Hardinge and Crowe. The most important feature was the emergence of the permanent secretary as an adviser on policy as well as an administrator, and the introduction of a registry system also enabled officials to have a greater say in policy. On the diplomatic service side, there was some liberalization of entrance procedures, and entry was still more closely geared to the Oxford and Cambridge examination system; there were also some temporary transfers between the Foreign Office and posts overseas. Little, however, was done to strengthen the service on the economic and commercial side. A royal commission reported on the eve of war in favour of more drastic reforms, but these had to wait. Nevertheless the substantial change from an office of clerks to a policy-making department had been accomplished.[2]

The principal leaders of the liberal government could hardly be faulted then on the question of preparedness; what could be alleged against them by their opponents was a certain insularity, an unwillingness to seek for sources of strength outside the British Isles. The liberal-imperialists were convinced that the Chamberlain view, that a system of preferential tariffs would promote imperial unity, was gravely mistaken. It would, on the contrary, set the interests of the homeland against those of other parts of the Empire, and render the whole idea of empire odious to the mass of the people.[3] The stimulation in Britain of the growth of an 'anti-colonial party' and the creation of 'a deep hatred of the colonies' would be the inevitable result of conceding the demand for preference; so Churchill told the colonial conference of 1907.[4] Similarly, although the desirability of building up the British element in the population of the dominions (especially in Australia with its fear of pressure from Asia) was generally accepted, it was the settled policy

[1] Randolph S. Churchill, *Winston S. Churchill*, vol. II (1967), pp. 539–45.
[2] Z. Steiner, 'The Last Years of the Old Foreign Office', *The Historical Journal*, vol. VI, 1963.
[3] Semmel, *Imperialism and Social Reform*, pp. 61–4.
[4] Amery, op. cit., vol. 1, pp. 316–17.

of the British government not to assist the process out of public funds.[1] This policy was confirmed again in a cabinet minute of 15 March 1911.[2] With the exception of defence arrangements – to which we shall return – the liberal-imperialist attitude was essentially one of *laissez-faire*; allow the colonies to grow in stature through their own efforts with the minimum of interference, and rely upon common interests and common sentiment to act as the cement of the system. It was essential that the self-governing colonies should rid themselves of any sense of inferiority and the word 'Empire' itself began to seem inadequate, as did the word 'colonial'. By a paradoxical compromise, the colonial conference of 1907 decided that future conferences should be styled 'imperial', while at the same time the word 'dominion' was substituted for 'colony' where their members were concerned. Between that time and the outbreak of war, the word 'Commonwealth' began to be used fairly freely in place of 'Empire' and the desire thenceforward to distinguish the British from the German conception of empire accelerated the process. The writings of Lionel Curtis gave the new word increased currency, and in his speeches at the imperial war conference of 1917 Smuts talked of the 'British Commonwealth'.[3]

South Africa – The Touchstone

It is appropriate that it should be a South African who gave linguistic currency to the achievement, if negative achievement, of the liberal government in the sphere of imperial reorganization. For the counterpart of the liberal theory of empire was that no important white community should remain in a subordinate position. For this reason the restoration of self-government to the conquered Boer republics and the creation of the Union of South Africa with a status equal to that of the other dominions, was the positive aspect of the period in which liberals took most pride.

But although the liberals, and Campbell-Bannerman in particular, were committed by their past stand on South Africa to a policy of

[1] *C.H.B.E.*, vol. III, 480.
[2] Dep. Asquith, Box 6, Folio 18.
[3] S. R. Mehrotra, 'On the Use of the Term "Commonwealth"', *Journal of Commonwealth Political Studies*, vol. I, No. 1, 1963. Lionel Curtis (1872–1955), after service in the South African war, held various posts in the Transvaal before returning to England to lecture on colonial history and to devote himself, through the Round Table and other organizations, to promoting his own particular blend of imperialism and dominion autonomy. His books, *The Problem of the Commonwealth* and *The Commonwealth of Nations* appeared in 1916.

reconciliation, there was no complete discontinuity between the conservative and liberal administrations.[1] Milner, who had himself acquiesced in the granting of limited self-government to the Transvaal, had been succeeded by a conservative in the person of the Earl of Selborne. His appointment as governor of the Transvaal and high commissioner in South Africa was not revoked by the new government;[2] and a number of Milner's picked administrators – the so-called Milner Kindergarten – notably Lionel Curtis himself, Philip Kerr, Richard Feetham, Patrick Duncan, Robert Brand, and Geoffrey Robinson (the later Geoffrey Dawson) remained closely associated with the management of South African affairs.[3] Selborne himself was very conscious of the importance of securing the acquiescence of the Boers to a political settlement, in view of the danger of German troops entering South Africa if war broke out, and provoking a general rising.[4]

The first step was the new constitution which Smuts persuaded the incoming government to substitute for the Lyttelton constitution during his visit to London in January 1906. It has been pointed out, however, that this constitution, while satisfying to liberal sentiment in its generosity to the Boers, marked the first step towards a colour-bar in South Africa and all that this meant for the future. Although the liberals claimed that the treaty of Vereeniging prevented them insisting upon the point, some natives could have been given the franchise.[5]

The next step was closer union, pressed on Selborne by the kindergarten, largely for economic reasons – it was Selborne not Curtis who showed anxiety about its implications for the Empire's humanitarian tradition – and accepted by Selborne largely because of the need to create a British political majority before the German threat could materialize. On the British side there was also the hope that union might form a prelude to imperial federation. Union was acceptable to Afrikaner nationalists, who hoped that the Afrikaner element would

[1] For Smuts' later view that it was the magnanimity of Campbell-Bannerman that was decisive, see W. K. Hancock, *Smuts* (Cambridge, 1962), vol. 1, pp. 213–17.
[2] W. W. Palmer (1859–1942), later Viscount Wolmer, who became second Earl of Selborne in 1895, had been under-secretary of state for the colonies from 1895 to 1900 and first lord of the admiralty, 1900–5. He held his post in South Africa until 1910. President of the Board of Agriculture, May 1915–July 1916.
[3] This did not prevent Milner from regarding prospects in South Africa as 'very black, owing to the ignorance and evil dispositions of this wretched "pro-Boer" cabinet'. Milner Papers [Bodl. 269], Diary, 1906, 11 January 1906.
[4] Selborne to Lyttelton, 24 May 1905. Balfour Papers, B.M. Add. 49775.
[5] L. M. Thompson, *The Unification of South Africa* (Oxford, 1960), p. 24.

come out on top and be able to move towards complete independence – a belief that half a century of history was in the end to justify. Botha and Smuts, however, were convinced that the British and Boer strains could be merged in a single South African nation, and that the new Empire–Commonwealth system would give it all the freedom it required.[1]

When the results of the long negotiations over the form of union were presented to the British people and the liberal party, it was natural to stress the contribution which South African union could make to a consolidation of the system of self-governing dominions: 'If it should ever be the fact, as I hope it may, that it is found possible to solve the very difficult problem of co-operation all over the Empire in the policy of that Empire, to that achievement this Act of African Union is a necessary preliminary.'[2] Botha had indeed captured the imagination of the public when he attended the 1907 conference and seemed to present the image of a second Laurier destined to exorcize his people's anglophobia and to lead them along the path of imperial co-operation.[3]

Not everyone overlooked the fact that once again the victims of Anglo-Boer agreement had been the disfranchised majority. During the second reading debate on the South Africa bill, the veteran imperialist Dilke, said: 'I do not wish to be alarmist, but I do not think it can be said that we are strengthening the Imperial fabric in an Empire where there are 360 millions of coloured people under our rule, by this non-Federal Union in South Africa under such conditions.'[4] But it was clear that by now there was little option for the British government but to follow the course it had taken. If it were to amend the colour-bar provisions the South Africans would take their stand on the principle of colonial self-government and would probably be supported on those grounds by Canada and Australia. The goodwill of Botha and his friends would have been lost and the more extreme Boer leaders strengthened. In fact, the international situation was more than ever seen as the overriding factor; Britain could not afford to face war with a hostile population in South Africa, and in the event of war the Suez route might become unusable and the Cape route to the East recover all its former importance.[5]

[1] Ibid., pp. 64–82.
[2] Speech by Lord Crewe, House of Lords, 22 July 1909, quoted, ibid., pp. 419–20.
[3] Ibid., p. 398.
[4] Quoted, ibid., pp. 425–6.
[5] Ibid., pp. 398–400.

Anxieties about South Africa were enhanced by the fears that Germany was seeking to expand its own hold in Africa. Although colonial questions as such played little direct part in the diplomatic revolution that led to the making of the *ententes* Germany's attitude at the time of the Boer war was not forgotten, and the belief that Germany cherished an ultimate aim of promoting her own colonization of a Boer-dominated South Africa remained alive. It was for this reason that although Grey was ready to be easy over Africa where Germany was concerned, specific concessions were always unacceptable to his principal advisers. They argued for instance against the cession of Walfisch Bay, the British enclave on the coast of German South-West Africa, on the ground that its possession by the Germans would facilitate any operation against South Africa. German ill-treatment of the native Hereros provided an acceptable public reason for a refusal to contemplate any further expansion of German colonial rule. In particular, it helped to provide a reason for refusing to allow the Germans to acquire any part of the Congo as successors to King Leopold of the Belgians. The fear was that Germany would seek to create a belt of German territory linking her possessions in East and West Africa, thus cutting off Britain's southern African territories from Egypt and the Sudan, and putting an end to the 'Cape to Cairo' dream. In fact, most British humanitarian zeal was expended upon allegations of maladministration in the Portuguese and Belgian territories; and many Englishmen still respected the Germans for their efficiency and resourcefulness. E. D. Morel, the secretary of the Congo Reform Association, advocated Germany taking and purchasing most of the Belgian Congo and Angola; thus a leading British radical came to echo the basic thesis of the German imperialist school.[1]

Grey himself was still willing to consider a division of the Portuguese colonies should Portugal be ready to dispose of them; the Union of South Africa, he believed, would never rest till it had Delagoa Bay and he was prepared to modify Salisbury's 1898 agreement with the Germans on that subject. An agreement was in fact initialled in August

[1] Wm. Roger Louis, *Great Britain and Germany's Lost Colonies, 1914–1919* (Oxford, Clarendon Press, 1967), pp. 25–35. E. D. Morel (1873–1924) founded the Congo Reform Association in 1904 and was its secretary until 1919. He gave up his prospective liberal parliamentary candidature at the outbreak of the war which he opposed, was one of the founders and first secretary of the Union of Democratic Control and joined the labour party, sitting as a labour M.P. from 1922 to 1924. His career is dealt with sympathetically, in A. J. P. Taylor, *The Trouble-makers* (1957). Belgium acquired the Congo from King Leopold in 1908, though Britain did not recognize the annexation until 1913.

1913, but Grey's insistence (as a condition of signature) that it be made public along with the earlier one was not acceptable to the Germans, and with the outbreak of war these arrangements lapsed for good.[1] By the time the question of African boundaries became alive once more the South Africans were in a position to claim not only an independent but in some respects a decisive voice.

Imperialism, Tariffs, and Milner

For the central core of the unionist party the developing contest at home was of paramount importance. The main question to be decided was how far to make new fiscal arrangements central to their policy. Was it possible to prevent protection from appearing as a method of shifting the burden of taxation on to the masses – the political dangers of which had been amply demonstrated by the election of 1906; and could the argument be raised to a different level altogether.[2]

The difficulty was that it now appeared clear that complete free trade within the Empire was not consistent with the autonomy upon which the dominions set such store: 'The Imperial free trade system which Liberals would accept involves just the kind of highly centralized Imperial organization which they particularly detest.'[3] The solution would be the Canadian one by which each country would have a general tariff at whatever level it chose, while there would be a preferential tariff for the Empire which might eventually come to stand at a purely revenue level. This, it was argued, would mean a deliberate adoption of 'the Empire as distinct from the United Kingdom as a basis of public policy', its effects being measured not in purely economic terms 'but by the greater political or social stability or the greater defensive power of the Empire'.[4]

Such a *via media* did not satisfy either extreme wing of the party. For free-traders like Robert Cecil, imperial unity must be maintained by other methods; 'to make it depend on a corn tax must throw the

[1] Louis, op. cit., pp. 33–4.
[2] 'I am strongly in favour of Colonial preference if we can obtain a satisfactory arrangement with the Colonies, and I do not think such an arrangement should be rejected merely on the ground that it involves some taxation of the foodstuffs, so long as it does not carry in it any increase in the proportion paid by the working class to the general taxation of the country.' Balfour to H. A. Gwynne, 3 April 1908. Balfour Papers, B.M. Add. 49797.
[3] Hewins to Balfour, 15 February 1907. Balfour Papers, B.M. Add. 49779.
[4] Hewins to Balfour, 18 February 1907, ibid.

Empire into the melting pot of party politics'.[1] For Austen Chamberlain and his friends, the whole issue was not made central enough to the party's effort to recover power.[2] But in the end Chamberlain acquiesced in Balfour's pledge before the second election of 1910 to put tariff reform to a referendum if the unionists were successful, on the ground that party unity was the essential thing and that at least the unionists had by now been turned into a party practically solid for tariff reform.[3]

If tariff reform was to be regarded mainly as a policy for consolidating the Empire, then the views of the dominions, and notably of Canada the main exponent of preference, were all-important. Some free-traders refused to believe that it could make any difference: 'It passes the limits of my credulity to be told that the friendship of Canada depends upon our giving to the most prosperous of her industries the really trifling advantage of a 5 per cent duty in our markets.'[4] For others, it was the only way of preventing Canada from being swallowed up by the United States.[5] The matter became of practical importance when Laurier reached a reciprocity agreement with the United States in November 1910.

The imperialists in the party argued that the essential thing was to secure Laurier's defeat and the success of Borden and the Canadian conservatives in the forthcoming elections and that the unionists should end their preoccupation with constitutional issues at home and put tariff reform back into the centre of the picture. It was even argued that it was the failure to have done this sooner that was in part responsible for Laurier's acceptance of the American reciprocity proposals.[6] In the event, it was not the course of British party politics but the clumsiness of some Americans, who allowed it to be shown that they regarded reciprocity as only a stepping-stone to annexation, that brought Laurier down to defeat in September 1911. In June next year Borden visited London and was sounded out by the new unionist leader Bonar Law

[1] Robert Cecil to Balfour, 30 June 1907. Balfour Papers, B.M. Add. 49737.
[2] Chamberlain discussed with the German ambassador in 1908 whether such a system of preference would raise objections and was told that there would be no objection provided duties were not so high as to exclude other countries from trading with the Empire – that would lead to a combination of other countries against Britain. Chamberlain, *Down the Years*, pp. 49–50.
[3] Petrie, *Chamberlain*, vol. 1, pp. 266–72.
[4] Robert Cecil to Balfour, 17 January 1907. Balfour Papers, B.M., Add., 49737.
[5] From the beginning of 1909 'Canada and the Preference scheme' became a refrain in the Northcliffe press. A. M. Gollin, *Proconsul in Politics*, pp. 147–8.
[6] Richard Jebb to Milner, 26 July 1911. Milner Papers, A. III, Letters, 1908–12. Richard Jebb to Milner 29 July 1911. Milner Papers, C. LXXIV, 1908–17, Canada [Bodl. 169].

on the value that Canada would attach to imperial preference involving British taxation on foodstuffs.[1] By now the enthusiasm for protection was waning in the conservative ranks,[2] though the principle of a referendum on protection after a party victory remained party policy until the whole issue was for the time being swallowed up in the new problems of the war.[3]

Aloof from the main body of the conservative critics of the government, and uninvolved in their heart-searchings over preference, Lord Milner fulfilled a curious role in the background of British politics – the only British statesman of the period with a real ideological streak.[4] Milner regarded himself as working with the conservatives rather than for them: 'I do not see, under present circumstances,' he wrote, 'how Imperialists can work with anyone else, not that I love the Conservative Party so much as because the behaviour of their opponents on Imperial questions has been so detestable that one is obliged any way to go against *them*.'[5] It is thus still puzzling to find that his admirers should have gone on believing long after his death that he would be placed by history 'in the forefront of the statesmen who shaped the course of our Commonwealth in the opening years of the present century'.[6]

Milner differed from the bulk of conservative as from the bulk of Liberal opinion in his indifference to and indeed contempt for party politics. Expressions of dislike for party politics and of his view that,

[1] Randolph Churchill, *Lord Derby* (1959), p. 162. Bonar Law had succeeded Balfour after the latter's retirement in November 1911 – a compromise after a deadlock between Austen Chamberlain and Walter Long.
[2] Petrie, op. cit., pp. 326–9.
[3] A memorandum written by Hewins in October 1913 suggested that in fact Cobdenism was on the wane even in the liberal party and that there were signs, in practice, of a tendency towards imperial preference: 'It is clearly not possible to have an Army or Navy policy adequate for the defence of the Empire unless the economic interests of the Empire are maintained in relative predominance over those of foreign powers.' Hewins, 'The Tariff Commission, 17 October 1913', Balfour Papers, B.M. Add. 49779.
[4] For this reason, he may have been easier for continental scholars to appreciate, see Vladimir Halpérin, *Lord Milner and the Empire* (1952). Cf. Edward Crankshaw, *The Forsaken Idea. A Study of Lord Milner* (1952).
[5] Milner to F. H. Corydon, 18 March 1905, Milner Papers.
[6] Broadcast by L. S. Amery on the centenary of Milner's birth, *The Listener*, 1 April 1954. The survival of animosity towards Milner on the left may be gauged from a comment by Gilbert Murray; who in a private letter denounced the 'absolute glorification of Milner by the B.B.C., without a single word of doubt about his making of the Boer war and opposition to the peace of Vereeniging. It fills me not only with indignation but with something like alarm. I thought that type of imperialism was dead and damned. What an effect it is likely to have in South Africa and in Europe.' Murray to Barbara Hammond, 27 March 1954 (Hammond Papers, Bodleian Library, MS. Hammond, 31, Folio 112). It is interesting to note that as late as this, the old pro-Boers were still concerned with South African feelings along British–Dutch lines, not with *apartheid*.

among other things, they made impossible a proper settlement of the South African question appear in his letters from early on in the South African war.[1] 'Here is everything depending,' he wrote in 1905, 'on this rotten assembly at Westminster and the whole future of the Empire may turn upon the whims of men who have been elected for their competence in dealing with Metropolitan tramways or country pubs.'[2]

No doubt much of this animus reflected his preoccupation with South Africa. More than any other person, he had been responsible for the war;[3] and then it appeared that its fruits were to be thrown away. His interest was not in renewing the ascendancy that Britain had possessed over the Boer Republics, but in the full-scale anglicization of the whole of South Africa. His programme, it has been pointed out, was in many respects similar to that which Lord Durham had envisaged in 1839 for the elimination of French-Canadian individuality.[4] To bring it about he was prepared for uncompromising assertion of imperial rule. No wonder that an indignant liberal called him 'the Strafford of South Africa'.[5] Above all, he held to the supremacy of the English language: 'I always was and am, opposed to equality of language. I hold that the English language ought to occupy the first position in every country under the English flag.'[6] The mine-owners' profits were no great matter where he was concerned. Far more typical was his hope that South Africa could be used for training the home army: 'There is no country in the world for turning boys, and indeed children, into men like South Africa.'[7]

It is not surprising that Milner's ideas of imperial union, which were far-reaching but had little relevance to economic matters, should have been puzzling to men for whom tariff reform was the major concern.[8] Milner's attitude was basically a racial one and his essential point was that the drift towards autonomy of the peoples of British stock should be compensated for by the creation of real federal institutions. Uncon-

[1] Wrench, *Milner*, p. 233; Gollin, *Proconsul in Politics*, 34–5, 46–8, 65, Thompson, *Unification of South Africa*, p. 16.
[2] Milner to George Parkin, 24 July 1905. Milner Papers, A. 1, Letters, 1905–6. Parkin had now left Canada for England and was (the first) secretary of the Rhodes Trust.
[3] Eric Stokes, 'Milnerism', *Historical Journal*, vol. V, 1962.
[4] Thompson, *Unification of South Africa*, p. 8.
[5] Courtenay Ilbert to Bryce, 28 December 1905. Bryce Papers, English Correspondence, vol. 13.
[6] Milner to John Martin, editor of the *Bloemfontein Post*, 30 October 1911. Milner Papers, III A. Letters, 1910–13.
[7] Milner to J. Rendel, 12 January 1903. Milner Papers, loc. cit.
[8] Hewins, op. cit., vol. 1, p. 39.

cerned with the parliamentary game at home, he was quite ready to see all Britain's 'world business' looked after by a 'real imperial council' while existing parliaments restricted themselves to these matters of local concern which he found so uninspiring.[1]

Such ideas were not only alien to a Britain deeply engaged in one of its periodic bouts of internal reform but also to the overseas democracies of the dominions. The Pacific dominions, where sympathy for the idea of imperial unity was strongest, he did not know at first hand; and towards Canada, which he visited in 1908 and 1912, Milner's feelings were ambivalent.[2] He wrote to a correspondent that he was anxious to dispel any impression that he had come to lecture the Canadians; he had come, he said, to learn not to preach.[3] But his views were not secret. When in 1909 the governor-general, Lord Grey, wrote to him about the tactlessness of the British press in talking about the need for Canadian loyalty to Great Britain, Milner replied that this was a misunderstanding – Canada and England should each be loyal to the whole of which they were each a part. He did not agree, however, that there was no danger to loyalty in the true sense: 'The "Americanization" of great part of the Canadian west is a danger on that side, just as the cosmopolitan internationalism which has so strong a hold on England, especially in the leaders of the working-class, is a danger on this.'[4] He thus welcomed the impulse to Canadian national feeling given by the reciprocity controversy, since Canadian national feeling could be reconciled with imperial unity; the 'one real danger' was 'continentalism'.[5]

From 1906 onwards Milner was rather a focus for activity among the tory imperialists than a leader of them. Often the initiative and ideas came from Leo Amery,[6] though Milner with his powerful links with the right-wing press played an important part in influencing opinion.[7]

[1] Gollin, op. cit., p. 106; Amery, op. cit., pp. 179–80; Thompson, op. cit., p. 5.
[2] For a Canadian's reactions to Milner's imperial attitude, see the extracts from Mackenzie King's diary for 1908 in Dawson, op. cit., pp. 168–70.
[3] Milner to Col. Denison, 20 September 1908. Milner MSS., C. LXXIV, 1908–17, Canada [Bodl. 169].
[4] Milner to Earl Grey, 25 February 1909. Milner MSS., A. II, Letters, 1907–9.
[5] Milner to Col. Denison, 10 April 1911. Milner Papers, C. LXXIV, 1908–17. Canada [Bodl. 169].
[6] Gollin, op. cit., p. 184 fn.
[7] Ibid., p. 134. Milner was very conscious of the importance of the press and particularly worried about the poor reporting of news as between one part of the Empire and the other. See the letter to Earl Grey, cited above. An imperial press conference did indeed meet in London in July 1909 for the purpose of discussing imperial problems as they related especially to journalism; but the only subject seriously canvassed was that of naval defence. Otherwise

What he hankered after was something outside the ordinary confines of British politics, a single imperial-unionist party with branches all over the Empire which would cut itself adrift from mere local parties.[1] In fact, he drifted into the die-hard camp after the upheaval of 1910–11 and with his strong military connections, enhanced by his work for the National Service League, he was an important figure in the agitation among the officer corps in the Ulster crisis of 1914.[2]

The Round Table

It was natural that Milner should also have been involved at the beginning in the affairs of the Round Table group, the successor to the Coefficients and Compatriots of the preceding decade, and the longest-lived of the more or less 'open conspiracies' – in H. G. Wells' telling phrase – which high-minded men embarked upon in order to strengthen the hands of statesmen in dealing with the problems of empire, and to guide their steps in the directions that the imperial faith appeared to dictate.[3] Indeed, an American historian who has done much work on the history of the Round Table has expressed the view that its origins actually date back to Milner's Canadian visit in September–November 1908 and the groups he there assembled for the discussion of imperial federation.[4] A club formed under Milner's inspiration in Toronto by Arthur Glazebrook appears to have been the nucleus of the later Canadian Round Table group.

It was, however, Lionel Curtis who supplied the driving force of the new movement and suggested its basic techniques when, with the success of the movement towards closer union in South Africa, a number of members of Milner's Kindergarten found themselves ready to move on to the wider imperial scene. Of those who took part in the round of talks in London in the summer of 1909 (out of which the Round Table

---

the delegates were treated to a number of speeches from leading British political figures and to sightseeing tours throughout the United Kingdom. R. Cook, *The Politics of John W. Dafoe and the Free Press* (Toronto, 1963), p. 37.

[1] Milner to Amery, 29 June 1909, quoted in Gollin, op. cit., p. 163.

[2] Ibid., pp. 188, 195, 200–1. His own preference was for a federal United Kingdom; see the precis of his political views dated, 18 September 1911, and forwarded to Austen Chamberlain in a letter of 10 October. Austen Chamberlain Papers, AC. 9. 18.

[3] For a recent summary of the early years of the Round Table, see Gollin, op. cit., pp. 164–7.

[4] Carroll Quigley, 'The Round Table Groups in Canada 1908–1938', *Canadian Historical Review*, vol. XLIII, September 1962. This article contains information about the founding and scope of the movement as a whole, as well as about its Canadian components.

proper emerged) besides Milner himself, Lionel Curtis, Geoffrey Robinson, Philip Kerr, W. S. Marris, Lord Lovat, and R. H. Brand had served in South Africa in one capacity or another. Rhodes's associate Dr Starr Jameson, who had played a leading role in the South African constitutional convention, was in London during part of the time and involved in some of the meetings. The South African financier Sir Abe Bailey, another of Rhodes's disciples, who had financed *The State* (the organ of the closer union movement in South Africa) was to be an important source of finance, particularly for the movement's journal, *The Round Table*, which began publication in 1910; the other principal source of finance was the Rhodes Trust itself. Others who took part in the early discussions were F. S. Oliver, the politically oriented draper whose biography of Alexander Hamilton (1906) had been curiously transmuted into an argument for South African union, Arthur Steel-Maitland, a rising young tory with an interest in social reform who had accompanied Milner to Canada as his secretary, the banker, R. M. Holland Martin, G. L. Craik, Lord Howick (son-in-law of Lord Selborne, and thus another link with South Africa), and Lord Selborne's heir, Lord Wolmer.

The purposes of the new movement were summarized in a printed memorandum of the 'conversations which took place between a few English and South African friends at intervals during the summer of 1909'.[1] In its analysis of the 'problem' the document made it clear that the defence issue, precipitated by the fact that South Africa would now be responsible for its own defence, was at the root of the matter. Britain's share was still too large: 'the existing position may be summed up by saying that four of the five self-governing communities have not vindicated the claim they are making to being considered as sovereign nations, so long as the burden of protecting the five is borne with difficulty by the fifth alone'. Such an arrangement must, it was felt, end in disruption; some kind of union was the 'only means of securing the political ideals of the race – a real nationality and self-government to those capable of exercising it, and to those which are not government in the interest of the governed themselves'.

The means to bring about change were seen as the setting up of groups of 'carefully selected men' in each country by the visit of a deputation from the original nucleus; these should remain in constant contact through the visits of an itinerant delegate and through corre-

[1] Copy in Lothian Papers, Box 210.

spondence with the London group which would 'undertake to collect, to digest, and to disseminate information'. The need for magazines, to attract press and public attention to the movement's ideas, was also recognized. These proposals were responsible for the characteristic organizational features of the movement, including the regular London meetings or Moots which determined the content and character of the journal and which took collective responsibility for editorial matter and the regular appearance in it of anonymous reports on conditions in each of the dominions.

The memorandum laid it down that the 'Movement should avoid any savour of advertisement or mystery' – but avoiding the former tended to promote the latter, and the precise influence of the movement on later policy-making in the Commonwealth field as distinct from the influence in their own capacity of some of its members remains difficult to establish.[1] It was also laid down that 'for the present it would be inexpedient to seek or allow identification with any party'.

The freedom from party ties seemed of particular importance to Kerr; the cause suffered already in his view from the fact that the unionists claimed a monopoly of imperial virtue which made the dominions feel that it was not a national cry in England and made liberals take a more anti-imperial stance than their convictions really required them to.[2] The fact was that the ideas of *The Round Table* seemed too remote from practical politics to appeal to the party leaders. 'Balfour,' wrote Lothian, 'accepts all the future seems to hold for the necessity of consolidation and the granting to the colonies of a share in Imperial control. But to him it is a misty if fascinating speculation. He cannot afford to let his imagination riot in the future or govern his tongue.'[3] Amery also, after participating for three years in the Moots,

---

[1] No full-scale history of the *Round Table* has been published and none of the principal figures in it has had a biography, except for Philip Kerr (Lord Lothian). *Lord Lothian* by J. R. M. Butler (1960), while a sympathetic study of the man and his opinions, is conceived on too small a scale to deal with his many-sided contribution to the history of his times.

[2] Undated pamphlet (probably 1910 or 1911) entitled *Imperial Union and Federation for the United Kingdom*, written by Kerr. Lothian Papers, Box 210. Kerr (1882–1940) (succeeded as eleventh Marquis of Lothian in 1930) had held various posts in South Africa between 1904 and 1909, culminating in the editorship of *The State*. He was editor of *The Round Table* from 1910 to 1916, when he became one of Lloyd George's secretaries, a post he held till 1921. He was chancellor of the Duchy of Lancaster from August to November 1931 and parliamentary under-secretary at the India Office from November 1931 to September 1932 when he left the national government with the other liberal free-traders. Ambassador to the U.S.A., August 1939 to December 1940. Secretary of the Rhodes Trust, 1925–39.

[3] Kerr to Brand, 1 January 1910. Brand Papers, Lothian Correspondence.

found that they were too dominated by Curtis and his ideas of federal union, and he himself dropped out.[1]

The first step after the formal organization of the English group at the beginning of September 1909 was the dispatch of a delegation to Canada composed of Curtis, Kerr, and Marris.[2] A shipboard letter from Kerr shows that he was not confident at all about his mission. The South African Kindergarten seemed to him out of touch with English realities, and he could not see what could be offered to Canada to bring her closer as there was nothing that England could offer that the United States could not offer just as well. The best hope was to postpone the issue for a quarter of a century until assiduous propaganda and the experiences of imperial conferences had done their work.[3] From Winnipeg he wrote more encouragingly, finding 'practically everybody disposed to the ideas of a big Empire' but feeling it necessary for something more than just a combination for defence to be offered, if people's imaginations were to be caught.[4] Marris confessed himself uncertain of the future, though he was fairly confident that Canada would succeed in keeping out of the American orbit. He noted the difference that had developed between Kerr's pragmatism and Curtis's conviction that anything short of 'organic union' was apostasy from the original ideal.[5] Nevertheless a Toronto Round Table group was successfully launched and a number of eminent Canadians gravitated towards it; additional groups were created in other Canadian centres and for a decade, the movement remained very active in the dominions.[6]

The founding meeting in September 1909 had given the movement as its first task the drawing up of 'a full and reasoned statement of the

[1] Amery, op. cit., vol. 1, pp. 347–8.
[2] W. S. Marris (1873–1945) (knighted, 1919), was a member of the I.C.S. lent to the Transvaal government in 1906; he was to hold important positions in India between 1917 and 1927 and was responsible for drafting the Montagu–Chelmsford report.
[3] Kerr to Brand, 23 September 1909. Brand Papers, Lothian Correspondence. R. H. Brand (1878–1963) (created baron in 1946) held various posts in South Africa between 1902 and 1909. He subsequently became a banker and between 1915 and 1922 held a number of government posts dealing with transatlantic supplies and with European financial questions. He was head of the British food mission in Washington, 1941–44, and treasury representative there from May 1944 to May 1946; he was chairman of the British Supply Council in North America, April–November 1942 and June 1945–March 1946 and the U.K. delegate at the Bretton Woods and Savannah conferences. Between 1909 and 1917 Brand and Kerr shared a home in London.
[4] Kerr to Brand, 20 October 1909. Brand Papers, Lothian Correspondence.
[5] Marris to Brand, 31 October 1909. Brand Papers, Lothian Correspondence.
[6] Quigley, loc. cit.; J. Eayrs, 'The Round Table Movement in Canada, 1909–1920', Canadian Historical Review, XXXVIII, March 1957.

Imperial problem, setting out the alternatives involved, the real import of disruption, the sacrifices necessary to avoid it, and the successive stages through which the ultimate goal' was to be sought. A meeting from 15 to 18 January 1910 took the project a stage further. Kerr, Curtis, and Marris were all present together with Brand and Craik of the original participants in the discussions, and three more members of the Kindergarten, Lionel Hichens, Patrick Duncan, and Richard Feetham.[1] They agreed that the ultimate aim should be an organic union in the form of an imperial government constitutionally responsible to all electors in the Empire. It would be the movement's task to prepare and publish a scheme of union and encourage any intermediate steps towards this aim.[2]

Full agreement remained out of reach; the members of the group, though agreed that closer union was essential, continued to differ on how best to attain it. Kerr had warned Brand from Canada that if Milner and Curtis insisted upon working for imperial federation in the strict sense he would be forced to withdraw altogether.[3] In fact, Curtis seems not to have pressed the point too far, and Milner does not seem to have taken a very active role once the movement was launched. On the other hand, when Milner suggested that dominion high commissioners should have ministerial rank and be grouped together under one roof, Amery objected on the ground that it would encourage the dominions to think of themselves as separate states and of their high commissioners as ambassadors. Curtis's comment was that Amery was like 99 per cent of those brought up in the environment of British politics, unable to think of constitutional development except in terms of a gradual evolution. Curtis took the view that this would not work; the dominions must be encouraged to think of themselves as separate states and then come to see for themselves the advantages of a federal union.[4]

---

[1] Lionel Hichens (1874–1940) had served as a financial expert in Egypt, South Africa, and India, and was son-in-law of Sir Neville Lyttelton, British chief of staff, 1904–8. He had a subsequent career in private business but remained an active member of the Round Table group throughout his life. Patrick Duncan (1870–1943) (knighted, 1937) had been private secretary to Milner at the Board of Inland Revenue before going to South Africa in 1901. A long public and political career in South Africa culminated in his appointment as governor-general in 1937. He held the post until his death. Richard Feetham (1874–1966) began his South African career in 1902 as deputy town clerk of Johannesburg and subsequently held high judicial office.
[2] Minutes of meeting at Ledbury, 15 to 18 January 1910. Lothian Papers, Box 210.
[3] Kerr to Brand, 1 November 1909. Brand Papers, Lothian Correspondence. There was another crisis in 1912. Kerr to Brand, 18 September 1912. Ibid.
[4] Curtis to Kerr, 10 September 1910. Lothian Papers, Box 210.

Even more fundamental was the problem that was bound to face the Round Table as it did all the other advocates of imperial union – the future of the Empire's non-white majority. What was to be the ultimate destiny of the black man in southern Africa? Curtis seemed to believe that he would somehow disappear; but Marris did not regard this as realistic. Where too would India fit in, now that Morley and Minto had launched her, however tentatively, along the road of representative institutions – could these fall short of autonomy and what then?[1] In default of answers to these questions what could the Round Table do but react to the stream of events and insert its particular point of view whenever occasion offered?

One such opportunity looked like being presented by the 1911 imperial conference which was timed to coincide with the coronation. Kerr hoped that, like the Diamond Jubilee, the South African war, the coronation of Edward VII, and the dreadnought scare, it might help to 'raise the temperature of imperial patriotism' and to educate the democracies of the Empire to the point at which they would be willing to digest the doctrines of organic union. If the Irish question could be solved by a federal scheme for the whole United Kingdom in the coming year, then the crucial stage in the consolidation of the Empire might be at hand. Curtis, on his way to Australia, was urged to suggest to the Australian leaders that they ought to insist on the discussion of problems of foreign policy, notably the Anglo-Japanese alliance, and that this should be followed by some regular arrangements for direct access to the Foreign Office by dominion ministers. Instead of wasting time over preference, time should be given to the discussion of defence; discussion of the strategic needs of the Empire would make the dominions realize 'the importance of unity in preparation and unity of control, with its obvious corollaries about constitutional unity'.[2]

As we shall see, the discussions at the imperial conference, though they covered this ground, had none of the expected consequences. Upon Kerr these setbacks had a salutary effect. He began, as he wrote on his way to India next year, to realize that the world and imperial problems were too big for any single mind to grasp and that the Moot system, suitable in South Africa where the original Kindergarten shared the same experience and the same point of view, was not easy to trans-

[1] Marris to Brand, 12 February 1909. Brand Papers, Lothian Correspondence.
[2] Kerr to Curtis, 29 July 1910. Lothian Papers, Box 210.

fer into the more complex English environment.[1] But Curtis was undis-
mayed, believing that the imperial problem had only to be correctly
presented and discussed by men of goodwill in Britain and all the
dominions for action to follow.[2]

The activities of the Round Table groups in the various countries
and the publication of the journal kept the movement in being despite
the fact that on so many of the fundamental issues agreement had not
been obtained.[3] Curtis remained the dominant figure but Milner was
its political hope, and the conservative party's equivocations on the
preference issue made the political approach to the imperial problem
seem the more hopeful of the paths available.[4] But it was only the crisis
of the war that was to give the group the opportunity of influencing
action.

Radical Attitudes

The relationship of the imperial cause to the radical and socialist
impulses in British political life was a complex one.[5] For most of its
protagonists, tariff reform, the revenue for social services it would provide, and the opportunities it would open for trade and employment at
home provided the only alternative to socialism, whose growing appeal
appeared to be indicated by the labour party's advance in the 1906
election.[6] Yet the element of purposeful development in both the
socialist and imperial creeds seemed to some men on both sides to be a
common ground separating them from the radical exponents of free
trade and *laissez-faire*; this was in part Milner's own view.[7] On the
other side, the Fabians found themselves divided over tariff reform.
Bernard Shaw, one of the sympathizers with the tariff reformers, was

[1] Kerr to Brand, 30 January 1912. Brand Papers, Lothian Correspondence.
[2] Lecture by Curtis, Toronto University, 18 November 1913. Lothian Papers, Box 210.
[3] There is an unpublished Washington University thesis on this subject: DeWitt Clinton
Ellinwood, Jnr, 'Lord Milner's Kindergarten, the British Round Table Group and the
Movement for Imperial Reform, 1910–1918' (1962). See also J. R. M. Butler, *Lord Lothian*
(1960), ch. III.
[4] In December 1912 Bonar Law said that the proposed duties on foodstuffs would not be
imposed without another imperial conference and then only if the dominions thought it
essential. Amery, op. cit., vol. 1, pp. 413–14.
[5] On the relationship between tariff reform and social reform in the thinking of Joseph
Chamberlain, see Peter Fraser, *Joseph Chamberlain* (1966), pp. 286 ff. Cf. Koebner and
Schmidt, *Imperialism*, ch. X.
[6] Petrie, *Austen Chamberlain*, vol. 1, pp. 200–2, 239.
[7] Thornton, *The Imperial Idea and its Enemies*, pp. 254–82.

chosen to draft the pamphlet *Fabianism and the Fiscal Question* which disavowed the idea that socialism opposed protection as such, and pointed to the importance of not allowing Britain to become a parasite on her colonies. But Fabians as 'sincere imperialist enthusiasts' could not co-operate with the tariff reform movement, which was interested in tariff reform merely as a means of reducing direct taxation.[1] An even closer alignment appeared possible when Robert Blatchford and his *Clarion* espoused tariff reform and compulsory national service.[2] But an associate of Milner's, approaching Blatchford for a socialist–unionist alliance, found that the socialists were unavailable because of their theoretical position and their enmity to privilege and religion.[3]

The imperialist wing of the Fabians never quite lost in the pre-1914 period their admiration for Milner. 'In his desire for the integrity of the Empire,' the *New Statesman* wrote, 'Lord Milner, like the Socialists, is really concerned about the breeding of "an Imperial race" and necessarily finds himself demanding legislation essentially Socialist in character.'[4] But the main body of the Fabians was closer to the liberal imperialists, believing with them in the superiority of British (and indeed of western European) civilization and regarding its rule over backward peoples as, on the whole, beneficial. They approved of the extension of the principle of full self-government to the dominions, subject to the protection of aboriginal peoples, but not to India which was not yet capable of using it properly. But these views – formulated at the time of the South African war in *Fabianism and the Empire*, drafted by Bernard Shaw, which appeared in 1900 – were not of major importance, as from 1904 to 1911 the society was almost wholly absorbed in internal affairs.[5]

On the whole the left did not contribute much to the development of a coherent philosophy to govern the relations of Britain and the Empire during this period.[6] For the most part, the labour party, in and out of parliament, found its more natural partners in the radical wing of the

[1] Semmel, *Imperialism and Social Reform*, pp. 129–32, 238–9.
[2] Robert Blatchford (1851–1943) had founded the *Clarion* as a socialist weekly in 1891. His jingoism and opposition to organized religion separated him from the main socialist fold.
[3] Herbert MacIlwain to Milner, 25 June 1910. Milner Papers, III A, Letters, 1910–13.
[4] *New Statesman*, 1 May 1913, quoted by Semmel, op. cit., p. 140
[5] A. M. McBriar, *Fabian Socialism and English Politics, 1884–1918* (Cambridge U. P. 1962), ch. V.
[6] For a general view of attitudes to empire in the period, see A. F. Madden, 'Changing Attitudes and Widening Responsibilities, 1895 to 1914', *C.H.B.E.*, vol. III, ch. X.

liberal party, many of whose most prominent members they were ultimately to absorb.

For the time being, however, the position was different. The liberal party being now in power, its leaders of both wings – little Englanders as well as imperialists – were ministers and fully occupied with the tasks of government. The radicals, as normally happens on such occasions, found themselves bereft of leadership and reduced to a number of individuals who carried little weight either in themselves or as a group. The labour party was rather stronger, but its strength still depended on a tacit electoral alliance with the liberals and it could clearly not combine with the conservative opposition. The dominant element in the party, as far as international and imperial affairs were concerned, was the I.L.P. – which had taken a line contrary to that of the Fabians both on the Boer war and on the imperial issues generally. It was free trade, anti-conscriptionist and cherished a belief in international working-class solidarity as an obstacle to war that extended almost to a formally pacifist position. For overseas territories, self-government was more important than any contribution the colonial powers could make to the spread of civilization. In terms of the labour party's trade union wing and its electoral following, such sentiments were probably rather far remote from reality, as the war itself was to prove, but with bread-and-butter issues absorbing most attention the parliamentary leadership could bang the radical drum without fear of disavowal.[1]

As far as the Empire and imperial unity was concerned, the radicals did not for the most part assail the existing system. There was some fear that there might be a revulsion in England against paying taxes for the protection (as it seemed) of wealthy dominions which used their growing powers of self-government to protect themselves against British exports and which were the source of complications with foreign governments. A desire to 'cut the painter' might consequently grow.[2] But this aspect of mid-nineteenth-century radicalism did not in fact play much of a role.[3] More important, as in the case of Morel, was the blending of

[1] McBriar, op. cit., pp. 290, 305 ff., 337–8. On the general position of European socialism in relation to imperialism and international relations at this period, see James Joll, *The Second International* (1955).
[2] Earl Grey to Fabian Ware (the editor of the *Morning Post*), 28 October 1907. Copy in Milner Papers, CLXXIV, 1908–17, Canada [Bodl. 169].
[3] For a general presentation of imperialist and anti-imperialist ideas in fictional form, see John Buchan, *The Lodge in the Wilderness* (1906). Buchan (b. 1875) who had been Milner's private secretary in South Africa from 1901 to 1903 did not become involved with the rest of the Kindergarten in the Round Table movement, though he shared some of its ideas, and

anti-imperial with humanitarian sentiment, and this could lead in the opposite direction.[1] Labour members of the House of Commons joined the radicals in opposing the draft South Africa act in 1909, on the ground that inadequate protection was being given to native interests.[2] Generally labour sentiment, as set out in Ramsay MacDonald's book *Labour and the Empire*, published in 1907, was hostile to the control of non-white peoples by white minorities.[3] Labour sympathies with the Indian national movement also continued to be strong.[4]

In relation to foreign affairs there was some persistent anxiety about the extent to which the country appeared to be engaging in policies which parliament was given too little opportunity to discuss or approve.[5] Radicals also objected to the creation of the committee of Imperial Defence, on the ground that it would reduce the influence of the cabinet

in his fiction gave classic expression to some aspects of the imperialist ideology. He was later a conservative M.P., 1927–35 and, as Baron Tweedsmuir, governor-general of Canada from 1935 to his death in February 1940. See the biography, *John Buchan*, by Janet Adam Smith (1965).

[1] On the other hand, most humanitarians were driven into supporting direct British rule and even its extension as an instrument for fighting evils such as slavery. See Madden, in *C.H.B.E.*, vol. III, pp. 351–3.

[2] Thompson, *Unification of South Africa*, p. 401.

[3] James Ramsay MacDonald (1866–1937), secretary of the labour representation committee and then of the labour party, 1900–12, and treasurer 1912–24, was chairman of the I.L.P., 1906–9. He entered parliament in 1906 and was leader of the party from 1911 to 1914. Unlike nearly all his fellow-socialists, he spoke of foreign and imperial questions on the basis of first-hand knowledge. He made a world tour in 1906, and visited the continent on political business every year from 1907 to 1916. He visited South Africa in 1902, and India in 1909 and 1912. After his partial eclipse during and immediately after the war, owing to his opposition to it, he re-entered parliament in 1922, becoming chairman of the labour parliamentary party and leader of the opposition. He was prime minister and foreign secretary, January–November 1924, prime minister, 1929–35, and lord president of the council, 1935–7. The vendetta pursued against him even posthumously, for his break with the labour party and formation of the 'national government' in 1931, and the breakdown of his physical and mental powers in his last years, have curiously obscured the fact that he was the one statesman of international calibre so far produced by the labour party and one of the few exceptions to the generally insular outlook of its leadership.

[4] See Ramsay MacDonald, *The Awakening of India* (1910), *The Government of India* (1919). MacDonald was a member of the royal commission on the Public Services in India, 1912–14.

[5] In a letter from L. T. Hobhouse to Gilbert Murray on 30 October 1912 he called attention to a conference of the 'Foreign Policy Committee' to meet on 26 November at which he hoped Murray would support the resolution 'That it is essential to the interest and safety of the country that steps should be taken to secure adequate Parliamentary control of foreign affairs, and that in particular no engagements, formal or informal, involving national responsibilities should be permanently binding until confirmed by Parliament.' Lord Courtney was to be in the chair and it was hoped that there would also be present: Sir John Brunner, Arthur Ponsonby, M.P., E. D. Morel, Ramsay MacDonald, Philip Morrell, Charles Trevelyan, G. P. Gooch, W. Anderson, the Rev. Silvester Horne, and C. Roden Buxton. The combination of radical high-mindedness, basic sympathy for Germany and socialist internationalism is well represented by this list. Gilbert Murray Papers. Cf. A. J. P. Taylor, *The Troublemakers*, ch. IV.

and hence of parliamentary control.[1] But for the most part the radicals tended to take up not so much the central issues of politics as some of the side-effects of the government's actions. In the case of the *entente* with Russia, for instance, objections were raised to the establishment of spheres of influence in Persia, which the agreement entailed and which it was held spelled death to nascent Persian democracy.[2]

One anti-imperialist of an older generation, Wilfrid Scawen Blunt, attacked Grey throughout not only for his Persian policy but for other actions tending to alienate the Moslem world, both in the Middle East and in India. Grey, he pointed out, had been Cromer's private secretary and fully inherited his overbearing attitude towards Egypt, and the principle of its separation from the Turkish dominions. In an article in 1912 Blunt attacked Grey's conduct over the Balkan war, asserting that his joining with Russia to coerce the Turks would result in the growth of German influence at Constantinople.[3]

Blunt was not a figure of great importance, but it is interesting to note that it was now possible for radicalism to identify itself with the Turkish cause instead of with the Christian minorities, as it had a generation earlier. It is also significant that Blunt's pro-Moslem and arabophile outlook began a trend in a section of British opinion which was to be much reinforced by Britain's involvement with the Arab nationalist movement in the first world war. Its basic assumption, that of a natural coincidence of interests and outlook between the British and the Arabs, was to develop in some quarters almost into a dogma and was to prove a most important factor in policy-making over some decades.[4]

Where Blunt was more prescient than many other radicals of the

[1] Monger, *The End of Isolation*, pp. 285 fn., 309 fn.
[2] The foreign secretary wrote to J. A. Spender on 24 September 1912: 'I am bombarded by letters here from people who want me to break with Russia over Persia: how on earth can we help Persia if we do? And it is these same people who denounce partition because it would increase our responsibilities.' Spender Papers, B.M. Add. 46389. As editor of the *Westminster Gazette* from 1896 to 1922, J. A. Spender (1861–1942) was the principal journalistic exponent of liberal imperialism, and on close terms with that wing of the Asquith cabinet.
[3] Lord Lytton, *Wilfred Scawen Blunt* (1961), pp. 125 ff. W. S. Blunt (1840–1922) had been in the diplomatic service from 1858 to 1869 and had subsequently travelled much in the Middle East and India. He had been imprisoned in Ireland during Balfour's chief secretaryship in connection with his activities on behalf of Irish nationalism. His pro-Arab inclinations arose in part from his interest in breeding Arab horses – an interest shared with his wife, Byron's granddaughter.
[4] It is also interesting to find that Blunt blames England's 'betrayal' of the Moslem cause on the 'power of the alien gang of Jew financiers which has captured the House of Commons'. The connection of a pro-Moslem with an anti-semitic viewpoint thus antedates the Palestine question and the 'Balfour declaration', and cannot simply be attributed to the quarrel over Zionism.

pre-1914 era was in his perception of the lack of hold that empire, as such, had among the British masses.

> The English [he wrote to an Indian Moslem leader] are not by taste a military nation, and less than ever now will they be induced to accept universal service in the army, while financially there are great difficulties ahead which will limit the development of the fleet. No country in Europe is less inclined than ours to the sacrifice demanded by the needs of an overgrown Empire. If the lessons of history teach us anything, they teach us that a nation cannot retain other nations in subjection unless it is ready at all points to fight. The English nation is already overburdened with its dependencies and though everyone talks the language of Imperialism, the will to defend the Empire is altogether lacking.[1]

The course of two world wars and the efforts made by the British might seem on the surface to have given Blunt the lie, yet in a deeper sense, the root of the matter is perhaps there. For the challenges of the two wars if they included a threat to the Commonwealth and Empire were both ultimately the product of Britain's European position. When it came after 1945 to the direct question of whether the Empire should be held by force or not, public opinion again and again showed itself fundamentally hostile to the idea of making the necessary sacrifices, as well as unconvinced of the morality of doing so.

The Dominions' Differing Views

Some months after the liberal government had taken office, Clarke wrote to Balfour that the 'difficulty of steering the Empire' was increasing and that he was inclined to fear that domestic developments would make it harder to deal with imperial questions.[2] In fact there was no break in the machinery, and the actual course of institutional development followed a line that was little affected by British political debate.[3]

---

[1] This passage and the passages summarized in the previous footnote appear in a letter from Blunt to the Indian Moslem leader Syed Mahmud of 28 July 1913, quoted in Lytton, op. cit., pp. 182–8.
[2] Clarke to Balfour, 20 September 1906. Balfour Papers, B.M. Add. 49702.
[3] See J. A. Cross, *Whitehall and the Commonwealth*, British departmental Organization for Commonwealth Relations, 1900–1966 (1967), and in *C.H.B.E.*, vol. III, ch. XI, by J. E. Tyler, 'Development of the Imperial Conference, 1887–1914', and ch. XIX, by R. B. Pugh, 'The Colonial Office, 1801–1925'.

The imperial council proposed by Sir Frederick Pollock and embodied in Lyttelton's dispatch of April 1905 had found little favour in Canadian eyes, although Pollock himself had tried in vain to convince Laurier of the merits of the idea.[1] But Canadian liberalism was opposed to all extensions of imperial machinery as necessarily entangling Canada in matters not her concern and therefore as likely to weaken rather than strengthen imperial ties. Nothing could be so dangerous as the growth in each dominion of parties based on an imperialist versus anti-imperialist division.[2] As the leading Canadian liberal journalist had put it at the end of 1905: 'The Imperial ideals to which the British statesmen in office during the past ten years "had been wedded" looked to a centralization of power in the capital – the Roman plan modified to meet twentieth century requirements.' Laurier had defeated these attempts.

> Canada under the Laurier régime [he continued] has taken steps which have strengthened the Empire, not by consenting to the appointment of some fussy bureaucrats dominated by some fads, to meddle with colonial affairs, but by enormously increasing the power and resources of this country. Canada, in taking over the entire responsibility of her defence, in modifying her militia system, in making a start in the establishment of a Canadian navy, makes it very clear that she intends to be a factor in world politics in alliance with the Motherland. But it will be an alliance not a merger.[3]

What Canada could afford in aloofness from British policy-making was less acceptable to the Pacific dominions with their worries about imperial rivalries in the Pacific. Alfred Deakin, the dominant figure in Australian politics, had an imperial vision of his own, centred upon a belief that the governments of the dominions could work direct with the United Kingdom government and avoid the irksome tutelage of the Colonial Office. Basing himself on the 'Britishness of the Empire' he was suspicious of Boers and of French Canadians.[4] It is not surprising, there-

---

[1] Hewins, op. cit., vol. 1, pp. 120 ff. There may be an echo of this proposal in a suggestion made by Esher to Balfour in October 1910 that the Joint Council which had been suggested as a way of resolving disputes between the two houses of the U.K. Parliament might be extended into an Imperial Senate through its afforcement by delegations from one or more of the Dominions as occasion demanded. Balfour Papers, B.M. Add. 49719.

[2] Mackenzie King to Amery, 2 April 1907. Dawson, *Mackenzie King*, vol. 1, p. 148 fn.

[3] The (Winnipeg) *Free Press*, 9 December 1905, quoted by Cook, op. cit., pp. 23–4.

[4] J. A. La Nauze, *Alfred Deakin* (Melbourne, 1965), vol. 2, pp. 480–501. Deakin's imperialism totally disregarded both the position of the tropical colonies – 'Britain's Empire' as opposed

fore, that the 1907 colonial conference largely took the form of a clash between Laurier and Deakin, with the latter receiving some support from Starr Jameson, now premier of the Cape. The upshot was that Laurier, backed by Botha, got his way and the only concrete proposal that survived the conference was for a permanent secretariat to function between what were to be the regular quadrennial imperial conferences of the future. For the imperialists who had done their best to lobby its members on tariff reform and who were able to point to a number of preferential arrangements made between the other parts of the Empire in recent years, the conference of 1907 was of course a disappointment.[1] Nevertheless their tendency to blame the liberal ministers at home was unjustified. Amery records that he found Churchill (under-secretary to Elgin at the Colonial Office) not only dogmatic in his free-trade views but also strongly opposed to consulting the dominions about foreign affairs until they were military powers whose alliance could be of value.[2] But the fact was, loath though Amery and his friends were to accept it, that the Canadians in particular were averse to being involved through consultation in matters over which they could not exercise control.

Much more significant was the steady accretion of autonomy in practice, even in the field of foreign relations. In international law, and by foreign powers, the Empire was regarded as a single whole. The dominions had no regular representation abroad, and any agreements they made had to be signed by a British minister; but this did not prevent them pursuing vigorous negotiations of their own, particularly in the commercial field, so that the imperial signature could be regarded as a mere formality. For an imperialist of the Amery brand the idea of a Canadian representative at Washington, or even of a Canadian attaché or department within the British embassy, seemed alarming. Grey, however, showed himself fairly favourable to the idea put to him by Mackenzie King in 1909 that there should be a permanent representative of Canada attached to the British embassy in countries of

to the 'British Empire' – and India. 'I laugh when I think of a man who blows the imperial trumpet louder than other people and yet would banish India which is the most stupendous part of the Empire – our best customer among other trifles – into the imperial back kitchen.' Morley to Minto, 2 April 1907. Quoted, ibid., pp. 480–1. The liberal ministers had other reasons for objecting to Deakin who maintained close contact with the opposition during his visit for the conference and made public speeches defending tariff reform.

[1] Hewins, op. cit., vol. 1, pp. 197–8, 205.
[2] Amery, op. cit., vol. 1, p. 302. The Elgin–Churchill relationship has been fully explored in Ronald Hyam, *Elgin and Churchill at the Colonial Office* (London, Macmillan, 1968).

especial interest to Canada, in particular, the United States, China, and Japan; but the suggestion was not followed up.[1]

The only change in Britain's arrangements brought about by the conference of 1907 was the constitution within the Colonial Office – not, as some of the prime ministers might have expected, outside it – of a separate department of which the secretariat of the conference in fact formed an integral part. In 1911 the posts of head of the conference secretariat and of head of the dominions department were actually combined. The full responsibility of the Colonial Office for relations with the dominions was thus reaffirmed and the views of those who had urged that the difference between the two kinds of task represented by colonial rule and quasi-diplomatic relations with other autonomous governments should receive formal recognition were implicitly rejected.[2]

The idea of a separate office was mooted again by Laurier in 1909, perhaps under pressure from Earl Grey, but finding his principal colleague opposed to it he let the matter drop. In London pressure from imperialist circles inside and outside parliament led to a cabinet reconsideration of the whole problem and of various possible solutions, including the creation of a dominions department with the prime minister as its head. Had there been dominion pressure at the 1911 conference the government would have assented at least to the bifurcation of the existing Colonial Office with two permanent undersecretaries. On the whole, however, neither of Elgin's successors at the Colonial Office, Crewe and Harcourt, was favourable to change.[3]

Apart from the practical problems which seemed to crop up as an obstacle to each proposal for change, there was also an objection, at least in Harcourt's mind, to basing a new pattern of organization upon the existing distribution of imperial responsibilities.

It appears almost certain [he wrote in a memorandum (not communicated to the dominion governments)] that in a future not very remote the Dominions in temperate zones will desire to acquire for

[1] Dawson, *Mackenzie King*, p. 194.
[2] The division of the office also seemed essential from the point of view of ensuring a more vigorous policy of development in the Crown colonies. Amery, after visiting East Africa, was convinced that the existing Colonial Office was too *laissez-faire* for the task. Amery, op. cit., vol. 1, p. 321.
[3] Lewis Harcourt (1863–1923) (created Viscount Harcourt, 1916) had sat in the cabinet since March 1907 as first commissioner for works – a post he had held since 1905. He was secretary of state for the colonies from November 1910 to May 1915, and first commissioner again until December 1916.

themselves 'hot houses' for consumable luxuries and other purposes. It is not unreasonable to contemplate the ultimate absorption of the West Indies by Canada; of the Pacific Islands by Australia and New Zealand; of Rhodesia and the native Protectorates (even of Nyasaland) by South Africa.

If the Colonial Office were bifurcated the dominions would be divorced far more completely 'from any knowledge of or interest in, or indirect influence over their neighbouring Crown Colonies'.[1]

Had Deakin remained in office until the imperial conference of 1911 assembled there might have been more of a clash between the advocates of change and the defenders of the *status quo*. Deakin's idea had been that the secretariat should act not only as a bridge between conferences but also as a link between governments superseding the Colonial Office:

> My idea is, Imperial Secretariat only to be under Prime Minister for control of office matters – not as a member of British cabinet – but as head of Imperial representatives who control it . . . We have a new Department under new joint control and at joint cost – the first Department of a future Imperial service to embrace Army, Navy, and Treaties, i.e. Foreign Affairs. We cut entirely free of the Colonial Office and have nothing of its Minister except as to matters apart from our self-governing powers which have no political complexion.[2]

But Deakin, whose views were not generally supported by Australian labour, ended his third and final term as prime minister in April 1910. It looked as though the Canadian view of the proper course of imperial development had triumphed; such was Dafoe's conclusion from what he had heard leaders of both parties declare at the imperial press conference in 1909.[3] As Mackenzie King put it the most lasting develop-

---

[1] Cross, op. cit., p. 33. The assumption that the Protectorates of Bechuanaland, Basutoland, and Swaziland which now formed enclaves within the Dominion of South Africa would eventually be absorbed within it was common at the time to both the British and the South African governments; but opposition to extending South African racial legislation to further territories remained an obstacle that no British government ultimately found it possible to defy.

[2] Deakin to E. Morris Miller, 30 December 1909, in La Nauze, op. cit., vol. 2, p. 504. In fact, the British government was not happy about the way in which dominion governments were by-passing the Colonial Office and going directly to the departments involved in the particular matter in which they were interested, and on 30 March 1911 Harcourt sent a circular to seven of his ministerial colleagues deploring this practice. Cross, op. cit., pp. 37–8.

[3] Cook, op. cit., p. 38.

ments in the new empire would be 'more unconscious than determined'.[1]

Nevertheless, the federal theme did receive one final airing in the proposals put forward by the New Zealand Premier Sir Joseph Ward at the imperial conference in 1911.[2] His suggestion was that 'there should be an Imperial Council of State, with Representatives from all the constituent parts of the Empire, in theory and fact advisory to the Imperial Government on all questions affecting the interests of His Majesty's Dominions overseas'. But it has been pointed out that what he really had in mind was 'the representation of the United Kingdom and the dominions on a proportionate population basis in an imperial parliament of defence'.[3]

Sir Joseph Ward's proposals would seem largely to have emanated from the fertile brain of Lionel Curtis who, during his visit to Australia in 1910, had sent him some suggestions through the governor, Lord Islington.[4] But if they commended themselves to the New Zealand government, it was largely because New Zealand's own sense of remoteness made her seek for some voice in imperial affairs that might help to secure more rapid and safer communications between herself and other parts of the Empire.[5] The new Australian prime minister, Andrew Fisher, was not ready to go the whole way with Ward, though he would have liked some kind of advisory council with which the United Kingdom might keep in touch especially at times of crisis. But the Canadian objections to any such development were irremovable,[6] and those of South Africa no less formidable;[7] the British government had no difficulty in keeping things as they were.[8]

[1] Mackenzie King to Amery, 16 July 1910. Dawson, op. cit., p. 219.
[2] On the 1911 conference, I have been able to make use of the unpublished Oxford B.Phil. thesis by Mr I. R. Hancock.
[3] C.H.B.E., vol. III, pp. 432–3.
[4] J. E. Kendle, 'The Round Table Movement, New Zealand and the Imperial Conference of 1911', Journal of Commonwealth Political Studies, vol. III, 1965.
[5] New Zealand's main immediate purpose was to get Australian backing for the establishment of a new imperial route via Canada; but Australia had banked her future on the Indian Ocean and the Suez Canal route (Hancock, pp. 28–9).
[6] 'Thus we find ourselves on the old abandoned ground of a centralized Empire with the Dominions in subordination to the central power', (Winnipeg) Free Press, 8 May 1911. Cook, op. cit., p. 40.
[7] 'We easily quashed the Imperial Council of State . . . I have never heard of a more idiotic proposal . . . as far as I can see Lionel Curtis is really the proposer . . . Laurier and I have renewed our friendship . . . He and I agree about everything.' Botha to Smuts, 13 June 1911. Hancock, Smuts, vol. 1, p. 351.
[8] Much of this discussion must be regarded as somewhat academic in view of the lack of interest in the imperial conference and its work shown by the parliaments of the Empire, and

The only important innovation of the 1911 conference was the invitation to the dominion prime ministers to attend a special session of the committee of Imperial Defence where they were able to receive a confidential briefing on the major questions of foreign and imperial policy that the Empire now faced. The practice of occasional attendance by dominion ministers now became established,[1] but this was not held by the British government to involve any acceptance of the principle that the dominions were entitled to participate in the formulation of foreign as well as of defence policy although Borden seems to have been given the impression that this was now the case.[2]

To some extent, such arguments were once again academic. Where questions of foreign policy directly involving a specific issue of interest to a dominion were concerned, their governments were bound to seek a means of seeing that their influence was felt and of protesting if their opinions were not sought.[3] But on the great issues of European and so of world policy with which Britain was wrestling they neither had specific counsel to offer, nor alternative sources of information with which to support any views they might have, nor was it felt that their actual or presumed contributions to the Empire's fighting strength were such as to give them a prescriptive right to take part in the making of the vital decisions.

The main example of a matter of primary interest to a dominion was the Anglo-Japanese alliance.[4] There had always been a problem in the

the unwillingness of the governments to consult them. The Empire Parliamentary Association proposed by Amery and set up in the form of independent branches in each dominion came to be a useful means of informally exchanging views but no more. Amery, op. cit., vol. 1, p. 351.
[1] C.H.B.E., vol. III, pp. 434-6.
[2] Hankey to Drummond, 11 December 1912. Dep. Asquith, 24. M. P. Hankey (1877-1963) (knighted, 1916), a Royal Marine, had been assistant secretary to the C.I.D. from 1908 to 1912 when he became its secretary, holding the post till 1938; secretary to the cabinet, 1916-38, clerk to the privy council, 1923-38, secretary to imperial war cabinet, 1917 and to imperial conferences, 1921, 1923, 1926, 1930, 1937; secretary to British delegation, Paris Peace conference, 1919, and at principal international conferences for next twelve years. Created Baron, 1939. Minister without portfolio, war cabinet, September 1939-May 1940; chancellor, Duchy of Lancaster, May 1940-July 1941; paymaster-general, July 1941-March 1942. (James) Eric Drummond (1876-1951) (knighted, 1916, succeeded as sixteenth Earl of Perth, 1937) entered the Foreign Office in 1900 and acted as one of the prime minister's secretaries from 1912 to 1915. Private secretary to foreign secretary, 1915-19. Secretary-general, League of Nations, 1919-33; ambassador to Italy, October 1933 to May 1939.
[3] Fisher felt that Australia should have been consulted about British policy at the second Hague conference of 1907 and on the Declaration of London of 1909. On their importance, see C.H.B.E., vol. III, pp. 702-10.
[4] I. H. Nish, 'Australia and the Anglo-Japanese Alliance', Australian Journal of Politics and History, vol. IX, 1963.

background arising out of the discriminatory legislation of the Australians against Asian immigrants; but the British government regarded immigration policy as something with which the imperial authority should not interfere, and the Japanese were for their own reasons unwilling to make an issue of it. As Japanese naval power grew, the possibility of a challenge to Australia's policies became more likely; and there were fears in Britain, when the question of renewing the treaty came up, that there might be an outcry from Australia and indeed from Canada also, where something of the same problem existed in respect of British Columbia. It was therefore suggested that the matter had best be discussed in the 1911 Conference. Although Asquith at first thought this highly inopportune, and although the Foreign Office made it clear that the maintenance of the alliance was far too vital an imperial interest for the imperial government to accept any kind of veto on the part of the dominions, this was agreed to. The alliance was therefore the main subject of discussion at the special meeting of the C.I.D. on 26 May; and indeed, the need to find some way of dealing with it may have been the reason why this meeting was originally envisaged. In the end, the renewal of the alliance was unanimously approved, it having been made plain that it would make no difference to the dominions' immigration policies, against which indeed Tokyo now ceased overtly to protest.

The alternative, given the need to provide for the defence of Hong Kong and of Australia, would have been to strengthen British naval forces in the Pacific – an idea that was difficult to reconcile with the current trend of naval policy.[1]

Similarly, South Africa was consulted directly about the negotiations with Germany on colonial matters in 1912 when, as has been said, the Union government proved adamant against any extension of German territory.[2]

The Dictates of Defence

The one area in which a constant dialogue between the United Kingdom and the dominions governments was maintained was that of defence, but of necessity the discussions were largely confidential and

[1] Minutes of 108th meeting of C.I.D., 26 January 1911. Dep. Asquith, Box 132.
[2] Exchange of telegrams between Harcourt and Viscount Gladstone, governor-general of South Africa (1910–14), 29 May, 12 June 1912. Viscount Gladstone Papers, B.M. Add. 45997.

public opinion – except occasionally in Britain over naval construction – was not easy to arouse. Between 1897 and 1907 two points of deep significance had emerged and they retained their importance between 1907 and the outbreak of war. The defence interests of the United Kingdom were different in kind and in degree from those of the colonies, and those of the colonies – and particularly those of what were now styled the dominions – differed profoundly from each other. The historic defence needs of Britain had been to maintain a navy strong enough to protect the British Isles, to sustain the imperial lines of communication and to cut the communications of any enemy or groups of enemies; and to maintain an army able, when the need arose, to reinforce any threatened part of the Empire. To these requirements the change in the diplomatic position had added a new one, that of being able to intervene on the continent in sufficient strength to give reality to Britain's support for French independence and to protect, if need be, the traditional danger points along the southern shores of the narrow seas. The Haldane army reorganization, with its provision for an expeditionary force of some 167,000 men, was the method chosen to meet this new demand. It presupposed – as did most military thinking of the time – a short war in which instant readiness and technical skill would make up for the numerical advantages enjoyed by the continental powers, with their reliance upon general conscription and their ability in case of war to mobilize very large numbers of trained reserves.

There were three lines of possible criticism against a military policy of this kind. There was, first, that of the radicals, which was based essentially upon a denial of the presumption that Britain need be concerned about the balance of power in Europe, and which tended to discount the evidence of German hostility to Britain, or argued that it was the talk of tariff reform and of curtailing Germany's commercial opportunities overseas that explained Germany's persistence in naval competition. Secondly, there was the attitude which regarded the scale of the enterprise as altogether too small, and which could see no way of avoiding compulsory service.[1] The failure of the national service proposals to make headway has already been noted; but its advocates were not easily silenced and there grew to be an uneasy suspicion in some liberal

[1] 'Indeed, I think I go rather further than you do,' wrote Milner to Lord Roberts on 22 July 1905, 'at least than anything you have said yet. I don't believe we can escape – I don't see why we should – from one universal, personal service which all other great nations of Europe have adopted, and from which, I believe, none of them dream of going back.' Milner Papers, A. 1, Letters, 1905–6.

circles that the War Office's mind was not altogether closed on the subject.[1] Finally, there was the argument that the preservation of naval supremacy made the land effort unnecessary and withdrew funds which could be used for social purposes at home.

This position was well expressed by Churchill, President of the Board of Trade, in a memorandum for the cabinet committee on the estimates in 1908. The expeditionary force now available was more than double the force considered necessary before 1899, and much larger than that asked for by Brodrick the last conservative secretary of state: 'No other nation has ever made so dangerous and provocative a provision as a force of 166,000 expressly ready at a month's notice to cross the seas and effect a descent upon the territory of any Power.'[2] In another document, Churchill argued that it was not possible to provide in peacetime for perils of the first magnitude, such as a struggle with Russia on the Indian frontier or with Germany in Europe. The present force could meet all possible minor emergencies such as might arise in Egypt or India; nothing more need be done immediately; ultimate safety could only lie in 'the possession of undisputed naval supremacy' which could enable Britain in the end to 'realize and apply the whole energies' of the British people and of other peoples under Britain's 'control'.[3]

The assumption that the strength of the dominions was still under British 'control' was obviously deep-rooted as the dominion nationalists suspected; nor, of course, did Churchill's argument make allowances for the fact that Britain's allies in Europe might be crushed before Britain's strength could be summoned to their aid. It was indeed a

[1] In April 1913 the *Westminster Gazette* published an article contending that the War Office 'blind to every other military need except a desire to intervene in the Continent of Europe, forgetful of the necessity of a supreme Navy, were pressing for a large increase in our forces, presumably on a compulsory basis, in order to enable us to intervene in European quarrels'. Writing to Spender, Seely, the secretary of state for war argued that even leaving Europe out of consideration, British responsibilities in Egypt and India, to say nothing of the Mediterranean and China, were such as might require the entire expeditionary force to enable Britain to hold its own. Nevertheless, he assured Spender that the government still adhered to the voluntary principle. Spender Papers, B.M. Add. 46392. John Edward Seely (1868–1947) (created Lord Mottistone, 1933) was under-secretary for the colonies, 1908–11 and for war, 1911–12. He was secretary of state for war from June 1912 until March 1914 when Asquith took over the War Office after the 'Curragh mutiny'. After war service during which he commanded the Canadian cavalry brigade, Seely became parliamentary under-secretary at the Ministry of Munitions from July 1918 to January 1919 and under-secretary of state for air from January to November 1919.
[2] Winston Churchill, Memorandum for Cabinet Committee on Estimates, 18 June 1908. Asquith Dep. Box 98.
[3] Winston Churchill, Note upon British military needs, 27 June 1908. Ibid.

vision of British strategy which was inspired, even if not consciously, by the experience of the struggle against Napoleon since when much had changed. But it was certainly in tune with dominant naval thinking at the time and even later.

Fisher had always claimed that for Britain a continental struggle by regular land warfare was impracticable, and that the correct strategy was to make use of combined naval and military expeditions against the outlying possessions of the enemy.[1] Nor would the naval experts agree that invasion of the home islands was a possibility justifying vast military expenditure. Lord Roberts and other military experts urged upon Balfour in July 1907 that now that Germany was the presumed enemy the chances of a serious invasion were much greater than when they had been ruled out by the defence committee in 1902–3, and that in the new circumstances there would be a role for land forces as well. Clarke, to whom Balfour passed on these views, found them unacceptable and maintained that the question was still a purely naval one.[2] This was certainly Fisher's view and one reiterated by him as late as May 1914.[3] In 1908 the C.I.D. had in fact looked at the matter again and come to the conclusion that so long as naval supremacy was assured against any reasonable combination of powers, no invasion was possible.[4]

Defence against invasion was not, however, the only problem facing the fleet in this period. The Mediterranean and its defences retained a high priority in the thinking of the naval strategists, and became even more important when the navy turned over to oil for fuel and, consequently, relied on stability in the Persian Gulf and swift access to the area by the shortest route.[5] It would, furthermore, be a serious matter if Egypt and Cyprus were prone to attack so that reinforcements could not be brought to or drawn from them, as it would take five or six weeks

[1] Fisher to Edward VII, 4 October 1907. Marder, *Fear God and Dread Nought*, vol. 2, p. 143.
[2] Balfour to Clarke, 20 July 1907; Clarke to Balfour, 18 August 1907. Balfour Papers, B.M. Add. 49702.
[3] Fisher to Prince of Wales, 16 October 1907; to Edward Goulding mid-November 1908; to Asquith early May 1914. Marder, op. cit., pp. 147, 201, 504.
[4] Minutes of 100th meeting of C.I.D., 22 October 1908. Dep. Asquith, Box 132.
[5] Oil gave ships greater speed, a greater radius and the possibility of refuelling at sea instead of having to put into coaling stations. The changeover began before 1911 for the smaller vessels. The estimates of April 1912 included provision for fast oil-burning dreadnoughts. A Royal Commission was appointed to study the whole question and on 17 July 1913 Churchill announced that the basic decision in favour of oil had been taken. Cf. Churchill, op. cit., vol. 2, pp. 607–9. Marder, *From Dreadnought to Scapa Flow*, vol. 1, pp. 269–70. It is interesting to note that the fact that Britain's arrangement with the Russians gave her control over the main Persian oilfields was an accident; in 1907 their importance was still unguessed.

to bring troops from India. Reinforcements to and from Australia and New Zealand would also have to take the long route round the Cape.[1] Indeed, some students of war were opposed to the whole policy of denuding the Mediterranean, 'permanently the centre of naval gravity in Europe' for the sake of the North Sea.[2] It was also held that it was no use depending upon alliances for this purpose: 'Britain either is or is not one of the Great Powers of the World. Her position in this respect depends solely upon sea-command and sea-command in the Mediterranean.' And this, of course, was supported by the thesis that Britain was primarily a trading nation which would be 'mad' to entangle itself 'in a continental strife on land'.[3]

For the government, the choice could not be made in such absolute terms; the Admiralty might decry all alliances and be in favour of meeting all Britain's needs by increasing the number of ships. The army and Foreign Office were, as we have seen, in favour of an active understanding with France. The original compromise was on a fleet strong enough to deal with either France or Italy. Italy's position became stronger after her conquest of Tripoli in 1911, and in May 1912 Anglo-French naval conversations were begun. The French brought about a concentration of their fleet in the Mediterranean equal to that of the Austrians and Italians together. A policy which seemed to imply dependence upon the French – which Churchill and the Admiralty would have denied was the case, on the ground that Britain's own naval dispositions were the same as they would have been in any case – was not palatable to all the cabinet.[4] His predecessor as first lord, McKenna, wrote: 'If it is accepted as an axiom of British naval strategy that our dispositions are to be made with a view to limiting our operations to the North Sea, while upon France is to fall the duty of building against and holding in check the German allies elsewhere, our colonies and our trade will depend not on British power but on French goodwill.'[5] The argument was accepted in so far as the naval co-operation agreement

[1] Memorandum by secretary of state for war, 9 May 1912. Dep. Asquith, Box 107.
[2] Esher to Spender, 5 June 1912. Spender Papers, B.M. Add. 46392.
[3] Esher to Balfour, 30 May 1912. Balfour Papers, B.M. Add. 49719.
[4] Churchill, op. cit., pp. 580–96.
[5] Memorandum by McKenna, 3 July 1912. Dep. Asquith, Box 107. These sentiments did not prevent McKenna from being among the six ministers who wrote to Asquith on 29 January 1914 protesting against the increase in the naval estimates now being demanded. Simon Papers. Cf. Churchill, op. cit., pp. 655–86. Reginald McKenna (1863–1943), M.P. since 1895, had been financial secretary to the treasury and president of the Board of Education before becoming first lord of the admiralty in April 1908; he was home secretary, October 1911–May 1915 and chancellor of the exchequer, May 1915–December 1916.

of February 1913 was a technical one, and did not include any commitments. But the French use in July 1914 of the argument that the British were now in honour bound to defend their northern coasts which they had denuded for the sake of the Mediterranean, gave force to the argument that in defence matters no agreement is a purely technical one.[1]

What is perhaps most startling in retrospect is the fact that the improvements in the capacity of British forces, both on land and at sea, were not accompanied by any agreement on the strategic doctrine for their use. Neither Fisher nor his successor, Sir Arthur Wilson, believed in using the machinery of the C.I.D. to agree with the army upon the course to be followed in case of war. They believed that the war plan was a matter for the first sea lord alone, and should be divulged to the army only when war broke out. In fact, Fisher was too immersed in other matters to work out a war plan at all.[2] The discussions held at the War Office and the C.I.D. during the imperial conference of 1911 showed how significantly different were the expectations of the two services. Only at the time of Agadir was it made clear that the army had won its battle and that the navy's first task would be safely to transport to France Britain's new expeditionary force.

The Dominions and Naval and Military Dispositions

From Fisher's point of view the dominions were at first no more reliable than foreign allies: 'The Colonies one and all grab all they possibly can out of us and give nothing back. *They are all alike.*'[3] But for the British cabinet, faced with the mounting bill for defence, the question of the role of the colonies could not be dismissed so easily, and throughout the period efforts were made to discover the ways in which they could best contribute to the common defence without weakening their local capacities, and without upsetting their national susceptibilities. In April 1907 Haig, soon after having been brought back from India by Haldane, drew up a memorandum pointing out the need for uniformity between the British army and their forces in organization, tactics, administration, and equipment; and this was generally found acceptable.[4]

[1] Marder, op. cit., pp. 287 ff.
[2] Marder, *Fear God and Dread Nought*, vol. 2, pp. 215–16.
[3] Marder, *Fear God and Dread Nought*, vol. 2, p. 139.
[4] Nowell-Smith (ed.), *Edwardian England*, p. 533. Douglas Haig (1861–1928) (knighted 1909, Earl Haig 1919) was (between two spells of staff work in India) at the War Office between

But although Haldane talked of making common plans for the concentration of the various local forces in an emergency,[1] it was not the military but the naval side of possible imperial co-operation that bulked largest.

Although the preparations for the special imperial conference on defence held in July 1909 included correspondence about the chief of staff's proposals,[2] the main accent was on naval affairs. The imperial conference of 1907 had shown that there was agreement that something should be done, particularly since neither Australia nor Britain was satisfied with the existing naval agreement, but there was no unanimity of view on the way forward.[3]

From the Admiralty's point of view, the question of central control was still all-important in wartime, though it was prepared to accede to the dominions' insistence on the peacetime control of their own forces, while pointing out that this made it difficult to envisage exchanges of personnel as a method of obtaining a common training.[4] Now that New Zealand was prepared to offer a battleship, Canada to assume more responsibility for local defence and to spend some money on a naval service, and Australia to build upon a local naval force, the conference

---

1906 and 1909, where he was responsible for the scheme for the Imperial General Staff organization. He returned to England in 1911, took the first army corps to France in August 1914 and succeeded Sir John French as commander-in-chief in December 1915. Commander-in-chief, home forces, 1919–21.

[1] Haldane to Kitchener, 8 July 1909. Balfour Papers, B.M. Add. 49724.

[2] Dep. Asquith, Box 101, Folios 6, 23, 47. Nothing seems to have come of a suggestion made in 1905 that New Zealand should offer a regiment or battalion to serve in India, paid by and under the control of the Indian military authorities, with a linked regiment or battalion in New Zealand, exchanging stations at regular intervals. Lord Plunket, governor-general of New Zealand to Lord Crewe, 14 June 1909. Dep. Asquith, Box 101, Folio 40. The idea of associating Australia and New Zealand with the defence of British interests on the mainland of Asia was a tempting one to the imperially minded. During a tour of Australia in 1913, Amery delivered a speech at Melbourne on the 'Twin Empires' in which he urged Australia to look beyond the conception of a White Commonwealth to the future development of Asia and especially to India as an ally there. Amery, op. cit., vol. 1, p. 430. But such ideas were very premature in the Australian context. Australian eyes were fixed upon the immediate proximity of the Germans in their Pacific colonies, and on the more distant pressure from Japan and China for outlets for their surplus population. Australia looked north and north-east, not north-west – except as its line of communication to Britain itself.

[3] Deakin had tried the idea in 1905 that the Australians should pay and maintain a national steamship line whose ships could be converted to armed cruisers in time of war; but this had not been thought practicable. Australian opinion was now in favour of a flotilla of torpedo boats rather than of contributing a dreadnought which might never be seen in Australian waters. Lord Dudley, governor-general of Australia to colonial secretary, 22 July 1909. Dep. Asquith, Box 101, Folio 38.

[4] Note by J. R. Chancellor, secretary colonial defence committee, 20 May 1909. Dep. Asquith, Box 100.

could, it was hoped, make useful proposals 'in furtherance . . . of the simple strategical ideal that the maximum of power would be obtained, if all parts of the Empire contributed according to their needs and resources, to the maintenance of the British navy'.[1]

The Canadians were once again the most insistent on their independence of a central control. President Roosevelt had wished for an invitation for the American fleet (busy showing the flag in the Pacific in order to warn the Japanese of its power) to visit Vancouver. Mackenzie King was opposed to this, lest it encourage a feeling of dependence on the United States and strengthen annexationist sentiment in the west. What the situation revealed was the need for Canada to have her own navy; although this would not mean Canada acting independently of Britain, she would better be able to control the use to which her money would be put than by making financial contributions to the expansion of the British navy.[2] In March 1909 the Canadian House of Commons unanimously adopted a resolution calling for the establishment of a Canadian naval force; but although this was done on conservative initiative, the unanimity did not last and some conservatives demanded instead that Canada contribute dreadnoughts to the British navy. The separate naval force became liberal policy.[3] This was accepted at the 1909 conference with the intention that the fleet should be divided between the Pacific and Atlantic.[4] The main positive result of the conference was, however, the proposed remodelling of naval dispositions in the Far East. A Pacific fleet was to be set up consisting of the East Indies and China squadron owned and controlled by the British admiralty, and an Australian squadron owned and controlled by the Australian government.[5] For the moment even Fisher's enthusiasm was aroused at the prospects for the future which this scheme held out: 'It means *eventually* Canada, Australia, New Zealand, the Cape (that is South Africa), and India *running a complete Navy*. We manage the job in Europe. They'll manage it against the Yankees, Japs, and Chinese, as occasion requires out there.'[6]

[1] Memorandum by first lord of the admiralty, McKenna, 20 July 1909. Dep. Asquith, Box 101, Folio 87.   [2] Diary, 27 February 1908, quoted Dawson, *Mackenzie King*, pp. 160-1.
[3] Cook, *John Dafoe and the Free Press*, pp. 36-9.
[4] On the 1909 conference and its results, see W. C. B. Tunstall, 'Imperial Defence, 1897–1914', *C.H.B.E.*, vol. III, ch. XV.
[5] New Zealand was to pay for a battle-cruiser for the China squadron, and pay towards the squadron's maintenance.
[6] Fisher to Esher, 13 September 1909; cf. Fisher to the naval journalist, Gerard Fiennes, 14 April 1910. Marder, *Fear God and Dread Nought*, vol. 2, pp. 266, 321.

But both the Canadian and the Australasian solution proved abortive. Canadian opinion was not wholly converted to the idea of a Canadian navy and to the amount of money which would be entailed in its creation.[1] When Laurier arrived at the imperial conference of 1911, the policy was still unchanged and some steps had been taken to implement it. But the Admiralty's interpretation of the position appeared to Laurier to suggest that its centralizing philosophy had not been abandoned and he claimed in return that Canada could not merely determine to what use her fleet should be put in time of war but even decide whether or not she took part in a United Kingdom war at all. It would, in his view, be Canada's duty to go to war against Germany but not necessarily against Germany's allies; technically, of course, the dominions would be at war whenever the United Kingdom was, but this did not oblige them actually to engage in operations.[2]

In the event, the discussion was an academic one. When Laurier went down to defeat over reciprocity in the election that year, the Canadian navy was sunk with him. His conservative successor Borden abandoned the Laurier programme and instead put forward in December 1912 a proposal to appropriate $35 million to enable the British government to build three dreadnoughts. This followed a visit to London by Borden who attended a meeting of the C.I.D. at which naval defence was discussed as well as future dominion representation at the C.I.D.[3] But the idea of a direct contribution was not to the taste of liberal opinion which could not see a direct connection between the German threat to Britain's naval supremacy and a Canadian contribution.[4] The French Canadian leader Bourassa also took the view that Canada's duty was her own defence; if she contributed to 'imperial armaments' it could only be on the basis of representation in the organs which decided upon the policy that might lead to their use.[5] The result

[1] On Canadian policy from 1909 to 1914, see Preston, op. cit., chs. 12 to 14.
[2] Minutes of 112th meeting of C.I.D., 29 May 1911. Dep. Asquith, Box 132.
[3] Minutes of 119th meeting of C.I.D., 1 August 1912. Dep. Asquith, Box 132. This was followed at Borden's request by a written statement from Churchill emphasizing the importance of the proposed contribution the absence of which would necessitate still further efforts from the United Kingdom. Dep. Asquith, 107, 108. Cf. Randolph Churchill, *Winston S. Churchill*, vol. 2, pp. 629–30.
[4] Cook, op. cit., pp. 57–64.
[5] Henri Bourassa to Milner, 7 October 1912. Replying, Milner who was in Montreal at the time, wrote that he agreed that contributions should not be given without representation: 'I believe . . . that the policy of the Empire would be a better policy – broader, simpler, more pacific as well as more effective, if it were the result of deliberations of men from all parts of the Empire, than it is now decided by British statesmen who are mainly preoccupied with

was that the liberal-controlled senate rejected Borden's bill in April 1913, and Canada entered the war with scarcely any naval armaments to speak of.

The Admiralty under Churchill's rule showed itself lukewarm to the Pacific fleet idea.[1] Progress towards building up strength in the Far East was slow. Churchill's scheme for an imperial naval squadron based on Gibraltar, consisting of the three proposed Canadian-financed dreadnoughts, H.M.S. *New Zealand* and the projected H.M.S. *Malaya*, made no impact and nothing came of it.[2] Instead, both Australia and New Zealand moved towards becoming naval powers on their own,[3] though H.M.S. *New Zealand* was in fact used in the North Sea.

After all the talk and thought given to the naval question, it was the Admiralty's policy that prevailed when war came; the domination of home waters, the control of what warships the dominions possessed, and the invoking of the Anglo-Japanese alliance to deal with Germany in the Pacific. On the military side, which had bulked less large in debate, what had been done was more impressive. The influence of the new imperial general staff, as the general staff was styled as a result of the 1909 conference, was increased by the setting up of sections in Canada, Australia, and New Zealand; the development of local forces was stimulated by the visits of Sir John French to Canada in 1910, and by Kitchener to Australia and New Zealand in 1909–10, when each dominion agreed to adopt schemes for compulsory military training. Amery's proposal that a large permanent force of troops should be kept in South Africa and counted as part of the home establishment so as to be an imperial reserve did not gain acceptance,[4] as most British troops were going to be needed nearer home; but a new territorial army was created in the Union itself.

The means by which the dominions were to make their important

---

purely British not to say local interests and considerations . . .' Milner to Bourassa, 9 October 1912. Milner Papers, CLXXIV, 1908–17, Canada (Bodl. 189). But this echo of federalist ideas was scarcely in tune with either the British or the Canadian mood of the time.

[1] Fisher blamed his successor for the failure to proceed with the scheme: 'Of course, the real culprit is A. K. Wilson who will not understand that our great colonies are practically independent nations and are not going to subscribe to other people's navies.' Fisher to Sir Reginald Henderson, 10 February 1914. Marder, *Fear God and Dread Nought*, vol. 2, 266 fn.

[2] On the developments of this period, see Gordon, op. cit., pp. 242 ff. Churchill, op. cit., vol. 2, chs. 15 to 17.

[3] New Zealand's anxieties and intentions were explained to the C.I.D. by her defence minister early in 1913. Minutes of 122nd and 123rd meeting of C.I.D., 6 February and 11 April 1913. Dep. Asquith, Box 132. Cf. Gordon, op. cit., ch. XII.

[4] Amery's proposal was made in 1909. Balfour Papers, B.M. Add. 49775.

contributions to the struggle against Germany were thus in process of creation by 1914, and in some cases the preparations were far advanced; but their share in the making of the main strategic plans was unimportant. By 1911 the British army was committed to operations as 'left-flank appendage of the French army'.[1] The British cabinet as a whole was by 1912 aware of how far the military talks had gone and contained within it an opposition which objected not to the actual military proposals but to any suggestion that this implied a binding commitment to enter into a Franco-German conflict should one break out. Opposition was strengthened by the naval agreement of 1912 and by the exchange of letters between Grey and the French ambassador, Paul Cambon, on 22 November 1912, in which the two governments agreed to consult together should there be reason to fear an act of aggression or a threat to the peace. They had their way in that the formula was less definite respecting joint action than that originally proposed by the French, and it was formally laid down that consultation between experts was not to be regarded as a commitment to action on the part of either government.[2] Nevertheless, the commitment was there; and since all planning on the British side was based on the arrangements made, there was no question but that unless Britain remained militarily inactive, a continental strategy would be adopted. Since the bulk of the members of the British cabinet itself were thus left with only a partial understanding of the position, it would have been remarkable if dominion statesmen had been any clearer on the subject; 'to what extent the Dominion governments were eventually informed (about the military conversations) is uncertain'; Borden's memoirs are silent as to his having been told during his visit to London in 1912.[3]

Indian Nationalism and Defence

One problem continued to baffle the imagination and intelligence of liberal and imperialist alike; what to do about India. 'The English rule in India is surely one of the most extraordinary accidents that has ever happened in history. We are there like a man who has fallen off a ladder

---

[1] Tunstall, in *C.H.B.E.*, vol. III, p. 593. The principal author of the plan was Sir Henry Wilson (1864–1922) (knighted 1915, baronet 1919) who was director of Military Operations, 1910–14, and after holding important posts in France, C.I.G.S. from 1918 until February 1922 when he was elected to the House of Commons for an Ulster seat. He was assassinated by Sinn Feiners in June of that year.

[2] Taylor, *The Struggle for Mastery in Europe*, pp. 480–1.

[3] Tunstall, loc. cit., p. 592.

on to the back of an elephant and doesn't know what to do or how to get down. Until something happens he remains.'[1] Something now looked more likely to come from Indian developments than from British decisions at home. Curzon, for all his great qualities, had underestimated the strength of the nationalist movement. The question for his successors was whether self-government within the Empire was a conceivable goal, and an experiment based on liberal beliefs was now inevitable. Minto, appointed by Balfour, was from December 1905 to November 1910 responsible to Morley as secretary of state: 'for five crucial years a whig viceroy and an Indian minister of advanced liberal views faced demands for constitutional reform, and the problems posed by the rise of a terrorist movement and of organized Muslim nationalism'.[2] They also faced a body of opinion which held to the view, with which they themselves sympathized, that western parliamentary institutions, in however diluted a form, were unsuitable to Indian conditions. If concessions were once made the result would be anarchy or foreign conquest.[3] Yet how could an absolutist régime in India be fitted into an Empire that was in other respects taking on the aspect of a Commonwealth of self-governing nations?

One of the difficulties in handling these issues was that no regular means existed of keeping parliament in touch with Indian affairs. The suggestion of a royal commission on constitutional reform made by Gokhale in 1906, and Morley's own suggestion of reviving the parliamentary joint committee that had existed in the time of the East India Company, were both rejected by Minto.[4] Nor was the Council of India a suitable body for looking after India's interests and for screening her from party pressures in Britain.[5] Indian policy remained in this period something apart from the general run of affairs, only called to mind by some manifestation of nationalist feeling or direct threat from outside.

In these circumstances, it is not surprising that the House of Commons itself showed little interest in the Morley–Minto reforms which led to the India Councils act of 1909 and the modest enlargement of the

[1] H. G. Wells, *The New Macchiavelli* (1911), Penguin edn, p. 267.
[2] R. J. Moore, *Liberalism and Indian Politics, 1872–1922* (London, Arnold, 1966), p. 81.
[3] S. R. Mehrotra, *India and the Commonwealth, 1885–1929* (1965), pp. 51, 56–8.
[4] Moore, op. cit., p. 124.
[5] 'My experience tells me that there are no more dangerous advisers than the retired Indian official . . . The ideas of the retired Anglo-Indian have crystallized under the influence of the local atmosphere and surroundings in which he lived in years gone by. Those ideas are out of date but they still serve to guide the people of England.' Minto to Morley, 14 July 1910. M. N. Das, *India under Morley and Minto* (London, Allen & Unwin, 1964), p. 70.

representative principle that it embodied.[1] The sympathies of the labour party and of many liberals for the congress party did not stir the government side of the House to action.[2] Even so, Minto himself was convinced that it was agitation in Britain that produced demands in India for a pace of advance that could not be accepted.[3]

Some of the anxiety was over Minto's need to use stern measures to deal with the terrorist section of the national movement and advocates of boycott and physical force.[4] But there was also the fact that neither he nor Morley conceived of their reforms as a step on the road to responsible government, and so were liable to criticism for having ruined the prospect of co-operating with the Indian moderates in an agreed programme of constitutional advance.[5] In a curious way this reflected not so much imperial pride as historical resignation. British rule in India was only a passing phase and nothing could be done to give it roots. 'We all feel,' wrote Minto to Morley, 'that we are mere sojourners in the land, that we are only camping and on the march'; and he contrasted the coming and going of Englishmen in India with the permanence of the British element in Canada. 'Your way of putting this,' replied Morley, 'helps me to realize how intensely artificial and unnatural is our mighty Raj. And it sets one wondering whether it can possibly last. It surely cannot and our only business is to do what we can to make the next transition whatever it may turn out to be something of an improvement.'[6]

In 1910 the ageing Morley was succeeded by Lord Crewe, and Hardinge achieved his ambition of becoming viceroy. Between their assumption of office and the outbreak of war things in India went some-

[1] For the Morley–Minto Reforms, see Moore, op. cit., pp. 84–101, and the documents in C. H. Philips, *The Evolution of India and Pakistan*, pp. 80–91.
[2] On the divisions over India in British politics, see S. R. Wasti, *Lord Minto and the Indian Nationalist Movement* (Oxford, 1964), p. 10.
[3] 'Our great danger is at home – if we were only left to look after ourselves here it would be alright – but idiotic questions in the House of Commons do needless harm and agitators in the old country assisted by people whom one hates to recognize as one's fellow-countrymen keep up a constant correspondence with agitators here – and people at home have become so sensational – if a squib went off in a Calcutta street they would think India was in a blaze.' Minto to General Hutton, 2 February 1909. Hutton Papers, B.M. Add. 50081. 'Our great danger is the House of Commons . . . and if India becomes a playground for party politicians at home we shall have such an awakening here some day as will strain our strength to the uttermost.' Minto to Hutton, 23 October 1909. Ibid. Cf. the letters from Minto to Morley in 1906 and 1907, quoted by Das, op. cit., pp. 66, 72.
[4] Moore, op. cit., pp. 94–8.
[5] Ibid., pp. 98–101; cf. Mehrotra, op. cit., pp. 58–9.
[6] Minto to Morley, 24 July 1907; Morley to Minto, 15 August 1907, quoted by Das, op. cit., p. 51.

what more easily. The spirit of the régime was one of guarded liberalism. The reunification of Bengal, the removal of the capital to Delhi the seat of the Moghul emperors, a further devolution of powers to the provinces (especially in financial matters), and the setting up of a royal commission on recruitment to civil service with a mandate to look into the barriers against the recruitment of Indians, all helped to improve the atmosphere.[1] The royal durbar of December 1911 might be regarded as marking the last occasion on which the idea of peaceful Indian evolution under the British crown as an acceptable and agreed goal was given appropriate ceremonial expression, with a very large apparent measure of Indian consent. But it was also made clear that the more far-reaching explanations of the government's purposes, such as that given in a speech by the new under-secretary, Edwin Montagu, were not to be regarded as committing the government to a plan for creating in India a federation of autonomous provinces only loosely held together at the centre.[2] The repudiation of such intentions did not prevent Curzon and other representatives of the conservative view from making it their business specifically to repudiate any notion that India could aspire even in the distant future to the status of a dominion, with an Indian prime minister and an Indian commander-in-chief.[3]

One aspect of Indian affairs which directly affected imperial policy was the attitude of the Moslems, who insisted successfully that any increase in the elected element in Indian government must allow them separate electorates so that they should not be swamped by the Hindu majority.[4] Much was to be made later of the allegation that on this and other occasions the British deliberately encouraged Moslem political ambitions so as to split the nationalist movement. But this was not true of Minto.[5] Indeed, the history of the granting of self-governing and representative institutions all over the Empire shows that the immediate effect of a movement in this direction has always been to increase the fears of local minorities; and a knowledge of European history, particularly, for instance, of events in the Habsburg empire, should have prepared people for this phenomenon. The device of separate electorates was the obvious one for the Moslems' purpose.[6]

---

[1] Moore, op. cit., pp. 107–8.   [2] Mehrotra, op. cit., pp. 60–4.
[3] Philips, op. cit., pp. 91–5.
[4] See the Muslim address to Lord Minto, 1 October 1906. Philips, op. cit., p. 190, and the documents that follow.
[5] Wasti, op. cit., p. 13.
[6] Hardinge's reversal of Curzon's partition of Bengal was, however, regarded as a set-back

What is true, is that the British were particularly worried about Moslem opinion because of their involvement in the politics of the Moslem world as a whole. The Indian Moslems had been unhappy about the deterioration of Anglo-Turkish relations which had been going on since the 1890s. What would be their attitude in an Anglo-Turkish war? The *entente* with Russia and its consequences in Persia did nothing to diminish these Moslem anxieties, and there was disappointment when Britain failed to support Turkey against Italy in 1911 and over her attitudes at the time of the Balkan war of 1912. On the British side there were anxieties lest Germany exploit this situation,[1] and these proved not unfounded.[2] By 1914 there had been a *rapprochement* of Moslem and non-Moslem opinion in India and of the moderate and extremist wings of the nationalist movement, so that, although the Indian role in government was principally a matter of the provinces, Britain could not afford to ignore the fact that in giving its advice on imperial policy the government of India was obliged to take account of an already far from negligible body of opinion.

Britain was affected in its capacity for solving India's problems by the unhelpful attitude of other Commonwealth countries. The problem of discrimination against Indians in the dominions was discussed at the 1911 imperial conference with reference to merchant shipping, but by now the imperial government could do little but offer sympathy.[3] The most important single cause of difficulty was presented by South Africa. Discrimination by the Transvaal had led the Indian community under Gandhi's leadership to take the imperial side in the Boer war, but Milner proved no more sympathetic to its claims after victory. Once self-government was granted, the position worsened further, and Gandhi made his reputation by his passive resistance movement. The Indian nationalist leader, Gokhale, went to South Africa in 1912 to negotiate on behalf of the Indian government and in November 1913 the viceroy, Hardinge, publicly expressed 'the sympathy of India, deep

for the Muslim League, and made some Moslems feel that they would after all do better to throw in their lot with Congress. Moore, op. cit., p. 109.
[1] Of Marschall von Bieberstein, the German ambassador at Constantinople from 1897 to 1912, Fisher wrote, 'For years now I've been trying to make people in authority realize that he is the greatest man in Europe . . . He understands that Islam is the key of the British Empire.' Fisher to Arnold White, 21 May 1912. Marder, *Fear God and Dread Nought*, vol. 2, p. 129 fn.
[2] Fritz Fischer, *Germany's Aims in the First World War* (1967), pp. 120 ff.
[3] I. R. Hancock, 'The 1911 Imperial Conference', *Historical Studies: Australia and New Zealand*, vol. XII, October 1966, pp. 356 ff.

and burning, and not only of India, but of all lovers of India' like himself 'for their compatriots in South Africa in their resistance to invidious and unjust laws'.[1] Some of the most immediate grievances of the Indian community were redressed by an act of the South African parliament in July 1914; but fundamentally there could be no meeting-place between the Indian demand for at least ultimate equality of opportunity, and the dominant racial instinct of Boer nationalism.[2] Indians were therefore bound to regard with suspicion any plans for a reorganization of the Empire which would give the dominion governments a greater voice in general matters of imperial policy. The leverage, political, economic, and sentimental, that India might hope to exercise over Britain itself would not exist in the case of governments with no responsibility for India and little concern for the interests or feelings of her people.[3]

The changes in Britain's relations in Europe were, of course, directly significant where the defence of India itself was concerned, as the *entente* with Russia entitled the home government to believe that the threat to India's frontiers was no longer immediate. Morley was thus able to refuse much extra military expenditure, and the question was now rather whether India could itself contribute forces to the European theatre in the event of war with Germany. Kitchener's successor in 1909, General Sir O'Moore Creagh, found that this was not contemplated by either the Indian government or the India Office which had not equipped the Indian army for this purpose.[4] But in October 1911 the viceroy was surprised to find that the War Office was in direct correspondence with the Indian military authorities about the dispatch of troops to Europe in the event of a crisis. Crewe informed him that the cabinet had not assented to such a plan, and that Asquith and Grey believed, as did Crewe himself, that they would never agree to it.[5] Nevertheless another inquiry from the War Office came in July 1913, though by the time an answer was received hostilities had already broken out.

It was not only India's northern frontiers that concerned the Indian

[1] E. Thompson and G. T. Garratt, *Rise and Fulfilment of British Rule in India* (1934), pp. 585–7.
[2] See the account of the relations between Smuts and Gandhi in Hancock, *Smuts*, vol. 1, pp. 321–47.
[3] Only Kerr of the Round Table group seems to have favoured Indian representation in the proposed imperial parliament. Kerr to Brand, 18 April 1912 and 25 April 1912 (Brand Papers). See his article 'India and the Empire', *The Round Table*, September 1912.
[4] Nowell-Smith (ed.), *Edwardian England*, p. 525.
[5] Lord Hardinge, *My Indian Years* (1948), pp. 32–3.

government from the point of view of defence. The Indian Ocean and the Persian Gulf also came within the sphere of its responsibilities. At a meeting of the C.I.D. in 1911, Kitchener emphasized the importance of the Gulf and declared that if the Turks established control over Kuwait, the loss of prestige that this would entail would be damaging in India itself.[1]

The Indian government devoted itself to fostering the independence of the Gulf sheiks on the Persian side of the frontier just as the British government upheld those on the other side with whom it had entered into treaty relationships. The political officers there were appointed by the government of India, which also supplied any military forces which were necessary. Relations with the government at Teheran, which wished to assert its authority, raised difficulties; and at Teheran it was the United Kingdom not India that was represented, so that it was not easy to keep policies in step.[2] Oil provided a new and vital factor in the whole situation, and the overlap between the London-based Empire and the empire based on New Delhi and Simla was to continue to cause trouble during the war and even afterwards.

The Intractability of the Irish Question

If it seems that the British statesmen of the period left the great and decisive issues of defence and foreign policy very much in the hands of professionals, the reason lies not only in the important developments that were going on in the country, but also in continued preoccupation with the Irish question. This became even more pronounced when, after the elections of 1910, the liberals' parliamentary position became dependent upon the Irish, and the parliament act of 1911 removed the powers of the House of Lords indefinitely to obstruct a home rule measure. The existence of a hostile and sullen Ireland was not a matter which could fail to concern any British government at a time of international tensions; nor could the government overlook the impact of Irish discontent upon opinion and even policy in the United States, Canada, and Australia.

The liberal party's commitment was to home rule, and by 1914 a high proportion of the energies of the party and government were devoted to the passage of the bill and to finding a solution to the problem of

[1] 110th meeting of the C.I.D., 4 May 1911. Dep. Asquith, Box 132.
[2] John Marlowe, *Late Victorian, The Life of Sir Arnold Talbot Wilson* (1967), pp. 42, 89.

Ulster which in the spring of that year brought the country to the verge of civil war. Conservative imperialists were divided between the totally intransigent, and those who believed that the Irish problem might be turned to positive advantage in making for a political recasting of the imperial structure as a whole.

If devolution could be an acceptable solution, if the United Kingdom itself were to be turned into a federation, then the wider federal scheme might at last get a fair hearing.

A Federation of the British Isles which will give each portion of the United Kingdom provincial rights like those enjoyed by the pro- vinces of Canada with a representation proportionate to its popula- tion in the Central Federal Parliament sitting in London, offers the only means that I am aware of [wrote Earl Grey] for reducing the over-representation of Ireland at Westminster to its proper limits without making a present of a new grievance to the Irish people. . . . To Canadian thinkers [continued Grey (who claimed that Laurier had read his letter with approval)] the Federation of the United Kingdom is a condition precedent to the Federation of the Empire. As soon as the United Kingdom is federated, Canada, or any other of the self-governing Dominions will have the power of entering the Federal Union as soon as they are prepared to adopt the Federal Tariff.[1]

Grey repeated the same views in a letter of 12 October 1911, but his correspondent replied that the Irish nationalists would never accept a status similar to that of Quebec in Canada; they would insist on home rule proper and the liberals would introduce a bill on the 1886 model.[2] On the liberal side, Churchill was attracted for a time in 1911–12 by a devolution scheme as a means of meeting Ulster's case.[3] Other liberals, however, dismissed this as a reversion to Churchill's earlier toryism, perhaps due to the persuasion of his 'young friends of the Round Table'.[4]

Milner himself, although approving of devolution for its own sake,

[1] Grey to Lord Brassey, 5 March 1910. Austen Chamberlain Papers, AC. 8/10. Cf. Grey to Balfour, 23 February 1910. Balfour Papers, B.M. Add. 49697.
[2] Grey to Lord Balcarres, 12 October 1911; Balcarres to Grey, 16 December 1911. Bryce Papers, U.S.A., vol. 33.
[3] Amery, op. cit., vol. 1, pp. 404–7.
[4] Correspondence between Sir Courtenay Ilbert and Lord Bryce. Bryce Papers, English Correspondence, vol. 13.

did not believe that it would be a basis for imperial federation; Ireland, with Canada's degree of autonomy would have taken a step towards a total dissolution of the tie with Britain, while an Ireland with no more autonomy than Ontario would have no imperial significance.[1] His own suggestion, that tariffs could be the clue and that if the Irish were offered a preference in the British market more favourable than that enjoyed by Canadians or Australians they would settle for less than dominion status, was no more promising.[2]

By 1914 there was a state of deadlock. The liberals were determined to press on with home rule, and many of them attached first priority to passing the measure. It is worth noting that the six ministers who protested against the naval estimates at the beginning of 1914 gave the need of maintaining party solidarity and of taking no risks with home rule as a principal reason for their stand.[3] On the other side, the danger of civil war in Ireland leading to trouble in India and foreign complications was the reason urged by Lord Roberts for not using the army to coerce Ulster.[4] Milner was among the intransigent. He refused to consider a Round Table plan for a federal solution to the Ulster issue which had been put forward by Edward Grigg and which had won Churchill's support.[5] But some conservatives were by now not ready to follow Milner all the way in tampering with the army in Ulster's support because of the growing threat from Germany.[6]

A real compromise was, however, impossible. There was no formula, as the Buckingham Palace conference showed in July 1914, that would satisfy the Irish and their supporters overseas and also meet the claims of Ulster; and the war brought about a suspension of the conflict, not

[1] Milner letters. Balfour Papers, B.M. Add. 49647.
[2] Protection for the United Kingdom including Ireland was also the burden of L. S. Amery, *The Case Against Home Rule* (1912).
[3] Letter signed by Beauchamp, McKenna, Simon, Hobhouse, Runciman, McKinnon Wood, 29 January 1914. Simon Papers.
[4] Roberts to Asquith, 20 March 1914. Dep. Asquith, Ireland, 1914.
[5] Gollin, *Proconsul in Politics*, pp. 212–13. Edward Grigg (1879–1955) (knighted 1920, created Baron Altrincham 1945) was an important figure on *The Times* and from 1913 to 1914, joint editor of *The Round Table*. After war service he was in 1919, secretary of the Army Reorganization Committee, military secretary to the Prince of Wales on his dominion tour in 1920, and private secretary to Lloyd George, 1921–22. He was M.P. 1922–5; secretary of Rhodes Trustees, 1923–5. Governor of Kenya, 1925–31. M.P., 1933–45. Parliamentary secretary, Ministry of Information, 1939–40, financial secretary, War Office, 1940; joint parliamentary under-secretary for war, 1940–2; member of the cabinet committee on India, 1942 and minister resident in Middle East, 1944–5. Editor *National Review* (later *National and English Review*), 1948–55.
[6] Gollin, op. cit., p. 191.

its resolution.[1] The Home Rule bill was allowed to pass in September with an act suspending its operation until after the war, the government giving an undertaking meanwhile to bring in a special bill to deal with Ulster.

The North Atlantic Triangle

The sensitivity towards Ireland was in part due to the proved Irish ability to affect American opinion and to the growth of the belief that good relations with the United States were essential to British security. The possibility of challenging the United States at sea had been virtually ruled out before the liberals took office. A combination between Germany and the United States was all Britain had to fear; but such a combination was most improbable. In 1907 the C.I.D. concluded an examination of the position with the reflection that an Anglo-American war would not merely be 'the supreme limit of human folly' but was also so unlikely as to be a contingency against which it was 'unnecessary to make provision'.[2]

Britain could thus concentrate against the German menace at sea without worrying about the other great naval power. But were there prospects here of actual support from the United States in her world-wide tasks? Some people felt that the next step should be a positive one – the creation of some form of English-speaking or Anglo-Saxon confederation which could unite Britain and the United States and the white dominions. Success would guarantee peace on the oceans; failure might see the United States developing imperial ambitions, which must involve a conflict with Britain.[3]

[1] 'I do beg you to consider as a military measure the importance of giving the Irish their bill and so bringing them round in England and in America to our side. The denial of this will certainly be paid with disloyalty and rancour and an element of weakness and discord introduced into our affairs. It is well worth while giving them their trophy subject to proper conditions and to postponement of operations and amendments.' Churchill to Cecil, 8 September 1914. Cecil Papers, B.M. Add. 51706.
[2] Marder, *From Dreadnought to Scapa Flow*, vol. 1, pp. 124, 142–3, 182–4.
[3] These ideas were expounded in a paper sent by Philip Kerr to Roosevelt in 1909 in preparation for the ex-president's visit to England. Sending a copy to Balfour, Kerr admitted that these ideas were for the future. But one of Germany's objectives in building up her fleet was to be able to challenge imperial preference; if she could range the United States against it, it might be impossible for Britain to put it through. It was therefore essential to put ideas to Roosevelt which might prevent him being attracted by an American–German combination. This paper is referred to in Kenneth Young, *Balfour*, pp. 281–2, as being by Balfour himself; this is clearly not the case. See Balfour Papers, B.M. Add. 49797, and letter there to Balfour from Kerr of 3 May 1909.

Such assumptions were neither justified in the event nor widely shared in imperialist circles. Milner was particularly insistent that, while it was important to keep on good terms with the Americans, it was unnecessary to suggest the establishment of a relationship which would only be appropriate inside the 'family' of the Empire.[1] Some liberals who were struck by the absence of divergent interests, and who regarded the United States as 'scarcely a foreign country', felt that it was important that the imperialists should not be allowed to capture American opinion for their own version of the British future.[2] Neither sector of British opinion fully understood the transformation that was coming over the United States in these years or the new forces that were at once pushing it forward into a greater world role and pulling it backwards from any commitments to other countries. Certainly the Foreign Office, preoccupied with events in Europe, did not pay excessive attention to American developments and tended to be irritated by the somewhat inchoate and amateur aspects of American diplomacy, forced as it was to steer an uncertain course between the perceptions of secretaries of state and the prejudices of Congress: 'The office is so anti-American,' wrote a correspondent of Bryce's, 'that it is always difficult to discuss American affairs with them.'[3] Bryce as ambassador did much to insulate Anglo-American relations from these irritations; his successor, Spring-Rice, selected for the post because Grey despaired of finding anyone to come up to 'the American ideal of being outside the diplomatic service and of world-wide reputation', was less successful.[4]

The principal factor in the relations of the two countries remained the position of Canada. Canada had found a new bond with the United States in their common hostility to Japanese immigration, and the Canadian government provided a channel for American approaches to Britain for a common policy on the subject.[5] American hostility to the

---

[1] Milner to Col. Denison, 3 November 1909. Milner Papers, CLXXIV, 1908–17, Canada [Bodl. 169]. Milner to Haslam, 24 May 1912. Milner Papers, Imperial Union [Bodl. 167]. Cf. Gollin, op. cit., p. 130. Not only did Lord Charles Beresford, the principal opponent of Fisher's naval reforms openly propose an Anglo-American alliance but Fisher himself had by 1907 been converted to the idea of 'the federation of all who speak the English tongue' and in 1909–10 was doing his best to popularize the idea. Marder, *Fear God and Dread Nought*, vol. 2, pp. 191, 298, 343–8, 361–2.
[2] Gilbert Murray to J. L. Hammond, 29 January 1907. Gilbert Murray Papers, Hammond Correspondence.
[3] George Young to Bryce, 13 July 1911. Bryce Papers, U.S.A., vol. 32.
[4] Edward Grey to Bryce, 5 October 1911; Bryce to Grey, 28 October 1911. Bryce Papers, U.S.A., vol. 32.
[5] Dawson, op. cit., vol. 1, pp. 146–58, 163–5.

Japanese alliance also fortified Canada's suspicions, and dominion assent to its renewal in 1911 was only secured by the inclusion of the saving clause that prevented Britain from being drawn into a war against the United States. Even neutrality in an American–Japanese war might be thought incompatible with keeping the Empire together.[1]

Even more serious notice was taken of the U.S. attempts to bring about the commercial reciprocity with Canada which British observers feared would give the United States such a leverage in Canadian affairs as to force Canada into adopting an American stance on all international issues.[2] Other observers regarded the situation with more equanimity, and attempts were made through Bryce to find out how opinion in Canada could be calmed down over the provocative speeches made by some American politicians.[3]

The defeat of Laurier was an encouragement, although it was realized that in addition to 'self-preservation under the British flag', the selfish interest of protected Canadian industries had played an important role.[4] For the moment the future of Canada ceased to be an open question. The British government hoped that some advance could be made towards obviating other sources of friction between the two countries. Much hope was placed in the project of a general arbitration treaty, not only for the two countries themselves but also as an example to other European countries of how to deal with disputes.[5] Nevertheless, there were doubts felt about those who were suspected of wanting to 'convert the treaty into a league, defensive and offensive against other nations, particularly Germany, and to drag France into it'.[6] But the matter was settled by the action of the American senate in refusing ratification.

Two disputes, linked in their settlement, clouded Anglo-American relations directly; the decision of the American Congress to exempt American coastal shipping from paying tolls on passing through the Panama Canal (in breach of the Hay–Pauncefote treaty) and British hostility to the course of President Wilson's intervention in Mexican

---

[1] Balfour to Esher, 4 February 1910. Balfour Papers, B.M. Add. 49719.
[2] See the correspondence between Hewins and Balfour, 1908–10, Balfour Papers, B.M. Add. 49779; and Hewins, op. cit., vol. 1, pp. 265–8.
[3] Earl Grey to Bryce, 1 June 1911, Bryce Papers, U.S.A., vol. 31; 2 September 1911, Bryce Papers, U.S.A., vol. 32. Charles D. Hilles to Bryce, 26 August 1911. Ibid. Laurier to Bryce, 4 September 1911. Ibid.
[4] Earl Grey to Bryce, 22 September 1911. Bryce Papers, U.S.A., vol. 32.
[5] Edward Grey to Bryce, 3 April 1911. Bryce Papers, U.S.A., vol. 31.
[6] Courtenay Ilbert to Bryce, 26 April 1911. Bryce Papers, English Correspondence, vol. 14.

politics – a hostility believed by the president to be due to Britain's concern being rather with oil supplies for the Royal Navy than with good government for the Mexicans. After the repeal in June 1914 of the canal tolls bill, Britain accepted the American lead on Mexican affairs – uncertain though it proved to be.[1]

But with the prospect of a major war in which Britain would be a belligerent and the United States a neutral, even graver problems lay in the background. The United States had traditionally been an advocate of neutral rights – though this position had been much modified by the North during the civil war. At the Hague conference in 1907, and at the London conference which sat from December 1908 to February 1909, the British negotiators had taken up a position much closer to that of the Americans than in the past. The reason for this was partly the assumption that in a European war Britain would be neutral, and partly the belief that in a war in which she was actually engaged the interception of commerce upon the high seas would be easier and blockade more difficult than in earlier centuries. For this reason the declaration of London included a definition of contraband which excluded from goods liable to seizure much of what made up the sinews of modern war.[2] By 1911, when the declaration of London came before parliament for ratification, the possible blunting of British sea-power in a war was a matter of greater concern, and the House of Lords rejected it.[3] Nevertheless, the ideas it contained provided arguments for the United States and other neutrals to use when, with the coming of war, Britain began to use the weapon of commerce interception against the central powers.[4]

From Peace to War

Although the impact of external events upon the British public mind may only have been intermittent, the transformation of Britain's posi-

---

[1] The Latin American policy of Woodrow Wilson is fully treated for American sources in Arthur Link, *Woodrow Wilson*, vol. 2 (1956). Unfortunately the '50 Year Rule' prevented his having access to British sources on the diplomacy and politics of the Mexican imbroglio.
[2] *C.H.B.E.*, vol. III, pp. 702–10; Admiral Sir Herbert Richmond, *Statesmen and Sea Power* (Oxford, 1946), pp. 279–83; Lord Hankey, *The Supreme Command*, vol. 1, ch. IX.
[3] Grey was, however, still convinced of its utility and had tried to get the United States to make public its hope for British ratification. Grey to Bryce, 20 March 1911. Bryce Papers, U.S.A., vol. 31.
[4] The subject is treated in detail in A. C. Bell, *The Blockade of Germany*, an official history printed for official purposes in 1937 and publicly released in 1961 (H.M.S.O.).

BRITAIN'S LIBERAL EMPIRE

tion from that of a power external to the European network of alliances and understandings to one deeply involved in it was fairly widely appreciated. In particular, it was clear that in so far as there was a French and a German camp, Britain, if she had to choose, would inevitably choose the former. Not merely the content of German foreign policy and her seeming determination to match her strength on land with an equal effort by sea, but still more the truculence of her methods and the overt jingoism of her ruling classes, seemed to make this choice inevitable. Indeed, so strong was this hostility towards Germany that a recent historian of the *ententes* has suggested that any attempts at a real *rapprochement* with Germany after 1903 were bound to be unwelcome to public opinion.[1] Positive satisfaction at a closer alignment with France was more rarely expressed, and felt perhaps in more restricted circles, but Austen Chamberlain felt able to assure the German ambassador in May 1908 that there had been a real desire for an understanding with France ever since the 1880s because the British 'thought there was a closer communion of ideals between these two great liberal nations than between themselves and any other'.[2]

Chamberlain himself came to believe that it was desirable to turn the *entente* into a full alliance so as to prepare for the possibility of war and that some such thing as a British Monroe doctrine might obviate misunderstanding as to the line Britain would draw in defence of her vital interests.[3] Balfour also felt by 1912 that Britain had the burden of an alliance without its advantages and urged Grey (as did Chamberlain) that a formal treaty should be concluded. The difficulty, as he admitted, was that while he would support fighting to avoid the destruction of France, he would not wish to see Britain drawn into a war for the recovery of Alsace-Lorraine. His suggestion for getting round the problem was that the signatories should pledge recourse to arbitration before treating any dispute as a *casus belli* and this would reassure public opinion, at home and in the dominions, in Europe and in the United States, as to the defensive nature of British policy and act as a brake on French chauvinism.[4]

[1] Monger, op. cit., pp. 225-6. One is tempted to speculate why German sabre-rattling should have been so rapid in its impact on the British press and public, while nazi behaviour of an even more provocative kind was generally passed over until 1939.
[2] Austen Chamberlain, *Down the Years*, pp. 52-7.   [3] Chamberlain, op. cit., p. 66.
[4] Memorandum of 12 June 1912. Balfour Papers, B.M. Add. 49731. Copy sent to Chamberlain on 4 July, in Austen Chamberlain Papers, A.C. 10/26. See also the exchange of letters between Chamberlain and Balfour's niece and biographer, Mrs Blanche Dugdale. Ibid., AC. 40/123.

172

The weaknesses of the movement for international arbitration, largely due to the half-heartedness of the Americans who were theoretically its principal protagonists, gave a rather unpractical air to suggestions of this kind. They are of interest rather as prefiguring Britain's later interest in the League of Nations machinery as a way out of similar dilemmas. Furthermore, as we now know, and as indeed the events of July–August 1914 were to demonstrate, the importance of the mobilization machinery of the continental powers and the rigid strategy and time-table that it imposed upon them, made such a pause between a dispute and its resolution difficult to envisage. But these were not the principal reasons which made it inevitable that Grey should reject suggestions of this kind. An overt alliance with France would not merely have been unacceptable to important elements in British society – the important commercial ties between Britain and Germany and the conviction that war would be an economic disaster made the 'City' on the whole an influence for peace. Even more important, a great part of the liberal party itself would have found it impossible to sustain a government that embarked on such a course. Prominent liberals regretted the hostility to Germany that they observed in British opinion and refused to believe that the faults lay all on the German side.[1] The uneasy compromise that endured until the war itself was the nearest the government could come to reconciling the different influences playing upon it.

Opinion was largely turned in favour of going to war in 1914 by the German invasion of Belgium, and this for two reasons. In the first place, the historic sensitivity of the country to events across the narrow seas was re-ignited. In a sense, Britain was responding to the same challenge as in the days of Philip II, Louis XIV, or Napoleon. In the second place, and even more important, the German repudiation of the international commitment to Belgian neutrality and its recourse to pure *raison d'état* enabled Britain with a good conscience to present itself as the guarantor of international order and good faith, and to connect their violators with the old idea of absolutism and militarism. In this way, the overseas democracies, the dominions in the first instance and later perhaps the

---

[1] See, e.g., Bryce to A. V. Dicey, 16 February 1909. Even after the outbreak of war Bryce held to his opinions: 'Why should England so far back as 1905 or 1906 have made a special friendship with France and begun to cultivate a special hostility against Germany? We had no cause of quarrel with Germany yet ever since 1906 we have been working everywhere against her. Had we been on friendly terms we might probably have stopped her from touching Belgium.' Bryce to Dicey, 20 August 1914. Bryce Papers, English Correspondence, vol. 4.

United States, might be brought to see that Britain was fighting for no selfish interests but for ideals in which they too shared.[1]

Except for the ideologues of the extreme left, opposition to the war was at first limited to the sophisticated. There is much evidence to the effect that the war when it came was widely welcomed, both because of the feeling that a trial of strength with Germany was inevitable and because of the appeal it made to the strain of idealism in the national make-up. A sense of righteous exhilaration in a largely inarticulate public and a feeling of moral purpose lasted nearly to the end.[2]

To declare war was not, of course, to decide how it should be fought. Some people believed that while the British would support a largely naval war of the traditional kind, they would never accept large-scale involvement in continental fighting and that this would in the end mean disillusioning France of her expectations.[3] The preparations made did imply the immediate sending of an expeditionary force, though without providing the organization of trained reserves, or for the production of war materials that would be needed to back up the effort on land, should most prophecies be falsified and the war prove to be a long one. As late as 4 August the cabinet were hesitating about sending over the expeditionary force partly because they thought that if it were retained at home it might become the nucleus of a more powerful one, partly because troops might be needed overseas, and partly because of a revival of the invasion bogy and the thought that a denuded Britain would hamper the mobility of the fleet.[4] But in the end the government accepted the estimates agreed upon some years earlier as to the minimum requirements for home defence; and the 'mercenary army' went forth.

The debates over foreign policy and over its military implications were not stilled for long, and the wartime arguments over strategy and over war aims are incomprehensible without this background of uncertainty. Nor were the repercussions of these uncertainties ended by the

[1] The mood of the time is best captured in H. G. Wells's novel, *Mr Britling Sees It Through*, published in September 1916.
[2] A. Marwick, *The Deluge* (1965), pp. 27, 49. Men who lived through both wars were struck and worried by an absence of similar exhilaration in the second. See, e.g., Harold Nicolson, *Diaries and Letters, 1939–1945*, p. 245 and *passim*.
[3] 'As the people of this country will never permit an English soldier to fight on the Continent of Europe in a Franco-German war, there will later on be a hell of a row with France as to "Perfide Albion!"' Fisher to Julian Corbett, 1 December 1913. Marder, *Fear God and Dread Nought*, vol. 2, p. 495.
[4] Conversation between Balfour and Haldane, 4 August 1914. Notes made by Balfour on 5 August. Balfour Papers, B.M. Add. 49724.

victory of 1918. The various schools of thought had their representatives both in the discussions over peacemaking, and in settling what Britain's policy should be and still more what it should not be, in the post-war years. Some people were converted by their wartime experiences to new points of view, but the majority showed the usual human tendency to find in events confirmation for what they had always believed. They faced, however, a new difficulty in that the international and imperial position of Britain and the general international context of the post-1919 decades were very much changed as a consequence of the war itself; so that the correctness or otherwise of the criticism or the defence of pre-1914 policy may have had less relevance than they thought for determining the new course.

With the advantages of a longer perspective and more information, particularly about foreign countries and governments than was earlier available, it is clear that the liberal empire faced a real dilemma. It was able to resist the temptations of the course suggested by Joseph Chamberlain and his spiritual heirs, that of meeting the German challenge by accepting for the Empire the German idea of the *geschlossene Handels-Staat*. This was not merely because it was out of harmony with the liberal vision of an international community harmoniously acting in accord through the lubricating influences of international commerce, and the parallel circulation of social and political ideals, but also because even if Britain had espoused the idea, it could not have made it work. The Germans might continue and extend the work of German and central European unification beyond the point at which it had been interrupted by the work of Bismarck; but whatever territories they might rule or come to control, it was German national feeling and its sense of solidarity that they would be relying upon. Whatever role overseas colonies (existing or to be acquired) might play it would be a wholly subordinate economic and strategic one and the colonies would not count for anything in the German political process. The British Empire presented problems of a very different kind.

The inhabitants of the British Isles represented only a small proportion of those owing allegiance to the British crown; although, as events were to show, the fellow-feeling of men of British descent wherever resident in the Empire was to be an important factor in the Empire's war effort and make possible the pooling of its resources without the need for new formal institutions. Only in the Australasian dominions were those of British stock in a position to translate their wishes immediately into national policy; and even in those dominions, to say nothing of Canada and South Africa, the very logic of representative institutions and of responsible government made their leaders conscious all the time of the importance of their own imperative local concerns as well as of those of the Empire as a whole. The policy of the Empire in war and peace depended upon a series of informal understandings and gentlemen's agreements, which were no doubt highly characteristic of the political genius of the British race but which were always prone to bring about critical confrontations if pressed too far.

In Ireland and in India, national aspirations to self-government, at least on the model of the older dominions, were theoretically, and in Ireland's case indeed genuinely, acceptable to liberal opinion. But their translation into fact had been delayed in Ireland by the unsolved problem of the Ulster protestant minority, maintained and supported by the unrepentant protestant ascendancy of the south. In India's case, the minority problems – and notably that of the Moslems – were reinforced in their effect upon liberal opinion by the still widespread doubts of India's potential for democratic self-government. It is perhaps a testimony to the real strength of the liberal ideal both in Britain and India that independence on a model other than the Westminster one was not seriously advocated by any important body of opinion.

As for the colonies in Africa and elsewhere, where no important body of white population existed to claim self-government – the Rhodesias were doubtful ground – there was certainly no assumption of progress even along the gradualist lines followed in India. The British might reasonably argue that since foreigners were going to rule in any event, they were no worse than their rivals and indeed better than most of them. And indeed paternalism was in the ascendancy; but it was on the whole a passive paternalism. Individual enterprise might make this or that part of the colonial empire a useful source of this or that material, or even a market of definite if subsidiary importance for British industry; and no doubt the existence of so many and such scattered possessions was a stimulation to the mercantile marine, to Britain's lead in telecommunications and to other elements in the country's economic strength. But at a time when so much was being demanded – by contemporary standards – from the British taxpayer, the idea of a definite state-sponsored programme of development seemed as financially impracticable as it was out of harmony with the still predominantly individualist outlook of the period.

For Britain's leaders in 1914, however, no balance sheet of empire presented itself. The Empire had come into being as the result of a series of disparate events and in response to thrusts of many different kinds; the burdens of maintaining some parts of it could only be justified in terms of the defence needs of other parts. The India Office, the Colonial Office, the War Office, and the Admiralty each had a different picture of the system and its needs. But no one suggested that it should be dismantled, nor seriously denied that its survival was among the stakes of the new conflict.

If statesmen found it hard to see the Empire as a whole, this was even truer of the ordinary men. In the words of Wells's Mr Britling:

> Politically the British Empire is a clumsy collection of strange accidents. It is a thing as little to be proud of as the outline of a flint or the shape of a potato. For the mass of the English people India and Egypt and all that side of our system mean less than nothing; our trade is something they do not understand, our imperial wealth something they do not share. Britain has been a group of four democracies caught in the net of a vast yet casual imperialism; the common man here is in a state of political perplexity from the cradle to the grave.[1]

The conflict itself was, however, a European one; to call it the first world war – as became the habit after 1945 – was to overlook the fact that the vast bulk of the fighting took place in Europe and that the results of nearly all the campaigns outside Europe might well have been undone had the victory there gone the other way. In fact, whatever public opinion may have agreed to accept as the rallying cries of the time, the main argument that was decisive in the eyes of the men who made the fateful decision was the familiar one of the balance of power. If the European balance was to be upset to a catastrophic extent by Germany, then Britain's freedom of action overseas would disappear and even though the United Kingdom itself might reach some kind of tolerable arrangement with Europe's new masters, the imperial system could not survive. Such reasoning was not in accordance with what many liberals had believed to be the essence of their creed.[2] But

---

[1] H. G. Wells, *Mr Britling Sees It Through* (London, Cassell, 1916), p. 425.
[2] 'I can see no mortal reason why we should be dragged into this affair unless Grey has given pledges of which the House of Commons knows nothing . . . I also used to believe that the "balance of power doctrine" was a doctrine discarded by Liberals.' Lord Fitzmaurice to J. A.

taking responsibility for ruling a country in a competitive international system had made it impossible to contract out of the laws by which that system was governed.

The reasoning was even more repugnant to the political instincts of the dominions; yet for each one of them, it is clear that the breakdown of the imperial system, and of Britain's ability to come to their aid either physically or in economic terms, would have made a vital difference. For Canada it would have meant absorption into a North American system totally dominated by American capital and ruled from Washington. For Australia and New Zealand it would have meant vulnerability to the presumed threat from Asia before there was a serious possibility of United States intervening on their behalf. For South Africa it would have entailed the abandonment of the policy of Anglo-Dutch conciliation of Botha and Smuts and the domination of white South Africa by a new combination of Boer and German. The dominions' decisions to accept a share in the responsibility for defeating the German challenge cannot therefore simply be dismissed as an unavoidable entanglement in Britain's European policies; though some of their politicians would come to represent it as such. Nor was there in most cases the same degree of commitment to total war as Britain itself eventually achieved; nor of course was there the same confidence in the qualities displayed by Britain's military leaders.

The liberal Empire as tested by the fire of war did not come out too badly. The basic structure of its institutions, domestic and imperial, was modified to meet wartime exigencies but only within the basic rules of the game. The challenge of Germany was defeated, and if the Russian alliance in the end succumbed to the vulnerability that its opponents had detected in tsardom, the successful defence of the Western front in 1914 would not have been possible without Russia's role in drawing off German forces. And the steady effort to minimize sources of friction with the United States, despite some severe blows to mutual understanding at different stages in the war, culminated in an American intervention that might otherwise not have been possible. Pre-1914 British statesmanship and pre-1914 British diplomacy deserve more credit than they often receive.

The weakness of the liberal empire proved to lie in what seemed at first sight to be its most impressive professional performance, the pre-

Spender, 31 July 1914. Spender Papers, B.M. Add. 46392. For some further reflections on this theme, see Max Beloff, *The Balance of Power* (Montreal, 1968).

paration of the armed services. That both army and navy were far better prepared than in most previous British wars can scarcely be gainsaid. What was lacking was a full appreciation of what modern industrialism implied for the conduct of military operations, particularly against a country which was determined to make the fullest use of its own strength, and less inhibited than some by traditional distinction between the armed services of an enemy and the civilian population. British generals and admirals were clearly not the almost cretinous creatures, indifferent to human suffering, that a generation of 'debunkers' was to make them out to be, with disastrous results where future national morale was concerned. Within their limits, they were solid and dedicated professionals. But their service training had not inculcated that rare kind of imagination which enables men to plan not just for the exploitation of the existing state of their art but for its future developments also. Nor was there any possibility of civilians correcting their mistakes in time. Science itself was a remote world of specialists; industry, outside the few firms traditionally entrusted with the provision of war stores, was another world almost equally unknown; the politicians themselves were not much better placed for the most part, and the training they had received was just as little suited to the performance of this particular task as that of the soldiers and sailors for whom as fellow-professionals they also felt a perhaps exaggerated respect.

The political leaders of the liberal Empire had developed two aspects of leadership to great perfection; one (which they shared with their best civil servants) was what was known as judgement – facility in absorbing and rendering reliable opinions upon a complicated mass of factual material and devising a policy out of it. It was *par excellence* the quality attributed to the university training of the kind that most of them had enjoyed. Asquith, product of Jowett's Balliol, was its supreme exemplar. But judgement is useless unless the material is in the briefs, and for what was needed in military matters once the lines of trenches to the sea were completed, or at sea with the coming of the submarine, was not in the briefs. The second quality was the capacity to reconcile different trends in the body-politic and to embody the result in the form of political leadership. This capacity was developed to its fullest by Lloyd George, the former radical, and it carried Britain through the darkest hour.

It was then neither intelligence nor character that failed Britain but imagination, the ability to see facts afresh without professional blinkers. And since no political system has yet been found that guarantees the appearance and use of this rarest of gifts, its absence cannot perhaps be held against the liberal Empire. Neither the allied nor the enemy camp showed up in a much better light; and both paid the penalty in the holocaust of their youth. But because the world position of Britain was in a sense more of a *tour de force* than that of her rivals, because it depended on so unique a set of circumstances and the deployment of so wide a range of skills, the effect upon Britain was perhaps the greatest, though it took longest to show itself. Britain in 1914, by all the rules of politics, took the right decisions; but this did not and perhaps could not do more than postpone the dissolution of Britain's empire and the end of her world position; or perhaps it would be truer to say that the decision was responsible for it happening when it did in quite a different form. Had Germany's challenge been refused, or had Germany won, so much would have been different that it is impossible to visualize what the course of British history would then have been. In the jargon of the modern strategist we have no alternative 'scenario' to offer.

Chapter 5

WAR AND WAR AIMS

PART I. BRITAIN, THE EMPIRE AND EARLY PEACE FEELERS

Basic Considerations

British policy during the war years frequently involved objectives or institutional innovations for which no pre-war precedent existed, but no abrupt break in continuity occurred, as apart from anything else, there was very little change in the governing personnel of the country. It is true that the first coalition in May 1915, and still more the Lloyd George ministry of December 1916, brought in important figures from the conservative ranks, some of whom had not previously held ministerial office, but all of them except Smuts had played significant roles in pre-war British politics. The same was true of Arthur Henderson, the principal representative of labour in the government's ranks. And although Lloyd George brought into office a number of men from the business world and elsewhere who had had no previous political experience, none of them played any significant part in the debates over grand strategy and war aims. Among the government's military and naval advisers there were also no startling rises from obscurity; the key positions in the civil service and the diplomatic service remained in the same hands. And what was true of the British government was true also of the dominions. Those who led the imperial war effort, and made certain that imperial considerations would not be overlooked in the settling of peace terms, were familiar from pre-war gatherings: Borden, Botha, and Smuts, Hughes of Australia, Ward of New Zealand.

What did change was not the men but the circumstances. Objectives that had previously seemed difficult or impossible to attain became accomplished fact, because there seemed no other way of forwarding the victory which was the common aim of all. What would earlier have been resisted on principle – the creation of the imperial war cabinet, for instance – now appeared natural and inevitable. It is not surprising that some people thought that the old obstacles were removed for good, and that the war meant in this as in other spheres, a new beginning.

Regarding foreign policy proper, and particularly Britain's war aims, the picture is somewhat different. The fact of war meant that the map of the world was open for redrawing. Aims that could not have been avowed as a reason for going to war now became attainable, indeed, perhaps inevitable, since the alternative to a British solution for the new problems would have been one less favourable to Britain, or actually damaging to the Empire's security. As a result Britain – which by any standard was a sated power in 1914 – ended the war with the Empire enlarged to what was to prove its maximum extent; but fighting as she was, alongside allies and needing to make certain they remained in the war, and hoping also for new allies, she was bound to make concessions about the future political arrangements of the world which she would not have done had she remained completely free to choose for herself. All alliances involve servitudes.

The so-called secret treaties, with their far-reaching provisions for change in the Balkans, the Mediterranean, and the Middle East must therefore be interpreted as a direct consequence of the strategic situation of the first two years of the war rather than as embodying the arrangements that Britain would have thought ideal. Indeed, so far as the Balkans and the Middle East were concerned, the provisions for Russia to advance to the Straits and for the truncation of the Turkish dominions were clearly a second best, resorted to only because of the failure to keep Turkey neutral. But had not the concentration of the French navy in the Mediterranean on ferrying troops from North Africa to France, as well as a degree of incompetence in the command of the British squadron there allowed the German battle-cruiser *Goeben* and light cruiser *Breslau* to reach Constantinople and turn the tables in favour of Turkish belligerence, subsequent history might have been very different.[1] Once the future had been rendered malleable, then the precise share of the spoils claimed by Britain was dictated by a mixture of reflexes to the old problems – the route to India, the defence of Egypt and the Canal – and to the all-important new one, oil.

Even more important was the question of the new balance of forces in Europe that would be created by Germany's defeat. It is obvious that all debates over war aims within a coalition present this double aspect; the terms to be offered to or imposed upon the enemy, and the questions

[1] On this episode, see Marder, *From Dreadnought to Scapa Flow*, vol. 2, pp. 20–41.

that will arise between the allies, once the enemy is disposed of and the new area of bargaining defined. In practice, these aspects cannot be kept separate, since the greater or lesser degree of inter-allied agreement about the future may determine the acceptability of peace approaches from one or more members of the opposing camp.

The very recent alignment of Britain with France and Russia must not be forgotten. Those who had made the decision for war had been very much aware that Britain would be in almost as parlous a position if France and Russia defeated Germany without her aid, as if Germany itself were victorious; since they would then be able to dictate a peace without consideration for British interests, and Russia in particular would be able to renew its pressure upon India with impunity.[1] The possibility of a renewal of rivalries with them once the German danger was over was, therefore, present from the beginning, though it was scarcely a topic that lent itself to public debate. It was even more obvious that if Japan removed German influence in China and the Pacific and rendered naval assistance, the dangers of a confrontation with that power were being brought much nearer. Even if the pressing dangers nearer home assumed priority, the Pacific dominions would keep British statesmen alive to the issue.[2]

The fortunes of war were to bring about two quite different situations in France and Russia. The extreme importance that continued to be attached to the western front throughout the war, despite the efforts made to break away from it, had striking effects upon Anglo-French relations. The priority given to French military planning on the military side produced a sense of grievance that was significant later on, and it was matched by the unpopularity that the French inevitably incurred among the rank and file of the army and so among civilians at home in Britain.[3] Even more important was the strengthening of the feeling, never abandoned in some quarters, that the whole policy of a

[1] F. S. Northedge, *The Troubled Giant, Britain among the Great Powers* (1966), p. 8.

[2] See, e.g., Louis, *Great Britain and Germany's Lost Colonies*, pp. 80–1.

[3] For examples of feeling among the troops more hostile to the French than to the Germans, see Marwick, *The Deluge*, p. 217; Martin Gilbert, *Britain and Germany between the Wars* (1964), p. 2. The prevalence of popular francophobia, contrasted with the strong sympathy for France among an important section of the British upper class and in the literary and artistic worlds, is something to be kept in mind when one comes to examine Britain's policy in Europe between the wars and the extent of sympathy for the policy of 'appeasing' Germany at France's expense. There is a parallel to be found perhaps in the division in British sympathies at the time of the Suez expedition in 1956. Ordinary people many of whom had direct, or close second-hand, experience of the 'Desert War' had little sympathy for the Egyptians. On the other hand, pro-Arab sentiment in the foreign office and other sections of the 'Establishment' was an important source of opposition to the government's policy.

massive continental commitment was an error and that at some point
it would be necessary to escape from it and back to the wider area of
world politics where Britain's traditional forms of warfare would have
more scope.[1] The conscription act of 1916 rejecting Britain's traditional
reliance upon limited land forces was a turning-point of deep significance, since it meant that Britain was now trying to produce out of her
own resources mass-armies of the continental type as well as the naval
and industrial strength which had in the past been her principal contribution to coalition warfare. Some have argued that it was the excessive strain upon the country inherent in this effort that marked the
beginning of subsequent retreat and decline.[2]

Those who believed that a war of this kind had been brought about
by previous errors in policy, and in particular by a failure to develop
the imperial relationship, had at all costs to avoid sanctioning peace
terms that would make a recrudescence of the same situation probable.
French leadership, and while Russia was still in the war, Russian-
inspired aims, were alike suspect:

> This war against a German domination in Europe was only necessary
> because we had failed to make ourselves sufficiently strong and
> united as an Empire to be able to afford to disregard the European
> balance. When it comes to the terms of peace and after, we have got
> to get back to a British point of view and get rid of the echoing of
> French and Russian ideas cemented together by denunciation of
> Germany. And we shall have to fight against the people who will be
> prepared to sell every imperial gain the war may have brought us in
> order to secure what they think is the proper frontier between certain
> foreign nations in Europe or who after the peace will be hypnotized
> for years by the emotions and the claptrap of the war. And then will
> come the last chance of building up things, the chance that should
> have been taken after the South African war and was not.[3]

[1] 'You and I have always had this great bond of union, that we both instinctively felt sure
that the traditional action of the British Army was right, to act in subsidiary campaigns with
a limited responsibility in conjunction with the British Fleet *and not to take part in Continental
struggles*, except indirectly by means of subsidies and securing the passage of supplies overseas.'
Fisher to Hankey, 19 February 1918. Hankey in replying on 21 February agreed with Fisher
and went on to say that Britain should have equipped Russia's armies before her own.
Marder, *Fear God and Dread Nought*, vol. 3, pp. 511–13. Fisher was nearing the end of his life
but Hankey still had twenty years of vital influence before him and there is reason to believe
that in essentials his views did not alter.
[2] W. N. Medlicott, *Contemporary England, 1914–1964* (1967), p. 14.
[3] Amery to Milner, 25 May 1915. Milner Papers, Private Letters, 1915, vol. 2 [Bodl. 140].
The reference to the South African war is interesting in view of the fact that such views,

Such sentiments remained powerful throughout the war[1] and help to explain British reluctance to underwrite a French hegemony in Europe, as well as the speed with which France replaced Russia as the bogyman of the protagonists of British influence in the Middle East. The Bolshevik revolution and the apparent elimination of Russia as a major power greatly enhanced prospects for a French domination of Europe as well as nullifying the earlier undertakings to the tsarist government about eventual peace terms. But the revolution itself, and the threat that militant communism appeared to offer both in Europe and in the Empire, created new problems to replace the old. In particular, the appeal that communism was thought capable of exercising in India produced a new version of the old anti-Russia alignment of British policy, based upon the priority given to the security of India. Even before the war ended there was a readiness to consider Germany in the role of an anti-Russian barrier and balance.

The other principal limitation upon, and influence over, British policy was that of the United States. To make sure of its neutrality (and of a neutrality that would not prevent it from being a source of supply) was the principal task of British diplomacy from the beginning of the war, until, for reasons with which British diplomacy had little to do directly, the United States itself became a belligerent. During both periods it was necessary to reckon with an American outlook on the world that harmonized with neither of the main trends of thought in Britain. The United States was seemingly indifferent to the balance of power in Europe, and varied in its hopes for the future between relying on the 'justness' of an eventual territorial settlement, and putting its faith in some proposed universalist type of international organization. There was no diminution of the traditional American dislike of empires, and in particular of the British Empire, nor any new willingness to countenance measures looking to its consolidation.

imbued with a strong and persistent anti-French bias, were given a new weight with the arrival on the British scene of General (from 1941 Field Marshal) Smuts who became a member of the British war cabinet in June 1917. Jan Christian Smuts (1870–1950), after fighting in the Boer war, had held various posts in the Transvaal and South African governments, being minister of defence from 1910 to 1920. He was the commander in the East African campaign from 1916 to 1917. After resigning from the war cabinet in January 1919, he represented South Africa at the Paris Peace conference. He was prime minister and minister of native affairs, 1919–24; minister of justice, 1933–9; prime minister, minister of external affairs and defence, 1939–48.
[1] Two years later, Milner was arguing with Sir Henry Wilson that Britain had no need of continental alliances and that closer imperial ties would suffice to enable Britain to defy her enemies. Gollin, *Proconsul in Politics*, p. 529.

Even wider were the issues raised by the strain of the war upon Britain's resources and her consequent dependence upon the United States for financial as well as material support. Not only was this a limitation upon British autonomy inevitable in a debtor–creditor relationship, but it cast doubt upon the capacity of Britain, even if she wished to do so, to maintain in the future the level of naval armament that would alone give meaning to any reassertion of her independence. But the alternative might be to accept the American view of the freedom of the seas, with all that this implied for Britain's future world strategy, and the dissolving of the naval partnership with Japan. Wilson's universalist philosophy of international relations, and his denunciation of the whole apparatus of alliances and secret diplomacy awoke a highly responsive chord in those sections of British opinion that believed that the war would only be justified – if it were justified at all – by some complete remodelling of the international system.[1] Nevertheless, those responsible for guiding the actual course of British policy found the presence of the United States as an 'associated power', welcome for the assurance that it gave of Germany's ultimate defeat, but by no means an unmixed blessing.

The problem here as elsewhere was to strike the correct balance between the immediate requirements of the war and the long-term prospects of the country and the Empire. This problem was by no means unique but the decisions in the field of external policy were more concentrated, more decisive and more fateful than were those in other fields of endeavour. Much thinking and planning, official and unofficial, went on behind the scenes, and there was some public discussion, though obviously of a limited kind. But the basic decisions had to be taken by a handful of men, working under tremendous pressure, and often in circumstances of personal anxiety or tragedy.[2] As always, too, personal ambition became fused with adherence to rival schools of thought. The formal party truce did not inhibit the conflict of parties, factions, and persons although it altered its form, and it is not surprising therefore that the development of British policy during the war has yet to receive detailed study.[3]

[1] See L. W. Martin, *Peace Without Victory: Woodrow Wilson and the British Liberals* (New Haven, 1958).

[2] Both Asquith and Bonar Law, the two party leaders, lost their eldest sons in the war. Some of the atmosphere is conveyed in the diaries of Asquith's daughter-in-law Lady Cynthia Asquith, *Diaries 1915–1918* (1968).

[3] Delay in tackling the subject has been due, of course, in part to the long closure of the archives and to the failure to produce a series of diplomatic documents for the war years com-

The Political Machinery for Waging War

One underlying problem was present from the beginning of the war, and was later to prove the real cause of the political crisis of 1916 which resulted in the fall of Asquith from power. The traditional British cabinet, without secretariat or agenda, was not well designed for the rapid transaction of an ever-increasing load of business. More important still was the fact that much of this business related to matters of which there was no recent relevant experience, the mobilization for war purposes of the resources of a highly pacific society. But this was not all; resources had not merely to be mobilized, they also had to be used. Decisions had to be taken about basic strategy and about the complicated inter-relationships between military policy and diplomacy. The British governmental system was one in which the military arm was subordinate to the civilian authority. Military advice was made available through the responsible ministers, the secretary of state for war and the first lord of the admiralty. Haldane at the War Office had improved the organization for this purpose and the Admiralty was a fairly adequate instrument. Both services, and the navy especially, had shown some reluctance to embark on the road of inter-service co-ordination, despite the pressures from the C.I.D. But the original move of the expeditionary force to France was successfully accomplished.

Thenceforward the situation was affected deeply by the accident of personality. As secretary of state, Kitchener added a massive military reputation to the political authority inherent in the office, and commanded great popular support; but he was neither gifted at presenting a case, nor self-assertive in pressing it. Churchill as first lord possessed both of these gifts; Fisher whom he had brought back as first sea lord was uncertain of his political master's judgement but unwilling to pit himself against it. The constitutional issues were brought to a head by the belief of Churchill and others that the 'westerners' were accepting a war of attrition which might endure intolerably, and that the best hope of defeating Germany lay in finding a way round to the east.

The cabinet at the outbreak of war numbered twenty-two and was

parable to the pre-war and post-war series. Apart from such documents as the soviet government revealed, the material from the archives of Britain's allies has been even more scanty. For a preliminary sketch of the history of French war aims, see P. Renouvin, 'Les buts de guerre du gouvernement français, 1914–1918', *Revue Historique*, 1966. An abundance of American material has been some compensation in respect of those aspects of the story with which the United States was concerned. A pioneer attempt to look at the whole picture, is P. Guinn, *British Strategy and Politics, 1914–1918* (Oxford, 1965).

essentially an instrument for dealing with domestic policy; foreign and defence policy had, as we have seen, largely been dealt with by a group of senior ministers working through the C.I.D.[1] But already on 5 August 1914, the cabinet called into consultation a number of outside figures; and a similar meeting was held on the following day. But whereas the attendance of non-members at the C.I.D., a purely advisory body, created no constitutional problems this was not the case with the cabinet. The cabinet itself met almost daily during the early weeks of the war and at least twice a week after early September, but the important decisions that had to be taken day by day were largely left to the prime minister, Kitchener, and Churchill, with Grey, Lloyd George, and Runciman (president of the Board of Trade) brought in when necessary. In this sense there was from the beginning an inner cabinet, which caused the distrust always felt among those left outside. Even so there was no regular machinery for the study of long-range problems or for drawing up emergency plans; nor was there provision for systematic contacts with the service chiefs. Basically it was left to Hankey and the C.I.D. secretariat to do what they could.

The C.I.D. machinery then also co-ordinated the many committees set up either by itself or directly by the cabinet to deal with the supply side of the war effort. At the end of November 1914 the C.I.D. as such ceased to exist. It was converted into a war council, whose original members were the prime minister, the secretaries of state for war and foreign affairs, the chancellor of the exchequer, and the first lord of the admiralty; with Admiral Fisher, General Wolfe Murray, the C.I.G.S., and the inevitable Balfour, and Hankey as secretary. But the numbers tended to rise; Crewe was added in December, Haldane and the former first sea lord, Arthur Wilson, in January, and McKenna and Harcourt in March – bringing the total up from eight to thirteen. Other persons attended by invitation, as with the C.I.D. The status of the war council – which met at Downing Street and not at the C.I.D. headquarters – was, however, more ambiguous. In practice its decisions were acted on at once, though formally they were to be reported by the prime minister at the cabinet proper. The war council also followed

[1] The principal first-hand source for the machinery of government in the first world war is provided by Lord Hankey in his books, *Government Control in War* (1945), *Diplomacy by Conference* (1946), and *The Supreme Command, 1914–1918* (1961). See also, John Ehrman, *Cabinet Government and War* (1958); F. A. Johnson, *Defence by Committee* (1960); J. Mackintosh, *The British Cabinet* (1962); H. Daalder, *Cabinet Reform in Britain, 1914–1963* (Stanford University Press, 1964).

cabinet practice in having no agenda or minutes, and it made little use of prepared papers, relying upon oral briefings from the service ministers for following the progress of the war.

But the war council did not supersede either the cabinet or smaller and less formal meetings, and it met only irregularly; for instance, not at all between 19 March and 15 May 1915. Its handling of some of the main problems was investigated by the two commissions set up under the Special Commissions (Dardanelles and Mesopotamia) act of 1916. Although the commissions were part of the internal political struggle that eventually brought about the displacement of Asquith, they also threw some light on the weaknesses of the system in making decisions and allocating responsibility.[1]

The idea of helping the Russians by forcing the Straits was an appealing one, once the difficulties of gaining a victory by a break-through on the western front began to be fully appreciated. But while Fisher was an enthusiastic supporter of the plan he envisaged it as a major military operation, and when the War Office refused to make sufficient troops available and the war council accepted Churchill's view that a mainly naval operation would suffice, Fisher did not dissent; nor indeed did Arthur Wilson. Behind the scenes, Fisher expressed his doubts to Hankey, but he took the view that it was for his political chief, not for him, to speak at the war council, and the council was therefore entitled to assume that their professional naval advisers were in accord with their policy. In January 1915 after initial misgivings, Fisher went along with Churchill for a time, but after the military had in the end agreed to participate and the landings at Gallipoli had run into fierce resistance, Fisher again refused to run the risk of losing important vessels in a new naval effort to force the Straits. Fisher resigned after the war council meeting of 14 May, at which Kitchener had warned his colleagues that should Russia collapse an invasion of the British Isles might follow, and at which Churchill had been persuaded to add to the naval force. Fisher's resignation together with the outcry about the shortage of shells on the western front were the proximate causes of the fall of the administration, and Asquith's creation of the first coalition.

When the Dardanelles commission came to report on these events, the majority censured Fisher and Wilson for having remained silent at the meetings of the war council: 'We think that there was an obligation first on the First Lord, secondly on the Prime Minister and thirdly on

[1] See especially Dardanelles Commission, *First Report* (1917, Cd. 8490).

other Members of the War Council to see that the views of the Naval Advisers were clearly put before the Council, we also think that the Naval Advisers should have expressed their views to the Council, whether asked or not, if they considered that the project which the Council was about to adopt was impracticable from a naval point of view.' They also wrote that they were unable 'to concur in the view set forth by Lord Fisher that it was his duty if he differed from the Chief of his Department to maintain silence at the Council or to resign'. In their view 'the adoption of any such principle generally would impair the efficiency of the Public service.' Disagreeing with this, the former Prime Minister of Australia, Andrew Fisher, declared that it was wrong for departmental advisers to offer opinions except through the responsible minister or when specifically invited to do so, and that it 'would seal the fate of responsible government' if 'servants of the State were to share the responsibility of Ministers to Parliament and to the people on matters of public policy'. The New Zealand high commissioner, Sir Thomas Mackenzie also dissented, holding that Admiral Fisher had done all he need.

Perhaps too much should not be read into the fact that it was the two dominion members of the commission who took the most severely legalistic view of civilian responsibility, and who were least prone to allow the experts a more direct say in policy matters in wartime. The personal equations were all-important, and posed a problem for which there can be no ideal solution, and which different democracies have faced in different ways. The fall of Asquith did not resolve it, since the essential issues were inherent in the nature of Britain's participation in the war, and in the inevitably greater inclination of the civilian leaders to seek other paths to victory than the terrifying record of attrition tempered by misplaced optimism which was all that the generals had to offer.

The new coalition government replaced the war council by the Dardanelles committee which, though initially concerned with the final stages and liquidation of the Gallipoli expedition, was gradually drawn into dealing with the whole problem of British strategy. It was composed of five members from each of the two parties, and was regularly attended by the professional heads of the services. In November 1915 this committee was replaced by a new war committee, originally limited to six members but which grew to number eleven; the first sea lord and C.I.G.S. were again regular attenders. The size of these bodies aroused criticism, and Asquith's insistence on referring matters of importance to the full cabinet added complications; the delays over the evacuation of Gallipoli were due to this fact rather than to weaknesses in the war committee, which on this matter functioned with dispatch. Equally, however, the role of the service advisers was not clarified, and the lines of responsibility remained indistinct.

Imperial Factors, the Dominions and Ireland

The strength of the imperial factor in British wartime thinking was due partly to the new opportunities afforded to its proponents by the course of domestic policies, but also to the fact that the Empire was making an indispensable contribution to the total war effort, and this in the case of the dominions of their own free will.[1] Precise figures are difficult to establish, but of their whole male populations, 13·48 per cent of Canadians, 11·12 per cent of South Africans, 13·43 per cent of Australians, and no fewer than 19·35 per cent of New Zealanders served abroad.[2] The Indian contribution was numerically larger than that of all the dominions combined; and almost all the other colonies made contributions to combatant or non-combatant service.

The local effects of this participation differed in different countries. In the case of Australia and New Zealand, a particularly dramatic quality attached to their participation in the gallant though ultimately unsuccessful Gallipoli campaign in 1915. Blame for the failure could rightly be attributed to confused and divided counsels in London, and to the hesitancies of the British naval command in the initial stages.[3] The glory remained with the fighting-men. 'Anzac day' became the national holiday of both dominions, and the Australian national war memorial at Canberra provides a unique reminder both of an attitude to the war very different to that which came to dominate opinion in Britain, and of the extent to which the Australians continued to be a martial people.[4]

[1] See for a summary of the imperial contribution, C. E. Carrington, 'The Empire at War, 1914–1918', C.H.B.E., vol. III, ch. XVI.
[2] Australia with a population of about 5,000,000 all told suffered more fatal casualties than the United States with a population about twenty times as great. New Zealand's casualties were proportionately even higher than Australia's; it is not surprising that their leaders were unimpressed by American moralizing over the selfishness of their war aims.
[3] For a recent account of the Gallipoli campaign and its significance, see R. Rhodes James, Gallipoli (1965).
[4] In his diary for 24 February 1942 Harold Nicolson noted that the future historian of the British Empire's decline and fall would give an important role to the cartoonist David Low

Nevertheless, the Australians, like the citizens of the other dominions were further removed from the heart of the conflict than the British; and as the accent in the war moved from reliance upon initial enthusiasm and upon patriotic self-sacrifice to the impersonal organization of manpower and other resources, they like everyone else had to take account of the dissident and the lukewarm. From quite early in the war the question of conscription became a public issue with strong opposition coming from labour organizations, which were supported, particularly after the Easter rising in Ireland in 1916, by a section of Catholic opinion under the leadership of an Irish prelate, Archbishop Mannix. The Australian labour prime minister, William Morris Hughes, returned from his visit to England in 1916 a convert to conscription but in trying to minimize objections within his party, he put the issue to a referendum in which the proposal was in fact defeated. There followed a confused political period which ended when Hughes became head of a national government that included the conscription dissidents from his own party, and leaders of the former opposition. The new nationalist party secured a large majority in the election of May 1917, but nevertheless felt obliged to hold a second referendum before imposing compulsory service. This proposal was defeated for a second time, and despite the urgent appeal from Britain for reinforcements, Australia retained the voluntary principle until the end of the war. The suggestion of conscription had exacerbated political tensions without contributing to the war effort. In New Zealand, though a national government was also formed (in August 1915), reliance on voluntary service for duty overseas was maintained without dissent.

Canada's experience was even more politically abrasive than Australia's. By the end of 1916 conscription had become a burning issue, and an attempt was made to meet the emergency by inviting the liberals under Laurier to join Borden in a coalition government. The long-drawn-out negotiations created a national government; but it lacked Laurier and his personal followers, largely because of Laurier's refusal to admit that the militia act of 1904 imposing service 'anywhere in Canada and also beyond Canada for the defence thereof'

---

for having in his creation 'Colonel Blimp' sapped the nation's discipline and morale (Harold Nicolson, *Diaries and Letters, 1939–1945* (1967), pp. 213–14). Low was born in New Zealand and worked in Australia before coming to England in 1919, where his attacks on Hughes had drawn attention to him. One might hazard the guess that his acid pencil would have found less acclaim had he remained in the antipodes.

could be held applicable to the war in Europe. Laurier was thus effectively denying that the Canadian expeditionary force was fighting in Europe in defence of Canada. Borden introduced a conscription bill in June 1917, and the voting on it showed an almost clear division on straight racial lines. The conscriptionist victory was upheld in the election of December 1917, which greatly reduced Laurier's following outside the province of Quebec. The numbers of those claiming exemption under the conscription act suggested that there was more lip-service than enthusiasm for the policy in English-speaking Canada, and enabled the French Canadians who had made important (though by no means equivalent) contributions in volunteers to back up their pro-tests against charges of lack of patriotism. But the issue was not closed with the end of the war: 'English Canada soon lost most of its bitterness against Quebec as time passed, but French Canada never forgot the troubles of 1917–18, which served to nourish a new nationalist move-ment which was distinctly provincial and sometimes separatist in out-look.'[1] Almost equally important for the future of the Empire was the lesson drawn by men like Mackenzie King, that Canada could only survive as a nation with a working political system if it were insulated as far as possible from external complications over which the two founding races would always differ.

In South Africa the situation was vitally affected by political de-velopments between the creation of the Union and the outbreak of war. In 1912–13 the more extreme wing of the Afrikaners broke away from Botha's leadership and set up a separate nationalist party under General Hertzog. Nationalist feeling was further inflamed by the decision of the Botha–Smuts government after the declaration of war against Germany not only to take responsibility for local defence, re-leasing 6,000 imperial troops for service elsewhere, but also to invade German South-West Africa. This move helped to precipitate a rebel-lion which lasted until December and involved all the provinces except Natal. The degree to which the invasion of German South-West Africa merely brought to a head a movement for complete and re-publican independence, which was anyhow in the process of moving towards overt action, has been questioned; but that such a movement existed cannot be doubted, nor the intention of some of its leaders to

[1] Mason Wade, *The French Canadians, 1760–1945* (London, Macmillan, 1955), pp. 768–9. Chapters XI and XII of this book give the most detailed account available of the impact of the war on Canadian feeling and politics. The author, a Harvard professor and Catholic convert, is strongly sympathetic to the French-Canadian viewpoint.

secure German support. More important than its origins were its consequences, which despite the government's leniency served to add to the nationalist martyrology, and to deepen the rift between the Commonwealth aspirations of Botha and Smuts and the irreconcilables of Afrikanerdom.[1] For the rest of the war, South Africans were mainly engrossed first with the conquest of German South-West Africa and later with the long-drawn-out campaign in German East Africa. Nevertheless important forces also fought in Europe, and it was there that South African casualties were heaviest; some South African forces also took part in the Egypt-based campaign against the Turks. This important contribution to the allied war effort was attained without conscription, but the political consequences of the war were in the long run perhaps even more momentous than in the case of Canada.

In Ireland it was the evolution of internal politics after the Easter rising, the demise of the old home rule party, and its replacement by the irreconcilables of Sinn Fein that were crucial rather than events directly connected with the war. Ireland was exempted from the conscription act of 1916, but in the desperate temper of the spring of 1918 when a new conscription act was passed widening the age limits, the pressure to extend it to Ireland seemed hard to resist. Lloyd George coupled this move with an assurance that it would not be enforced before home rule was granted, but this did not mollify the Irish, who treated the act as a direct attack upon their separate national identity. It was at this point that the home rulers seceded for good from the parliament at Westminster, and although conscription was never in fact applied in Ireland, the resistance measures taken in protest against it provoked the government into a direct attempt to break the revolutionary movement by widespread arrests. Ireland was thus by the end of the war in a state of acute revolutionary tension, and the initial rallying to the common cause a thing of the distant past.

India and the War

The war was to prove a particularly crucial factor in the political development of India. In 1914 the rallying of most Indian opinion to the allied side, and the ability of Britain rapidly to denude India, if only temporarily, of all but 15,000 British troops, showed that the German expectations of using Indian nationalism as an agent of Ger-

[1] T. R. H. Davenport, 'The South African Rebellion, 1914', in *E.H.R.*, vol. LXXVIII, 1963.

man policy were unfounded; but by the end of hostilities the situation had changed again. Indian nationalism had received a new stimulus to which the Irish example had contributed, so that the majority of educated and articulate Indians was no longer prepared to accept British rule, nor an indefinite period of transition to self-government. On the British side, despite the existence of a formidable body of die-hard opinion, the idea of permanently maintaining the Indian empire by force of arms was equally unacceptable.[1]

At the outbreak of the war the British army in India was about the same size as it had been ever since the Mutiny, some 75,000 strong. The Indian army under its British officers numbered about 160,000. Both were regarded largely in connection with local defence, and had been starved of modern equipment. The letter from the War Office about the aid that India could send in the event of war in Europe, though drafted in December 1912, was not dispatched until July 1913, and the reply only reached the War Office after the hostilities had broken out.[2]

The Indian government was able in fact to send more troops over-seas than had been bargained for and to replace the bulk of British regulars with British territorials.[3] The Indian army itself was consider-ably expanded; recruitment totalled more than 800,000 fighting troops and about half that number of non-combatants. Although the Meso-potamian campaign, fought in a region of direct interest to India, took a high proportion of her manpower, India was represented by fighting-men on almost every front, in Europe and Africa as well as in Asia. The government of India did not, however, prove well-equipped to deal with an effort of this magnitude; the Mesopotamian campaign suffered from administrative weaknesses as well as military miscalcula-tion; and control was transferred to the War Office in February 1916.[4]

[1] Philip Woodruff (Philip Mason, pseud.), *The Men Who Ruled India*, vol. II (1954) edn 1963, pp. 226–9.
[2] Sir Llewellyn Woodward, *Great Britain and the War of 1914–1918* (1967), pp. 99–100.
[3] See the India Office memorandum of 11 March 1917 on the military assistance given by India during the War, prepared for the imperial war conference (Austen Chamberlain Papers, AC. 20/78). See also the memorandum from the Army Department in India to the war cabinet of 23 April 1918. Milner Papers, 108, Great War A 4. India and Afghanistan [Bodl. 108].
[4] Woodward, op. cit., pp. 100–13. For a description of the military organization of the government of India, see the extract from the *Report of the Mesopotamia Commission* (Cd. 8610, 1917) in Philips, op. cit., pp. 522–4. An attempt by Robertson to centralize the control of all military operations in the General Staff in London was however unsuccessful. The viceroy retained control in Persia, on the Gulf and on India's own frontiers. See the documents in Austen Chamberlain Papers, Box 20/83.

It also proved unable to channel fruitfully the enthusiasm that existed for the allied cause when the war began, and its bureaucratic complacency reopened the gap between government and opinion that had seemed to be closing a little.[1] Nor did its performance appear to indicate that imperial rule, as contrasted with self-government resulted in superior efficiency, though there were some people prepared to argue that even the limited degree of Indianization in the government that had taken place was itself an obstacle to it.[2]

Even with the Russian danger seemingly removed by the *entente*, the first responsibility of the Indian government remained the defence of India itself. Between November 1914 and September 1915 there were no less than seven attacks on the north-west frontier, and in 1915 the operations were on a larger scale than anything since 1897. There were also internal conspiracies, including a German-organized plot in Bengal.[3] It is therefore not surprising that in the autumn of 1915 the viceroy expressed anxiety about what might happen in the absence of so much of the Indian army on distant fronts, and that some of his anxieties were shared by London.[4] The absolute priority which Kitchener gave to France over India's needs was not universally acceptable.[5]

These anxieties did not materialize; but the defence of India was of course affected by the changing pattern of the war. The Japanese, though bound by treaty to the defence of India, might, once their own immediate objectives had been reached through the conquest of Germany's Far Eastern and Pacific possessions, undertake a reversal of alliances, as it was the British and Americans who would be the obstacle to their eventual domination of the Pacific area. There were reports of the Japanese assisting in the importation of German arms into India early in 1915, and of the encouragement given by them to

[1] L. F. Rushbrook Williams, 'India and the War', *Cambridge History of India*, vol. VI, ch. XXVI.

[2] After a visit to the Indian wounded in Mesopotamia an official of the British Red Cross Society wrote that their conditions were dreadful: 'The real culprits are the Government of India – and not the whole Government of India either – the introduction of an Indian into the Executive Council has resulted – as everyone who thought about it foretold – in ordinary members of the Council seeing fewer papers than they did before – you can't show secret documents from the British Foreign Office to an Indian councillor and consequently . . . they no longer circulate as they did.' Sir John Hewett to Milner, 8 June 1916. Milner Papers, Great War, Box 1, Documents of Interest, 1916 folder [Bodl. 116]. S. P. Sinha (later Lord Sinha) had been appointed to the council as the first Indian member in 1909.

[3] Lord Hardinge, *My Indian Years, 1910–1916*, p. 131.

[4] Correspondence in Dep. Asquith 4, Box 28, and Austen Chamberlain Papers, Box 20/79.

[5] Selborne to Austen Chamberlain, 24 October 1915. Austen Chamberlain Papers, AC. 13.

seditious movements. It was also noted with apprehension that Japan was extending its influence in Tibet and Yunnan, and that the security of India required on the contrary the exclusion of the Japanese from the whole 3,000 miles of the Sino-Indian border, even if this meant being accommodating to them in other parts of China. Closer relations with the Dutch and the Americans were also essential if Japan was to be contained.[1]

A more immediate threat seemed to be presented by the bolshevik revolution in 1917, both because of the opening that the collapse of Russian resistance might offer to German ambitions and because of the new Russian rulers own self-identification with the cause of Asian nationalism. In a declaration to the Moslems of Russia and the East on 3 December 1917, India was singled out as ripe for revolution.[2] In March and April 1918, anxieties about the bolshevik threat to the Empire and about German penetration into Asia figured prominently in the case for intervention in Russia pressed by the British representatives on the supreme war council.[3]

The result of these fears was the British intervention in the Caucasus and Transcaspia which was to last – though on a small scale – until April 1919 by which time it was felt that the British garrison in Persia were a sufficient cover for India.[4] On the whole, however, while the war against Germany lasted, India's demands tended to seem of secondary importance: 'The security of India or of any other subsidiary theatre must not weigh against the successful prosecution of the War at the decisive point – France.'[5]

Such expressions of official opinion did not mean, of course, that the importance of India was unappreciated, but rather that the authorities in London accepted the dominant military view that the security of India was being defended on the European front. Meanwhile, despite the disappointment felt in some quarters at the Indian government's handling of Indian national sensibilities, the need to woo Indian opinion did not pass unrecognized in London. Among the issues involved were

[1] General Staff Memorandum: 'Japanese Activities in China and India, 14 May 1916'; India Office Memorandum: 'Japanese Policy and its Bearing on India', 16 May 1916. Austen Chamberlain Papers, Box 21/88.
[2] R. H. Ullman, *Intervention and the War* (Princeton University Press, 1961), pp. 28–9.
[3] D. F. Trask, *The United States in the Supreme War Council* (Middletown Conn., 1961), pp. 112–13.
[4] Ullman, op. cit., ch. XI: 'The Defence of India: The Caucasus and Transcaspia.'
[5] War Cabinet Memorandum: 'Security in India', 30 April 1918. Milner Papers, Great War, Box A. 4, India and Afghanistan [Bodl. 108].

those of British war aims where Indian Moslem sympathies for Turkey still had to be taken into account. 'We should,' wrote a member of the council of India, 'ruin our credit in the East, where England's word is still taken at its face value, if after saying so many fine things at the start we ended the war in a scramble for the spoils of Turkey.'[1] Nor were Indian Moslems favourable to the developing tendencies to encourage Turkey's Arab subjects to revolt against her rule; indeed, educated Indian Moslems could not, it was argued, take the revolt seriously.[2] The project of a Jewish national home in Palestine stirred even more violent feelings. The zionists claimed that a regenerated Palestine would be an asset to the British Empire and that this was recognized by Germany,[3] and considerations of imperial strategy played a major part in winning for the zionist cause a man like Amery.[4] Nevertheless, the opposition which Edwin Montagu as secretary of state for India waged against the zionist claims was at least partly based on his view that to go along with them would alienate Moslem opinion. Montagu was himself in India by the time the Balfour declaration was issued 8 November 1917, and was obviously affected by the very different view of the war and of Britain's military and diplomatic requirements that prevailed there.[5]

For India also had its 'war aims', and these were not necessarily identical with Britain's. In 1915 the Aga Khan suggested that since Samoa had been promised to Australia, and German South-West Africa to South Africa, German East Africa should be given to India as a colony.[6] In so far as the object was to encourage Indian immigration, this proposal was contested by those in Britain who queried India's need for such an outlet.[7] The proposal was enthusiastically

[1] Memorandum by Sir Theodore Morison, 16 March 1915. PRO. CAB. (Public Record Office, Cabinet Papers) 37, 126.
[2] Views of an Indian Moslem forwarded by E. E. Long, a former editor of the *Indian Daily Telegraph*, in a note of 7 July 1916. PRO. CAB. 37, 152.
[3] Dr C. Weizmann, the zionist leader and later first president of Israel to Kerr, 7 June 1917, enclosing an article from a German newspaper referring to the utility for Britain of 'A Jewish Republic upon Palestinian soil as an intermediary between Egypt and India' and to the importance for Britain of a land-route for reinforcing India if it is to be prevented from falling to Japan. Cf. Weizmann to Kerr, 7 October 1917. Lothian Papers, Box 140.
[4] Amery, op. cit., vol. 2, p. 115.
[5] See the extract from his diary of 11 November 1917, in S. D. Waley, *Edwin Montagu* (Bombay, 1964), p. 141.
[6] Dep. Asquith, Box 27, Folio 31. Memorandum from the Aga Khan. He pressed for it again in 1916. Aga Khan to Sir T. Morison, 23 June 1916. Austen Chamberlain Papers, AC. 14, 39.
[7] Kerr to Chamberlain, 28 February 1917. Kerr argued against allowing Indian immigration into either German East Africa or Mesopotamia. Lothian Papers, Box 139. The Indian

revived by Montagu himself in July 1918, only to have it shot down by Curzon who doubted whether India either aspired to be, or was qualified to be, a colonizing power.[1]

But territorial questions overseas were secondary to the principal issues of the representation of India in the councils of the Empire, and the growth of her own self-governing institutions. In July 1915 a non-official member of the Indian legislative council gave notice of a resolution demanding that India should in future be represented directly, like the dominions, at all imperial conferences; and this demand was supported by the government of India.[2] The secretary of state made it clear that while the British government did not object to the resolution, admission to the conference was a matter for that body as a whole. India's demand was repeated by the new viceroy, Lord Chelmsford in 1916[3] and Chamberlain's reply again indicated that the problem would be to overcome the resistance of the dominions.[4]

The dominions' opposition was based in part upon the still vexed question of Indian immigration into the dominions and the treatment of Indians there.[5] But when the question of admitting India was first put to the dominion prime ministers, those of Australia and Canada were definitely opposed and those of South Africa and New Zealand non-committal,[6] which suggests that other factors entered into it. In the

---

delegation to the 1917 conference submitted a memorandum in favour of free Indian immigration to German East Africa. Austen Chamberlain Papers, AC. 20/78. On Mesopotamia Kerr may have been echoing the views of Curtis who had written to him arguing against Mesopotamia being treated as another province of India, since in India (unlike Mesopotamia) political organization would have to be fostered. Curtis to Kerr, 25 March 1917. Ibid. Amery argued at about this time for drawing a distinction between the government of India in its internal aspect where Indians might aspire to self-government, and India in the wider sense where the viceroy and foreign department would have an independent role. Memorandum on rearrangement of imperial administrative offices, 1917. PRO. CAB. 17, 190.

[1] Louis, *Germany's Lost Colonies*, pp. 113–15.
[2] On this question, see Mehrotra, op. cit., pp. 91 ff.
[3] Chelmsford had succeeded Hardinge in April 1916. F. J. N. Thesiger (1868–1933) (Baron Chelmsford 1905, viscount 1921) had held governorships in Australia. He remained viceroy till April 1921. First lord of the admiralty, 1924.
[4] Kerr had noted in 1912 that whereas hardly anyone in Britain wished to see the connection with India dissolved, what he called the 'Perish India' school still had adherents in the dominions. 'India and the Empire', *The Round Table*, September 1912.
[5] Curtis in a letter to the viceroy stressed his view that all settlement of Asiatics among white peoples was an evil, and objected even to a token acquiescence of the Indian demand for reciprocity such as the conference eventually accepted. Curtis to Chelmsford, 2 November 1916. Chelmsford himself was worried lest the proposed control by Australia and New Zealand after the war not only of the conquered German colonies but also of Britain's existing Pacific possessions would lead to the exclusion of Indians and to exasperating relations with Japan. Chelmsford to Chamberlain, 2 November 1917. Lothian Papers, Box 139.
[6] Petrie, op. cit., vol. II, pp. 73–4.

event, the British government got its way, and Indian delegates were invited to the conference which formally resolved in 13 April 1917 that India should in future figure as a regular member. India was also represented fully at meetings of the imperial war cabinet. The Indian delegation to London included, besides the secretary of state, an Indian civil servant, Sir James Meston (later Lord Meston), the Maharajah of Bikaner, and Sir S. P. Sinha, who had recently become a member of the Bengal executive council.[1] While this participation might be held to meet some of India's aspirations, there still remained the problem of associating an India for which the British government held ultimate responsibility in institutions alongside the dominions. It was unlikely that this gesture would, as some people seem to have hoped, prevent the Indian demand for self-government from being pressed.[2] And how would an imperial war cabinet so constituted deal with the problems of Indian government; could it in fact carry on into peacetime?[3]

The question of constitutional advance was not, however, to await the end of the war.[4] The need to do something had been pressed on the government by liberal-minded Englishmen as well as Indians from early in the war. The new viceroy found that the temper of Congress had become much more radical between 1915 and 1916, but it was December before his recommendations for constitutional advance reached the home government. Montagu, who had hoped to be viceroy, was appointed secretary of state in July 1917 and had to combat conservative hostility to his known sympathies with Indian nationalism. He found it difficult to get the war cabinet's attention for the subject of Indian constitutional reform despite the insistence of the viceroy and the provincial governors. Curzon successfully resisted his wish to make the new announcement of policy one unequivocally in favour of self-government. The formula, as the latter eventually drafted it, and as it appeared in Montagu's announcement to parliament on 20 August 1917, spoke of 'the increasing association of Indians in every branch of

[1] Sinha after serving on the viceroy's council in 1909–10 had been president of the Indian National Congress in 1915. He was to be a member of the Indian war cabinet in 1918, under-secretary of state for India, January 1919–September 1920, and governor of Bihar and Orissa, 1920–1.
[2] For this point of view, see Walter Long to Chamberlain, 30 December 1916. Austen Chamberlain Papers, Box AC. 16/52.
[3] Kerr to Curtis, 24 April 1917. Lothian Papers, Box 139.
[4] For developments in India from 1915 to 1919, see Moore, op. cit., pp. 113 ff.; Mehrotra, op. cit., pp. 100 ff.; R. Coupland, *The Indian Problem, 1833–1935* (1942): ch, V, 'The Montagu–Chelmsford Reforms'.

the administration, and the gradual development of self-governing institutions with a view to the progressive realization of responsible government in India as an integral part of the British Empire'.[1]

The view that cautious English liberals had expressed, that Indian pressure for greater concessions would halt progress, had proved incorrect.[2] As so often in the history of the transfer of power in the Empire, agitation had acted as a spur. Behind the scenes, the form of eventual self-governing institutions was argued. Greater measure of decentralization were generally favoured.[3] A discussion between the Round Table group and the Indian representatives at the 1917 imperial war conference concentrated on trying to distinguish between India's internal affairs, and those matters such as foreign policy and defence which must remain imperial;[4] but the Round Table as a group feared that Curtis' own rather advanced views in favour of Indian self-government would be held to reflect those of the whole of it.[5]

Curtis himself played an important part in the next stage of constitutional progress through winning over Milner and Curzon to the idea of dyarchy.[6] The Montagu–Chelmsford report, submitted to the war cabinet in April 1918 and published in July, was based on the principle of dividing the responsibilities of government into three levels. At the local level the greatest possible measure of popular control was to be given; at the provincial level, dyarchy was to reign with some departments in the hands of Indian ministers responsible to the legislature, while others remained in the care of the Governor. At the same time, more financial powers were to be transferred to the provinces. The viceroy's responsibility for the central government would remain intact but the legislative council was to be made larger and more representative. The appearance of a chamber of princes as another consultative body helped to emphasize the rather federalist inspiration of the proposals.[7]

---

[1] For extracts from the principal constitutional documents for this period, see Philip, op. cit., pp. 264–82.
[2] 'Any formulation during the present crisis of demands for further powers of self-government in India would, I think, be from the Indian point of view, disastrous. It would be construed as an attempt to extort concessions at a time of national danger,' Ilbert to Bryce, 6 November 1915. Bryce Papers, English Correspondence, vol. 13.
[3] Lord Willingdon, governor of Bombay to Spender, 25 April 1915. Spender Papers, B.M. Add. 46392.   [4] Kerr to Curtis, 23 April 1917. Lothian Papers, Box 139.
[5] Kerr to Curtis, 9 July 1917; Curtis to Kerr, 28 August 1917. Ibid.
[6] The idea had been suggested to the Round Table group by Sir William Duke, a member of the secretary of state's council in 1915. Waley, *Edwin Montagu*, pp. 151, 150, 167.
[7] The report was styled by Ilbert 'a typical Round Table production, very well-written, very

The report, of course, fell short of what Congress by now demanded. The memorandum presented by it to Montagu on his arrival in India in November 1917 had demanded a definite timetable over a period of about twenty-five years, at the end of which full self-government would have been achieved. It also demanded that full equality with the dominions should be recognized and that any imperial parliament or council that might come into being should have from the outset full Indian representation.[1] The expressions of disappointment by Congress and its demand for further important concessions led to the secession of the moderates, the later liberals, from its ranks.

What was important in the eyes of British supporters of the reforms was to make clear the extent of the British commitment to them.[2] The difficulty was the campaign against the government on this score which had gone on ever since Montagu's original pronouncement under the leadership of Lord Sydenham: 'By their jeers and flouts and jibes at the educated Indian,' wrote the viceroy, 'they are driving them to a state of exasperation which will seriously militate against the acceptance of any amending constitutional proposals.'[3] It was clear from the report that there would have to be increasing Indianization of the civil service to match the constitutional steps taken. And the partial closing of the opportunities to candidates from Britain may have been responsible for some of the hostility shown by the classes who had been wont to supply them. Certainly there had been cabinet opposition to the idea of a large-scale grant of army commissions to Indians on the ground that it would discourage future recruitment: 'Steps already taken to admit Indians have created distrust among parents and guardians.'[4] Again there was confusion as to whether Britain was in India for India's good as men like Montagu believed, or whether its main importance was its moral and material utility to Britain.[5] What was lacking was any forum in which these fundamental questions of the

doctrinaire, very ingenious but far too much influenced by colonial precedents'. Ilbert to Bryce, 30 August 1918. Bryce Papers, English Correspondence, vol. 13.
[1] Mehrotra, op. cit., pp. 107–9.
[2] Curtis to Neville Chamberlain, 18 July 1918. Lothian Papers, Box 139.
[3] Lord Chelmsford to Austen Chamberlain (extract), 17 May 1918. Printed as an appendix to a note for the war cabinet by Chamberlain on the situation in India, 26 June 1918. Austen Chamberlain Papers, Box 34/105, Secret G.T. 4956.
[4] Note of 26 April 1918. Lothian Papers, Box 139.
[5] The classical statement of the latter case is Curzon's lecture at Edinburgh, *The Place of India in the Empire* (1909), where he referred to India as having marked the British character by developing 'a sense of duty and a spirit of self-sacrifice, as well as faculties of administration and command'. Quoted Mehrotra, op. cit., p. 244.

Indian and imperial future could be hammered out and a consensus attained. The inadequacy of the Westminster parliament as an institution for handling imperial issues was once again illustrated: 'I feel more strongly than ever,' wrote Curtis to the Secretary of State, 'that Parliament's habit since Mutiny days, of ignoring Indian affairs, is at the root of all our trouble. No really informed opinion on Indian affairs can be created here unless or until Parliament reverts to its former practice of direct inquiry'.[1] But parliament had, as usual, other things on its mind. On the day that Curtis wrote, the last German offensive on the western front had been pushed back to its starting-point; and within less than a week, the allies were to take the initiative and hold it to the end.

Early War Aims and Peace Feelers

The war aims of Britain, as publicly professed and generally understood from early in the war, were the restoration of Belgium, the protection of France against aggression, the destruction of 'Prussian' military domination, and the defence of the rights of small nations. But these principles were – apart from the first – ambiguous in themselves, and took little account of the likely demands for territorial gains on the part of Britain's allies. It was, after all, improbable that she herself would surrender the German colonies which were being attacked by British, Indian, and South African forces in Africa, and by Australasian forces in the Pacific, or that the Japanese would give up their conquests.[2]

Territorial changes in Europe – the French recovery of Alsace-Lorraine, the establishment of a Polish state – which came within the scope of what British statesmen considered reasonable, raised questions of what the post-war balance in Europe would look like and whether or not a peace could be reached which would sufficiently satisfy Germany to make an Anglo-German reconciliation possible.[3] Otherwise the Empire might need to provide large-scale armaments to meet a renewal of the German threat in the future. It was true that by the end of 1914 German shipping had been swept from the high seas and the German main fleet apparently confined to harbour, and the battle of Jutland

[1] Curtis to Montagu, 3 August 1918. Lothian Papers, Box 139.
[2] On the conquest of the German colonial empire, see Louis, op. cit., ch. II.
[3] Harold I. Nelson, *Land and Power, British and Allied Policy on Germany's frontiers, 1916–1919* (1963), p. 7.

in May 1916 confirmed this aspect of Britain's naval supremacy.[1] But the revelation of the power of the submarine as a commerce destroyer, and the limitations upon the blockade of Germany imposed by regard for American neutral rights rendered Britain sensitive to the nature of a European settlement.

Meanwhile inter-allied negotiations were in any event limiting Britain's freedom of action. By the agreement of 12 March 1915, signed during the opening phase of the Gallipoli operations, Britain and France surrendered their historic objections to Russia's desire to become a Mediterranean power by agreeing to her annexation of Constantinople and the Straits.[2] The reservation of British and French claims on the Ottoman empire pointed the way to the creation of a new barrier for the defence of the Suez Canal and the Persian Gulf through Britain becoming the heir to the Ottoman domination of the Arab lands; but this was a second-best. The secret treaty of London of 28 April 1915, by which Italy was induced to enter the war, affected the British position less directly, despite the undertaking that Italy should get a share in any eventual partition of Turkey and colonial gains in Africa to balance what France and Britain might seize from Germany. But the commitment to Italy's claims made a compromise peace with Austria impossible later in the war, and this in turn ensured that the war with Germany would also be fought to the bitter end. Efforts to secure the co-operation of Balkan powers in the war occupied much of the Foreign Office's energies. In the end Rumania and, after an internal revolution, Greece (but only in June 1917) entered the war, but the military benefits hardly compensated for the further political commitments that this entailed.

With the diplomatic and military map in such flux in the east, and with the inexorable grinding down of British manpower on the western front, war aims had both a speculative and an immediate significance. It was possible to envisage a number of future situations depending on the completeness or otherwise of the allied victory; but a sudden

[1] On Jutland, see Marder, *From Dreadnought to Scapa Flow*, vol. III.
[2] Russian objections helped to prevent the use of the Greek army for a direct attack upon Constantinople. But British attempts to build up Greece as an alternative ally in the Eastern Mediterranean were to have a long history. It is a matter for speculation whether British phil-hellenism was a product of the importance of Greek in the education of the ruling class which remained more considerable than in most other countries. It was, anyhow, perhaps less important than Lloyd George's admiration for the Greek statesman, Venizelos. It is rather similar to the question of how far British familiarity with the Bible contributed to early sympathy for zionism, later increasingly balanced by Arabophile tendencies among archeologists working in the Middle East.

deterioration in the military situation of either side, or pressure for negotiations from the United States and other neutrals too difficult to resist, might force an immediate decision as to the priorities in British policy.

The first kind of speculation was indicated by Kitchener in April 1915. He emphasized the difference of view between Britain in her insular position and the continental powers who would probably continue after the war to maintain armies on their previous scale.[1] Germany's defeat would produce a Russian preponderance in eastern Europe, combined with a new role allotted to her in the Balkans and Mediterranean. France would probably join with Germany, Italy, Austria, and Rumania in a strong combination to resist the further advance of Slav influence. Britain's position would then be difficult. It would be unwise to take sides against Russia, since she would be in a position both to threaten imperial frontiers directly, and through her influence over the remains of the Turkish empire to exert considerable influence over the Moslems of India. A Franco-German combination would dispose of large fleets and a long coastline, and would be equally difficult to oppose. Britain would therefore have to try to preserve neutrality in such a conflict alongside the United States. There would be the danger, however, that Germany would not be content with this but would drag Britain into war, and the important thing therefore was to safeguard British territories by ensuring them such frontiers as would make a German attack on them extremely difficult. Britain should not, therefore, after the war be induced to occupy territories vulnerable to German (or even Franco-German) attack.

There was the further possibility of winning over neutrals – Holland, for instance, was thought of as possible – and there was always the chance of detaching Germany's allies. The military themselves felt that British influence in allied councils was not increasing to the extent justified by her contribution to the war. Russia should be persuaded to drop the claim to Constantinople so as to come to terms with Turkey. Some territorial bait should be found to detach Bulgaria from Germany. To all these possibilities the agreements with Russia, Italy, and Rumania offered obstacles which one should attempt to get round by revising them.[2]

[1] 'Future Relations of the Great Powers', observations on the lord chancellor's note by K., 21 April 1915. PRO. CAB. 37, 127.
[2] Memoranda by Sir William Robertson, 12 February 1916 and 29 March 1916. Austen Chamberlain Papers, AC. 20/78, 01/8/32, 01/92/267.

It was obvious that such agreements were not in fact easy to reopen without danger to the cohesion of the allies. One method of strengthening it might be to develop permanent economic ties, by prolonging into peacetime the new channels of trade necessitated by the blockade so as to provide an answer to the German ambitions for a dominant *Mitteleuropa*.[1] An allied conference in June 1916 agreed that for a period to be determined Germany should lose the benefits of the most-favoured-nation clause and be subjected to a system of prohibitions on her exports.[2]

The first exhaustive attempt to outline peace terms was made by the Foreign Office in a memorandum drawn up by Sir Ralph Paget and Sir William Tyrrell, dated 31 August 1916 and circulated to the cabinet, though not discussed by it or by any cabinet committee during the lifetime of the Asquith government.[3] This document envisaged both a peace after victory, and the possible position, if it were necessary, to accept a compromise settlement. In the former case, the principle of nationality was to be one of the governing factors, but no state should be so strengthened as to threaten future peace, and none was to be left at a grave economic disadvantage. Where allied claims conflicted with the principle, circumstances and British interests should be the guide. The greatest British need was for an enduring peace and for an end to the armaments race, and general arbitration treaties should be insisted upon. Belgium was a special case, and the memorandum advocated a permanent alliance between Great Britain, France, and Belgium to prevent a renewed German invasion – despite the objections traditionally raised to continental alliances.[4] An inconclusive peace would mean that heavy burdens would fall on Britain, because if Britain alone had escaped invasion it might be necessary to buy German withdrawals at the price of cessions in East Africa. The financial burden of rehabilitating Belgium would fall wholly on British shoulders, and it might even be necessary for Britain to struggle alone against Germany to secure Belgian independence while France and Russia profited by standing on the sidelines.[5]

[1] See papers in Dep. Asquith, Box 29.
[2] A. J. Mayer, *Political Origins of the New Diplomacy* (New Haven, 1959), p. 20.
[3] Nelson, op. cit., p. 8. Most of the memorandum is printed in D. Lloyd George, *The Truth About the Peace Treaties* (1938), vol. 1, pp. 31 ff.
[4] PRO. CAB. 29 1/1, Paper, W.C. 64.
[5] The *entente* was formally pledged by an agreement of 12 February 1916 to restore Belgian independence and to secure her an indemnity.

A general staff memorandum, signed by Sir William Robertson, was dominated by the fear that at a hastily summoned peace conference Germany might drive a wedge between the allies, and that Britain might be deprived of her claims, in particular to the German colonies.[1] The basis of peace negotiations should be the three principles for which Britain had so often fought in the past, and for which she was fighting now: (a) the maintenance of the balance of power in Europe; (b) the maintenance of British maritime supremacy; and (c) the maintenance of a weak power in the Low Countries.

The balance of power in Europe demanded a strong central European power which must be Teutonic, as any Slav power would lean towards Russia and therefore destroy the very principle which it was desired to uphold: 'On the other hand, as Germany is the chief European competitor with us on the sea, it would be advantageous to make such terms of peace as would check the development of her navy and of her mercantile marine. In other words, it would be in the interests of the British Empire to leave Germany reasonably strong on land, but to weaken her at sea.' The main suggestions made were the cession of Alsace and Lorraine; of East Friesland, Schleswig, and part of Holstein (thus depriving Germany of the Kiel Canal and important stretches of the coastline), and some cession of territory to a reconstituted Poland. Meanwhile Germany would be strengthened by the incorporation of Austria proper, or by a closer union with a much diminished Austria-Hungary. The proposals for dealing with Turkey would provide a barrier to German development in the Near East.

A not dissimilar line of thinking was that of the first sea lord, though he added the cession of Heligoland, either to Britain or to some weak neutral power after the demolition of its fortifications. All German overseas possessions were to go to the allies.[2]

Balfour had expressed a somewhat different point of view, being less confident that Germany would be so weakened by the war that the problem of Slav preponderance was the one that needed worrying about. The Germans could not have centrifugal tendencies imposed upon them, while the Slav countries were bitterly divided among themselves and the only great power among them, namely Russia, was

---

[1] Austen Chamberlain Papers, AC. 20/78.
[2] Note on the possible terms of peace by the first sea lord, Admiral Jellicoe, 12 October 1916. PRO. CAB. 29 1/1. Fisher's ideas were very similar; see his letters to Arnold White, 24 September 1916, A. S. Hurd, 16 October 1918. Marder, *Fear God and Dread Nought*, vol. III, pp. 373-4, 554.

likely to be torn by revolutionary struggles as soon as the pressure of war was removed. Germany would probably remain the country that threatened to upset the balance of power and this would make the preservation of the *entente* essential: 'Whatever trouble Russia may give us in Mesopotamia, Persia, and Afghanistan, I do not think she will attempt the domination of Europe, still less succeed in securing it.'[1]

The mood of all these documents suggested confidence that, whatever difficulties the future might bring, the allies would at some moment be able to rearrange the map of Europe. But Lord Lansdowne, then serving under Asquith as minister without portfolio, was sceptical. There seemed no immediate prospect of a knock-out blow, and the idea of two or three years more of war with the losses that this would inevitably entail was something which should not be contemplated if there were any possibility of exploring at once the grounds of a possible settlement: 'We are,' he warned, 'slowly but surely killing off the best of the male population of these islands.'[2]

Lansdowne noted in a postscript that the cabinet had learned on the same day, 13 November 1916, that the war committee had indeed decided upon explorations along the lines he advocated, and the pressures for peace that the United States had been exercising intermittently since the beginning of the year were now becoming difficult to resist, despite Lloyd George's public denunciation of external interference before the 'Prussian military despotism' was broken beyond repair.[3] The general situation was such that Britain might be regarded as being impelled to make peace under duress, particularly in the light of the growing success of the German submarine campaign, and the apparent threat to the British command of the narrow seas after the raid on the Dover Patrol on 26 October, and the subsequent suspension of troop transports to France.[4]

The deciding factor seemed to be the impossibility of shifting the military from their commitment to the view that a knock-out blow on

[1] Balfour, 'The Peace Settlement in Europe', 4 October 1916. Austen Chamberlain Papers, AC. 20/78, 1078–2.
[2] Memorandum by Lansdowne, 13 November 1916, ibid., 1266. Cf. Earl of Oxford and Asquith, *Memories and Reflections* (1928), vol. II, p. 142. 'Slowly' was an odd adjective in the light of the battle of the Somme, the main British military operation of 1916. For the four months, July–October, British casualties were 450,000, over 100,000 being fatal. Guinn, op. cit., p. 155.
[3] *The Times*, 29 September 1916. Lansdowne's support for a 'rational' approach to European problems did not make him any less a die-hard where Ireland was concerned, opposing every move towards agreement over home rule.
[4] Guinn, op. cit., pp. 170 ff.

the western front was still possible, and that there was no prospect of Germany making peace before that happened on any terms which the allies could accept. To leave the domination of Prussia intact would mean laying up trouble for the future, estranging the dominions and allies and sacrificing British interests.[1]

It is now fairly clear that Robertson was correct and that the Americans were over-optimistic in thinking that the Germans at this stage were contemplating a peace which would meet even Britain's minimum demands.[2] But even without knowing Germany's plans it was obvious that, at a time when all Britain's major allies were suffering different degrees of exhaustion and discouragement, to seek peace would give an impression of weakness, so that there was no option, in the view of ministers, but to continue the struggle.[3]

At this point, however, the uneasiness about lack of determination in the conduct of the war, and the demand of the military and others for a greater degree of mobilization of Britain's manpower and other resources, led to the overthrow of the Asquith coalition and to the installation of Lloyd George in the seat of power. Among those who left office with Asquith were Grey himself and Lansdowne. The task of answering President Wilson's last initiative in favour of peace fell to the new limited war cabinet; Lloyd George, Milner, Curzon, Arthur Henderson, and Bonar Law, with Balfour as the new foreign secretary.[4]

Lloyd George and Reorganization

The story of the way in which the change of government came about has often been told, and needs no detailing here.[5] It arose out of the

[1] Memorandum by Sir William Robertson, 24 November 1916. Austen Chamberlain Papers, 20/78, 01/56/181.
[2] See Fischer, op. cit., pp. 310 ff.
[3] See the Memorandum by Lord Robert Cecil, 27 November 1916. Austen Chamberlain Papers, AC. 20/78, 1319. Lansdowne himself protested that he had been misunderstood, that he did not propose an inconclusive peace but merely a stocktaking of the whole position. Memorandum of 27 November, ibid., 1321.
[4] One must not assume that opinion generally was not behind the resistance to peace-initiatives. Lord Bryce, who cannot be classed as among the bellicose, warned Wilson's confidant and intermediary Col. House on 31 May and again on 2 September 1916 that the time was some way off before the Germans would be brought to the point at which they would contemplate peace on any terms the Allies would find acceptable. (Communicated by E. Ions.)
[5] See most recently, Roy Jenkins, *Asquith* (1964). The most dramatic account remains that of Lord Beaverbrook in his *Politicians and the War* (1928). The episode marks the author's first important irruption into British politics as the friend and confident of Bonar Law. Max Aitken (1879–1964) (knighted 1911, Baron Beaverbrook 1917), a Canadian-born newspaper

stresses and strains of wartime politics in circumstances where parliament could not play its normal role and where recourse to the electorate was impossible,[1] and its ultimate impact was as important for domestic as for external affairs; for the Lloyd George formula for government differed radically from what had gone before. The new war cabinet replaced both the old war committee of Asquith's day, and the historic cabinet itself. The C.I.D. secretariat was finally taken over, to become the cabinet secretariat, and gave the new body the full apparatus of agenda, minutes, and a machinery for communicating and following up its decisions. Foreign and military intelligence was presented at every meeting, and the system of circulating papers enabled ministers who were not members to keep in touch with the war cabinet's work; some, such as Balfour at the Admiralty, saw all the papers. But what struck people most forcibly was the small size and frequent meetings of the new body, to which people could easily be summoned, and whose sub-committees (of which Milner and Smuts were usually chairmen) could rapidly deal with any matter of interdepartmental controversy.[2]

So important a change in the machinery of government inevitably attracted criticism; and even those who accepted the need for a small body for the conduct of the war objected to the demotion of the departmental ministers in favour of the 'half-dozen oligarchs' who now controlled 'the destinies of the country'.[3] There were also criticism of Lloyd George's personal power, and some confusion in the public mind between the war cabinet secretariat under Hankey and his private secretariat under W. G. S. Adams, the 'garden suburb'. But departures from the historic constitution were in fact less important than the

---

owner, was M.P. 1910–16. Chancellor of the Duchy and minister of information, February–November 1918; minister of aircraft production, May 1940–May 1941; minister of state, May–June 1941; minister of supply, June 1941–February 1942; minister of war production, February 1942 (and member of war cabinet during this period). Lord Privy Seal, September 1943–July 1945. He acquired control of the *Daily Express* in 1915 and created the *Sunday Express* in 1918. His influence was strongly imperialist with a particular accent on the economic side, and as strongly isolationist and anti-European.

[1] See A. J. P. Taylor, *Politics in Wartime* (1964), pp. 11–44.

[2] The original members of the war cabinet were Lloyd George, Curzon as lord president, Bonar Law as chancellor and leader of the House, and Milner and the labour representative Arthur Henderson as ministers without portfolio. The addition of Smuts in June 1917 brought the number of members up to six and that of Carson in July to seven. In August Henderson was replaced by G. N. Barnes. In January 1918 Carson and Barnes left, reducing the total to five again, and in April 1918 Austen Chamberlain replaced Milner when the latter took over the War Office.

[3] See the speech by the Lord Midleton in the House of Lords, 19 June 1918. Lord Lansdowne and Lord Salisbury were other critics.

continued failure to solve the overriding problem of civil–military relations. In part this was because Lloyd George, despite his apparent
personal ascendancy, was to some extent the captive of the conservatives who supplied the bulk of his parliamentary support; and in their
ranks, confidence in the professional soldiers tended to be high. Lloyd
George doubted the capacity both of Sir William Robertson who had
become C.I.G.S. in December 1915, and of his principal field commander, Douglas Haig, but he did not feel in a position to get rid of
Robertson until February 1918. Haig, secure in royal as well as
political backing, remained in command of the British armies until the
end though ultimately obliged to accept the overall authority of Foch.
At the Admiralty, Jellicoe likewise did not command Lloyd George's
confidence. It was in order to put in a new first lord of the admiralty
(Sir Eric Geddes) who would control Jellicoe that Carson was moved
up to the war cabinet in July 1917, and in December Jellicoe himself
resigned.

So difficult was the task of establishing civilian authority that both
Lloyd George and Milner were at times inclined to believe in the reality
of a plot by the army leaders to take over the government.[1] In the end,
the dangers on the western front and the patent needs of the alliance for
greater unity of control gave Lloyd George his opportunity. The new
C.I.G.S. Sir Henry Wilson was the most acceptable to him of the
soldiers, and from April 1918 Milner as secretary of state for war was in
direct authority over him.[2] In the spring and summer of 1918, it was not
so much the war cabinet as the so-called 'X committee' – Lloyd
George, Milner, and Wilson – who controlled the war. With the defeat
of the prime minister's critics in the 'Maurice' debate on 9 May, Lloyd
George's power reached its peak.[3]

The development of British government in wartime was thus in many
respects a break with past practice. Britain experienced the same concentration of authority as was practised in other belligerent powers. Although the party system continued to limit the prime minister's freedom
of choice in the selection of his colleagues, it was possible to bring in men
from outside the political arena in a way which would not have been

[1] Beaverbrook, *Men and Power* (1956). p. 222.
[2] Lord Derby's confidence in Robertson and Haig had been a major obstacle to change.
[3] On the 'Maurice' debate arising out of accusations by General Sir Frederick Maurice, a
close associate of Robertson recently dismissed, that Lloyd George had misled the House of
Commons about the strength of British forces in France. See Taylor, *English History, 1914–
1945*, pp. 104–5.

possible in normal times. But the very pressures of war and the inevitable tendency to overwork – on the part of men often themselves subject to deep personal anxieties – made it hard to give prolonged and undivided attention to issues other than those forced upon them by day to day events. Where the soldiers are concerned this explains, if it does not excuse, the delay in adapting tactics to new weapons or to the new use of existing ones; in the case of the civilians it helps to explain why some important political developments came upon them unawares – the Russian revolution, for instance – and why important miscalculations in handling the political aspects of the struggle were almost unavoidable. As in all wars, the pursuit of victory had the effect of making people forget why victory was desirable; ends were lost sight of in a preoccupation with means. In retrospect the errors bulked larger than the achievements, and people wondered how any nation could have accepted such losses for so little permanent gain (the enemy, once defeated, was forgotten), and criticism of what had been done led people to question both the skill of their leaders individually and the capacity of the class from which most of them were still drawn. Much of the existing structure of British government and society seemed to have been put into the melting-pot by wartime changes; it remained to be seen how much of it would come out again in the traditional shape.

The 'Left' Against the 'New Imperialists'

Lloyd George's accession to power appeared to be a victory for the believers in a more decisive war effort and no negotiation, and in that sense it would be true to say it represented a victory for the 'right'. The early part of the war had already marked a setback for the political 'left', inevitable when the choice had to be made between consistency of belief and the innate instinct not to rock the boat. The labour party had supported the war effort from the beginning, losing its leader, Ramsay MacDonald, and four of the other seven members of the I.L.P. in the parliamentary party. The I.L.P. itself, while opposed in its majority to the war, was split in opposition. Some were pacifist. A small minority was revolutionary, while Keir Hardie, MacDonald, and Snowden accepted the view that the war was now a fact and must, accordingly, be fought – although they did not absolve the government from its responsibility for its outbreak. Others of the left, like Blatchford and Hyndman, were militantly pro-war. The *New Statesman* was a strong believer in the justice of the allied cause and the wickedness of German militarism.[1] So were most of the leaders of the Fabians, though the society itself made no pronouncement, and a minority led by Clifford Allen followed the I.L.P. line.[2] Later in the war the inevitable tensions arising out of the new industrial scene brought about a new wave of radicalism which made its impact in both positive and negative ways. For the time being, however, with little practical to contribute, the ideologues of the Fabian society and the left-wing liberals, who had worked with them before the war, and who would most of them end up in the post-war labour party, could circumvent their frustrations by planning for a better world, democratic control of foreign policy, some form of League of Nations and so forth.[3]

The left found it difficult to make its voice heard in any coherent fashion when possibilities of peace through negotiation began to be glimpsed in 1916. Those who had been against the war from the beginning were not in a good position to take the lead, and none of them, not even MacDonald, possessed the political stature to do so. The anti-imperialist theoretician J. A. Hobson suggested to Sir John Simon, who had resigned from the Asquith government over conscription in January 1916, that he should take the initiative in pressing for negotiation. This might put him in a position of leadership for the post-war struggle: 'The endeavour to recover or retain the lost or imperilled fortresses of political and civil liberty, i.e. a fight against militarism, conscription, protection, and bureaucratic nationalism, for liberty, sound finance, and constructive internationalism.'[4] Simon did not respond to this flattering overture and preferred service with the R.F.C.[5]

Over Irish affairs the left felt that there had already been a grave departure from their principles. After the Easter rising of 1916 and the creation of martyrs for the nationalist cause by the executions that followed, the new attempt to find a solution had foundered on the in-

---

[1] Medlicott, op. cit., p. 26.
[2] McBriar, op. cit., ch. V. Clifford Allen, left-wing journalist and conscientious objector was as Lord Allen of Hurtwood, a labour peer, a national leader of the left-wing of the 'appeasers' of the 1930s. See Arthur Marwick, *Clifford Allen: the Open Conspirator* (Edinburgh 1964), and Martin Gilbert, *Plough My Own Furrow: the story of Lord Allen of Hurtwood* (1965).
[3] See A. J. P. Taylor, *The Troublemakers*, ch. V.
[4] J. A. Hobson to Sir John Simon, 25 May 1916. Simon Papers.
[5] J. A. Simon (1873–1954) (knighted 1910, first viscount 1950) was M.P. from 1906 to 1918 and 1922 to 1940. Solicitor-general, 1910–13; attorney-general, 1913; home secretary, May 1915–January 1916. Chairman, Indian Statutory Commission, 1927. Foreign secretary, November 1931–June 1935; and leader of the National Liberal party from 1931; home secretary, 1935–7; chancellor of exchequer, 1937–40; lord chancellor, 1940–5.

transigence of both sides; but it was natural that some home rulers explained failure by the inclusion in the Asquith coalition of such leading extremists on the unionist side as Bonar Law, Carson, and F. E. Smith.[1]

Should the change of government in December 1916 then be viewed as a further triumph for what many liberals and most labour men would have regarded as the powers of darkness? How true is it to say that 'for the first time in British history, the "New Imperialism" repudiated by the electorate in 1906 had captured the citadel of power?'[2] Two important arguments may be brought forward in defence of this thesis. In the first place, an important group of imperialists had been working for some time to overthrow Asquith and instal a more dynamic successor. This was the ginger group led by Milner which met weekly from early in 1916 to 1918. Its members included, Carson, F. S. Oliver, Geoffrey Robinson (Dawson), Waldorf Astor, and General Wilson. The organizer on Milner's behalf was Amery.[3] Milner himself had largely been devoting his energies during 1915 and 1916 to building up the nucleus of a new party out of the strongly pro-war elements in the labour movement. The British Workers National League was founded by him with the aid of money from Waldorf Astor. One speaker at its inaugural meeting in May 1916 was the Australian prime minister, Hughes.[4]

In the second place, in the new war cabinet, after Lloyd George himself the dominant figures were the two former proconsuls, Milner and Curzon. A number of members of the Milner Kindergarten, it has been said, received influential if junior positions, Astor (as the Prime Minister's P.P.S.), Curtis and Kerr in the prime minister's new personal secretariat – the 'garden suburb', John Buchan as deputy director of the new Ministry of Information, Amery and Mark Sykes in the new war cabinet secretariat with the duty, new for civilians, of preparing

---

[1] Medlicott, op. cit., pp. 36–43.
[2] Guinn, op. cit., p. 192.
[3] Quigley, 'The Round Table Groups in Canada, 1908–1938' *Canadian Historical Review*, 1962, p. 204 fn.
[4] Apart from recruits from the *Clarion* group and a number of labour M.P.s and trade union leaders, the League also attracted the support of H. G. Wells; the mixture in its propaganda of state control, efficiency, and imperial organization had similarities with some earlier Fabian ideas. It does not appear that there was much contact between the Milnerites and Lloyd George at this time, though Arthur Lee may have kept Lloyd George in touch with their doings. Steel-Maitland acted as a link between Milner and Bonar Law. See P. A. Lockwood, 'Milner's Entry into the War Cabinet, December 1916', *Historical Journal*, vol. VII (1964).

for ministers weekly summaries of intelligence.[1] W. G. S. Adams, another member of the secretariat, had been in contact with Milner, and the new minister of agriculture, R. E. Prothero (Lord Ernle) had been associated with Milner on the food production committee of 1915. The new minister of labour, John Hodge, was president of the British Workers League and two of its vice-presidents got lesser posts. Finally, F. S. Oliver, though not in the government, kept in close touch with his friends.[2]

But this line of argument must not be carried too far. Not all the imperialists were Milnerites, and Milner's own influence was by no means in a single direction. In Britain itself, since the beginning of 1915, there had been proposals for summoning a conference of dominion governments but no such gathering was held. Milner in a couple of speeches had stressed the need for imperial co-operation and his hopes for the establishment of an imperial cabinet.[3] Meanwhile the Round Table group, with which he was still connected, was continuing to build up its network of channels in the dominions and notably in Canada.[4]

At this point the differences within the movement came into the open. The Curtis draft of a programme for the future with its strong centralist bias would, it was pointed out to Milner, alienate more Canadians than it would win over.[5] But Milner himself emphasized that he was very far from subscribing to the Curtis scheme.[6] It was Canadian opposition apparently that caused the group to drop the idea of an agreed manifesto, and to allow Curtis to publish as his personal work only, the book *The Problem of the Commonwealth* in 1916.[7] Canadians who favoured imperial co-operation were fearful of the centralizing tendency of Curtis's thought, and refused to accept that there was nothing between total independence in foreign policy and federal institutions for the whole Empire.[8]

---

[1] These are the men named by Guinn, loc. cit. Waldorf Astor (1879–1953) (second viscount, 1919) was, however, not a member of the Kindergarten. His interests hitherto had been in medicine and agriculture, not external affairs. Mark Sykes (1879–1919) (baronet, 1913) an M.P. and expert on Middle Eastern affairs was not a member of the Kindergarten either, and had been on Hankey's staff before the change of government.

[2] Lockwood, loc. cit. Oliver had sent Milner a list of young men suitable for employment under the new administration. Gollin, op. cit., pp. 376–9.

[3] Ibid., pp. 352, 394–5.

[4] Quigley, loc. cit.

[5] Glazebrook to Milner, 15 February 1915. Milner Papers, Private Letters, 1915, II [Bodl. 140].

[6] Milner to Glazebrook, 8 March 1919. Milner Papers, Private Letters, 1916, IV [Bodl. 142].

[7] Vincent Massey, *What's Past in Prologue* (1963), pp. 34 ff.

[8] Cook, *John Dafoe and the Free Press*, pp. 58, 93–4, 177.

Kerr, who was to be the most influential of the group, was also a proponent of federation, as the only way in which the people of the dominions could exercise a democratic control of foreign policy. Departing from his earlier concentration on the Anglo-Saxon element, Kerr now talked of India and Egypt as potential members: 'It is on our success in uniting not only races, religions, and colours, but even nations comprising a quarter of the people of the earth, within a single stable state that the hope of humanity depends.'[1] But Kerr did not think that the necessary convention to draw up a constitution for the Commonwealth could be held in wartime, and historical experience in the United States and in South Africa suggested to him that steps towards organic union would come when it was found too difficult to solve immediate practical problems through the existing machinery. An imperial conference would be needed after the war to adjust the financial relations between the United Kingdom and the dominions arising out of it. Consideration of a permanent redistribution of the burden of defence, on the lines of the 1909 conference, would raise the problem of what would happen if a dominion's contribution was not forthcoming through a change of government or a failure to carry a dominion parliament. Foreign affairs would be forced on to the agenda by Canada if Borden were still in power, and probably by Australia as well. It would then be realized that there was no way by which the dominions could have a voice in foreign affairs without a constitutional change. Such a conference would thus be bound to decide that a convention would be needed to draw up a 'constitutional act' which could be submitted for its consent to every part of the Empire.[2] Whether Milner himself was fully a convert to this view is perhaps doubtful; but that this kind of proposal was in the air explains why so much was expected of his entry into the government. Milner's thinking on politics was not restricted to the imperial field. There was also his well-known antipathy to parliamentary government as such,[3] and this might not be an asset to a ministry still ultimately dependent upon parlia-

[1] Memorandum, 'The Case for Imperial Federation', by Kerr, 26 February 1917. Lothian Papers, Box 139.
[2] Kerr to Austen Chamberlain, 1 April 1915. Austen Chamberlain Papers, AC. 13. Curtis and Hichens had taken part in a discussion with Chamberlain along these lines.
[3] 'Whether the future of the British Empire', wrote Milner, 'is one of greater progress or gradual decay will depend in my opinion on the question whether we are presently able to cleanse the Augean stable at Westminster.' Milner to Cunningham, 13 November 1915. Milner Papers, Private Letters, 1915 [Bodl. 141]. Cf. Milner to Curtis, 27 November 1915, in Gollin, op. cit., p. 314.

mentary support, and whose leader was to be engaged in what could, from one point of view, be regarded as a struggle to retain civilian control over the war machine.[1]

But there was another aspect of Milner's position which was even more ambiguous. The main ostensible purpose of the governmental reconstruction was to ensure the total defeat of Germany leading to a peace in which the Allies would be able to dictate their terms; and these would inevitably be directed against the possible recrudescence of a German threat. Milner had never taken an extreme anti-German line, and he was to be driven by the logic of an imperial, as opposed to a European, outlook on affairs to become a principal protagonist of a negotiated peace.[2]

In other words, the idea of an imperialist takeover is too sweeping. The same problems existed after Lloyd George became prime minister as before; opinions within the government and the governmental machine continued to differ. It was important that the new modelling of the machine itself enabled more consideration to be given to the problems of the peace; it was also important, of course, that there were new positions from which the imperialist point of view could be argued. But it was not so much that the new British ministers or their underlings whose views gained added strength, as that the dominion leaders themselves were now to be associated much more closely with the conduct of the war. More important than the composition of the original war cabinet was the change in June 1917 when Smuts himself became a member. It was Smuts the loser in the Boer war not Milner the victor, still less the Kindergarten and men of the Round Table, whose voice was to be most effective in these matters.

The fears that the new cabinet would be unable to deal with the problem of a disaffected Ireland proved to be justified. But it is not clear that by this stage anything could have been done to stem the tide towards nationalism, and towards the rejection of any compromise with the idea that home rule for the entire country was the only solution. The suppression of the Easter rebellion and the executions that fol-

---

[1] Milner was not himself necessarily a man to appeal to all soldiers: 'Milner is intolerable, I should like to put him in the ranks for six months and teach him what soldiers are like, that would perhaps stop his continual sneering at soldiers as if they were all damned fools. If he only knew how the country generally and the Labour Party in particular hate and distrust him, he might learn a little wisdom.' Derby to Esher, 25 November 1917. Randolph Churchill, *Lord Derby*, p. 293. On Lloyd George's struggles with the generals, see in particular, Lord Beaverbrook, *Men and Power, 1917–18* (1956).
[2] Milner to Glazebrook, 5 December 1914. Milner Papers (Speeches, pre-war).

lowed, together with the conscription issue, were, as has been seen, sufficient in themselves to swell the tide in this direction. The 1916 agreement between Lloyd George and Redmond and his supporters had secured acquiescence from them in a home rule measure excluding Ulster, which he led Carson to believe would be permanent. It was not the contradictory nature of these assurances that caused the breakdown, but rather the opposition of the unionists in the Asquith coalition to relinquishing control over southern Ireland. In trying to meet the pressures upon him Asquith made concessions which Redmond could not accept,[1] and Lloyd George was, as already noted, no more successful with his own attempt to balance home rule against conscription in 1918. The war had exaggerated, not bridged, the gap between the dominant British and the Irish view of the world; and the course of an independent Ireland towards neutrality in the renewed struggle with Germany in 1939 could have been foreseen in this development.[2]

Imperial Consultation and Economic Cohesion

The new régime's imperial organization depended not only on the views of the British government but also on those of the dominions. In the early part of the war, during the period of Kitchener's domination of Britain's effort, the dominions seem to have fallen in with his decisions without protest and without contributing to them;[3] contacts with dominion leaders were haphazard. Borden on a visit to England was invited to attend a routine meeting of the cabinet on 14 July 1915. When pressed to send more Canadian troops to France, he demanded that the British war effort should be better co-ordinated. In 1916 the new Australian prime minister, W. M. Hughes, visited England and set in at a cabinet meeting on 9 March and 9 June 1916, as did Massey of New Zealand on 26 October. Together with the Canadian high commissioner, Hughes attended the economic conference in Paris in June and insisted that he came as Australia's plenipotentiary and not as

[1] A. J. P. Taylor, *English History, 1914–1945*, pp. 56–7, 70–1, 82, 104.
[2] It is also interesting to note how close is the parallel between Irish developments in the first world war and Indian developments in the second. In both cases Britain sought in vain for an interim arrangement with the nationalists and in both was frustrated largely though not exclusively by minority objections. Both Ireland and India achieved independence after the wars at the price of partition, though Ulster's aims were not those of Pakistan.
[3] *C.H.B.E.*, vol. III, p. 606. It is not clear whether Hughes, Borden, and Massey attended meetings of the war committee in 1916. Ibid., p. 631.

a junior member of the British delegation, though neither dominion dissented from the British stand.[1]

It was therefore difficult to know how far the dominions themselves were insistent upon a greater say in imperial strategy, apart from decisions over matters of direct local concern, and how much they were interested in a permanent voice in foreign policy, although such a demand was made from time to time. Milner's former secretary, Arthur Steel-Maitland, now at the Colonial Office, claimed in a private letter that when it came to the point they shied off, because the corollary or consultation was some central body upon which the dominions should be represented, and which should for certain purposes have power to bind them. But whenever this was mooted, they protested against the interference with their autonomy.[2] A few months later Steel-Maitland declared himself convinced that the need for agreement with the dominions on war aims made some machinery for consultation necessary before the end of the war, since the difficulties of transport would make it too late afterwards; it took twenty-nine days to come from Australia. As the interests of the dominions in international questions broadened, demands for a share in making policy would become harder to resist.[3] There could be no doubt that on some fundamental matters consultation was imperative, and one such matter was the question of peace approaches which was a dominating theme behind the scenes in the closing weeks of 1916,[4] when the regular meeting of the imperial conference was two years overdue.

In these circumstances Lloyd George announced, on 14 December 1916, the decision to call not only an imperial war conference but simultaneously with it what was called an imperial war cabinet, that is to say meetings of the British war cabinet attended by the dominions'

[1] Ibid. W. M. Hughes (1864–1952), born in Wales, emigrated to Australia in 1884, and entered politics in 1894. He held a number of offices in the Commonwealth government, beginning with external affairs in 1904 and ending with the navy department, 1940–1. He was prime minister from 1915 to 1923 beginning as head of a labour ministry, but forming as we have seen a national war government in 1917.
[2] Arthur Steel-Maitland to Basil Worsfold, 10 June 1916 (information from Mr C. L. Cook). Arthur Steel-Maitland (1876–1935) (baronet, 1917) had become parliamentary undersecretary for the colonies in May 1915 and held the post until September 1917 when he became head of the new department of Overseas Trade set up under the joint aegis of the Foreign Office and Board of Trade, a post he retained until September 1919. He was minister of labour, 1924–9.
[3] Steel-Maitland to colonial secretary, 6 November 1916. Milner Papers, Imperial Union [Bodl. 299].
[4] Hewins, op. cit., p. 101.

prime ministers present for the conference, the whole serviced not by the Colonial Office but by Hankey's new cabinet secretariat.[1]

It was agreed that the conference should be treated as a special conference to get over the difficulty of Indian representation, but there was some confusion in the ministers' minds as to whether participation in the imperial war cabinet was a substitute for the wider conference. There was some anxiety that the dominions should understand that it was not intended to keep their representatives in the imperial war cabinet permanently on hand in London. In the end, the colonial secretary got his way on the grounds that the dominions might wish to have subjects discussed that were unsuitable for the imperial war cabinet; and the two bodies were kept distinct despite the overlap of membership.[2]

The imperial war cabinet was attended during 1917 by the foreign secretary Balfour, the colonial secretary Walter Long, and by Austen Chamberlain, the secretary of state for India.[3] The first meeting was on 17 March, and they met on fourteen occasions during the following six weeks. The most notable absentee was Hughes of Australia, who could not leave his country during the election campaign.[4] There were further meetings in June and July 1918, and the imperial war cabinet was then summoned into session again to deal with the problems of peacemaking, holding its first session for this purpose on 20 November.[5]

While the meetings in 1917 took place at a critical period in the war, they also looked forward to the post-war position, and Milner and his friends did their best, though unsuccessfully, to persuade the conference to approve some form of federal system for the future.[6] Instead the conference agreed to remit the constitutional problem to a special post-war conference, but in a resolution (carried on 16 March) which

[1] Cross, op. cit., pp. 40–1. Cf. Hankey, *The Supreme Command*, vol. 2, ch. LXIV. Cross credits Milner and Amery with the initiative. The event marked a further demotion of the Colonial Office as an intermediary between the British government and the dominions. Walter Long who had done something to remedy the dominions' lack of information on the course of the war by a system of weekly telegrams, objected to the imperial war cabinet idea but was overruled by the prime minister after pressure from Milner and Curzon. Milner Papers [Bodl. 299]. Diary of Sir Hugh Thornton, 1916–17, pp. 18–19. Cf. *C.H.B.E.*, vol. III, p. 757.
[2] Minutes of meetings of war cabinet, 22 and 23 December 1916; Long to Lloyd George, 30 December 1916. PRO. CAB. 37, 162, Folios 11, 12, 30.
[3] The conference was also attended by three representatives of the Indian government itself, including the Maharajah of Bikaner and Sir S. P. Sinha (later Lord Sinha).
[4] *C.H.B.E.*, vol. III, pp. 631–2. The role of the Irish in opposing Hughes was one reason for the war cabinet's renewed attention to the Irish problem. Hankey, op. cit., pp. 657–8.
[5] *C.H.B.E.*, vol. III, p. 645.
[6] Gollin, op. cit., p. 398.

left no doubt but that any solution would be on quite different lines. It should be based 'upon a full recognition of the Dominions as autonomous nations of an Imperial Commonwealth and of India as an important portion of the same', and should 'recognize the right of the Dominions and India to an adequate voice in foreign policy and foreign relations and should provide effective arrangements for continuous consultation in all important matters of common Imperial concern, and for such necessary concerted action, founded on consultation, as the several Governments might determine'. As Smuts said, the idea of a future imperial parliament and a future imperial executive was 'negatived by implication' by the terms of the resolution. A South African colleague wrote to him exultantly, 'You have put the lid on Messrs Lionel Curtis & Co.'[1] In a speech to a meeting of members of both houses of parliament on 15 May 1917, Smuts underlined his own conception of the British system as something other than a state or an empire: a dynamic and evolving system of states which would better take for itself the new name of Commonwealth.[2] Milner, however, does not seem to have felt that he had been altogether defeated. He thought the proposed post-war conference would not go so far as Curtis's proposals but would set up 'some sort of halfway house by which the Dominions would have some permanent representation in an Imperial Cabinet dealing with Defence, Foreign Affairs, and Communications; and would undertake to provide in their own way for a certain definite proportion of the cost of the Navy and the Consular and Diplomatic Service . . . a lopsided sort of arrangement' but one that would enable them to 'carry on for a bit'.[3]

The possible permanent establishment of an imperial cabinet was in fact discussed during these meetings. Long, despite his earlier reservations, was now converted; on the understanding that only prime ministers attend – unless they were prevented from coming, and nominated a substitute from their own cabinet. The cabinet would only meet when summoned by the British prime minister for a specific date and when at least three of the other prime ministers could attend in person. Some provision would have to be made also for India to be

---

[1] Hancock, *Smuts*, vol. 1, pp. 427–30.
[2] Text in W. K. Hancock and J. van der Poel (eds), *Selections from the Smuts Papers*, vol. III (1966), pp. 506–17. Afterwards Lord Harcourt wrote 'Tonight was the funeral of the Round Table'. Ibid., p. 518.
[3] Milner to Glazebrook, 21 April 1917. Milner Papers, Private Letters, 1917, VI [Bodl. 144].

represented.[1] Some rather similar ideas seem to have been present in Borden's mind.[2] The idea was put to the imperial war cabinet itself on 2 May in a speech by Lloyd George, who expressed the view of its British members that it would be a great pity if this institution were not incorporated in the machinery of the British Empire.[3] On 17 May Lloyd George announced in the House of Commons his intention of arranging for future meetings so that the body would become an accepted part of the British constitution.[4]

For some members of the imperialist group this step forward was in itself enough. Amery believed that there should be a new post of imperial secretary separate from the British prime minister and that he and not the latter would come to preside over the imperial cabinet. For this role, he cast Milner. His argument was that the Round Table insistence on formal constitutional ties was anachronistic and that provided the imperial cabinet was equipped with staffs which would enable it to do the thinking for the Empire, not only in warfare but also in economic matters, the rest would follow: 'Whoever controls the thinking department and supplies the idea eventually controls the administration.'[5] A speech by Borden suggested that the idea of a permanent imperial executive was also acceptable to him.[6]

Borden was, a year later, to return to the theme with even greater conviction:

'For my part I see no incongruity whatever in applying the term Cabinet to the association of Prime Ministers and other ministers who meet around a common council board to debate and to determine the various needs of the Empire. If I should attempt to describe

[1] Draft minute for circulation to the cabinet by Walter Long, 27 April 1917. Austen Chamberlain Papers, AC. 16/52.
[2] Note by Chamberlain of conversation with Borden, 27 April 1917. Ibid.
[3] Imperial War Cabinet, 14, Minutes of meeting on 2 May 1917. PRO. CAB. 23. 40.
[4] Amery, op. cit., vol. 2, p. 108. Cf. Hewins, op. cit., pp. 233–8.
[5] Amery to Milner, 10 July 1917. PRO. CAB. 17. 190. The minute has as an enclosure a paper arguing for detaching dominion business fom the Colonial Office and putting it in a new department under the 'Imperial Secretary'. In another undated paper of this year, Amery points out that the division of responsibilities for dealing with overseas territories between the Foreign Office, Colonial Office, and India Office will become even more untenable when post-war accretions of territory have to be provided for, and suggests a four-fold division between a Dominion Office, a Middle Eastern Office, the India Office, and the Colonial Office virtually confined to Africa (ibid.). The setting up of a separate Dominions Office was made less urgent by the development of direct communications between the British and dominions' prime ministers and was only achieved in 1925 when Amery was colonial secretary. Cross, op. cit., pp. 41–9.
[6] Speech in Canadian House of Commons, 18 May 1917.

it, I should say it is a Cabinet of Governments. . . . I venture to believe that in it may be found a development in the constitutional relations of the Empire which will form the basis of its unity in the years to come.[1]

But Borden's enthusiasm was to some extent misleading. He assumed that the concern the dominions were showing when the existence of the Empire was at stake would continue when external developments seemed secondary to their own domestic development, and to the political considerations that it dictated to their leaders. He assumed also that there could in peacetime be some kind of common executive without any common machinery for controlling it, or for putting its decisions into practice. And it seems curious that a practised statesman of a country so jealous of its identity as Canada, could accept the intellectual constructs of Amery and his friends.

At the 1918 conference Hughes moved a resolution pointing out the necessity of some more direct form of communication between the dominions' and British prime ministers than that which went via the governors-general and the Colonial Office. Massey felt that the Hughes resolution contemplated a continuation into peacetime of the imperial cabinet, but argued that the dominions would not be satisfied with participation in the decision-making process for a month or six weeks in the year and that resident ministers would be needed.[2] When this was discussed at the imperial war cabinet, Hughes and Massey repeated their arguments, but Smuts thought that all constitutional discussion should be left until after the war. Balfour said that the crux of the matter was how several distinct states could have unity of control over a single foreign policy; it would mean the dominions exercising a share of control over a single Foreign Office. The discussion was resumed two days later when Long proposed a committee to examine post-war constitutional arrangements. Hughes strongly opposed this suggestion: 'He thought that the view of the Australian people would be that if Australian representatives were sent to a Council of Empire, they would be entangled and doubly committed if a war broke out, and that the last state would, in fact, be worse than the first.' Borden agreed that sections of Canadian opinion held this view but that he would sooner leave the Empire than hold it himself.

[1] Borden, Speech to Empire Parliamentary Association, 21 June 1918, quoted in *War Cabinet Report, 1918* (Cmd. 225).
[2] Imperial War Conference, 18 July 1918. PRO. CAB. 32. 1.

In the end it was agreed that direct communications between the prime ministers of the dominions, as members of the imperial war cabinet, and the British prime minister would henceforward be the rule, and that to give continuity to the work of the imperial war cabinet, the prime ministers should have the right to nominate substitutes from their cabinets. But the dominions' prime ministers meeting separately had agreed, so Borden told their British colleagues, that even an informal committee such as the British proposed for the discussion of post-war arrangements would be politically embarrassing and the idea was dropped.[1]

More important than the failure to bring about any constitutional change was the evidence that the 1917 meetings had already provided, that the main effect of the war upon the dominions had been to increase their own self-reliance and to diminish the prestige of the British government. The dominions, wrote Kerr, who had the benefit of close contacts with these proceedings, were tending 'more and more to conceive of the Empire as five nations deliberating on equal terms round a table' at which India would also be represented. Probable differences between them over peace terms could already be foreseen.[2] In that sense, Kerr reached the same position as Smuts: 'We must complete the process whereby the state to which we belong is converted in spirit, if not in name, from an Empire to a Commonwealth, from a state that is in which power and responsibility are concentrated in a few hands in a single part with one in which they are shared equally among all the self-governing nations of which it is composed.'[3] But although this formula realistically represented the new dominion mood, and, in the shape of the statute of Westminster, produced the Commonwealth that faced the next great world crisis, it did nothing to detract from the three principal reasons why Britain's position was emphatically not one of an equal among others. Britain was still, in terms of population and industrial strength, much more powerful than any of the self-governing dominions; she had and would retain under her control (for three more decades at least as it proved) vast dependent territories in many parts of the world; and most important of all, she was still an offshore island

[1] Imperial war cabinet, meetings of 23 July, 25 July, and 30 July 1918. PRO. CAB. 23. 41. Amery says that these discussions show that the intention was to keep the imperial war cabinet in more or less permanent session even after the war. Op. cit., vol. 2, p. 109. It is by no means clear that this was everyone's view.
[2] Kerr to Curtis, 22 July 1917. Lothian Papers, Box 139.
[3] Undated Memorandum, 'The British Commonwealth' (1918). Lothian Papers Box 139.

of Europe. The 1,413 civilians who lost their lives during the war in air raids on the United Kingdom were a token of the new significance to be attached to this geographical location.

The contribution of the Empire to the war had not been solely in terms of fighting-men. Direct gifts to the British treasury from all parts of the Empire, as well as the support by the dominions of their own armies, alleviated the burden on the exchequer. Agricultural and industrial development was hastened by the demands of war; and an important groundwork for future progress was laid in the provision of public works and new industrial plant.[1] In the post-war world the Empire's economic importance would be enhanced, and this told in favour of the proponents of imperial economic consolidation.

The importance of the Empire's economic resources had not been overlooked, even during the period when the free-traders seemed to dominate opinion, and in 1912 a royal commission had been set up to examine the resources of the Empire in primary products.[2] Once the war came the advocates of a positive policy of development could renew their efforts. In a memorandum by Hewins for the prime minister's committee on commercial and industrial policy, he pointed out that the dominions had now separated from the United Kingdom in their commercial policy and in any future negotiations for commercial treaties this would adversely affect the unity of the Empire. The only alternative was for a form of joint commercial negotiations, which would mean abandoning the existing system of 'most-favoured-nation' treaties. The same conclusion, he argued, followed from the resolutions of the Paris economic conference in favour of differentiating in post-war trade in favour of the wartime allies.[3]

In June 1916 a committee had been set up under Lord Balfour of Burleigh to look at the stimulation of trade within the Empire, and the manner of declaring and giving effect to a policy of imperial preference.[4] On 3 February 1917 the committee recommended an immediate declaration by the United Kingdom of its adhesion to a policy of

[1] C.H.B.E., vol. III, pp. 642–3. Canadians complained in the early part of the war that Britain preferred to place war contracts in the U.S.A. Glazebrook to Milner, 23 July 1915. Milner Papers, CLXXIV, 1908–17, Canada [Bodl. 169].
[2] C.H.B.E., vol. III, p. 757.
[3] Memorandum of 4 September 1916. Balfour Papers, B.M. Add. 49779.
[4] Hewins, op. cit., Vol. 2, pp. 71 ff. A. H. Bruce (1849–1921) (sixth Baron Balfour of Burleigh, 1869) had been secretary for Scotland from 1895 to 1903 when he resigned with the other unionist free-traders. From Hewins's approval of his appointment it would appear that he had become a convert to imperial preference.

preference, and that early attention should be given to imposing a wider range of customs duties on which preferences could be given.[1]

The agenda of the imperial conference of 1917 did not include a separate item on imperial preference, but it was clear that the British government assumed that the matter would be raised under the general heading of relations within the Empire.[2] The imperial war cabinet took the matter up on a resolution by Massey which linked preferences with the encouragement of immigration from the United Kingdom to the dominions. The Balfour of Burleigh committee had shown the dangerous extent to which the United Kingdom was dependent on foreign countries; so long as it retained control of the sea, the Empire could produce all that was necessary. On emigration, other countries would not tolerate the Empire possessing vast areas which it did not fill. Borden said that while favourable to preference, Canada could not wish to impose anything unwelcome to the people of Britain, and while agreeing with Massey on immigration, he did not think that emigration to the United States was wholly a loss to the Empire because of its effect upon feelings there.

Lloyd George agreed with Massey that the war was bound to change British feeling on the imperial questions but said that it was important, as Borden had put it, that Canadian prosperity should not be at the expense of the British working class who must come to regard the Empire as a source of prosperity as well as of glory. He preferred the idea of subsidized imperial shipping routes to preferences, since the principal wheat- and meat-producing countries were Britain's allies and preferences might look like an attempt to injure them. Measures for helping shipping could be justified on defence grounds, and were used by Russia and the United States themselves. Britain would also after the war have to pay special attention to her own defence-related industries.[3] Milner, as might have been expected, emphasized the political aspect of the matter, declaring that the principle of preference was more important than tariffs or shipping in themselves. Smuts argued for caution and postponement, saying that all that was necessary was that the principle of preference should be recognized in any

[1] Ibid., p. 115.
[2] Hewins, op. cit., vol. 2, p. 109.
[3] In 1915 the United Kingdom had placed restrictions on certain non-essential imports largely to save shipping space, the so-called McKenna duties. When most wartime limitations were removed in September 1919, a number of duties were retained as 'safeguarding' duties in respect of defence.

future system which included tariffs. It was clear that any resolution by the conference would have to be carefully drafted so as to avoid creating anxiety among the allies.[1]

The conference at its meeting on 25 April went publicly on record in favour of encouraging the development of imperial resources and of each part of the Empire 'giving exceptionally favourable treatment to the produce and manufactures of other parts of the Empire'. It also privately agreed to take measures to free the Empire and allied countries from their previous dependence on German controlled organizations for the supply of non-ferrous metals.[2] The advocates of greater imperial economic unity felt that the 1917 conference presented a chance that must not be missed, and they urged that steps should be taken at once to see that everything was in readiness for action when the time came.[3] A committee under Long with Hewins (who was made under-secretary of state for the colonies in September 1917) as vice-chairman was therefore set up, and much preparatory work was done to prepare for more detailed policy decisions in the 1918 conference. It was originally to have been called the committee on the trade relations of the Empire, but the dominions significantly objected on the ground that the trade relations between the dominions could not come within the purview of a British cabinet committee, and it was therefore styled the committee on the trade relations of the United Kingdom within the Empire. The principle of its operations was that an empire policy should be settled first, that on this basis relations with the allies should be settled in accordance with the resolutions of the Paris conference and that relations with the rest of the world would be dealt with last of all.[4] It was obvious, however, that this order of priorities might conflict with the growing requirements of inter-allied solidarity, and the need to consider especially the susceptibilities of the United States upon whose forces the hopes of a decisive victory now rested.[5] Worries were expressed lest the proposals for an inter-allied control of raw materials after the war should prevent Britain having a final say in the control of empire products, at least so far as her own supplies were concerned.[6]

[1] Minutes of meetings of imperial war cabinet, 24 and 26 April 1917. Austen Chamberlain Papers, AC. 20/77.   [2] Hewins, op. cit., vol. 2, pp. 141–3.
[3] Long to Balfour, 16 May 1917. Balfour Papers, B.M. Add. 49777.
[4] Hewins, op. cit., vol. 2, pp. 168–70.
[5] The United States declared war on Germany on 6 April 1917, though its forces on land were not expected to make their full impact until the summer of 1918 or even 1919.
[6] Lord Emmott to Lord Robert Cecil, 24 January 1918. Cecil of Chelwood Papers, B.M. Add. 51093. Lord Robert Cecil (1864–1958) (Viscount Cecil of Chelwood 1923). Under-secretary

The 1918 conference took some important decisions on the basis of the reports of Hewins's committee, notably on imperial arrangements for securing supplies of raw materials, but matters were again complicated by the commitments into which the British government had entered through the development of inter-allied supply and transport organizations.

> I hope [wrote Long to Cecil] it will not on any account be assumed that the Dominions and India will agree to post-war control by any inter-Allied organization of raw materials which they produce. Our experience at the Imperial War Conference was that they were most reluctant to commit themselves . . . It is therefore essential that in any negotiations you may have with the Allied Governments you should in no way commit the Dominions or India, without previous consultation with them.[1]

The importance attached to post-war economic arrangements as well as the territorial demands of the dominions influenced the successful efforts of Smuts, Borden, and Hughes to secure dominion representation at the peace conference as part of the British Empire delegation.[2] But in the new circumstances, the work of the 1918 conference and of Hewins's committee was pushed into the background. In January 1919 Long left the Colonial Office for the Admiralty, to be succeeded by Milner for whom these economic questions were of subordinate interest, and Hewins left office for good. Despite Lloyd George's apparent conversion to imperial preference, the time for Britain to change its policy had not yet arrived.[3]

---

for foreign affairs, May 1915–January 1919; minister of blockade, December 1916–July 1918. Chairman of supreme economic council and head of section of British Delegation to Peace conference dealing with the proposed League of Nations. Lord privy seal, 1923–4. Chancellor of Duchy of Lancaster, 1924–7. President, League of Nations Union, 1923–45.

[1] Walter Long to Cecil, 15 November 1916. Cecil of Chelwood Papers, B.M. Add. 51094.

[2] Hancock, *Smuts*, vol. 1, pp. 496–7.

[3] In a letter to Bonar Law in 1918 looking to the general election that would follow the end of hostilities, Lloyd George said that he accepted the principle of preference as the imperial conference had defined it – preference on existing duties, and on any new duties to be imposed in the future. Balfour Papers, B.M. Add. 49693. This was far from a commitment to the ideal of imperial economic unity, and although the coalition election programme included a mention of a measure of imperial preference, the issue did not figure prominently in the campaign. The aftermath of war was not a felicitous moment for the imposition of food taxes.

PART II. THE UNITED STATES AND VICTORY

Early Anglo-American Friction

One aspect of the war that had from the beginning loomed large in the minds of British statesmen had been the changing moods, intentions, and policies of the United States. Officially the United States stood neutral in the conflict, and this stand reflected both the point of equilibrium between the divergent currents of American opinion and the dominant conviction in President Wilson's own mind that it was the duty of his country to remain outside, and indeed above, the sordid quarrels of the old world. Britain's problem was that the interpretation of neutrality adopted by the United States might vitally affect allied prospects, and Wilson might at any time decide that American interests were so damaged by the continuance of the war that it would be worth exercising American pressure to the fullest extent in order to bring it to an end.

The effect of American attitudes, and particularly those of President Wilson, on British opinion was in the main contrary to his desires. So far from accepting the view that Americans, being outside the conflict, could see beyond immediate problems to some higher version of the common good, the hard-pressed British generally interpreted the American position as being dictated by a mixture of greed, cowardice, and moral obliquity. It was impossible for them to accept the view that there was no difference between the ravishers of Belgium and their own reluctant recourse to arms: 'There's two sorts of liberalism,' said Mr Britling, 'that pretend to be the same thing; there's the liberalism of great aims and the liberalism of defective moral energy.'[1]

To any pressure short of armed intervention the allies, and Britain in particular, were more vulnerable than the Germans. Once the war settled down into one of attrition, American supplies became of increasing importance, and dependence upon the United States for supplies inevitably led to dependence upon the ability to secure credit in the New York money-market.[2] By the summer of 1916 Britain's ability to pay was already doubtful and it was feared that resources would be

[1] H. G. Wells, *Mr Britling Sees it Through*, p. 353.
[2] Early in the war, Mackenzie King, then working in the field of industrial relations sent a message to the American secretary of state, W. J. Bryan, expressing the hope that the United States would use its financial power over the belligerents to bring the war to an end. Dawson, *Mackenzie King*, p. 257.

exhausted by June 1917.[1] Foreign Office opinion held that the United States would hardly be likely, whatever its irritation at British policy, to proceed to extremes in the form of a trade embargo because of its dependence upon the British Empire as a market and as a source of raw materials; but it admitted that the possibility of loans drying up was a real one and one that had to be taken into consideration in deciding policy.[2]

To avoid friction while Britain was at war and the United States neutral was impossible. Britain could not forego the weapon of her superior naval strength, and the right to impose restrictions upon neutral trade where this was helping the German war effort. The United States took its stand, as during the Napoleonic wars, on the rights of neutrals to do business as usual. Fortunately for Britain the argument cut both ways since submarine warfare, upon which Germany placed increasing hope, was liable to cause losses of life to neutral Americans proceeding upon their lawful occasions, and such action tended to push the United States towards the opposite camp.

The problem for Britain was therefore to get the maximum advantage from the blockade without irredeemably alienating the United States. At the beginning of the war an effort was made to induce Britain to accept the full limitations of the declaration of London.[3] Although this demand was abandoned by 21 October 1914 modifications in the blockading policy were made, and on 22 July 1915 the cabinet decided that, in view of the state of relations with the United States, no American ships outward-bound from Europe, even though presumably carrying German goods, should be stopped.[4]

Even these measures of appeasement did not prevent friction, and this in turn aided the anti-British elements in Congress and elsewhere.[5]

[1] Memorandum by R. H. Brand, 29 August 1916. Balfour Papers, B.M. Add. 49748.
[2] Foreign Office memorandum on relations with the U.S.A., 30 October 1916. Dep. Asquith Box 130.
[3] Bell, *The Blockade of the Central Empires*, pp. 54 ff. The anglophil American ambassador Walter Page threatened resignation if the demand was pressed. Arthur Link, *Wilson*, vol. 3 (1960), p. 123.
[4] Cecil to Balfour, 12 April 1916. Balfour Papers, B.M. Add. 49738. A Foreign Office memorandum in June 1915 discussed the danger of the use of 'British Navalism' as a propaganda weapon against Britain. PRO. CAB. 37. 130.
[5] 'Whatever England can do by way of a blockade in accordance with recognized international law, this country will accept, I think, without serious objection. When, however, she proceeds by irregular methods, and asks us to raise no objection, she in a certain sense asks the United States to become a party to her endeavour, as a belligerent, to starve or embarrass Germany a country with which the United States is at peace . . .' Seth Low to Bryce, 31 January 1916 (communicated by Mr E. Ions). One difficulty was, of course, the absence of 'recognized international law'.

It was obviously of great advantage to these circles that the opposition to the British blockade could be paraded under the appealing slogan of the freedom of the seas, which the Germans themselves advanced as a condition of peace without specifying its content. The rules of blockade, and the question of the immunity of private property at sea, appeared to be linked with objections to the maintenance of British sea-power at its former level of preponderance. To prove the validity of the British case it was necessary to convince Americans that the allies were fighting their battle, and that a triumphant Germany would menace the western hemisphere.[1] And to a people and a government which had repented of their brief immersion in world politics under Theodore Roosevelt and relapsed into the feeling that from a secure base they could impartially judge the behaviour of other nations, such argument sounded hollow. Nevertheless there was an element in British opinion so convinced of the ultimate significance of the Anglo-American relationship that it was willing to make major concessions for its sake.[2]

It was indeed difficult both to make out the extent of anti-British sentiment and to decide on the most prudent course of action. Some hostility – from German-Americans – had to be taken as inherent in the situation, as well as the inevitable hostility to the allies arising from the fact that imperial Russia was among them; for instance, in Jewish circles the wartime behaviour of that government did not do anything to diminish the animosity felt towards it.

Irish opinion might be affected by British policy; Grey, Bryce, and Redmond himself repeatedly pressed upon Asquith the importance of the home rule issue, and Redmond also pleaded for leniency after the Easter Rising.[3] Friendly Americans pressed the Irish cause on their British correspondents.[4] The feeling over Ireland was not confined in America to those of Irish descent. It fitted in well with the distinctive suspicion of Britain as an aristocratic and imperialist country as contrasted with democratic and peace-loving America. Even the mildest

[1] See Bryce's letters to Charles Eliot, 11 May, 1 July, 8 August 1915, and 29 January 1916. Bryce Papers, U.S.A., vol. 2. Eliot in a letter of 11 May argued that Britain could no longer rely on sea-power for security and that some kind of League of Free Nations would be a better alternative. (Ibid.); partly printed in Henry James, *Charles Eliot* (1930), vol. 2, pp. 263–5.
[2] Sir George Trevelyan to Bryce, 6 March and 9 October 1916. Bryce Papers, English Correspondence, vol. 18.
[3] Dep. Asquith, Boxes 7, 8, 30, 37, 131. Cf. Cecil's memorandum of 17 June 1916. Balfour Papers, B.M. Add. 49738.
[4] Charles Howland to Gilbert Murray, 7 March 1917. Gilbert Murray Papers, American Letters.

of Britons were occasionally driven to protest: 'We really do not cherish what you describe as an "imperialistic world-controlling policy",' wrote Bryce; the British people had been tricked into the South African war by 'Chamberlain and the mine-owning gang' but the people had never approved it.[1] Language of this kind was in some sense a hostage to the Americans, since it helped to bolster their suspicion of any movement towards a more closely knit Empire. The sympathetic attitude of neutrals towards the Empire was due, so an anglophil American historian argued, to the decentralized character that it bore and to the system of free trade prevailing over most of it. If Curtis and his friends got their way, other nations would be inclined to regard it as a menace.[2]

Friendly Americans felt that the British case would have been better understood if someone with Bryce's stature had been Britain's ambassador.[3] But Bryce himself was extremely dubious of the idea that any good could be achieved by propaganda. The facts must be allowed to speak for themselves.[4] Page, whose own opinions were little regarded in Washington, felt that lack of personal contact between the two administrations (there was not one member of one who knew one member of the other) was a serious handicap.[5] And Milner, who felt that Britain was not 'cutting a very good figure in the eyes of the Americans', concluded that Britain's failure to put its case well to foreigners was part of the general failure in the management of the war.[6]

Whatever his defects, Spring-Rice did not leave the Foreign Office in any doubt of the degree of hostility to Britain in powerful sections of United States' public opinion, and of the danger of relying on opinion to prevent the American government pressing its views.[7] And yet it was not only that some people in England found it hard to think of the United States as a foreign country, but that the Americans themselves were prone to act as though they had some special claim to consideration. In January 1917 Page asked the armament firm of Vickers to supply him with information about the construction of Zeppelins. Bal-

[1] Bryce to Charles W. Eliot, 23 September 1915. Bryce Papers, U.S.A., vol. 2.
[2] G. L. Beer to A. Glazebrook, 28 October 1914. Milner Papers, Imperial Union.
[3] A. Bullard to Gilbert Murray, 23 September 1916, Gilbert Murray Papers, American Letters. C. F. Adams to Bryce, 29 December 1914. Bryce Papers, U.S.A., vol. 3.
[4] Bryce to Ilbert, 9 September 1914. Simon Papers. Pro-British Americans supported this view, C. F. Adams to Bryce, 17 October 1914. Bryce Papers, U.S.A., vol. 3.
[5] Young, *Balfour*, p. 379.
[6] Milner to Glazebrook, 8 March 1916. Milner Papers, Private Letters, 1916, IV [Bodl. 142].
[7] See, e.g., Spring-Rice to Grey, 20 October 1916. PRO. CAB. 37. 158. Cf. Beloff, 'The Special Relationship', in Gilbert (ed.), *An Age of Conflict*.

four was inclined to give the information, since, as he remarked, the United States was unlikely to go to war with Britain, and if she did the only possible place where an American Zeppelin could do any damage was Canada. But, he went on, 'there is no doubt that America's behaviour is rather singular. They undoubtedly regard us as something quite different from the ordinary foreigner; but this does not the least prevent them making both the most dangerous requests for our assistance and the most offensive remonstrances whenever we do not do exactly what they like.'[1]

Wilson the Peacemaker

Wilson had early attempted to bring about peace. Colonel House visited Europe in the spring of 1915 but found the moment unpropitious. In the following winter he made a second attempt and in February 1916 came to what appeared to be an agreement with Grey that America would offer mediation on 'terms not unfavourable to the Allies' and that if Germany refused, America would enter the war. The basis would have been the restoration of Belgium, the return of Alsace-Lorraine to France and 'an outlet to the sea' for Russia. Germany would get compensation overseas. Wilson, however, inserted the word 'probably' before the undertaking to go to war, and in the circumstances the offer appeared too unattractive to follow up in view of the possible dangers to allied unity.[2]

Wilson's speech of 27 May 1916 again attracted attention to America's possible role as a peacemaker. America was not, the president declared once again, interested in the war's causes or objects, but she could not be indifferent to what went on in the world and would be ready to participate in 'an universal association of the nations to maintain the inviolate security of the highway of the seas for the common and unhindered use of all the nations of the world and to prevent any war begun either contrary to treaty covenants or without warning and

[1] Balfour to Carson, 12 January 1917. Balfour Papers, B.M. Add. 49709. Sir Edward Carson (1854–1935), the Ulster leader had been attorney-general from May to November 1915 and became first lord of the admiralty in December 1916, holding this post until July 1917 when he was removed from the Admiralty during the crisis over convoys. He then became a member of the war cabinet but resigned on the home rule issue in January 1918.
[2] Grey's account is in his *Twenty-Five Years* (1925), vol. II, ch. XXIII. For an account from the American side, see A. S. Link, *Woodrow Wilson*, vol. IV (1964), pp. 101–41. The memorandum of the House–Grey conversations was initialled on 22 February. The French who were kept informed were totally averse to negotiations at this stage.

full submission of the causes to the opinion of the world – a virtual guarantee of territorial integrity and political independence'.[1]

Allied opinion generally was not warm to the speech, which seemed to most people in England and France to ignore the cause for which they were fighting. The impossibility of attaining America's general objectives without an allied victory was the burden of Britain's official response. And there was also doubt, in view of America's refusal to throw her strength into the balance of the existing conflict, whether she could be relied upon as a guarantor of a future settlement.[2] Some dissentients from the official line, however, found encouragement in the president's words.

Noel Buxton (later Lord Noel-Buxton), a high-minded philanthropist who had been one of the liberal opponents of Grey's policy, visited the United States at this time and wrote a memorandum advocating that the British government publicly align itself with the president's proposals.[3] Spring-Rice, in commenting on it to the Foreign Office, pointed out that much of the speech was for internal consumption. The allies were to give up their means of pressure on the central powers for promises of support which no American president could constitutionally give. He was particularly worried at Buxton's suggestion that England alone of the allies might agree in principle to the president's suggestion, since this would fulfil Germany's intention of driving a wedge between them.[4]

Grey's interchanges with House on the president's proposals lasted till almost the end of August, and on 29 August 1916 Edwin Montagu, then minister of munitions, wrote a memorandum on the need to consider not only war aims but also whether the government should consider the terms for an armistice or neutral mediation. The only neutral mediator to be considered would be the U.S.A: 'And so contemptible and untrustworthy', he went on, 'does the American politician of all parties in recent international politics seem to me, that I hope this question can be answered in the negative.'[5]

---

[1] Link, *Wilson*, vol. V (1965), pp. 25–6. [2] Ibid., pp. 27–35.
[3] House's talk with Noel Buxton is recorded in a letter from him to Milner of 30 July 1916. Link, op. cit., vol. V, pp. 37–8.
[4] Spring-Rice to Foreign Office, 4 July 1916. PRO. CAB. 37. 151. Buxton sent House and other Americans a memorandum in October suggesting that Wilson go beyond his speech of 27 May by offering territorial and other bases for a mediated settlement along lines he suggested. See T. P. Conwell-Evans, *Foreign Policy from a Back-Bench, 1904–1918* (1932), pp. 120–3.
[5] 'The Problems of Peace', note by Mr Montagu. PRO. CAB. 29 1/1.

Wilson was, however, more than ever determined to make an effort to end the war rather than see the United States dragged into it. And it was clear that if he persisted he would be difficult to resist. A Treasury memorandum, drawn up by Keynes and presented on 10 October, showed how dependent upon the United States the financial effort of the war had made Britain;[1] the Ministry of Munitions also revealed the degree of dependence in which Britain stood in the field of war supplies. Grey, summing up the departmental briefs, argued for the maximum of concessions possible to American opinion in respect of the blockade, provided that no issue of principle was conceded. But he warned his colleagues that even greater concessions might have to be considered if the situation worsened. And by the end of the month further evidence of the financial weakness of the allies had come to light, and the chancellor of the exchequer, McKenna, found it necessary to remind his colleagues of the full gravity of the situation in a report on 24 October: 'If things go on as at present, I venture to say with certainty that by next June or earlier, the President of the American Republic will be in a position, if he wishes, to dictate his own terms to us.'[2] An indication that the president might do just that came in a warning to member banks in the federal reserve system against further unsecured investments in allied treasury bills.[3]

But the president's moves were overtaken by Germany's own peace offer of 12 December 1916 which the American government was asked to convey to the allies.[4] In doing so, however, Wilson made it clear that, although he was acting only as an intermediary, the United States was directly interested in the outcome; and he sent a note of his own on 18 December suggesting that soundings be taken to see what common ground there was upon which general peace might be established. Although this was a less direct move for intervention than Wilson had originally intended, or than the allies feared, it once again showed the gap between American and British thinking, particularly in his statement that the objects of the belligerents on both sides were 'virtually the same'.[5] Indeed, his adviser Colonel House was so affected by Wil-

---

[1] J. M. Keynes (1883–1946) (baron, 1942), a former civil servant and an academic economist, served in the Treasury from 1915 to 1919. He played the leading part in the financial negotiations with the United States in 1943–5.
[2] Link, *Wilson*, vol. V, pp. 178–84.
[3] Ibid., pp. 200–6.
[4] On the German offer which was made largely to satisfy the Austrians and to prepare the way for unrestricted submarine warfare when rejected, see Fischer, op. cit., pp. 295 ff.
[5] Link, op. cit., vol. V, pp. 214–19.

son's maladroitness, as he saw it, as to fear that war between the United States and Britain was a real possibility.[1]

Lloyd George made it clear in the House of Commons on 19 December that the German note gave no hope of the Germans accepting the allies' basic demands for reparation, restitution, and guarantees for future peace. It was obviously impossible, however, to dismiss the offer out of hand for fear of a hostile American reaction, and the new war cabinet was under conflicting domestic pressures in planning a reply. Their military advisers took the view that Germany would not be suggesting peace terms if they had thought they could get better terms later. A peace now would crystallize Germany's domination of central Europe and the Balkans and this was unacceptable.[2] But in some circles in Britain the importance of not alienating American opinion was stressed, and the belief expressed, that the United States was fundamentally at one with Britain on the nature of a future peace.[3] Those at the centre of the British war effort did not share the latter view; pacifism was much stronger in the United States and British motives were suspect; it would be better that France, as the victims of aggression, should take the lead in rejecting the German demands.[4] Balfour, in his draft of a possible reply to Wilson, denied that the wider aims of the president's policy would be unaffected by the immediate terms of peace. If the central powers were prepared to endorse the rights of nationalities, then they should apply at once to Belgium, Serbia, Rumania, and elsewhere. Nor would a mere reversion to the *status quo* suffice.[5]

The war cabinet discussed the German note on 18 December and the American proposals on 21 and 23 December.[6] The whole question was then dealt with at an Anglo-French conference in London on 26–28 December, at which Balfour gave a warning that the United States had it in its power to compel peace, and that something must be done to dispel the view that the war itself could be settled somehow or other by the belligerents, with the United States only joining in afterwards at

[1] Ibid., pp. 225–7.

[2] Note on the German peace proposals by Sir William Robertson, 14 December 1916. PRO. CAB. 29 1/1.

[3] Conwell-Evans, op. cit., pp. 123–8; Martin, *Peace Without Victory*, pp. 118–22. Memoranda by Noel Buxton of 15 and 29 December 1916, are in Balfour Papers, B.M. Add. 49738.

[4] Note on German peace offer by Lord Robert Cecil, 15 December 1916. PRO. CAB. 37. 161.

[5] Suggestion for British reply to the president of the United States by Balfour, December 1916. PRO. CAB. 37. 162.

[6] War cabinet minutes, 21 December and 23 December 1916. PRO. CAB. 37/162.

the head of the other nations of the world to lay the foundations of a universal peace.[1] The allied rejection on 30 December of the German note of 12 December was categorical, describing the Germans' offer as 'merely a manoeuvre to encourage their own people, mislead the neutrals and justify further German illegalities'. The reply to the United States required and received more careful consideration, and in its final form, as sent on 10 January 1917, gave a fairly full outline of the terms on which the allies would insist as part of any settlement and which indeed foreshadowed the reshaping of the map of Europe in the peace treaties.[2]

It has been pointed out by Wilson's biographer that the terms suggested closely resembled those suggested by Wilson's pro-allied secretary of state, Lansing, in earlier conversations with the French and British ambassadors at Washington. The object of stating terms that Germany could not be expected to accept unless defeated in the field may have been to force her into unrestricted submarine warfare and thus secure American belligerency on the allied side; however the available records do not resolve this reliably.[3] And this is to assume that the terms were harsher than were needed to maintain the unity between the European allies, or to justify to the allied peoples the heavy sacrifices of the war. There is little reason to believe that they would at this stage have been very different, even if the possibility of American belligerency had not existed.

In fact Wilson at the time was encouraged by his contacts with Germany to believe in the possibility of securing a negotiated peace, and House found it necessary to assure his British friends that the danger was that British intransigence, based on false confidence that another offensive could bring about victory, would prevent the president bringing about a settlement which would be fully in accordance with the allies' basic interests.[4] Wilson's own statement of the American position, in his speech before the Senate on 22 January 1917 – 'the peace without victory' speech – and his emphasis upon the freedom of the seas as a major element in a future settlement were not, however, calculated to reassure the British government, powerful though the appeal may have been to its critics on the left. Nor indeed had Wilson expected enthus-

[1] Minutes of Anglo-French conference, 26–28 December 1916. Austen Chamberlain Papers, AC. 20/76.
[2] D. Lloyd George, *War Memoirs* (edn 1936), vol. i, pp. 661–4.
[3] Link, op. cit., vol. 5, p. 239.
[4] Ibid., pp. 258–9.

iasm in London. His hopes were still fixed on Germany offering terms he could persuade or press the allies into accepting. But on 31 January the news of Germany's withdrawal of its pledge of the previous May, to refrain from unrestricted submarine warfare, ended these hopes for good. On 3 February the United States severed diplomatic relations with Germany.[1] And although Wilson hesitated at each stage in the inevitable course to war, the fears that Spring-Rice had expressed a year earlier, that if it came to the point the United States would rather fight Britain than Germany, could now be dismissed.[2]

Wilson was not, however, by any means won over to the allied views on war aims, in so far as they were a conflation of all the individual claims of the allied governments. On 10 February 1917 he intervened to urge the allied governments to guarantee the future integrity of the Austro-Hungarian empire, so as to induce its government to make a separate peace. Although this made no more impact than the other Austrian peace feelers which form so large a part of the background of wartime diplomacy, Lloyd George took the occasion to urge upon Wilson, through the American ambassador, that he should bring the United States into the war at once. This was not so much to help on the military side as to make sure that America's voice was fully expressed in the making of the peace; otherwise nothing, he argued, could prevent the present belligerents from seeking compensation for their losses by making concrete gains: 'Even Great Britain, who wants nothing for herself, will be prevented from returning the German colonies. South Africa and Australia will not permit the giving back of lands that would make them neighbours to German subjects and give Germany secret submarine bases throughout the whole world. The United States wants nothing but justice and ordered freedom and guarantees of these for the future.'[3]

---

[1] A. Walworth, *Woodrow Wilson*, vol. II (1958), pp. 78–85. On the basis of a record of a conversation between House and Sir William Wiseman the head of British naval intelligence in the United States and an increasingly important semi-official intermediary between the two governments, it has been suggested, first, that the British government knew from intelligence sources that unrestricted submarine warfare was coming and that it could therefore afford not to worry about Wilson's bid for mediation, and second, that fears about what the submarine campaign might achieve before America would effectively intervene and about the possibility of Russia being knocked out, actually made the British government favourable to American mediation at this juncture. Link, op. cit., pp. 280–1. But there is nothing else to confirm either hypothesis. On Wiseman's role, see Sir Arthur Willert, *The Road to Safety, a study in Anglo-American relations* (1952).

[2] Spring-Rice to Grey, 29 January 1916. PRO. CAB. 37. 141.

[3] Page to secretary of state, 11 February 1917. Quoted Link, op. cit., vol. V, pp. 317–18.

It is difficult to know how seriously Lloyd George took these sentiments, supposing they were uttered as reported. Did he think that an appeal of this kind would be more likely to move Wilson than one based on the allied needs in men, ammunitions, and ships? Or did he seriously wish to balance the Americans against the dominions, in the interests of a peace more directly prompted by considerations of long-term British security in Europe? In any event, there seems to have been no direct response. But on 26 February, after the knowledge of the Zimmermann telegram had reached Washington, Wilson asked Congress for the emergency powers which enabled him to establish a condition of armed neutrality by orders to the navy on 13 March. On 6 April Congress approved the resolution by which the United States declared war.[1] British discussions on war aims were thus henceforward conducted in the knowledge that the United States would be at the peace table and in a powerful position to make its wishes felt.

While the various demands which might together make up a peace settlement had been fairly widely canvassed already, it was not clear within what framework the British government envisaged the future. Would it be a settlement which Britain and its empire could unitedly hope to preserve against all-comers, or must the need for permanent alliances be faced? Or could there be substitutes for both 'splendid isolation' and the 'old diplomacy' in some new international organization capable of guaranteeing world order impartially against any aggressor?[2]

Later Imperial War Aims

In the war cabinet itself, the chief protagonist of the view that Britain could manage without alliances after the war, and that together with the dominions she could defy all-comers, was Milner; this view was linked with his disbelief in the likelihood of a complete military victory over Germany.[3] A meeting of the imperial war cabinet on 22 March

[1] The Zimmermann telegram of 19 January addressed to the German minister in Mexico suggested a German–Mexican alliance against the United States out of which Mexico might hope to recover Texas, New Mexico, and Arizona, and mediation by Mexico between Germany and Japan with a view to Japan's participation in the war against the United States.
[2] On the concept of 'splendid isolation' and its role in historiography, see C. H. D. Howard, *Splendid Isolation* (New York, 1967).
[3] See the note in Sir Henry Wilson's diary of the discussion between himself and Milner on board ship on 1 March 1917 on their way back from a mission to Russia. C. E. Callwell, *Field Marshall Sir Henry Wilson*, vol. 1 (1927), pp. 322–3.

heard Balfour expound his views about German objectives, which he saw as based on the idea of an overland expansionism 'largely directed to developing the communications between Germany, through Austria, through subordinate States like Bulgaria and Turkey to the Persian Gulf and ultimately to India and the Far East'. If Germany succeeded in this aim the whole world balance of power would be altered and Australia and New Zealand, as well as India, would be in a different position. The importance of this threat was underlined by Austen Chamberlain, who pointed out that the school which had always favoured the idea of an overland advance would have received additional strength, now that their ambitions for an overseas colonial empire had been defeated by the success of General Smuts's campaign in East Africa, and her other setbacks in that continent. For this reason enormous importance attached to the campaigns now being waged in the Middle East.[1] Milner, without disputing this analysis of the situation, raised the question as to whether insisting on secondary objectives in relation to the Balkans, Italy, and Poland might not make the central powers less willing to concede the objectives that mattered more, and whether indeed the war was not unnecessarily prolonged.[2]

At another meeting next day, Smuts raised the possibility of coming to terms with Germany if there was no military victory by the end of the summer. Milner was his only supporter, and the cabinet turned down a suggestion by him that a sub-committee should be appointed to decide upon a irreducible minimum for the allies terms. It was agreed that Balfour should prepare a memorandum on the question, but the matter does not seem to have been pursued.[3] At a meeting of the imperial war cabinet on 27 March, on the initiative of Smuts and Ward, a discussion took place on the need to arrive at some clear conclusion about war aims, and the fear was expressed that the British representatives at a peace conference would be in a minority among delegates primarily interested in central European affairs, and that they would

---

[1] Imperial war cabinet, *Procès-Verbal*, 22 March 1917. Austen Chamberlain Papers, AC. 20/77. By this time, of course, the Russian revolution of March 1917 had cast doubt upon the future of the eastern front, despite the proclaimed determination of the new régime to continue fighting for Russia's original objectives.
[2] For a general introduction to the subject of allied war aims, see A. J. P. Taylor, 'The War Aims of the Allies in the First World War', in R. Pares and A. J. P. Taylor (eds), *Essays Presented to Sir Lewis Namier* (1956).
[3] Milner Papers, Thornton's Diary, 1916–1917, 24 March 1917 [Bodl. 299]. Borden was among those who deprecated any modification of the allies' proclaimed objectives. *Memoirs of Sir Robert Borden*, vol. 2 (1938), pp. 689–70.

need to be able to defend British interests which were not primarily territorial but concerned rather with the effective defence of the communications between the different parts of the Empire itself. It was, however, accepted that Germany's power in the future would largely depend on the nature of the settlement in Europe, so that the two problems were in fact closely interconnected.[1]

It was indeed difficult to see how the renewal of a challenge to Britain's world position could be prevented in the long run and, equally, how successful the Empire would be after the war in making full use of its resources for mutual defence. The imperial war conference was exhorted by Ward to devote some attention to the role the dominions might play in the Pacific after the end of the war, but found the Admiralty unable to devote its attention to such far-off questions.[2]

An attempt to see the question in the round was made at this time by Amery in a memorandum for a committee which had been set up under Curzon's chairmanship to consider possible terms of peace.[3] Amery gave the standard defence of British intervention in European affairs in the past as having been based on an attempt to prevent the domination of the continent by a single military power capable of gaining control of the sea. The other equally important aspect of British policy has been the offensive use of sea-power to gain positions of strength outside Europe: 'It is this continuous creation of new sources of power in new worlds overseas to redress the balance of the Old World which is the really characteristic feature of British policy and accounts for the fact that an essentially defensive policy has led to the acquisition of so immense an Empire.' Now that British policy was 'no longer the policy of an island immediately adjacent to the coast of Europe, though drawing economic strength from overseas possessions', but that of a commonwealth of communities whose actual home 'was at' the four corners of the earth, the importance of the overseas, or oceanic, aspect of that policy 'was more important than ever'. It was Germany's extension of her European ambitions to challenge Britain's world interests that had been responsible for Britain's participation in the war, and it was this aspect of her policy that most concerned Britain in making the peace. Amery suggested that the technical and economic conditions of the conflict made it likely that Germany's position in Europe would

[1] Imperial war cabinet minutes, 27 March 1927, PRO. CAB. 23. 40.
[2] Imperial war conference minutes, 28 March, 30 March 1917. PRO. CAB. 32. 1.
[3] 'Notes on Possible Terms of Peace', by L.S.A., 11 April 1917. Austen Chamberlain Papers, AC. 20/78. Cf. Amery, *Memoirs*, vol. 2, pp. 104–6.

in fact be strengthened by it. There was little future for small countries like Belgium. The important thing was to concentrate on the imperial side, and Amery dealt not only with the Middle East in terms rather similar to Balfour's but also with Africa, since he foresaw the danger of a 'great German railway Empire continuous from Hamburg to Lake Nyasa'. The greatest dangers that could face the British Empire in the future would be German control of Palestine and the German re-acquisition of East Africa.

The territorial demands of the Empire should be governed by these considerations, and by the need to make sure that Germany had no network of overseas bases for either ships or aircraft. And this argument applied with particular force 'to that great southern half of the British Empire' which lay in 'an irregular semicircle around the Indian Ocean'. In Europe an attempt must be made to limit German strength by rearrangements of the map on ethnic lines, but this was not of as vital interest to Britain as to her allies, and the degree to which it could be pressed would depend upon the military situation. An eventual settle-ment would be at the expense of the outlying and less effectively organ-ized elements on each side: the German colonial empire, Turkey, and Russia. The actual situation at the time hostilities ceased would be all important; once the Germans had been driven from France and Bel-gium and the Turks from Palestine, Armenia, Mesopotamia, and Syria, negotiations could begin.[1]

The Amery memorandum was indeed the basis of the report of Curzon's committee on 'territorial desiderata'.[2] Priority was given to the acquisitions necessary for the security of the Empire, and it was to be made clear to the allies that the interests of the dominions and India were entitled to consideration over and above that given to the claims of the United Kingdom. It could indeed be argued that in putting for-ward this proposition, which was based on the importance of the mili-tary contributions of India and the dominions, the members of the committee were being somewhat disingenuous. The committee (like the imperial war cabinet) already contained representatives of these

[1] By now the tide was turning in the Middle East war; Baghdad fell on 11 March 1917, and the Turks had been driven back farther in Mesopotamia by the end of the year. By July 1917 the Arab revolt (begun in June 1916 by the Sherif of Mecca) had led to the fall of Aqaba; soon afterwards Allenby began his advance from Egypt which led to the capture of Jerusalem on 9 December.

[2] Imperial war cabinet, report of the committee on the terms of peace (territorial desiderata), 24 April 1917. Austen Chamberlain Papers, AC. 20/78. It is followed by minutes of meetings of the committee held on 17, 18, 19, 23 April.

countries who had had their say to the proposals the British government should put forward. Why, it might be asked, were they entitled to a second round of claims in the future negotiations themselves? The question was not an academic one. The claims to separate representation of India and the dominions were to be an important source of friction in the preparations for the peace conference, especially where the United States was concerned, and later in relation to the League of Nations. It might seem to a cynical foreigner that the British Empire, like some oriental deity, was single or multiple in its manifestations as best suited itself, and for men brought up within the legal concept of the state, this predilection of the British for vague notions not easy to fit into classical modes of legal thinking was a perfectly understandable source of irritation. The vagueness about status might suit the political purposes of a Balfour or a Smuts but there was no reason why those outside the charmed circle should lend themselves to these deliberate ambiguities.

In fact, the determination of the dominions to retain the German colonies they had seized was such that there could be no question of their being made to abandon them.[1] The idea of British strategists early in the war that they might just be seized as bargaining counters was thus illusory.[2] The feelings in military circles in 1916 that a policy of complete annexation should not be allowed to harden lest it prolong the war and that an outlet for German population in Africa would be less damaging in the future than a further increase in the German element in the United States, found equally little response; and the argument was indeed specifically repudiated by the Foreign Office, which denied that Germany required an African outlet for her labour.[3] Nor was there any chance of the British government accepting the idea of internationalizing the German colonies on the lines advocated by a section of the British left or that of creating a single central African area of commercial non-discrimination, including the allied possesssions there as adumbrated by the Board of Trade.[4] It is true that at the first meeting of the

[1] See memorandum by Hankey on the General Military Policy of the War, written for the prime minister, December 1914. Copy sent to Balfour 29 December. Balfour Papers, B.M. Add. 49703.
[2] That there would inevitably be major annexations overseas was admitted in a memorandum by the colonial secretary, Lewis Harcourt on 25 March 1915. Dep. Asquith, Box 114.
[3] See the documents of the 'Committee on Territorial Changes' from August 1916 to January 1917. PRO. CAB. 16. 36.
[4] See Louis, op. cit., ch. III, 'Internationalization or Annexation? 1917–18' where the subject is treated in detail.

imperial war cabinet Lloyd George argued that the question of the German colonies should not be considered from the point of view of any single part of the Empire but as part of the whole settlement of the war. But Massey's prompt intervention on the subject of New Zealand's demand to be allowed to retain German Samoa, showed that his appeal was falling on stony ground.[1]

In respect of Europe, the committee also repeated the essentials of Amery's argument. The settlement should be one that reduced the power and resources available to the central powers, corresponded as far as possible with the wishes of the populations, and was inherently stable. The creation of conditions of resentment likely to revive the arms race and bring about another war must be avoided. The hopes that these aims could be reconciled with each other were to prove vain, and it may be argued that their chances would not have been improved by carrying out the wishes of the committee on Economic and Non-Territorial Desiderata for excluding the Germans from participating in the future economic development of British overseas territories.[2] But the discussions show that British governmental circles realized that what mattered about a peace settlement was the likelihood of its proving durable and that this must ultimately depend upon its general acceptability. But it was not assumed that nations could simply give up objectives to which they had shown themselves attached, or that a new era would be inaugurated in which the normal considerations of power politics would cease to apply. Indeed, so far from being swayed by the passions of the moment into believing that Germany was the one and only eternal enemy, the committee on territorial desiderata expressed its anxieties about the future of Britain's position in the Mediterranean with special reference to France's ambitions in Greece.[3] It is clear that at this stage of the war, whatever the doubts there might be about the military situation, no one in authority doubted either the right of Britain to pursue national aims nor the capacity of the Empire to absorb yet further territories and responsibilities.

[1] Imperial war cabinet, *Procès-Verbal*, meeting of 20 March 1917. Austen Chamberlain Papers, AC. 20/77. Samoa had been partitioned between the United States and Germany in 1899. For New Zealand's interest in the islands from 1884 on, see B. K. Gordon, *New Zealand Becomes a Pacific Power* (Chicago, 1960), pp. 15–22.

[2] This committee was under Milner's chairmanship. Its report dated 24 April is in Austen Chamberlain Papers, AC. 20/78, together with minutes of its meetings on 16, 17, 19, 20, 24 April.

[3] The Salonika expedition of which the initial landings took place in October 1915 but which achieved no success of moment until the last two months of the war was very much the favoured 'side-show' of the French. See Woodward, op. cit., pp. 87–8, 97–8.

Continued uneasiness about the military results of accepting the orthodox view, that a decisive victory could be obtained on the western front, resulted in Lloyd George sending Smuts to France on a mission of inquiry in April 1917.[1] His report to the war cabinet at the end of the month emphasized the need to limit war aims along the lines suggested by the two committees. So far the two gainers in the war had been the British Empire and Germany; the defeat of the latter was therefore essential if the British gains were not to be menaced and this would depend upon political and psychological factors as much as on purely military ones. The Russian revolution might set in train a movement towards democracy in central Europe more important for achieving the destruction of the military predominance of the central powers than anything the allies could devise. Nevertheless, though modifications in the conduct of the war were recommended by Smuts, his report did little to suggest that there could be any basic departure from the course hitherto pursued.

A meeting of the imperial war cabinet to discuss peace terms, held on 1 May 1917, did not make any basic changes from the recommendations of the committees.[2] What was discouraging, as regarding prospects of achieving allied aims, was the deterioration of the situation in Russia.[3] Amery argued that the elimination of Russia made it more than ever necessary to guard against the German thrust in the Middle East, and not to try to woo extremist opinion in Russia by making declarations regarding colonial or Near Eastern matters that might prejudice British security in the future. France was more than ever necessary as a balance to the central powers, and Italy's role in the alliance had also become more important. In Amery's emphasis on explaining to the Americans the need to eliminate the German threat to India and the dominions in terms of an analogy with the Monroe doctrine, one can already trace the anxiety in London lest the American instinct to vie with the Russians in democratic and non-annexationist terms be used to thwart essential British interests.[4]

[1] Hancock, *Smuts*, vol. 1, pp. 448 ff. The text of his report is in the *Smuts Papers*, vol. III, pp. 482–92.
[2] Imperial war cabinet, minutes of meeting of 1 May 1917. PRO. CAB. 21/78.
[3] Memorandum by Lord Curzon for war cabinet, 12 May 1917. Austen Chamberlain Papers, AC. 20/78.
[4] Letter from Amery to Austen Chamberlain, 6 July 1917, enclosing memorandum written by him for the war cabinet, 20 June 1917: 'The Russian Situation and its Consequences', Austen Chamberlain Papers, AC. 20/78. The idea of the political history of Europe in 1917–18 as being the outcome of a tug-of-war between Lenin and Wilson is the theme of Arno J. Mayer, *Political Origins of the New Diplomacy* (New Haven, 1959).

It was indeed increasingly the problem posed by the Russian upheaval that had to be taken into account, along with American pressure by the makers of British policy; this was not merely the likely breakdown of resistance to the Germans in the east and the possibility this would give them of withdrawing forces to fight on the western front, but also the progress of anti-war propaganda and its appeal to the weary peoples of the rest of the belligerent countries. By this time Kerr was writing: 'Having broken away from autocracy the world is now rushing headlong towards the abyss of anarchy under the guidance of such phrases as "self-determination", "nationalism", "Home Rule" and so forth,'[1] but to deplore the fact was not enough. Nor must one forget the fact that 1917, even after the entry of the United States into the war, was the blackest year yet for the allies; and a particularly grim one for Britain. The failure of the Nivelle offensive in April brought about the mutinies in the French army that seriously reduced its capacity as a fighting force for several months. The weight of the fighting fell upon the British in the ill-conceived and tragic offensive in Flanders, which lasted from July to October and cost almost a quarter of a million casualties.[2] In such circumstances it is not surprising that the possibility of a negotiated peace should have been reconsidered.

From the late summer of 1917 Milner, at any rate, was feeling his way in that direction.[3] The initiative in securing a public debate on this theme was taken by Lansdowne, who sent Balfour a memorandum early in November outlining his argument for strengthening the peace party in Germany and Austria by disabusing the public in those countries of the view that Britain stood for a punitive peace.[4] In a private letter to Lansdowne, Balfour deprecated the idea that the moment was appropriate for a parliamentary airing of the subject of peace terms though he was not far apart from Lansdowne on the substance of a possible settlement. Lansdowne now sought to air his views in the press; and, *The Times* having refused to print a letter on the subject, it appeared in the *Daily Telegraph* on 29 November.[5]

In the light of what is now known about German peace aims, it is doubtful whether an initiative such as Lansdowne proposed could have

[1] Kerr to Curtis, 22 July 1917, Lothian Papers, Box 139.
[2] At the end of October the Italian defeat at Caporetto threw a further burden on the British and French armies.
[3] Gollin, op. cit., pp. 552–3, 561. In September there were approaches from the central powers.
[4] Lansdowne to Balfour, 16 November 1917, Balfour Papers, B.M. Add. 49730.
[5] On the whole episode, see Newton, *Lord Lansdowne*, ch. XX, 'The Peace Letter'.

achieved results. It is, however, clear that the belief he expressed, that the prolongation of the war would leave the nations too exhausted to profit from their recovered security, evoked many echoes.[1] Because 'peace' has been appropriated as an ideal largely by the left, and because Lansdowne was, in the phrase of a recent historian, a 'hardened reactionary',[2] his espousal of the cause – despite the fact that it originated, as we have seen, at least a year earlier – has been taken as an indication that right-wing fears of social revolution had made it respectable. And the fact that the bolsheviks had now come into power in Russia and were calling for uprisings against all the belligerent governments, as well as showing their own determination to quit the war, is thought of as having been the prime mover in all such talk.[3]

It is difficult to see why this argument for an early peace should be held to be discreditable. The fabric of British institutions did in fact hold fast, despite the growth of industrial discontent and social bitterness in the last phases of the war and during the immediately post-war period. Nor was the defeat of bolshevism in Britain, as in some other belligerent countries, merely a stage in the march to power of the radical right. But Britain did not come out of the war unscathed; on the contrary, it is possible that the losses of life, to which Lansdowne called attention, were paralleled by a loss of inner confidence among the living which made rational handling of future problems much harder to achieve. To some extent this was masked by the political longevity of the wartime, and even of some of the pre-war, leadership. It was only after the second world war that the survivors of 1914–18 came into their own. Save for the brief Churchill interlude of 1951–5 (during part of which ill-health prevented him from exercising full authority), Britain from 1945 to 1962 – the period in which the Empire was liquidated and the Commonwealth bereft of all but symbolical significance – was ruled by three men who had come alive through an experience in which most of their friends and contemporaries had perished: Major Attlee, Captain Eden, and Captain Macmillan.

It is not necessary to limit one's arguments to the doubtful ground of individual psychology. The demographic blow struck at the British

---

[1] 'I have received an extraordinary number of letters, from people whom no one would include in the category of cranks, showing that I am by no means alone in the opinion which I tried to express.' Lansdowne to Chamberlain, 2 December 1917. Austen Chamberlain Papers, AC. 13.
[2] Marwick, *The Deluge*, p. 215.
[3] See Gollin, loc. cit., and Mayer, op. cit., pp. 282 ff., 322, 334, 370.

ruling class was paralleled by an understandable doubt about its capacities, and hence about its prescriptive claims. The edges of political debate, partially muted during the war, became harsher. The destruction of the historic liberal party, which had acted as a bridge between different social classes and groups and enabled democratic reform at home to be combined with the maintenance of a British imperial system overseas, was a direct product of the divisions introduced into it by wartime pressures.[1] There was soon to be no alternative between the rule of one or other party anchored to a class-basis, wholly unsympathetic to and even uncomprehending of each other. In such circumstances, continuity and coherence in external policy could scarcely be expected. It was a high price to pay for victory, and the only serious defence of Lansdowne's opponents must be that nothing short of victory would have prevented a German-dictated peace whose upshot would have been no less disastrous.

It is from this point of view that the history of the British reaction to the new soviet régime in Russia must be viewed. An interpretation of British policy that ascribes to it a considered intention to obliterate the new régime and enforce some preferred alternative upon the Russian people, will not survive serious examination. That it still underlies, if not always explicitly, much writing on the subject, is due to a number of reasons. In the first place, it is often forgotten that the soviet attitude of complete hostility to the capitalist world as a whole did not arise from the early experiences of the revolutionary government itself, but was implicit in its basic philosophy. If Lenin is to be treated as a serious historical figure one cannot ignore one of the main pillars of his creed. In the second place, the régime itself, whatever its claims to speak in the name of the people, had come into power by violence and maintained itself only through violence. Its appeal to the principles of self-determination was therefore an equivocal one. This fact was overlooked or disparaged by large sections of the British left, and the readiness of the labour party to accept at the hands of the Russians what they would not have accepted from any normal government was one of the primary obstacles to a long-term consensus on British foreign policy. Again, it was the soviet government that deserted the alliance and repudiated the agreements to which its predecessors had given their assent. There was thus no compulsion upon the allies to look after Russia's interests at the expense of their own peoples, and the British government cannot

[1] See Trevor Wilson, *The Downfall of the Liberal Party, 1914–1935* (1966).

therefore be blamed for considering policy towards Russia in the light of its general position and aims.

It has been suggested that during the weeks immediately following the Lansdowne letter, British statesmen toyed with the idea of using Russia's plight to make a deal with the Germans at Russia's expense.[1] For the existence of such plans the evidence is too scanty to be convincing. It was indeed the opposite policy that prevailed and which eventually brought about British and allied intervention; that of trying at all costs to revive the eastern front, either through some arrangement with the soviet régime, should the German demands upon it drive it to resistance, or through bolstering up elements in Russia friendly to the allies and hostile to the soviet régime. That the policy failed can be explained not by its inherent difficulties, still less by its alleged immorality, but by the confusion that prevailed in the allied capitals about the real situation in Russia and about the possible utility of external interference.[2]

In so far as there was time to sit back and coolly consider what the desiderata of British policy might be, it was obvious that there were a variety of possible outcomes to the situation, most of them unpalatable. Russia might succumb to anarchy, which would be intolerable, or she might fall under the virtual control of Germany, which would effectively mean the establishment of a German preponderance in the whole of eastern Europe. Nor would a general international scheme of control involving the western allies and the central powers after the peace be without danger from the British point of view. Russian independence was the best safeguard for Britain's imperial interests.[3] The difficulty was to find any alternative to bolshevism. In 1918 American suspicions became vocal, to the effect that British conservatives yearned to restore tsarist autocracy, but as Balfour pointed out, tsarist militarism had always been regarded as a major threat to the Empire; and unless the German autocracy collapsed as a result of the war, a restored tsardom would almost inevitable be dependent on Germany and so a greater menace than ever.[4] But the alternative idea which Lloyd George ex-

---

[1] Mayer, op. cit., pp. 324–5, 374–6; Gollin, op. cit., p. 525 fn.
[2] It would seem unnecessary to traverse the ground covered in R. H. Ullman, *Intervention and the War*, where the course of British policy is fully documented.
[3] Proposals for the reorganization of British interests in Russia by Major-General F. C. Poole, February 1918. Lothian Papers, Box 141. Poole had been chief of the British Artillery Mission with the Russian army and was to command the British troops sent to Murmansk.
[4] Balfour to Lloyd George, 16 July 1918. Ullman, op. cit., p. 223.

pressed, of letting the Russian people choose their own form of constitutional government, was found to ignore the realities of the situation.[1]

From November 1917, therefore, the British government faced a
novel situation to which historic policies had to be adapted. As between a communist Russia dedicated to the overthrow of all imperialist
governments, and the possible emergence of a powerful Russo-German
political bloc controlled by Berlin, the choice was an unpleasant one.
It is no matter for surprise that a consistent policy in this area should
have been difficult to arrive at or to preserve.

The American Susceptibilities and Claims

Suspicion of the motives behind Britain's Russian policy was only one
aspect of the more important and wider problem of Anglo-American
relations in the period after the United States became a belligerent.
The United States refused on principle to regard its status as merely
that of an additional ally of the *entente* powers. Though fighting in conjunction with them, she was fighting, as far as was practicable, a
separate war. The attempt to organize and dispatch her land forces in
such a way that they could fight as independent units was justified on
military grounds, but political considerations were not absent. In particular, when the supreme war council was set up in November 1917 in
the wake of Caporetto, the United States co-operated in its military
work but steadfastly refused to get involved in its political aspects. The
American government wished to keep its hands free to secure its own
war aims, which differed from those to which the *entente* powers and
Italy were committed.[2] And Wilson was certain that the preponderance
of power that America would enjoy in face of an exhausted Europe
would enable him to get his way.[3]

British policy had to take these facts into account, as well as the survival within the United States, and indeed within the administration,
of elements unfavourable to the war and to be on the alert for potential
support for Britain and its Empire. These difficulties affected the two
fields in which American help was most urgently needed – finance and
shipping[4] – but were overcome. The financial assistance to the allies con-

[1] Notes by Lloyd George on Lord Reading's telegram from Washington, 13 July 1918.
Balfour Papers, B.M. Add. 49692. The telegram is in Ullman, op. cit., p. 220.
[2] See Trask, *The United States in the Supreme War Council*.
[3] See, e.g., Wilson to House, 21 July 1917. Quoted Mayer, op. cit., p. 188.
[4] See the letters of Spring-Rice to Balfour and Cecil in the summer and early autumn of 1917.
Balfour Papers, B.M. Add. 49738, 49740.

tinued, and the United States turned its energies into a massive ship-building programme and agreed eventually to join in a system of shipping allocation and control, essential if American troop shipments to Europe were not to upset the general supply position. But it was obvious that the main reason for the success of the British negotiators in bringing this about was the fact that, despite the heavy losses she had incurred, Britain was the one member of the alliance with shipping surplus to her own requirements and that this gave her an important advantage.[1] Even so, all was not smooth going, partly because the new tonnage being built in the United States turned American minds to a post-war situation when it was hoped that America's mercantile marine could be revived and successfully compete with Britain's.[2] The United States was prepared to accept the full rigours of commercial warfare against the central powers now that it had ceased to be a neutral, but it did not accept the idea that American and British interests were in natural and permanent harmony. On the British side, it was felt that the United States might use its political influence, for instance in Latin America, and exploit Britain's much greater absorption in the war to build up commercial positions of strength at Britain's expense.[3]

The intricate, delicate, and often highly technical nature of Britain's relations with the United States during the remainder of the war had clear implications for British representation in the United States, and Balfour, who went to Washington to examine the whole situation, became convinced that Spring-Rice should be replaced.[4] A good deal of correspondence ensued as to who the proposed ambassador should be. Balfour's first choice was Grey. Other names suggested were those of Austen Chamberlain and the newspaper magnate, Lord Northcliffe. In the end, the choice fell on Lord Reading, then serving as lord chief justice, first as special envoy and then as ambassador. Northcliffe's claims were met by sending him on a special mission to the United States from June to November, to do information and propaganda work.[5] In addition there were, of course, many other British officials on

[1] See the comments of Britain's principal negotiator on shipping questions, Arthur Salter (Lord Salter) in his *Slave of the Lamp* (1967), chs 3 and 5.
[2] See the correspondence about the proposed American purchase of ships on order for Britain at the time America entered the war. Balfour Papers, B.M. Add. 49693.
[3] Balfour to Wiseman, 5 March 1918; Balfour to Eric Drummond, 14 March 1918. Balfour Papers, B.M. Add. 49741.
[4] Balfour, telegram from Washington, 6 May 1917. Balfour Papers, B.M. Add. 49692.
[5] There were considerable anxieties about the Northcliffe mission both in respect of the character of its head and in the light of the feeling that any direct propaganda in the United

temporary or permanent assignment to Washington to handle the increasing press of military and other business. For the first time British officialdom was required to inform itself about American methods of doing business, and about the nature of American politics. Not all of them learned their lessons equally well. There was a natural temptation to seek the company of those most friendly to Britain who were often to be found in the ranks of the opposition: 'There are still some of our people here who are carrying on flirtations with Roosevelt and the Republicans. They don't seem to grasp the simple fact that whether we like it or not, Wilson will be President for another three years, and that it must be the height of folly to side with his political opponents.'[1] As far as direct connections with the president were concerned, William Wiseman continued to perform his special functions, occupying as he put it 'practically the position of political secretary to [Colonel] House'.[2]

Indeed, even though Britain might appear, to American public opinion, the most vulnerable of the allies, it was obviously easier for linguistic and other reasons for the British to deal with the Americans than for officials of other nationalities. This was not without political implications,[3] but this did not mean that there was any serious possibility of turning this wartime co-operation into something more permanent. Balfour told his cabinet colleagues in December 1917 that he would like a defence alliance with the United States,[4] and among liberals, Walter Runciman and the extreme radical, Josiah Wedgwood,

---

States by Britain would only do harm. Drummond (from Ottawa) to Hankey, 27 May 1917, ibid., B.M. Add. 49704. The French, it was felt, could do more in this respect with safety. Balfour to Cecil, 3 June 1917, reporting on conversations between House and Spring-Rice, ibid., B.M. Add. 49738. Wilson also made it plain that he did not approve of direct propaganda either by Englishmen in the United States or Americans going to Britain. Willert, op. cit., p. 94. On the other hand, some people felt that the absence of British propaganda signified to Americans a deplorable indifference to world opinion. Mrs Burnett-Smith to Lloyd George, 18 December 1918. Balfour Papers, B.M. Add. 49692. On the Northcliffe mission itself, see Stanley Morison, 'Personality and Diplomacy in Anglo-American relations, 1917', in R. Pares and A. J. P. Taylor (eds), *Essays Presented to Sir Lewis Namier* (1956).
[1] Wiseman to Drummond, 25 January 1918, ibid., B.M. Add. 49741.
[2] Wiseman to Drummond, 27 April 1918. Ibid. B.M. Add. 49741. Note by Balfour, Willert, op. cit., p. 82. Wiseman became in 1919 the adviser on Anglo-American relations at the Paris Peace conference.
[3] 'I am very much struck by the way all the officials are turning to the English for co-operation as opposed to the rest of the Allies. It is generally realized (though of course never mentioned) that the war has come to be a struggle between Germany on the one side and England and American on the other.' Wiseman to Drummond, 25 January 1918. Balfour Papers, B.M. Add. 49741.
[4] Young, *Balfour*, pp. 385-6.

proclaimed the desirability of an Anglo-American link.[1] But despite the profusion of hands-across-the-sea style oratory, the reality was very different.

Quite apart from the conflicts of interest between the two countries and the distance between them over war aims, the Americans' belief that Britain was an undemocratic society was still a powerful factor in determining their attitudes.[2] And these views were no doubt fortified by the continuing connections maintained by influential Americans with the British left.[3]

It thus became necessary to consider American susceptibilities on all aspects of war aims that concerned the Empire. In commenting on a paper drawn up by Smuts for the war cabinet in December 1917, on the possible lines that peace talks might take, Kerr wrote that it would be 'absolutely fatal' to suggest that the German colonies should be retained because they were essential to communications. The United States would not look at that for a moment because it would lead to the proposition that every coaling station and port in the world should belong to Britain for the same reason. The case for the retention of the Germany colonies should rest on the 'best interest both of the inhabitants and of the world'. They should be attached either to a neighbouring country, as with German South-West Africa, or to a power with great colonial experience, like Britain or France. He believed this argument would prevail 'where the purely British argument would not'.[4]

The antipathy to Britain as an imperial power was fanned by the continued hostility of the Irish, and events in Ireland were not such as to cause any diminution of the feeling. Balfour consulted Colonel House as to the likely effect on American opinion of the scheme to associate the introduction of conscription into Ireland with a measure of home rule.[5] But Irish policy could not be decided wholly by considerations of its impact abroad; and the problem continued to envenom Anglo-American relations, despite the fact that some of the more established Irish-Americans were alarmed at the evidence that Irish nationalists would

---

[1] Mayer, op. cit., p. 332.
[2] The president's reference in a speech on female suffrage on 30 September 1918 to 'old Governments like that of Great Britain which did not profess to be democratic' annoyed both Reading and Balfour a good deal. Telegram of 3 October 1918. Balfour Papers, B.M. Add. 49741.
[3] Martin, op. cit., pp. 132 ff.; Mayer, op. cit., 335–7.
[4] Kerr to Smuts, 14 December 1917. *Smuts's Papers*, vol. III, p. 576–7.
[5] Balfour to Wiseman, 1 April 1918. Balfour Papers, B.M. Add. 49692.

be willing to see Germany establish a naval base on the Irish coast which would be used against the Americans.[1]

A positive factor, however, was the continued improvement in Canadian–American relations which led the British government to look favourably on the proposal that Canada should have its own representation at Washington.[2] A special Canadian war mission was established there in January 1918, although agreement on regular diplomatic representation had to wait till 1920.[3]

The Middle East

It was clear from the beginning that the main effort of the United States would be on the western front. Until the late summer of 1918 the general allied expectation was that the war would go on well into 1919, since only in that year would the new weight of the American ground forces be able to play a decisive role. In the other theatres of war, the Americans neither claimed nor played a part – yet it was in the east, and in particular in the Ottoman empire, that some of the major decisions would have to be made. No one seriously suggested that the areas detached from Turkish rule should be restored to it; indeed, even part of the Anatolian peninsula itself seemed a possible area for foreign control. In that sense the campaigns and bargaining that went on were a continuation of a process long familiar to European statesmen as the 'eastern question'. With the weakening in the position of Russia and the possible collapse of its power altogether, visions of a revival of the German *Drang nach Osten* began to haunt British planners. The barrier to an overland advance against India required strengthening. Egypt must be retained and the power that was exercised from the Egyptian base developed in an eastward direction across Sinai and into Palestine. Mesopotamia so hardly won must be retained, both to protect the Gulf and in the light of the growing significance of oil. Britain's allies – France and perhaps Italy – might have to be allowed some share of the Turkish spoils, but it was not Britain's intention to give away anything that would diminish the strength of Britain's own position. If the Americans could be brought in to share the burden it must be in a way which suited the general purposes of British policy.

[1] Spring-Rice to Balfour, 27 September 1917. Balfour Papers, B.M. Add. 49740.
[2] Robert Cecil to Spring-Rice, 14 April 1917. Balfour Papers, B.M. Add. 49777.
[3] Roger Graham, *Arthur Meighen* (Toronto, 1962), vol. 2, pp. 55–7, 60. No appointment was made until February 1927.

It thus came about that the British Empire which had entered the war in a wholly defensive spirit, and with essentially defensive aims, emerged with a largely expanded Middle East empire whose subsequent dissolution was to be more bitterly contested, and led to more disagreements over timing and method, than any other aspect of the imperial retreat save only that from India.[1] During the period of retreat which began in the 1930s, and of which the penultimate stage was reached with the hurried and messy exodus from Aden at the end of 1967, it became fashionable to blame the policy-makers of the war years for their muddled thinking and contradictory promises. As so often criticism of this kind overlooked the conditions under which wartime policy had to be made, and there was also, as we have seen, the plurality of decision-making centres; Whitehall itself, New Delhi and Simla, Cairo – not to mention, in relatively primitive countries with a less well-developed network of communications, some initiative by the men on the spot.

But the real point that should be made is quite a different one. The records show that so far from being the victims of sentiment – though sentiment played its part – the makers of British policy were fairly clear as to their objectives; and within a mental framework of which imperial thinking was still a part, their position was a perfectly coherent one. Indeed, despite the beginnings of a liquidation of the position in the 1930s, the Middle East barrier played in the second world war precisely the role that the imperial planners had envisaged for it. The advance of the Germans to join up with their Japanese allies was in fact prevented by British military control, retained or established in the Middle East. And against Russian and communist infiltration, the line held for even longer.

What was missing in 1914–18 was a proper appreciation of the fact that it was not possible simply to replace Turkish control over the non-Turkish parts of the Empire by the rule, direct or partially disguised, of Britain or indeed of any other distant country. Other forces had to be taken into account, including the various nationalisms of the indigenous peoples.[2] The more or less primitive desert Arabs had long enjoyed

[1] The affairs of the Middle East take up for instance a quite inordinate share of A. P. Thornton, *The Imperial Idea and its Enemies*, despite the fact that the author's understanding of the politics of the question leaves much to be desired. An essential though controversial introduction to the theme is Elizabeth Monroe, *Britain's Moment in the Middle East, 1914–56* (1963).
[2] On this aspect of the matter, see the important studies by Elie Kedourie, especially, *England and the Middle East* (1956) and *Nationalism* (1960).

British sympathies of a kind so easily meted out by travellers and explorers to the exotic. In raising the Arab revolt, T. E. Lawrence and his coadjutors were exploiting links that already existed to however minimal a degree. Far more important, though less appealing to most Britons, was the more modern nationalism of the urban Arab – and principally that of the intelligentsia – to Egypt and the 'fertile crescent'. In speaking the traditional language of oppressed nationalities claiming self-determination, these Arabs could make the same kind of appeal to British idealism as had the Turks' Balkan subjects in earlier generations, and the Indian Congress. Finally, there was the Jewish nationalist movement, known as zionism, which looked forward to solving the quite separate problem of persecuted European Jewry by settlement in Palestine under autonomous Jewish institutions – a Jewish national home.[1]

It was not that any of these local or external forces were ignored by British policy-makers. On the contrary, they were concerned throughout to win their support, the more so since they were directly competing in each case with the Germans.[2] The difficulties were to be found in operation, not in conception. In the first place, the forces at work were not in harmony with each other and their interests were not easily reconcilable. In the second place, it was not to be expected that they would lend themselves to manipulation for purely British interests; they had to be convinced that their own purposes would best be secured by accepting British rule or suzerainty. Finally, there was the question of the representation on the ground of British power; and the difficulties of finding the right kind of men were considerable despite the experience that had been gained in Egypt. Neither India, nor still less the colonial world of Africa, provided a useful parallel.[3] The traditional difference

[1] See Christopher Sykes, *Cross Roads to Israel* (1965); B. Halpern, *The Idea of the Jewish State* (Harvard University Press, 1961), and Leonard Stein, *The Balfour Declaration* (1961).
[2] That this was true of the Moslem world has already been noted; it was equally true of the zionists where the Germans could until 1917 point to the presence of the anti-semitic tsarist government on the allied side. The Germans were handicapped as to what they could promise by their own alliance with the Turks whose territory was in question.
[3] Of course, the problem was recognized from the beginning by those who knew the area and the peoples involved. At a meeting of the war committee in July 1916 Sir Mark Sykes who played a leading part in policy-making and diplomacy with respect to the Middle East, urged on the government a definitely pro-Arab policy which should be free from social discrimination or the idea of a ruling race . . . 'in my opinion Arabs cannot be run on the lines of the "white man's" burden. The Arabs have many faults and failings, but they have physique, fire and nimbleness of mind and a sense of breed which makes it impossible to adopt the white versus coloured attitude towards them.' PRO. CAB. 17. 176. The zionist settlers in Palestine were even less amenable to treatment as a 'colonial' people.

in outlook between the British and Indian governments and the differences between the approaches of the military, the Foreign Office and the Colonial Office had all to be taken into account as well as the personal character of the Lloyd George governmental machine. And within the British parties as well as between them there were clashes of interpretation and preference.

Nor was it to be expected that the British (or even the British and French, when in agreement) would be allowed to settle the fate of the area entirely as seemed good to them. The historic and contemporary importance of the whole region (Palestine's special significance to the world's three great monotheistic religions) meant that it was impossible to imagine that other countries would refrain from having their say. But it must not be forgotten that, when the final decisions came to be made the area concerned had in fact been liberated from Turkish rule not by its inhabitants, actual or presumptive, but by allied arms, locally primarily by the British but also – since Turkish defeat was bound up with Germany's – by the allied and associated powers together. Neither Lawrence's Arab irregulars nor the Jewish legion in Allenby's forces were more than marginal elements in the final victory. It was in full consciousness of this prospect, and later of the fact itself, that British wartime planning for the Middle East proceeded. At the time no one doubted that victory gave rights to the victors.

The flight of the Khedive to Turkey at the outset of the war had forced the British government to take steps about the status of Egypt, and the long equivocation about Britain's position there was ended with the declaration of a protectorate on 18 December 1914. To enlist Egyptian sympathies with the war thus became important and from Indian quarters came suggestions that this could be done by conciliation and by concessions to the demand for self-government.[1] Henceforward, as was to happen in country after country and was already the case in India, the British had continuously to balance sacrifices of security and efficiency, inevitable in the transition to self-government, against the long-term desirability of securing the maximum degree of local consent for overall British control.[2]

The question of extending the area of British control in the Middle East arose not from the actual position in Egypt, but from the Gallipoli

[1] Note on the situation in Egypt by the Aga Khan and M. A. Ali Baig, 12 January 1915. Dep. Asquith, Box 113.
[2] See Marlowe, *Anglo-Egyptian Relations*, ch. IX, 'The Protectorate'.

expedition, Russia's demand on 4 March 1915 for Turkey and the Straits which Britain conceded on 12 March and the French four weeks later, and the French demand for Syria including Palestine. But consideration of the future shape of the area predated these events. Palestine in particular, with its propinquity to the Suez Canal, was not a country that Britain could ignore, and its future was raised in cabinet as early as 9 November 1914. On the same day, the home secretary, Samuel, suggested to Grey that as the European powers would object to any one of them getting the country, Jewish national aspirations might be fulfilled by restoring a Jewish state there, to be neutralized but set up under conditions which would give Britain a considerable influence. Shortly afterwards Samuel modified his views to advocate complete British control, and between January and March 1915 he circulated documents to his colleagues outlining this idea.[1]

In its final form, Samuel's paper met with strong opposition from Montagu, who represented that section of Anglo-Jewry which felt the recognition of a Jewish national entity would worsen the position of the Jewish community in Britain itself and elsewhere.[2] As Asquith was also hostile the scheme made no progress at the time, but in April 1915 the cabinet set up a committee on Desiderata in Asiatic Turkey. Even before this the Indian government had pressed for the permanent establishment of British power in Mesopotamia,[3] but there was no unanimity in the India office as to the extent to which Turkey should be shorn of her territories.[4] Kitchener felt that any settlement should allow for the possible future hostility of France and Russia, and also thought that Alexandretta should be acquired to provide for the defence of Mesopotamia.[5] The Admiralty wanted the prestige that Russia would acquire in the Middle East by its promised acquisition of Constantinople to be balanced by Britain's establishment in Mesopotamia, and on the eastern shore of the Mediterranean:

As has been our constant habit in building up the Empire we have in this case hung back reluctantly for nearly a century from the in-

[1] Stein, op. cit., pp. 103 ff.
[2] Memorandum, 'Jews and Palestine', by E.S.M. Dep. Asquith, Box 27.
[3] Note by viceroy of India, 'The Future Status and Administration of Basra', 24 February 1915. PRO. CAB. 27. 1.
[4] See the notes by General Sir Edmund Barrow, the military secretary of the India Office, 16 March; Sir Arthur Hirtzel, the permanent secretary, 17 March, and the secretary of state, 6 April 1915. Ibid.
[5] Memorandum by Lord Kitchener, 16 March. Ibid.

creasing burden of our destiny. We have hung back, as we always did, till it is no longer possible with safety to avoid that destiny. We have never had cause to regret such a step when the moment was forced upon us, and everything points to such another moment being at hand.'[1]

As far as Arabia itself was concerned, the India Office thought that some kind of British influence must be made to predominate in the peninsula though it deprecated any attempt at direct administration.[2]

The committee on Asiatic Turkey, whose chairman was a Foreign Office official, Sir Maurice de Bunsen, and of which Hankey was secretary, reported on 30 June 1915. It stated the need to balance any improvement in Britain's position, following a territorial rearrangement in the area, with the 'inevitable increase of Imperial responsibility'. The Empire was large enough already and should be consolidated so that the current generation could pass on to their successors 'an inheritance' standing 'four-square to the world'. The security of the Gulf was in its view the key consideration, and because India would have difficulty in supplying troops if Russia invaded Mesopotamia there had to be a backdoor to the Mediterranean. The role that Kitchener assigned to Alexandretta was allotted to Haifa. As additional security a belt of French territory should be inserted between the British-held area of Mesopotamia and the Russian frontier; though, of course, a revival of the pre-1904 fears of a Franco–Russian combination against Britain would make the proposed Haifa–Euphrates railway valueless. The main proposals were put forward on the assumption of an allied victory, though a rather narrower set of claims in respect of the territory to the north of the Gulf was set out in the event of a negotiated peace.[3]

It was in the following month that the approach was received from the Sherif of Mecca, Hussein, about the raising of revolt against the Turks, and this led to the assurances given him by Sir Henry MacMahon

[1] Memorandum by the Admiralty, 'Alexandretta and Mesopotamia', 17 March 1915.
[2] Note by the India Office: 'Arabia', 26 April 1915. Ibid.
[3] 'Report of the Committee on Asiatic Turkey', 30 June 1915. Austen Chamberlain Papers, AC. 1958. Sir Mark Sykes who had taken part in the committee's deliberations signified his agreement to the report but was unable to sign it owing to absence abroad. Not everyone shared the committee's moderation. Sir Valentine Chirol felt that the committee underestimated the danger to Britain's position of pan-Islamic propaganda and also that there was no proof that a boundary with Russia itself was more likely to engender trouble than any system of buffer states. Chirol: Memorandum on the Committee Report, forwarded by Sir Mark Sykes. Ibid. Valentine Chirol (1852–1929), a former director of the foreign department of *The Times*, was sent on a mission to the Balkans in 1915. He was a prominent authority on both Indian and Middle Eastern affairs.

on 24 October 1915. The ambiguity of these assurances, in relation both to the need to satisfy France's aspirations and to the special situation of Palestine, inspired the later arguments that the Arabs had been misled into believing that the entire area to be taken from the Turks would receive its immediate independence. Historians have continued to differ on this score, but it is clear that the planners in London, with their immediate concern over the German threat to the Gulf and their preoccupation, as far as the future was concerned, with a revived Russian (and even French) threat, took for granted the desirability of some British foothold on the Eastern Mediterranean. It was on the basis of the report of the de Bunsen committee that Sykes pursued his negotiations with the French in the winter of 1915–16; and these talks into which the Russians were drawn in March, culminated in the Sykes–Picot agreement which was given final form in a letter from Grey on 16 May 1916.

The Sykes–Picot agreement envisaged Arab independence for most of the area, but assumed that the Arabs would need foreign assistance, to be given by the French in the area from Damascus to Mosul, and by the British in the area from Gaza to Kirkuk.[1] Britain's foothold on the eastern Mediterranean was to be a small enclave including Haifa and Acre, annexed outright, and Palestine was to be internationalized.

Meanwhile this drastic rearrangement of the map was queried, and some people in the India Office urged that part of the Arab lands should remain under Ottoman rule.[2] The need to destroy the link between Turkey and Germany was generally agreed. If German forces were in Turkey when peace came, she would have a military base from which to threaten India and Egypt, a political base for fostering discontent among the Moslems of the Empire, an 'international pawn' in Palestine which would give her a hold over the zionists, the papacy, and the orthodox church, a stranglehold over Russia at the Bosphorus, and the monopoly of certain essential oilfields.[3]

[1] The texts of the letters composing the Sykes–Picot agreement are printed in *D.B.F.P.*, series 1, vol. IV, pp. 241–51.
[2] India Office memoranda on the war with Turkey, 25 May and 13 June 1916.
[3] Memorandum by Sir Mark Sykes, 'The Problem of the Near East', 20 June 1916. CAB. 17. 175.

The Balfour Declaration

Given the immense importance attached to the Middle Eastern question and the British suspicions of her present allies as well as her present
enemies, it is not surprising that the Sykes–Picot agreement did not
ultimately satisfy Britain's requirements. It is also not surprising that
playing the zionist card assumed an attractiveness absent when Samuel
made his original suggestions early in the war. Indeed, with the background of these discussions the emphasis laid upon the effects of zionist
propaganda, the personality and services to the war effort of the zionist leader, Dr Chaim Weizmann, and the personal sympathies of Lloyd
George in the history of the Balfour Declaration of 2 November 1917
in favour of a Jewish national home in Palestine, take on their proper
proportions. Later on, as the reality of Arab nationalism asserted itself,
some historians argued that this identification of the British and the
zionist cause had been a cardinal error, as otherwise the British might
have built up and sustained a presence in the Middle East on the basis
of Arab consent.[1] There are many reasons – such as France's experience
in Syria and the Lebanon – for thinking that this commitment was not
the decisive factor that is suggested. But whatever the verdict on that
may be, it is clear that at the time the enterprise was thought to be
directly useful to the Empire and in no sense a charitable or merely
idealistic gesture – though one should not underrate the very real appeal of zionism to some prominent Englishmen. The point needs
emphasis not only because the Jewish presence in Palestine was connected with the maintenance of British imperial interests by the enemies
of those interests, inside and outside the Middle East, but because the
wing in British politics that was most sympathetic to imperialist ideas
was also favourable to the zionists. Despite the traditional, if mild and
veiled, anti-semitism of the British upper classes, it was from the conservatives that most of the zionists' best friends were drawn.[2]

[1] 'Measured by British interests alone, it was one of the greatest mistakes in our imperial
history', Monroe, op. cit., p. 43. 'No greater disservice was ever rendered to the cause of
British imperialism than by its own support of the Zionist movement', Thornton, op. cit., p.
184.
[2] There were, of course, liberals and even socialists who also espoused the zionist cause but
it is grotesque to say as Thornton does that 'the labour party was always a strong supporter
of Zionism' (loc. cit.). The labour party's natural affiliations were with nationalists opposing
British colonial rule, and the Palestine Arab was a much more obvious object of favourable
attention than the Jewish immigrant, despite the 'socialist' character and of much early
Jewish settlement and the generally socialist ideology of much of the zionist movement.

What is undeniable, however, is that the zionist appeal to British policy-makers was from the beginning a mixed one. A largely Jewish Palestine might be a future bastion of Britain's position in the Middle East; the immediate question was whether espousal of the zionist cause would secure for the allies the sympathies of the Jewish communities of eastern Europe, particularly Russia, and above all of the United States. This notion prompted Grey's inquiry of the French and the Russians, on 11 March 1916, as to how they would view a declaration guaranteeing Jewish rights in a liberated Palestine.[1] Henceforward the interconnection between the two ideas was bound to be maintained, and it was this duality in the British attitude as much as the contradiction between the MacMahon–Hussein correspondence and the Sykes–Picot agreement that needs to be noted. The need for a British presence in the eastern Mediterranean was not something that the rest of the world would regard as self-evident, and least of all, the Americans. The return of the Jews to their historic homeland had a more universal appeal.

The report of the imperial war cabinet committee on the terms of peace of 24 April 1917 emphasized the importance of Britain controlling both Palestine and Iraq and the need to modify the Sykes–Picot agreement with this in mind . . . 'the ultimate connection by railroad of Egypt, Palestine, Mesopotamia, and the Persian Gulf is an object to be kept steadily in view'.[2] By this time a formal agreement had been drawn up by the Foreign Office embodying an international administration for Palestine, arising from the discussions with the French and Italians at St Jean-de-Maurienne on 19 April. Sykes was busy on the cabinet's instructions trying to get the French to revise the Sykes–Picot arrangements and on 25 April Cecil, in charge of the Foreign Office during Balfour's absence, told Weizmann that it would strengthen the British position if the zionists would ask for a British Palestine.[3] The complicated negotiations between the zionist leaders and the allied governments, that occupied the spring and summer of 1917, were thus carried on in the knowledge that the war cabinet had accepted the idea of a special status for the Jews in Palestine. However, it was obviously to the interest of Britain that the initiative should appear to come from the Jewish side lest the British, a Christian power, appear to be forcing on the

[1] Stein, op. cit., p. 223.
[2] Imperial war cabinet, report of the committee on terms of peace (territorial desiderata), 24 April 1917. Austen Chamberlain Papers, AC. 20/78.
[3] Monroe, op. cit., p. 42.

Arabs the realization of zionist aims.[1] And this of course meant delicate handling of the anti-zionist element in British Jewry itself. The draft declaration was actually prepared on the zionist side and sent to Balfour by Lord Rothschild on 18 July, although it did not come before the war cabinet until September. The principal objector in political circles was again Montagu (recently made Secretary of State for India), moved both by his assimilationist attitude to the Jewish question and by his concern about the effects of the declaration upon Moslem opinion in India. The discussions were prolonged and it was not until October that a working draft, largely composed by Amery under Milner's authority, was put before the war cabinet. It was thus from Milner and the imperialist group concentrated in the war cabinet secretariat that the impetus came; and this was fully appreciated by the zionist leaders.[2]

The need to secure the assent of President Wilson caused delay but urgency was introduced into the situation by renewed reports of a possible counter-offer by the Germans. The most weighty sceptic was Curzon, who pointed out the danger of raising hopes that could not be fulfilled, but he did not press his opposition and on 31 October the war cabinet gave its assent. The argument from Balfour that finally carried the day was based almost exclusively on the immediate advantages of the declaration to allied propaganda. Indeed, over the next few weeks, there was some discussion of the United States rather than Britain being made the protecting power.[3]

In fact, the declaration made little impact by comparison with the other great events of the end of 1917; the bolshevik revolution brought a new turn to the whole problem of the eastern Mediterranean, and the Middle East and zionism was not one of the foremost issues during the conquest and occupation of the area in 1918. The form British in-

[1] Minute from W. Ormsby-Gore to Hankey, 18 August 1917. CAB. 21. 58. W. Ormsby-Gore (1885–1964) (Baron Harlech, 1938), M.P. 1910–38, had been an intelligence officer in the Arab bureau before returning to London in 1917 as P.P.S. to Milner and an assistant secretary to the war cabinet. He was under-secretary for the colonies, 1922–4, and 1924–9. P.M.G., 1931; first commissioner of works, 1931–6; secretary of state for the colonies, 1936–8. High Commissioner in South Africa, 1941–4.

[2] 'It is true that British help, if it comes now, will be invaluable to us, but it is equally true that a reconstructed Palestine will become a very great asset to the British Empire', C. Weizmann to Kerr, 7 October 1917. Quoted Stein, op. cit., p. 519. Smuts who had turned down the offer of the military command in Palestine was another supporter of the zionist cause, a fact curiously omitted by his biographer, Sir Keith Hancock, and on which the published Smuts paper are silent. On the role of British imperial interests in the Palestine question, see also Halpern, op. cit., pp. 271 ff.

[3] Stein, op. cit., pp. 606–14.

fluence should take in the different parts of the area, and the line to take with the French held priority. When Clemenceau came to London at the end of November 1918 for preparatory talks on the peace conference, Lloyd George persuaded him to agree to a British instead of an international administration for Palestine, subject to an agreement about the holy places. He also secured the transfer of the Mosul oilfield from the French sphere in Syria to the British sphere in Iraq.[1]

The Foreign Office, which had shown little enthusiasm for the zionist cause, was inclined to put its trust for the future in the forces of Arab nationalism; if that force could be won over it would be possible to establish a link between Egypt and India without taking France into partnership: 'the permanent political advantages of the Arab movement for British policy outweigh its comparative military ineffectiveness and the diplomatic embarrassment which it may cause'.[2] Where Palestine itself was concerned, however, some of those concerned on the British side took the view, on closer acquaintance with the country and its peoples, that only a Jewish Palestine would serve imperial interests; 'if this splendid country is ever to be properly developed and still more if it is ever to be British, it is only the Zionists who can accomplish these two aims.'[3] By the end of the war, the chief power to be considered in the Middle East was France; the idea of involving the United States was not completely dropped, but it was not a very serious alternative in the areas of direct British interest.

The United States and Peace Terms

In all other respects, British war aims had to accommodate the development of American thinking and the public pronouncements of President Wilson,[4] the importance of which rested as much upon the relative growth of American power, as upon the effectiveness of Wilson's appeal to public opinion in both camps. It was obviously in Britain's interests that the two countries' policies should coincide as far as possible, and that the burdens of sustaining a future settlement should be equitably shared. But this line of policy was difficult to follow in the

[1] Stein, ibid., pp. 614–16.
[2] Foreign Office memorandum, 'French and Arab claims in the Middle East in relation to British interests', 19 December 1918. PRO. CAB. 29. 2.
[3] Ormsby-Gore from Tel Aviv–Jaffa to Hankey, 19 April 1918. PRO. CAB. 21. 58.
[4] See especially, Nelson, *Land and Power*, ch. III, 'The American Factor and British Policy, 1917–1918'.

absence of any notable American interest in sharing the burden and in view of the revealed antagonism of the United States to British naval strength and to the British imperial system as a whole. Where Europe was concerned, the Americans were informed by Balfour as early as 28 April 1917 of the engagements taken by the European allies to each other, though by this time the Russian revolution had clearly called some of these arrangements into question.[1]

The detailed terms of a settlement could, however, only be framed in relation to the circumstances under which hostilities were ended. On the day the Lansdowne letter was published, a meeting of allied leaders in Paris agreed to take up peace soundings from Austria and entrust the talks to Smuts, but it became clear that there was no prospect of Austria discussing a separate peace. Smuts had no powers to discuss a general one, but in spite of this he was hopeful that the Austrians might persuade the Germans to enter into peace talks, and thought it essential to make a public statement that British war aims did not involve ruining the enemy countries.[2] Balfour, commenting on Smuts's paper, was much less optimistic about the possibility of bridging the gap between the two sides, and doubted the wisdom of proposing terms in which all the concessions, as he pointed out, would be made at the expense of Serbia, Rumania, Italy, and possibly France, and none at the expense of Britain and America.[3] There were also dangers, he thought, particularly in respect of the German colonies, of following the bolshevik line on self-determination; while even in Europe there was a conflict between that principle and the survival of the Austrian empire.[4]

The outcome of the talks with the Austrians was communicated to Wilson on 2 January,[5] and was thus in his hands when he made the 'fourteen points' speech on 8 January.[6] Three days earlier Lloyd George had publicized the British position in a speech to a meeting of trade union delegates. Since the declaration had been discussed with the labour and liberal party leaders as well as with some of the dominions' representatives, it indicated the ground on which Britain now stood.

---

[1] Northedge, *The Troubled Giant*, pp. 24–5. Wilson's denial of all knowledge of the 'secret treaties' cannot be accepted.   [2] Hancock, *Smuts*, pp. 466–8.
[3] Balfour, note on Smuts's 'Paper on Peace Conversations', 15 December 1917. Balfour Papers, B.M. Add. 49697.
[4] Balfour to Cecil, 26 December 1917. Ibid. Smuts, Cecil, and Kerr who had been in contact with the Turks had been asked to draw up a statement on war aims.
[5] Text of telegram in Balfour Papers, B.M. Add. 49738.
[6] Text in H. S. Commager (ed.), *Documents of American History* (New York, 1940). 423

Lloyd George was largely in accord with what Wilson was to say three days later.[1] The principle of self-determination was accepted as the basis of settlement in Europe and, more guardedly, in Turkey in Asia. The disposition of the German colonies was to be settled by a conference which should have primary regard to the wishes of the native inhabitants as to their most suitable protector. Three conditions were essential if a lasting peace were to be achieved: 'First the sanctity of treaties must be re-established; secondly, a territorial settlement must be secured based on the right of self-determination or the consent of the governed; and lastly, we must seek by the creation of some international organisation to limit the burden of armaments and diminish the probability of war.'

It has been suggested that the most striking difference between the two speeches, not so much in their texts as in the public comment on them in the two countries, was in their treatment of the proposed post-war international organization.[2] For Wilson it was to be the cornerstone of a new world order.[3] British ideas were both less precise and more moderate in their aspirations. The League idea had, of course, been canvassed in Britain since early in the war, and had many distinguished supporters.[4] But in British governmental circles it was suspected as being a substitute, and almost certainly an ineffective one, for Britain's maritime supremacy. The whole idea of an international force intervening to prevent a struggle, or to save one of the combatants from the consequences of a breach of the rules of war by the other, so Hankey had argued as early as June 1915, ignored human nature. Men did not fight in support of abstract principles but only when they felt that some vital concern of their own was at stake.[5] The following year he returned to the argument, in connection with proposals for compulsory arbitration of international disputes with some kind of international sanction behind the tribunal's awards. For a generation after the war such pacific procedures would be successful as Germany would not have re-

[1] Text in Lloyd George, *War Memoirs*, pp. 1510–17.   [2] Northedge, op. cit., pp. 35–6.
[3] Wilson's admirers on the left in Britain were, of course, more sympathetic to his views. The labour party memorandum on war aims of 28 December 1917 had proposed the transfer of all European colonies in tropical Africa to the League of Nations to be administered under the authority of its 'Legislative Council' as a single independent African state. Mayer, op. cit., p. 319.
[4] On the intellectual antecedents of the League idea and the British share in the origins of the Covenant, see Alfred Zimmern, *The League of Nations and the Rule of Law, 1918–1935* (1936); H. R. Winkler, *The League of Nations Movement in Great Britain, 1914–1919* (New Brunswick, 1952).
[5] Hankey, 'Memorandum on "Freedom of the Seas"', 11 June 1915. PRO. CAB. 17. 130.

covered sufficiently to renew her challenge. Meanwhile, the nation would be persuaded into relaxing its efforts and diverting its energies away from military preparations; and then Germany would reappear and get her way. No other country, and least of all the United States, could then be relied upon to come to Britain's assistance.[1] An almost equally sceptical examination of the idea was put forward by Balfour a few months later. The commitments to go to war, or at least to break off all commercial and diplomatic relations with an offending state, would have to be binding ones, if the proposed League were to have any chance of success; and there was no chance of it being a practicable proposition unless the United States took a leading part and abandoned her traditional isolation.[2] Lord Robert Cecil supported the project,[3] but his paper on it underwent a devastating analysis from Eyre Crowe. Quite apart from the familiar and general objections to such an institution, Crowe pointed out that its creation would be particularly dangerous for Britain: 'A substantial majority of the Powers could almost at any time be found for measures ostensibly designed to favour the general cause of peace, but in effect calculated to curtail British supremacy at sea.' This would particularly affect a move to limit armaments. 'It is well to remember,' he added, 'that almost the whole energies of the Second Peace Conference at the Hague in 1907 were unmistakably directed to the weakening of our sea-power.' If there were to be a League of Peace, the sanctions it possessed would be crucial, and the ultimate in commercial sanction must be military force. Such a League must possess from the outset organized military forces greater than those of a potential challenger.[4]

It is not surprising therefore, that faced with such penetrating (and as it was proved, prophetic) advice, the war cabinet was not enthusiastic about the idea though accepting it in principle. The best guarantee of peace remained British sea-power, conjoined to the sea-power of the United States;[5] but this, of course, assumed that the British Empire

[1] Hankey to Balfour, 25 May 1917. Balfour Papers, B.M. Add. 49704.
[2] Memorandum by Balfour: 'Irresponsible Reflections on the part which the Pacific Nations might play in discouraging Future Wars'. PRO. CAB. 37. 141.
[3] Robert Cecil, 'Memorandum on Proposals for Diminishing the Occasion of Future Wars' (? October 1916). Austen Chamberlain Papers, AC. 20/78.
[4] 'Notes by Sir Eyre Crowe on Lord R. Cecil's Proposals for the Maintenance of Future Peace', 12 October 1916. Ibid.
[5] Imperial war cabinet: terms of peace committee, minutes of meeting of 20 April 1917. Austen Chamberlain Papers, AC. 20/78. Imperial war cabinet meeting of 1 May 1917. PRO. CAB. 21. 78.

remained a powerful force in world affairs. Milner took the view that the League of Nations, if it did come about, should have no coercive powers and should concern itself with peace-keeping among its own members, the belligerents with the possible addition of the United States (which was still neutral when he put forward these views to an American correspondent). In such a League, a united Empire would be a major force for peace.[1]

For those who thought in non-coercive terms, the British Empire as a grouping of autonomous nations might indeed seem a model for the future League, rather than a rival to it. Smuts early took this view and presented a paper on the subject to the imperial war cabinet on 16 December 1918.[2] The new League of Nations would, however, as he conceived it, hardly offer the cut-and-dried guarantees demanded by British critics for the country's security. It was to be a flexible association, as was the Commonwealth, and co-operation rather than coercion was to be its watchword. Where his thinking did approach that of Balfour and the others was in his recognition that only American participation would make the thing meaningful. To support Wilson's plan for a League would be one way of ensuring the continuation of American influence in Europe.

The conversion of the British government to the League idea was thus due rather to the pressures exerted upon it, both at home and abroad, than to intellectual conviction. Furthermore, it was clearly understood that this must not detract from the determination to pursue as a major war aim 'the security and integrity of the British Empire and of the nations' by which it was composed.[3] And by 1917 it was clear that this integrity was menaced. The call for independence for India, Ireland, and Egypt had been made by the German socialists at the international Stockholm conference in June 1917.[4] It was now echoed by the bolsheviks, and it was not a call that fell harshly on American ears. When, in connection with the British wish to bring Japanese troops into Siberia as a part of the efforts to reconstitute the eastern front, it was publicly suggested that this was important in order to block the German road to India or Persia, it was also pointed out that it was undesirable to stress this aspect of the matter since American opinion would react unfavourably to a policy which had imperial interests as its

[1] Milner to Dr Tryon, 29 August 1916. Milner Papers, Private Letters, 1916, IV [Bodl. 142].
[2] Hancock, *Smuts*, vol. 1, pp. 438, 457, 467, 500–3.
[3] Imperial war cabinet, minutes of meeting of 1 May 1917. PRO. CAB. 21. 78.
[4] Mayer, op. cit., p. 126.

core.[1] Wilson's Mount Vernon speech on 4 July 1918, in which he seemed to be applying the principles of government by consent and self-determination in a universalist fashion, also produced anxieties in British circles. 'Are we,' asked Derby, 'to give up Arabia, Palestine, and the German colonies and are we to give Ireland, Egypt, and even India such governments as the people there can be said to want?'[2] In the light of all this it is not surprising that some dominion statesmen were concerned with their participation in an eventual peace conference, and with securing prior agreement on the Empire's aims.[3]

Peace – The Final Pressures

In Britain itself, while the left as we have seen was sympathetic to the Wilson approach and Henderson, labour's representative in the war cabinet, had made it clear that he could not support any territorial annexations by Britain,[4] most of those involved with the war effort had no such scruples. Britain had devoted blood and treasure to the common cause and was entitled to such annexations as would afford her 'a strategical security which will enable that southern British world which ran from Cape Town through Cairo, Baghdad, and Calcutta to Sydney and Wellington, to go about its peaceful business without constant fear of German agression'.[5] Amery argued that it was useless to draw the Americans into remote problems such as Palestine just for the sake of involving them in world affairs. It was more profitable to view the world as a series of Monroe doctrines, with each of the main powers, including Britain, responsible for its own area of primary interest.[6]

[1] Wiseman to Drummond, 10 March 1918; Wiseman's comments on telegram to Reading, 19 April 1922, sent to Balfour on 22 April and approved by him. Balfour Papers, B.M. Add. 49741. Wilson's attitude towards intervention in Russia was coloured by his growing suspicion of Japan's intentions and it was largely to keep an eye on the Japanese that American troops were sent. The anti-Japanese slant of American policy was shared by the Canadians and the Colonial Secretary insisted that their representatives in Washington should be consulted on the question of Japanese intervention in Russia. War cabinet minutes, 25 February 1918, Cecil of Chelwood Papers, B.M. Add. 51103.
[2] Derby to Balfour, 8 July 1918. Balfour Papers, B.M. Add. 49743.
[3] Imperial war cabinet, minutes of meeting of 14 August 1918. PRO. CAB. 23. 42.
[4] Imperial war cabinet, meeting of 1 May 1917. CAB. 21. 78.
[5] Amery to Lloyd George (? summer of 1918). Amery, *Memoirs*, vol. II, p. 161.
[6] Amery to Balfour, 16 August and 22 August 1918. Balfour Papers, B.M. Add. 49775. As late as August 1918, Amery was still contemplating the likelihood of a peace which should leave Germany dominant in Central Europe up to the frontier with Russia of the Brest-Litovsk treaty of March 1918.

And these arrangements would be the necessary prerequisite to an effective League of Nations.[1]

Amery and those most concerned with relations within the Empire saw the problem of the German colonies in the light of the future security of the British possessions around the Indian ocean; the Foreign Office view, as represented by Balfour, tended to regard them in the traditional way, as pawns to be used in bargaining over the terms of a general settlement. Smuts preferred outright annexations but was prepared to consider an international system for tropical Africa as an alternative method of getting the security that Britain required. On this he got Borden's support, on the ground that it might help to persuade Canadians as well as Americans that the war had not been fought for selfish reasons. And he was keen if possible to get the Americans to take over some of the territory, so as to ensure that they continued to play a leading part in world affairs.[2] Long, for the Colonial Office, deprecated any form of condominium, and argued that it would be possible to guarantee freedom of commercial access to friendly powers without surrendering political control.[3] In the last months of the war therefore, the disposition of colonial territories was largely considered from the point of view of whether the United States could be induced to play a positive role, and if so, whether perhaps after all Palestine or German East Africa might be the required inducement. But although Lloyd George might play with these ideas, neither Amery nor Smuts from their different points of view was sympathetic.

The decisive factor was that by the end of hostilities Britain was in fact in possession of the territories she felt she needed in order to preserve command of the seas, access to raw materials, and the security of imperial communications. To these she intended to hold 'as grimly as possible'.[4] The different preoccupations of the various groups that together made up the conspectus of British official opinion must not make one overlook the fact that in 1918, as in the earlier years of the war, all was subject to the dramatic changes in the military situation itself. The elimination of Russia from the war, and the prospect that Russia's resources could be exploited to make up for Germany's shortages, made

[1] Amery to Reading (? October 1917). Amery, op. cit., pp. 162–3.
[2] Louis, op. cit., pp. 104 ff.
[3] Imperial war cabinet, memorandum by Long: 'Our Desiderata in regard to the Disposal of Territory taken from the Enemy', October 1918. PRO. CAB. 29. 2.
[4] Smuts's imperial war cabinet memorandum of 24 October 1918. Quoted Louis, op. cit., p. 116.

the summer of 1918 a dark one for the allies. The gravity of the military situation did indeed at last force on the soldiers the unity of command for which Lloyd George had been striving but Germany's warmaking capacity was not exhausted. In June 1918 it seemed possible that both France and Italy might be forced to abandon the war, and Milner contemplated a virtually new war in which Britain, the dominions, the United States, and Japan would have to fight the central powers with southern Asia and Africa as the stakes.[1] In mid-August Smuts still could not see the war ending before 1920.[2] However, the final allied offensive had in fact already begun, and the Germans knew they were defeated. The imminence of victory affected the perspectives of peace. Between March and July 1918 the temptation to seek an arrangement with Germany at the expense of Russia had been at its greatest.[3] Now it was a question of whether to negotiate on the basis of the 'fourteen points' (which Germany was to accept in principle on 4 October) or to continue to the point of unconditional surrender, so that the war should end with the allies on German soil, and the Germans be deprived in future of any opportunity of questioning the reality and magnitude of their defeat. On 17 October Milner made public his own conviction that to crush Germany completely would be to remove its stabilizing influence in eastern Europe and to make easier the spread of bolshevism. Even an insistence that Germany change her internal institutions – which had been common form among the allies – might offer possibilities for the spread of bolshevism in Germany itself. Balfour and Smuts also spoke in cabinet in favour of minimizing the territorial demands made upon Germany, and against the fragmentation of eastern Europe which would result from the imposition of the terms demanded by the French, the Poles – Wilson in their support – and the other allies. Even the union of the Germans of Austria – the Austro-Hungarian empire having by now visibly collapsed – with Germany itself appeared tolerable to Balfour.[4] Self-determination in a Europe as heterogeneous as its history had left it, was not in itself an adequate answer to all problems.

On the whole it was the voices of moderation which triumphed in the British cabinet, and they dominated the discussions with the Americans

[1] Milner to Lloyd George, 9 June 1918. Gollin, op. cit., pp. 565–6.
[2] Imperial war cabinet, meeting of 14 August 1918. PRO. CAB. 23. 42.
[3] Mayer, op. cit., p. 325 fn.
[4] Martin Gilbert, *The Roots of Appeasement* (1966), pp. 37–42; Gollin, op. cit., pp. 568 ff.

and the other allies in the period between the German offer of 4 October and the signature of the armistice on 11 November.[1] Milner denied that he wished to save the Hohenzollern system. His insistence was on armistice terms that would render it totally impossible for Germany to fight again; to add more than that might jeopardize the acceptance of those terms for the sake of gratifying 'feelings of anger or indignation'.[2] The cause of the nations newly liberated, or with territorial or other claims against Germany, did not lack adherents in Britain. But what British statesmen realized, whatever they might say on public platforms or in the heat of electioneering, was that Germany was a permanent factor in the European balance, and the question was how its continued and inevitable presence on the scene could best be reconciled with Britain's own imperial interests.

The other major issues between Britain and the United States over these decisive weeks were naval ones; the surrender and disposal of the German fleet, and the questions of disarmament and the freedom of the seas which had figured so prominently in Wilson's 'fourteen points'.[3] On the first there was no substantial disagreement; on disarmament, since the financial burdens of arms would be an obstacle to post-war recovery, the chances of agreement seemed present if a formula could be found, though it would have to be one that preserved Britain's existing lead. On the freedom of the seas, the opinions of the two governments were as wide apart as ever. It was true that Wilson himself was not always prepared to avow the full extent of the American interest in securing an abandonment by Britain of her historic claims. In an interview with Wiseman, on 16 October 1918, he said that he recognized that the British navy in the past had served as a sort of world police force, a role which the British people had never abused and which he himself would be prepared to leave with them. But many nations chafed under Britain's predominance and he felt that Germany's unjust jealousy of the British navy was the 'deepest cause' of the war. Wiseman was left with the impression that the president recognized the fact that the submarine had altered conditions at sea and made it necessary to revise maritime law, and that he was seeking a way in which the British navy might be used as an instrument of the League of

[1] Nelson, op. cit., pp. 40 ff.
[2] Milner to Thornton, 31 October 1918. Milner Papers, Private Letters, 1918, VII [Bodl. 145].
[3] M. G. Fry, 'The Imperial War Cabinet, the United States and the Freedom of the Seas', *Journal of the Royal United Service Institution*, vol. 110 (1965).

Nations.[1] In fact, of course, there would be no dispute in a 'League' war, since by definition there could be no legitimate intercourse with an out-lawed nation. The dispute was over the use of naval power in other conflicts, and here the American position was again based on the absolute right of neutrals to trade at will with the belligerents. In bringing pressure on Britain to accept his views, Wilson could have recourse to two threats. One was to make a separate peace with Germany and opt out of the war itself. The other was to outbuild the British navy, which the United States was clearly in a position to do if its people so chose. In the end the efforts of Wilson's advisers, notably House, who were anxious not to destroy the allied concord, produced a compromise in an acceptance of a British reservation to the 'fourteen points'.[2] Both sides appear to have thought they had gained a victory; the Americans in preserving the substance of the principle, the British in the view that they could now regard the issue as closed. In that they were rapidly to be disappointed. A desire to end hostilities and to prevent Germany recovering lost ground through last-minute dissensions among the allies were powerful motives for agreement until the armistice was signed. Thereafter, the new alignments revealed in the hectic exchanges of the last few weeks of the war were to provide the basis from which all British policy would require reconsideration.

[1] S. P. Tillman, *Anglo-American Relations at the Paris Peace Conference* (Princeton, 1961), p. 43.
[2] 'They must point out, however, that clause 2, relating to what is usually described as the Freedom of the Seas, is open to various interpretations some of which they could not accept.' Supreme war council to President Wilson, 4 November 1918. Lloyd George, *War Memoirs*, p. 1979.

Chapter 6

THE EMPIRE AND THE PEACE

The Demand for Security

The armistices that brought the great war to an end did not and could not bring about the peace that was so generally desired. It was not even the case that all hostilities had ceased. The Russian civil war, merging as it did into wars between the new soviet régime and parts of what had formerly been the Russian empire; the struggles between the newly emancipated countries of eastern Europe over boundary claims, the unreconciled conflict between Greek and Turk; the problem of the succession to Turkish rule in the Arab lands – all these were to be productive of continued armed struggles on a greater or lesser scale from which the world would not enjoy a general breathing space for another four years and more. In some of these struggles Britain was directly involved, as in the intervention in Russia that had begun on several fronts in 1918. From none could she afford to be aloof, since no country had a greater interest in a restoration of general tranquillity and a resumption of ordered economic intercourse. But Britain had even more immediate concerns. In Ireland the end of the war released the final surge of nationalism, leading first to armed repression by the government and then, after the signature of the treaty establishing the Irish Free State in a partitioned island, to further fighting between those who had accepted the settlement and the bitter-enders. In India the new phase in opposition political activity was also accompanied by acts of violence, and although in the end relative calm was restored and some constitutional advance made, the effect of the turmoil was disheartening to all protagonists of an agreed and peaceful evolution. In Egypt likewise, a nationalist challenge had to be faced.

The Lloyd George government fortified by its overwhelming election victory in November 1918 (in which the nature of the peace settlement was not the main issue) had, as we have seen, no qualms in seeking the greatest possible degree of advantage for Britain and her Empire.[1]

[1] On the election of 1918, see Wilson, *The Downfall of the Liberal Party*, part II: 'The Coupon Election'.

Its principal leaders were well aware of the limits of the possible, and were blinded neither by a utopian idealism nor by insensate feelings of revenge. But they strove to achieve their purposes under considerable handicaps.[1]

In the first place there was the pressure from public opinion, transmitted through the new conservative-dominated House of Commons, for peace terms that would somehow contrive to shift the financial burden of the war and reconstruction off the shoulders of the British taxpayer and on to those of the defeated enemy.[2] Of this, historians have made much.

Secondly, there was the acute consciousness that the German bid for domination of Europe by military means had been replaced by the even greater, if vaguer, communist revolutionary challenge to traditional society as a whole. It is easy in retrospect to say that in the light of Russia's weakness at the time, these fears were exaggerated. It was to be some time before it was clear that revolution, though it had spread to central Europe, was not yet capable of taking hold there, and that it would remain for the time being contained within whatever area the Red Army could control. It was natural to connect all the symptoms of industrial and social unrest that appeared inevitably in war-weary Britain and her equally war-weary allies, with the machinations of Moscow,[3] and it was also true that many of the energies of the communist movement appeared to be directed against Britain's imperial position, notably in India. At a time when the nationalist movement

[1] Lloyd George formed a new cabinet on the old style with twenty-one members in January 1919, but owing to Lloyd George's preoccupation with peace-making and consequent absences from London, it did not begin to act until October that year. In the interim, a war cabinet made up of Lloyd George, Curzon, Bonar Law, Barnes, and Chamberlain continued to function; Smuts resigned in December 1918 to head the South African delegation at Paris. The relevant ministries were held as follows: Foreign Office: Balfour; Colonies: Milner; War: Churchill; India: Montagu; Admiralty: Long. In October 1919 Curzon became foreign secretary and Balfour succeeded him as lord president. Churchill replaced Milner at the Colonial Office in February 1921. Although much attacked, the cabinet secretariat survived – as did the 'garden suburb' till Lloyd George's fall.

[2] It is true that parliamentary pressure was limited to a small number of issues, notably reparations, and that on much that was involved in the Paris negotiations, the British delegation was left a free hand. Northedge, op. cit., pp. 91–2. See for the development of British opinion on the peace settlement, R. B. McCallum, *Public Opinion and the Last Peace* (1944).

[3] It is worth noting that despite the fear of bolshevism, there was no 'red scare' in Britain at all comparable with that which the United States underwent in 1919–20 and this despite the fact that the war had laid an incomparably greater strain upon British than upon American Society. The fact is perhaps indicative of the continuing strength of the British social fabric and of the British commitment to legality; though communism was more active in the United States, appealing especially at first to Jews, Finns and other *émigrés* from Russia. Trotsky had been resident in New York.

was in an activist phase, this was bound to cause additional and understandable disquiet.

One difficulty was, of course, that it was hard to envisage the simultaneous alienation of Germany and Russia; if this were to come about, how could their junction be prevented? It was one thing to contemplate some satisfying of Germany's ambitions at Russia's expense when there seemed no other way of ending the war without disaster in the west; it was quite another to bring this about as an act of deliberate policy at a time when Germany had been defeated and Russia greatly weakened. For those who looked at the world between the blinkers of the professional economist, like J. M. Keynes, it seemed easy to say that the sensible thing to do was to harness German entrepreneurial skills to Russian resources and thus once more make the latter generally available for the markets of the world.[1] But this was to assume that power-politics had come to an end in some Wilsonian paradise and that Germany would not use such resources to re-establish her military and political power, and renew her world challenge.

Neither could the British feel convinced about the French solution of the problem, of which Clemenceau had already made himself an exponent before the end of the war. This was to use and fortify the nationalisms of Poland and of other eastern European nations recently emancipated from tsarist or Habsburg rule to form a belt of friendly states, linked to the west by treaty and equally opposed in their external policies to Russia and Germany. The fact that such a grouping did come about, and with British assent, does not indicate a general British acceptance of the French thesis. It was due partly to the realization that there was no prospect of restoring the empires that had been destroyed by the war, partly to some sympathy with the Wilsonian principle of self-determination, and partly to the fact that most of the nationalities concerned had some means of bringing their case to British attention and some links with the policy-making organs of the government.[2]

[1] For Keynes's scheme, see J. M. Keynes, *The Economic Consequences of the Peace* (published December 1919), pp. 270–7.

[2] The development of British opinion during the war in respect of the problems of the small nations of eastern and south eastern Europe was complicated and to some extent paradoxical. Their cause was espoused by some of the Right who believed they provided a means of disrupting Germany's ally, Austria, and by a group of liberal sympathizers of whom the most important were the historian, R. W. Seton-Watson, and the foreign editor of *The Times*, Henry Wickham Steed. On the other hand the extreme left, of the Union of Democratic Control variety faithful to its general pro-German bias and in some cases conscious of the economic benefits of large single markets, remained opposed to the break-up of the Habsburg

The difficulty of preventing any renewal of the Bismarckian alignment of Germany and Russia was only the principal one among the
inevitable preoccupations of Lloyd George and his advisers. Britain
had also to take account of her relations with the other great powers.
Clemenceau's east European plans were only part of what looked like
an attempt to use the fleeting moment of victory to impose upon Europe
a French domination that would itself revive fears of less than a generation back. The clashes in the Mediterranean, into which Britain was
forced by an unwillingness to see the Sykes–Picot agreement implemented at the expense of the Arab national movement she was now bent
upon cultivating, helped to embitter disagreements over the European
settlement. It was, however, understood better in Britain than in
America that much of France's apparent search for aggrandizement
was due to concern over her ultimate security, and that unless she could
be assured of external support in the event of a renewed German threat,
she would be bound to take what physical guarantees she could get.

In the end neither the United States nor Britain was in a position
to give such guarantees; the Americans because of their basic reluctance
to become involved in European politics (which the Wilsonian experience was to fortify rather than to weaken), the British because,
among other things (including anti-French feeling), of a similar
reluctance on the part of the dominion governments without whose support no British government any longer felt it prudent or right to act. A
joint guarantee with the Americans might be acceptable, perhaps
because it was unlikely to be called upon and also because the dominions
would henceforward feel secure only when they had assurances of
American as well as British support. Despite the opposition that Hughes
put up against the Americans where Australia's own narrow claims
were concerned, this basic strategy was now as much that of the
Australasian dominions as of the Canadians, who were its principal
advocates. The reason for this shift lay in the change of relations

---

Empire to the very end. Propagandists for the southern Slavs (who themselves had to contend
with pro-Italian elements) appealed to British imperialist sentiment with the argument that
a strong southern Slav state would provide the best bulwark against the German push towards
the Middle East. In October 1916, shortly before his death, Lord Cromer the former Consul-
General in Egypt accepted the presidency of the British Serbian society on these grounds.
As we have seen, there were hopes in governmental circles of a separate peace with Austria,
and it was only in the spring of 1918 that these were abandoned and only on 9 August that
the British recognized the Czech National Council in Paris. There is much valuable material
on this aspect of British war aims and on exile propaganda in England in Henry Hanak,
Great Britain and Austria-Hungary during the First World War (1962).

between Britain and Japan. It was Canada that took the lead in pressing the abrogation of the Japanese alliance upon Britain as part of the post-war settlement; but once it was at an end it was the Australians and New Zealanders who were most threatened by the changing balance of maritime power in the Pacific.

It was in the field of Anglo-American relations that the peace-making years were most momentous. The war had altered the balance between Britain and America for good; in the economic sphere by turning Britain into a permanent debtor and making it impossible for London alone to continue as the principal effective financial centre of the world, and also in the military and naval sphere. The Americans were quite prepared to use their resources to outbuild Britain at sea unless they could get agreements on naval and other issues that suited them; and the British had to decide whether to take up the challenge or not. Because they decided not to, a permanent shift in world power was consummated without a shot being fired. The fact that the shift was disguised (mainly on the British side) as an acceptance of partner-ship was necessary for political and psychological reasons, but it did not disguise the brutal truth.[1]

Whether Britain could have acted differently is a matter of specula-tion. While the government and its professional advisers might be resolute in the pursuit of national and imperial interests, they could not rely upon popular support if it involved further sacrifice. Much of the criticism of the peace treaties assumes, it has often been pointed out, that the allies had it in their power to enforce whatever terms they chose. This was untrue generally, and particularly untrue of Britain where the clamour for demobilization and for liquidating all further military commitments was irresistible.[2] It was fortified by the belief that the economic problems of the post-war period could best be solved by the practice of rigorous governmental economy; and in such a situation, the armed forces were the historic and natural targets of the economy drive.

But above all there were the never-to-be forgotten losses of the war itself and the burden, material and psychological, which they imposed upon the survivors. The 745,000 dead (9 per cent of all men under forty-five) had been the cream of the country's young manhood. Of the

[1] Marxist publicists went on predicting an inevitable Anglo-American war, oblivious of the fact that the war had already taken place – though bloodlessly.
[2] One can compare the pressure on the American government after the second world war in relation to the criticisms of 'Yalta' and 'Potsdam'.

1·6 million wounded, a high proportion had been gravely mutilated, and losses fell particularly heavily upon the volunteer officers, who would in the normal course of things have been the leaders of the next generation. Oxford sent 14,561 men to the colours – 2,680 were killed. It has also been argued plausibly that there was no mediatory agency between the older generation, entrenched in power by the 1918 election, and the younger generation that grew up in the war years and responded to very different appeals.[1]

When one looks at the different aspects of policy between the end of the war and the partial stabilization that set in in 1921, one must then constantly reflect how difficult, how novel, and how inextricably confused were the issues that fell to be resolved. Nor could they be separated neatly from each other as they can be by a historian writing years afterwards. Lloyd George and the other British and dominion statesmen – like the leaders of the United States, France, Italy, and the other allies – had to deal at one time with almost all of these issues, often at the very same meetings. History did not stand still while they negotiated on the territorial or economic clauses of the peace treaties or on the language of the League Covenant. Day to day decisions had to be taken as well. Perhaps this aspect of the matter is too easily overlooked when we look at some of what appear to be the loose ends or dead ends of some ventures – contacts with the Russians, for instance. The wonder is not that Paris killed Wilson but that Lloyd George, Clemenceau, and Orlando survived; not that the treaties were imperfect but that they were concluded at all.[2]

The Empire and Peace Terms

The need for some decision on Empire requirements and the means of obtaining them, emerged during the hectic series of consultations with the dominion leaders and allied statesmen that took place in London between the armistice and the informal opening of the peace con-

[1] Marwick, *The Deluge*, pp. 290–1. See also F. W. Hirst, *The Consequences of the War to Great Britain* (1934).

[2] We can also see why it has been recognized that as historical material for the peace conference period, personal diaries where things are set down as they occur are more revealing than formal documentation. See, e.g., Harold Nicolson, *Peacemaking 1919* (1933); Lord Riddell, *Intimate Diary of the Peace Conference and After* (1933); Stephen Bonsal, *Unfinished Business* (1944). The most revealing picture of the 'Big Four' in action is that contained in the notes of their interpreter, Paul Mantoux, *Les Deliberations du Conseil des Quatre* (2v) (Paris, 1955; English edition of vol. 1, Geneva, 1964). For the formal layout and timetable of the Conference, see F. A. Marston, *The Peace Conference of 1919: Organisation and Procedure* (1944).

ference on 12 January 1919.[1] A note by General Smuts, written shortly before his resignation from the war cabinet, asserted that the war had left only three great powers in being, Great Britain, the United States, and France. British policy in the past had been to maintain the balance of power by supporting the weaker side on the continent, but now she must side with the United States against France since the latter was imperialist, a bad neighbour, and hoped to dominate Europe by keeping Germany in subjection. Britain had been over-generous to France in the wartime negotiations, in agreeing to allow her two of the best German colonies in Africa and also in the Sykes–Picot agreement, which she could hope to break only with American support. By aligning herself with Wilson's policies, Britain would be following the true line of the future which would no doubt 'link the two great Commonwealths in a common destiny'. The interests of Canada, Australia, and New Zealand pointed the same way. If Britain supported Wilson over the League, he might drop some of the more contentious points in his proposals. The League itself should be the reversionary of the conquered empires, and under a mandatory system based on the principle of the open door Britain would have nothing to fear, since it was certain that those countries in which she was primarily interested would select her tutelage or friendship.[2]

While suspicions of French policy in both Europe and the Middle East were of course widely shared, the view that the policies of the British Empire and of the United States coincided so neatly was not acceptable to all Smuts's British or dominion colleagues. Indeed, it was not only the question of the international status of the dominions but also a direct interest in the terms proposed that inflated the question of dominion representation at the peace conference.[3] It had been foreseen even earlier that on some non-European questions the dominions might take independent views and would wish to be able to express them.[4]

At a meeting of the imperial war cabinet on 6 November, Hughes protested against the British government's acceptance of the 'fourteen

[1] The first formal plenary session was on 18 January. On these discussions in the Imperial war cabinet, see Nelson, op. cit., ch. V.
[2] 'Our Policy at the Peace Conference.' Note by General Smuts, 3 December 1918. Cecil of Chelwood Papers, B.M. Add. 51076. PRO. CAB. 29. 2/1. The strong anti-French bias which Smuts showed in this paper was to be a permanent element in his approach to British policy up to and including the second world war.
[3] Neither the Canadian nor the Australian cabinet was as convinced as were Borden and Hughes in London that the dominions ought to have separate representation. Graham, *Arthur Meighen*, vol. 1, pp. 216–17, 224–5; A. Farmer Whyte, *William Morris Hughes* (Sydney, 1957), p. 379. [4] Kerr to Curtis. 22 July 1917. Lothian Papers. Box 139.

points' without consulting the dominions: 'The removal of economic barriers' might affect the right to make commercial treaties, and prevent the growth of preferential trade within the Empire. The League of Nations, unless merely a pious aspiration, might be a direct threat to the British Empire and its autonomy. If Japan were to be present at the peace conference, how could one exclude Australia which had made greater sacrifices than Japan and regarded Japan as a daily menace?[1] Amery seized upon Hughes' outburst to urge separate dominion representation at the peace conference; otherwise, a serious and perhaps irremediable blow would have been struck at imperial unity and the centrifugal tendencies in the Empire would begin to get the upper hand. He also argued that the imperial war cabinet should remain in session during the period of the peace conference, and that all matters arising should be referred to it directly and not to meetings from which dominion representatives were excluded.[2]

Amery's views did not prevail and at an inter-allied meeting on 2 December it was arranged that dominion representatives should attend as extra members of the British delegation when some matter of direct interest to them was under discussion. This agreement was strongly challenged by Borden at a meeting of the imperial war cabinet on 31 December,[3] and Lloyd George agreed that the British delegation of five should include one dominion prime minister taken in rotation, and that the dominions (other than Newfoundland) as well as India should also be represented in their own right on an equal footing with the lesser allies such as Belgium.[4] The dominions and India were among the signatories to the treaty.

These preliminary discussions already foreshadowed the important differences of opinion and attitude that would reveal themselves in the actual negotiations; Borden, like Smuts, was determined to press for the closest co-operation with the United States; Hughes was highly suspicious of Wilson's intentions.[5]

[1] Imperial war cabinet, minutes of meeting of 6 November 1918. PRO. CAB. 23. 44.
[2] Amery to Hankey, 13 November 1918; Amery to Kerr, 14 November 1918. Lothian Papers, Box 140. Amery to Balfour, 14 November 1918. Balfour Papers, B.M. Add. 49775. Amery did not foresee the fact that for the period up to the conclusion of the German treaty the basic authority in British affairs would be located in Paris rather than in London. See Amery, op. cit., vol. 2, pp. 177–8.
[3] Imperial war cabinet, meeting of 31 December 1918. PRO. CAB. 23. 42.
[4] Marston, op. cit., pp. 62–3. See also Clement Jones, 'The Dominions and the Peace Conference' (1920). PRO. CAB. 29. 80.
[5] On Canada's position, see G. P. de T. Glazebrook, *Canada at the Paris Peace Conference* (1942), pp. 22–42.

Borden did not, however, merely advocate good relations with the United States and point out that there would be no support in Canada for co-operating with any European nation against her; his view was also that the Empire 'should keep clear as far as possible of European complications and alliances'. The war into which Canada had been drawn by long-standing pledges, and more recent understandings of which the dominions were not even aware, had strengthened these convictions.[1] Such opinions contrasted sharply with those of the Foreign Office, which held that the balance of power was a fundamental British interest and would remain one after the setting up of the League of Nations, and regretted that public opinion now felt it could safely be neglected. The establishment of new nation states would be an appropriate means to this end, though Britain had no direct interest in the territorial arrangements that might be made respecting them. Since the Foreign Office also emphasized the continued importance of the coastline of the narrow seas, clearly nothing in its picture of the European situation suggested any need for a fundamental change in Britain's policy.[2] All could agree in the desire to avoid a renewed entanglement in a continental war; but while Borden wished to keep away from any commitments in Europe, the Foreign Office held that it was only if wars could be prevented from breaking out, by the creation of stable conditions, that this objective could be attained. Both Borden and Smuts made it clear that if it was hoped participation in the imperial war cabinet would lead dominion statesmen to see Europe and the threats from Europe as British statesmen saw them, then it was a vain hope. If Britain were to take an active share in re-shaping Europe and in upholding a European settlement, then she would sooner or later be forced to contemplate parting from the dominions. This eventuality was not one which imperialist opinion, still very strong, was prepared as yet to contemplate. The unity of the Commonwealth would come first. The road to 'Chanak' and 'Munich' lay ahead.

The unity of the Commonwealth did not concern only dominion spokesmen. The Board of Trade also emphasized that the American principle of the 'open door' could not be fully applied to the former German colonies, as this would not be consistent with the 'trend of British Imperial Policy towards an inter-Imperial preferential system'.

[1] Imperial war cabinet, meeting of 30 December 1918. PRO. CAB. 23. 42.
[2] 'Europe', Foreign Office memorandum (probably December 1918). PRO. CAB. 29. 2.

Nor could British commercial interests in Iraq and free scope for the projected Egypt–Palestine–Gulf railway, be disregarded.[1]

The Canadian emphasis on good relations with the United States was of direct concern to other dominion governments over the question of the former German colonies. In July 1918 Smuts had argued that the dominions should retain colonies contiguous or adjacent to their territory and conquered by their forces: New Guinea for Australia, Samoa for New Zealand, and German South-West Africa for the Union. But quite apart from these claims the security of the British Empire, the greatest political system the world had ever seen and one 'founded on human liberty and aiming at peaceful development and free international intercourse', was at stake. This meant that no colony from which the Empire's communications might one day be threatened should be returned to Germany.[2]

At a meeting of the imperial war cabinet on 20 December, Borden argued that American goodwill was one of the principal assets of the war, and that it was therefore necessary to avoid giving the impression that Britain was interested in territorial aggrandizement. South Africa, Australia, and New Zealand should only retain territories that were necessary for the security of the Empire; the rest should go to which-ever states were appointed as mandatories by the League. Hughes, however, pointed out that he had already told Wilson that Australia's demands for islands in the Pacific were being put forward for the sake of Australia's own security, not in the interests of the Empire.[3]

In addition to the dominions, the Indian government also claimed its right to a voice in the settlement, and its demands were by no means modest. No part of Mesopotamia should be given up, and the foreign relations of all Arab states should be in British hands. In the Arabian peninsula a sort of British 'Monroe Doctrine' should prevail and the question of British protectorates in the Gulf principalities should not even be raised lest some sort of international right to judge of Britain's vital claims should be conceded. India would be opposed to a trans-Persian railway project but was deeply interested in Persian stability, and a British mandate would be the best means of ensuring it. East Africa should be retained to prevent the Germans using it for naval

---

[1] 'Economic Considerations Affecting the Terms of Peace', memorandum by the Board of Trade, November 1918; revised December 1918. PRO. CAB. 29. 1/3.
[2] 'The German Colonies at the Peace Conference', memorandum by General Smuts, 11 July 1918. Ibid.
[3] Imperial war cabinet, minutes of meeting, 20 December 1918. PRO. CAB. 23. 42.

bases, and Indian immigration should be allowed there so that Indian soldiers in the war could be rewarded by land grants. A plea was made for handing it over to India to administer. Finally, Japan should be kept away from Chinese provinces bordering India and Tibet.[1]

At the meeting at which Borden had spoken out against annexations, the British members of the cabinet had been chiefly exercised as to the region in which the United States itself might most usefully be offered a mandate. Smuts preferred to keep the United States out of Africa (as did the colonial secretary, who felt that there was no guarantee that the United States knew how to govern 'natives') and would have preferred to see her in Palestine. Curzon, who had talked of the possibility, if the Americans accepted mandates at all (which was by no means certain), of their preferring Constantinople or Armenia to anything in Africa, pointed out that having accepted the principle of self-determination Britain should abide by it, and that both Jews and Arabs in Palestine preferred the British to the Americans. Lloyd George was against allowing the United States into Europe and in particular into so dominating a position as that at Constantinople; he had also changed his mind about having the Americans in Palestine, which would put 'an absolutely new and crude Power' in the midst of all Britain's complicated interests in the area and provide a focal point for all the discontents that British policy might engender. Armenia would be the best thing, with East Africa as the least undesirable alternative. Churchill was for allowing the United States to have German East Africa, since Britain already had more territory in the area than she could develop and it was better to keep the United States out of the Mediterranean lest she be tempted to become the greatest naval power. Admiral Wemyss, the first sea lord, supported Churchill's view. Balfour, however, felt that there was no reason why the policing duties of the United States should lead her to maintain a large fleet in the Mediterranean, while Borden, true to the major premiss of his whole position, did not regard the presence of an American fleet in the Mediterranean with any apprehension.[2]

The views of the Admiralty must be taken in the context of its knowledge that the question of the 'freedom of the seas' had by no means been

[1] 'Indian Desiderata for a Peace Settlement,' note by political department of India Office, 4 December 1918. PRO. CAB. 29 2/1. A British mandate as the thing to aim for in Persia was accepted by the Foreign Office. 'Policy of H.M.G. towards Persia at the Peace Conference', Foreign Office memorandum, 19 December 1918. PRO. CAB. 29. 2.
[2] Imperial war cabinet, minutes of meeting, 20 December 1918. PRO. CAB. 23. 42.

solved by the pre-armistice formula. Indeed, it was actively canvassed in both British and American circles throughout the period between the armistice and the opening of the peace conference. Borden once again urged the merits of close relations with the United States as the essential thing at which to aim. Although it was clear that in the event of war Britain would never surrender her right to use her naval power, Lloyd George gathered from Wilson, during his visit to London at the end of December, that provided the League idea was accepted he would not oppose leaving the issue of the freedom of the seas until that institution had proved itself. The British government was encouraged in its stand by the knowledge that Wilson's own position on naval questions met by no means with universal approval in the United States itself, and the issue was indeed eventually submerged in the wider question of the League and did not as such appear at the peace conference itself.[1]

The Paris Peace Conference

The peace conference took an unexpected form. Instead of a preliminary inter-allied conference followed by one in which the allies would be joined by the ex-enemies in order to hammer out the final terms of the peace, the inter-allied gathering became the conference itself.[2] It devoted itself primarily to working out the text of a treaty with the Germans who were handed the draft on 7 May, and on 29 May presented their counter-proposals. The allied reply to these was handed over on 16 June. The allied terms were accepted on 23 June and the treaty (of Versailles) with Germany was signed on 28 June, after which Lloyd George and Wilson left Paris.

Meanwhile the settlement of the issues arising out of the war in eastern and south-eastern Europe had also been under discussion, and an incomplete draft of the Austrian treaty went to the Austrians on 2 June. The completed treaty was presented on 20 July. After counter-proposals and an allied reply, the Austrian treaty of St Germain was signed on 10 September. The Bulgarian treaty of Neuilly was signed on 27 November and the Hungarian treaty of the Trianon on 4 June 1920.[3] The

---

[1] M. G. Fry, 'The Imperial War Cabinet, the United States, and the Freedom of the Seas', *R.U.S.I. Journal*, vol. 110, (1965).
[2] The bewildering chronology of the conference is conveniently set out in Marston, op. cit., pp. 234–46.
[3] The Hungarian question was complicated by a communist coup at Budapest on 21 March 1919, after the provisional government had resigned rather than accept demands for terri-

abortive treaty of Sèvres with the Turks was signed on 10 August 1920. In addition to the treaties with the ex-enemies the minority treaties governing the conduct of the successor states had also been dealt with and a great deal of other business transacted.

While all of this concerned the British delegation, it was clearly the nature of the settlement with Germany that was the key issue and it was here that dominion pressures were at their strongest. The German treaty was of such importance not only because Germany was the principal enemy state, but also because Wilson had got his way as against the French in having the League of Nations covenant made an essential part of the treaty rather than postponing it until after the conclusion of a territorial settlement. The main issues were therefore the nature of the covenant, the territorial frontiers of Germany and the fate of the German colonies, German disarmament, the military occupation of German territory and finally reparations. But they could not be dealt with separately, nor was it possible to ignore the repercussions of what was done under these heads on other countries in Europe, and notably on the great absentee, Russia.

British policy was throughout never independent of imperial considerations, though (as previously) this did not mean that all the dominion statesmen were unanimous on what needed to be done. On reparations, Hughes was on the committee set up to advise the prime minister and as it also included Hewins and Long among its members, the imperial aspect could hardly be overlooked. It was this committee's estimates of the possible sums obtainable which both Lloyd George and the Treasury experts saw to be impracticable. But the important thing was to decide what categories of injury should be taken into account in assessing Germany's obligations, since if only material damage were included, Britain would have little to claim beyond merchant shipping, as compared with the claims of France and Belgium on whose territories the war had actually been fought, and the dominions even less. It was Smuts who found the formula at the conference by which expenditure on pensions and separation allowances was to count in assessing compensation for 'civilian losses'. It was therefore Smuts, later the main critic of the harshness of the peace, who was responsible for one of the main items causing future trouble.[1]

---

torial cessions to the Rumanians. The communists were overthrown by Rumanian military action with allied backing on 4 August.

[1] On Smuts's role in this respect, see Hancock, *Smuts*, vol. 1, pp. 539–42.

The problem that was to seem increasingly the most important one, that of getting Europe back on its feet economically so that trade could revive, was more directly a United Kingdom problem and of less direct and immediate relevance to the dominions. And Hughes in Paris, as in London beforehand, was the most vigorous and uncompromising exponent of the view that Germany could and should pay for the war, no matter what effect the transfer problems might have on European recovery.[1] There were also strong elements in British opinion who argued the reparations question from the opposite point of view, believing that to impose an indemnity upon Germany, and so to relieve the British taxpayer, was essential if Britain were to be able to compete commercially both with Germany herself and with other industrial countries, particularly the United States.[2]

Reparations were linked to the problem of security by the French demand for a long-term occupation of key areas in western Germany, and by the relation of this demand to French wishes for territorial annexations (other than the recovery of Alsace Lorraine), and for the political separation of the Rhineland if annexation proved inadmissible. On one aspect of the matter, the Saar, Britain's main concern was to mediate between the strongly opposed positions of Wilson and Clemenceau; and the ultimate compromise of temporary internationalization of the area under the League was devised in order to prevent an open breach between France and the United States which might lead the United States to retire back into isolation.[3]

On the main issue it was the British who found themselves directly opposed to France, with Wilson on the whole, though not consistently, accepting the British view. Although autonomist circles in the Rhineland tried to use British suspicions of French 'imperialism' to get support for their claims,[4] British policy was opposed to a permanent separation of the Rhineland from Germany, and also to long-term provisions for maintaining troops on German soil because she had to

[1] See W. Farmer Whyte, op. cit., ch. L, 'Hughes and Reparations'.
[2] 'British Empire Interests', an unsigned paper included in a file of peace conference material sent by Lloyd George's private secretary, A. J. Sylvester to Kerr, 1 April 1919. Lothian Papers, Box 141.
[3] These questions are treated by Northedge, op. cit., pp. 93 ff.
[4] An unsigned memorandum filed with a speech by the burgomaster of Cologne at the end of January 1919 on the 'Question of the Formation of a West German Republic' suggests that in some British quarters, this was regarded as preferable at any rate to French annexation. The argument used is an economic one; Germany must be given openings for trade with the West, lest it turn to Russia. Lothian Papers, Box 142. The burgomaster was Konrad Adenauer.

take into account her likely shortfall in military manpower. It was only with difficulty that Lloyd George had secured the prolongation of military service for one more year, and a Britain that returned to the voluntary principle would have few men to spare for police duties on the continent. The War Office indeed felt the time had already come by the spring of 1919 to withdraw troops from Europe – including of course those in Russia – and to concentrate them in the British Isles, where growing social unrest was feared, and at the storm centres of the Empire, notably Egypt and India.[1] Furthermore, as Kerr told Tardieu (the French member of the committee on German territorial questions) on 11 March, while the British government believed it had dominion support on measures needed to enforce German disarmament should these be required, the dominions would not 'bind themselves to interfere in any way in purely European questions such as the future of the Rhineland'.[2]

What in the end persuaded the French to accept demilitarization of the disputed territory as a substitute for annexation was the offer to France by Britain and the United States of guarantees against unprovoked German aggression. The offer was made on 14 March 1919, but the proposed treaties went through a number of revisions before the final texts were agreed upon and signed on 9 October, since they had to wait upon agreement over the question of the occupation of the area. This the French secured for a fifteen-year period, with a loophole for escape in the provision that this could be reconsidered if the guarantees against German aggression should by then appear insecure – and this of course allowed for the possibility that the treaties would not be ratified.[3]

It is not possible to accept at its face value Lloyd George's assertion in the House of Commons that the pacts were not in fact a *quid pro quo* for the abandonment of French claims to the left bank. What is more surprising is that the House of Commons were prepared to accept so major a departure from traditional British policy as that implied in what a labour member called a 'new triple alliance' after so perfunctory a debate.[4] It has been suggested that Lloyd George's main

[1] See the views of Sir Henry Wilson and Churchill, Nelson, op. cit., pp. 242, 328.
[2] Ibid., p. 214.
[3] For the evolution of the guarantee treaties, see Hankey, *The Supreme Control at the Paris Peace Conference, 1919* (1963), pp. 100, 102, 144–5, 173, 186–7.
[4] After a long debate on the peace treaty itself on 21 July, the House went on at almost 3 a.m on the morning of the 22nd to deal with the bill for giving effect to the treaty with France. It was approved without a division in less than an hour.

objective was to use American concern for French security as a lever for involving the Americans in a permanent and precise commitment to Europe.[1] It may well also have been the knowledge that the two guarantees stood and fell together that reassured the British negotiators and parliamentary opinion.[2]

For the dominions, however, the prospect was more alarming. A discussion by the British Empire delegation on 5 May revealed that Hughes and Massey would have preferred a simpler pledge of assistance to France against unprovoked German attack, while Borden and Botha were both doubtful of their countries' support for the treaty.[3] It was the South Africans who seemed to have been most vocally apprehensive. Botha wrote to Lloyd George on the next day to express his fears of a one-sided undertaking that did not bind France even to good behaviour in the occupied areas.[4]

As a result of the discussions with the dominion leaders, the British government informed the French that the treaty would only be considered effective if approved by the league as being consistent with the covenant, and that it would not be binding on the dominions unless ratified by their own parliaments.[5] Botha expressed his satisfaction at this concession but went on to point out that it meant that in some future continental war, Britain might be involved and one or more of the dominions remain neutral; but this result, he said, was inevitable and flowed from 'the status of independent nationhood of the dominions'.[6]

Somewhat similar pressure was exerted by the South Africans in the other major territorial question, that of the boundaries of a reconstituted Poland. Here Britain's own feelings were, however, not so distant from those of the dominions. A Foreign Office memorandum of 9 December 1918 had warned the government that it would be danger-

[1] Nelson, op. cit., pp. 219 ff.
[2] The hope of American ratification of the treaty of guarantee lapsed with the senate's defeat of the peace treaty in March 1920. The fact that Britain's obligation lapsed also was greeted with relief in London. Northedge, op. cit., p. 160.
[3] Nelson, op. cit., pp. 245–6.
[4] Botha to Lloyd George, 6 May 1919. *Smuts Papers*, vol. IV, pp. 150–1. As might be gathered from the anti-French tone of this letter, it was drafted by Smuts.
[5] Despite Borden's hesitations in Paris, the Canadian government finally decided to put the treaty before parliament for ratification, but the hesitations expressed there over the league covenant may have helped to decide to delay the matter and the adverse decision in the United States made it unnecessary to put it to the test. Glazebrook, op. cit., pp. 124–5.
[6] Botha to Lloyd George, 15 May 1919. *Smuts Papers*, vol. IV, p. 159. The letter was drafted by Smuts.

ous to endow the new Poland with territories whose inhabitants might desire union with Russia or Germany, because these two countries were bound to re-emerge as the strongest powers in eastern Europe and the conditions for a new partition of Poland would have been created.[1] There was also the fear that Balfour had expressed as early as March 1917, that an independent Poland would cut off Russia from western Europe, and prevent it from coming to the aid of the western powers in the event of a renewal of German aggression.[2]

The Bolshevik revolution had helped to force on some revision of British policy, but the British at the peace conference found themselves opposed to the more strongly pro-Polish sentiments of both the French and the Americans and engaged in a fairly vigorous contest with them on the future of Danzig and of Silesia. In a letter in March 1919 Smuts expressed strong anti-Polish opinions, particularly on Danzig, his principal reason being the conviction that Europe could not be saved from destruction without the co-operation of Germany, and that the peace settlement would be worthless if it did not meet with Germany's acceptance. Neither Poland nor Bohemia was politically viable except with Germany's goodwill and assistance.[3] His concern was not simply to contain the spread of bolshevism – though this objective also was strongly present – but to prevent the peace taking a wrong turn through neglect of the inevitable future primacy of Germany in Europe.

A similar demand for meeting reasonable German complaints was made by Smuts in a memorandum on 17 May,[4] and his sentiments did, of course, find an echo in both British and American circles.[5] The issue came to a head at meetings of the British Empire delegation held on 30 May and 1 June to discuss the German observations on the draft treaty.[6] Smuts extended his criticisms to almost every aspect of the terms of the treaty, in respect of Europe as well as to the exclusion of Germany from the League, and claimed that 'the roots of war' were in the document. Massey and Hughes, while not accepting most of Smuts's case, agreed that a case might be made for some revision of frontiers on

---

[1] Nelson, op. cit., p. 98.
[2] Northedge, op. cit., pp. 109–10.
[3] Smuts to Lloyd George, 26 March 1919. *Smuts Papers*, vol. IV, pp. 83–7.
[4] 'Negotiations for the Peace Treaty': memorandum by General Smuts, 17 May 1919. PRO. CAB. 29. 14.
[5] Cecil to Lloyd George, 27 May 1919. PRO. CAB. 29. 15.
[6] Clement Jones, 'The Dominions and the Peace Conference' (1920), pp. 162 ff. PRO. CAB. 29. 80.

the east. It is clear that Smuts's colleagues were anxious that he should not carry out his threat to withhold his signature and wanted to meet him where possible,[1] and Lloyd George conveyed these sentiments to his colleagues on 2 June. He secured some concessions to the British viewpoint,[2] but the main outlines of the treaty structure could not be revised at this late stage. In the end Smuts felt the concessions made to meet his criticisms would justify his signature,[3] particularly because a formal peace was needed to give Europe a chance of recovery which would be made greater by the creation of the League of Nations, but partly because of purely South African considerations. He did not wish to separate himself from his leader Botha as this might jeopardize national harmony. He saw that Botha had to sign lest South Africa be left in limbo, not taking advantage of her new status in the Commonwealth or of membership in the League of Nations and unable to take up the mandate for South-West Africa.[4]

Smuts however made it plain, in a protest issued at the time, that his signature did not imply approval of the treaty's terms, and that it was confidence in the league's potential that was the decisive factor in his decision.[5] He decided against a general attack on the treaty as this would serve no constructive purpose.[6] But on finally leaving England, in a public statement which was largely devoted to the importance of the new role of the dominions and the desirability of solving other constitutional questions within the Empire, he returned to the theme that a reconciliation with the new German republic was essential: 'You cannot have a stable Europe without a stable settled Germany; and you cannot have a stable, settled prosperous Great Britain while Europe is weltering in confusion and unsettlement next door. In our policy of European settlement the appeasement of Germany becomes one of cardinal importance.'[7] This was to be the burden of Smuts's contribution to British policy for the next two decades.

[1] Waley, op. cit., pp. 211–12.
[2] Northedge, op. cit., pp. 108–9, 114–16.
[3] Hancock, *Smuts*, vol. 1, pp. 532–8.
[4] Lloyd George had pointedly asked Smuts whether he was prepared to return German South-West Africa or German East Africa to the Germans as a concession to help them to sign the treaty. Lloyd George to Smuts, 3 June 1919. *Smuts Papers*, vol. IV, pp. 217–18.
[5] Press statement, 28 June 1919. Ibid., pp. 256–9.
[6] Smuts to Keynes, 17 July 1919. Ibid., p. 266.
[7] Press statement, 19 July 1919. Ibid., pp. 268–75.

The Dominions, The League and Mandates

Smuts's optimism about the League of Nations was in line with his own lead in the war cabinet, advocating the setting up of such an institution and setting out the main features of a possible structure for it.[1] For him there was no conflict between the interests of the Commonwealth and the giving of powers to the new league; indeed, in so far as it could become the successor of the defunct empires it would bridge the gap between a policy of 'no-annexations' and the needs of British and Commonwealth security. But although British governmental opinion had come round to the view that the need to go along with the United States, as well as the pressure of British opinion, made adherence to the proposal inevitable, there had been and would remain an understandable undercurrent of anxiety.

In April 1917 it was already being argued that while the combination of British and American sea-power was the best hope for preserving the peace in the future, an attack on it would undoubtedly be one of the first things that would be attempted within the framework of the proposed league.[2] It was clear that even in Britain the league was regarded as a substitute for preserving the margin of armed strength that had hitherto been thought necessary, and that it was not widely realized that the league would actually place new burdens on Britain if it involved a binding commitment to action against a future aggressor.[3] In the discussion by the imperial war cabinet of Smuts's proposals, Churchill presciently pointed out that the league would only work if the great powers were united and that a complete understanding between Britain, the United States, and France was the only possible basis for its creation.[4]

Even more anxious were those who did not accept Smuts's view that the league would be just the British Commonwealth writ large. In a memorandum in November 1918 Lord Eustace Percy, then serving in the Foreign Office, argued that it was important, from the point of view of future arrangements for economic co-operation within the

---

[1] Smuts's memorandum to the war cabinet of 16 December 1916 (PRO. CAB. 29 2/1) was printed as a pamphlet in the following month under the title *The League of Nations: A Practical Suggestion.* Hancock, *Smuts,* vol. 1, pp. 500 ff.
[2] Imperial war cabinet, meeting of 26 April 1917. PRO. CAB. 23. 40.
[3] Admiralty memorandum: 'Naval Aspects of a League of Nations and Limitation of Armaments', 23 December 1918. PRO. CAB. 29. 2.
[4] Imperial war cabinet, meeting of 24 December 1918. PRO. CAB. 23. 42.

Empire, that the League of Nations should not have any economic functions.[1] At the imperial war cabinet Hughes argued that Smuts's proposals went too far, and would create closer links between Britain and foreign countries than those between Britain and the dominions. And Balfour was anxious lest the league should claim rights in respect of Indian or Egyptian demands for independence.[2]

At the conference, however, Britain and the dominions stood together against the idea of turning the league into an instrument for perpetuating the *status quo* through policing measures and in favour of emphasizing its conciliatory aspect. It was clear that revision of the treaties rather than their enforcement was in the forefront of the British mind,[3] and it had been obvious that Britain would have to accept the separate representation of the dominions in the organs of the league,[4] although some effort was required to get American support for their inclusion and for that of India.[5]

The separate representation of the dominions was not, however, universally agreeable to those who had the cause of Empire at heart. Richard Jebb, for instance, regarded the decision as a step towards dissolution and regretted that 'family differences' might now be aired before a foreign tribunal. The league ought to be made up of groupings of states rather than of individual members and there should be a specific reservation in the covenant about imperial preference.[6] Similar apprehensions were expressed by Hewins.[7] It is true that the Foreign Office did not share these anxieties altogether, because of its assumption that Botha was wrong and that one part of the Empire could not be at war without the rest. For this reason the Foreign Office held that in the assembly the votes of the six British Empire members should not be cast in any dispute to which any part of the Empire was a party.[8] Milner, who seems originally not to have feared the conse-

[1] 'League of Nations': memorandum by political intelligence department, Foreign Office. PRO. CAB. 29. 2.
[2] Imperial war cabinet, meeting of 24 December 1918. PRO. CAB. 23. 42.
[3] Northedge, op. cit., pp. 116–21. See the (undated) memorandum by Kerr: 'The League of Nations'. Lothian Papers, Box 139.
[4] Meeting at Foreign Office, 1 January 1919, to consider position of dominions and India in relation to proposed League of Nations. Cecil of Chelwood Papers, B.M. Add. 51102.
[5] Tillman, *Anglo-American Relations at the Paris Peace Conference*, pp. 124–5.
[6] 'The British Empire and the League of Nations': memorandum for British Empire delegation, by Richard Jebb. PRO. CAB. 29. 14. It was published as an article in *Production* (April 1919).
[7] Diary entry, 10 July 1919. Op. cit., vol. 2, pp. 186–7.
[8] Foreign secretary to Grey (Washington), 24 October 1919. PRO. CAB. 29. 4.

quences of separate membership, later expressed his anxiety on this score also,[1] suggesting that there should be a clearing-house in London through which all communications to the league should be routed. But Australia, though a partisan of an imperial secretariat, did not wish it to intervene between the dominions and the league, nor, of course, was Canada prepared to accept an intermediary.[2]

Writing in 1928 an eminent historian discounted such fears and suggested that separate league membership had enhanced rather than weakened the ties between Commonwealth countries, since they were reminded at Geneva of what they had in common, while at imperial conferences it was their divisions that were uppermost.[3] Until the critical years of the thirties, many agreed with him, and thought that the problem of harmonizing the foreign policies of the British Commonwealth had been solved because the policy of each member was based upon the covenant of the league; as there could be no wars but league wars, the vexed question of a dominion remaining neutral while the Empire was at war could hardly arise.[4]

It should have been clear how great was the share of illusion in this attitude. The covenant might bind; but each member-state interpreted the obligation in the light of its own outlook and interests, which in times of difficulty were likely to come to the fore. Autonomous foreign and defence policies would clearly have developed even if the league had never been created, but membership of the league showed the outside world that this process had already gone a long way. Only in the economic field, where the league's powers and even influence were unimportant, were moves towards imperial unity unimperilled by its existence.

More important still was the fact that for some of the dominions – and notably Canada – the League of Nations added to the prevalent sense of security and provided an additional reason for neglecting the problems of defence. The league could look after Europe, and Canada could avoid being dragged into war again by the insensate rivalries of the continent.[5]

---

[1] Milner to Thornton, 17 January 1920. Milner Papers; letters to Thornton.
[2] Conferences of British Empire delegation at Foreign Office, 8–9 November 1920. PRO. CAB. 29. 28. 2.
[3] A. J. Toynbee, *The Conduct of British Empire Foreign Relations since the Peace Settlement* (1928), pp. 52–3.
[4] W. K. Hancock, *Survey of British Commonwealth Affairs*, vol. 1 (1937), pp. 307–8.
[5] James Eayrs, *In Defence of Canada*, vol. 1 (Toronto, 1964), introduction.

It was not, however, the impact of the league's creation upon opinion in the dominions that was the vital thing, but its impact in Britain. The reservations held by diplomats and servicemen about the futility of the covenant if Britain and its other major supporters were not sufficiently well-armed to enforce its provisions were not shared by the general public, which regarded the league as a means of shelving responsibilities, not of adding to them. Often, as an acute observer pointed out before the treaty was signed, those most vocal in their advocacy of the league idea were most resolute in their insistence upon disarmament.[1] And as usual pacifism and 'economy' went hand in hand.

The most important positive aspect of the league at the beginning was the opportunity it provided for dealing with the former German and Turkish possessions outside Europe.[2] It was indeed a Commonwealth rather than a specifically British policy that resulted in the mandates clause of the covenant,[3] and Smuts, Hughes, and Massey all argued that colonies with which their countries were directly concerned should be annexed.[4] Lloyd George had first to persuade them that mandates were an alternative, and then to convince Clemenceau and Wilson.[5] The idea of 'C' mandates, which allowed contiguous territories to be governed as though part of the territories of the mandatory power, and which provided a way out of what otherwise looked like deadlock, was itself of Australian origin.[6] The dominions were less interested in the precise delimitation of colonial boundaries in Africa and the compensations granted to, or claimed by, the other allied powers, France,

[1] Eustace Percy to Col. Fisher, 20 May 1919. Gilbert Murray Papers. On the other hand, Percy feared lest an international force be created to be used in conjunction with foreign statesmen for ends for which one would not like to use British troops – 'a kind of imperialistic fraud'. Percy to Gilbert Murray, 5 June 1919. Gilbert Murray Papers.
[2] For the British case on the German colonies, see the memorandum of January 1919. PRO. CAB. 29 1/3 P. 34. Not all British statesmen were convinced that a further extension of the Empire was to be welcomed. Montagu gave among his reasons for doubting its wisdom his belief that it would be difficult to find the men to run the new territories since people had been complaining already of the difficulty of recruiting good men to the Diplomatic service and the I.C.S. owing to the competition of industry and commerce and to the diminution in size of the country middle-class family as well as to the wartime losses. Montagu to Balfour, 20 December 1918. Balfour Papers, B.M. Add. 49748.
[3] This point is illustrated in detail by H. Duncan Hall in 'The British Commonwealth and the founding of the League of Nations Mandate System', in K. Bourne and D. C. Watt (eds), *Studies in International History* (1967).
[4] Clement Jones, 'The Dominions and the Peace Conference', ch. VI, 'Mandates'. CAB. 29. 80.
[5] Kerr to Milner, 31 January 1919. Lothian Papers, Box 187.
[6] Hall, loc. cit., p. 359.

Italy, Belgium, and Portugal; but these issues also required settlement and were in some cases fairly strenuously contested.[1]

The exclusion of Germany from Africa seemed sufficient for the security of the Indian Ocean area and Atlantic communications, but the Pacific was still vulnerable. The Australians believed that Wilson wanted to introduce the mandate system into the Pacific to prevent the Japanese from fortifying their acquisitions from Germany, and thus increasing the strength of their position; the Shantung settlement added to apprehensions on this score. The Australians were sceptical of the league's power to prevent the Japanese doing as they wished, and Hughes was concerned to make it clear that he was accepting the mandate system only under duress.[2]

The 'C' mandates, like the 'B' mandates in Africa which included German East Africa (Tanganyika), were thought of as colonial possessions; the 'B' mandates were subjected only to the principle of commercial non-discrimination. Despite the importance attached in the British case for their retention to the welfare of the inhabitants, it was assumed that this would be a matter for the administering powers and that a devolution of political authority was not contemplated. Nationalism in Africa was not yet an issue. But in the 'A' mandates which were devised for the ex-Turkish possessions, and where political advancement was among the duties of the mandatory, the issues were, as has been seen, much more complicated. Britain in Egypt, like France in Morocco, had consolidated its position as a result of the war; and this was bound to reflect on the attitude towards them of Arab opinion elsewhere. In the Middle East settlement, however, which took much longer to arrive at than the African and Pacific one, the dominions took no active part, though the interests of the Indian government in it were never neglected. It was Britain herself that had to accommodate competing Arab, Jewish, and French claims, and America that claimed the right both to be heard, and to avoid direct responsibility.

[1] On the negotiations at Paris, see Louis, op. cit., ch. IV, 'Mandates'. In view of later events, it is worth noting Milner's warning that Britain had in Ethiopia a vital interest, the headwaters of the Blue Nile upon which cotton-growing in the Sudan depended. 'Equitable compensation for Italy in Africa', memorandum by Milner, 30 May 1919. PRO. CAB. 29. 25.
[2] On Hughes's position, see his memorandum to the British Empire delegation, 8 February 1919: 'The Pacific Islands'. PRO. CAB. 29. 8. The attraction of the 'C' mandate was that it would enable Australia to introduce the 'White Australia' policy into the islands. Britain felt itself bound to support Australia on this issue for imperial reasons. See the memorandum on 'Mandates' (probably by Eyre Crowe) in Balfour Papers, B.M. Add. 49734.

The Middle East Settlement and Relations with France

The long-drawn negotiations over the Middle Eastern aspects of the peace settlement were important partly for their contribution to the growing alienation between Britain and France. Although Britain could not in the then state of Europe contemplate a final breach with France, and had in the end to subordinate some aspects of her Middle East policy to European requirements,[1] enough bad feeling was created for these discords to have importance[2] – as well as a permanent echo which was to continue reverberating in the very different circumstances of the post-war settlement of a quarter of a century later. After the turn of the century it had never been possible for Britain to contemplate an active role in Europe without active and far-reaching co-operation with the French; this might be understood in London, but it also had to be conveyed to those working on the imperial frontiers. The pro-Arab elements who had wanted to stake Britain's future on an understanding with Arab nationalism – and those in particular of the school of T. E. Lawrence who saw this cause embodied in the persons of Hussein, the Sherif of Mecca, and of his sons (particularly Faisal) – could not be restrained from acting in ways that bolstered French claims that the British were actively engaged in stirring up the population against them, even in those areas of the Middle East where Britain had accepted French pre-eminence.[3] When he visited London in December 1918, Clemenceau agreed that Palestine and Mosul should be allotted to the British sphere of influence; but why, he asked, should France give up her claims in Syria and the Lebanon when Britain clearly intended to keep Mesopotamia?[4] Nor, indeed, would British interests as they had previously been defined suffer from the carrying out of the Sykes–Picot agreement with these modifications. The Admiralty was still arguing for a route from Egypt through Palestine, Mesopotamia, and southern Persia to Baluchistan and India.[5] The retention of Mesopotamia in the form of a British-protected Arab state

[1] Monroe, *Britain's Moment in the Middle East*, p. 63.
[2] It is well reflected in fiction in Pierre Bénoit, *La Châtelaine du Liban* (Paris, 1924).
[3] Kedourie, *England and the Middle East* (1956), pp. 131, 144. On French suspicions of Britain, see the report to Curzon from the British embassy in Paris, 12 August 1919. Lothian Papers, Box 142. On Lawrence as an irritant in Anglo-French relations, see Clark-Kerr to Vansittart, 21 August 1919. *D.B.F.P.*, series 1, vol. IV, pp. 354–5. Memorandum by Balfour, 'Syria, Palestine and Mesopotamia', 11 August 1919. Ibid., pp. 340 ff.
[4] Kedourie, op. cit., p. 137.
[5] 'Summary of Admiralty Policy in Relation to the Peace Settlement', January 1919. PRO. CAB. 29. 7.

was being advocated in order to keep any other rival great power away from the littoral of the Persian Gulf and so away from waters that adjoined the Indian Empire.[1] Nevertheless, from the moment of the armistice with the Turks, Britain claimed a special role in everything to do with the Moslem world; and although British statesmen might assure the French that Britain had no wish to encroach upon the areas allotted to her ally, and that all the troubles arose from the French unwillingness to come to terms with Arab nationalism, British pretensions to mediate between the French and the Arabs could not improve French tempers. And British fears that an Arab rising in Syria would spread to British-held territories were not in French eyes an adequate excuse.[2]

The San Remo conference in April 1920 allocated the Middle East mandates on the basis of the Sykes–Picot and other inter-allied wartime agreements, Mesopotamia and Palestine to Britain, Syria and Lebanon to France. All hope of American participation had by now evaporated. A month earlier, Faisal, who had come to Syria in the wake of the British conquest, had accepted the role thrust upon him by local nationalism and accepted election as king of an independent Syria. He now repudiated the San Remo treaty and the French moved against him in force. By July he was in flight and the issue of Syria's future was settled for the time being.[3]

At this point, however, the affairs of Faisal became involved with the plans for that portion of the Arab world that had been allotted to Britain. Mesopotamia, as we have seen, had been conquered by an expedition originally mounted from India and it was expected that it would be ruled rather in the fashion of Cromer's Egypt. But the authority of Arnold Wilson and his school with their Indian background was undermined by propaganda from the Sherifians and from Lawrence and his friends, to bring Mesopotamia under the Sherifian (Hashemite) dynasty. A popular consultation embarked upon by the authorities was clearly not likely to be of much help, and expert opinion was doubtful of the validity of any but paternalist government on the Indian model until enough local administrators had been trained to run a modern-style government.[4] But firm government depended upon the presence of military strength and the large British military establish-

[1] 'Mesopotamia,' memorandum by Sir Erle Richards, January 1919. PRO. CAB. 29. 2.
[2] Kedourie, op. cit., p. 137.
[3] Ibid., pp. 172–4.
[4] Gertrude Bell to Montagu (from Baghdad), 4 January 1920. Lothian Papers, Box 142.

ment in Mesopotamia was a natural target for the economizers at home. There were major British troop withdrawals early in 1920 and it was argued that Indian troops were only an irritant to the population. From March to October 1920, thus coinciding with the French troubles in Syria, there was a major tribal rising in Mesopotamia, and much official opinion came round to the view that the only hope of checking the nationalist tide was to go along with it. In December 1920 Faisal was offered the throne of Iraq, as the new mandated state was styled, and this settlement was confirmed at a conference at Cairo in March 1921. Britain now had its 'solution' for the Mesopotamian question and the new state was eventually endowed in 1926 with what proved to be the rich oilfields of Mosul. But the implanted Hashemite dynasty proved unable to cope with the religious and political dissensions of the country, and Britain found itself saddled with the unpopularity of its protégés; though once again a good deal of time was to elapse before the full consequences of this fact became apparent.[1]

Even more difficult were the problems of reconciliation that faced Britain in carrying out the Palestine mandate, which included the pledge to assist in creating a Jewish national home.[2] The Foreign Office saw the need to devise a scheme which would both protect Arab interests and give effect to the national aspirations of the Jews, and it was not keen to see either France or the United States make the attempt. The importance of Palestine was as a buffer-state for Egypt,[3] and in this view the Foreign Office supported the C.I.G.S., who had written of 'the creation of a buffer Jewish State in Palestine'. Though the state would be weak in itself, it would be 'strategically desirable' so long as it could be created 'without disturbing Mohammedan senti-ment', and provided, of course, that it was not controlled by a potenti-ally hostile power.[4]

But Islamic sentiment was not a fixed quantity, its role would fluctu-ate according to the encouragement it received. This fact was clearly seen

[1] Kedourie, op. cit., pp. 175 ff. For earlier British interest in Mesopotamian oil, see Platt, *Finance, Trade and British Foreign Policy*, pp. 195 ff.
[2] The period between the Balfour declaration and the San Remo conference is dealt with from the Jewish side by Stein: *The Balfour Declaration*, pp. 559–663. Cf. Sykes, *Cross Roads to Israel*, pp. 29–75; Ben Halpern, *The Idea of the Jewish State* (Harvard U.P., 1961), pp. 301–22; Jon Kimche, *The Unromantics* (London, 1968), pp. 42 ff.
[3] 'Memorandum Respecting Palestine', by Sir Erle Richards, January 1919 (for consideration of the Eastern committee of the war cabinet). PRO. CAB. 29. 2.
[4] Memorandum by C.I.G.S.: 'The Strategic Importance of Syria to the British Empire', 13 December 1918. Ibid.

by Mark Sykes who warned the government that British officers were foolish in giving ear to anti-Jewish (and anti-French) sentiments because these would turn out to be the forerunners of anti-British agitation; indeed, there was a danger of Arab nationalism developing into a general Islamic movement against the infidel.[1] Nevertheless, the British military authorities under Allenby tended to regard the Arabs as their principal clients (despite the fact that of all the Arabs the Palestinians had been the most pro-Turk) and to show ill-concealed impatience at the Jews' pretensions to enjoy the fruits of the Balfour declaration.[2] Faisal himself had some dealings with the zionist leaders during his visit to Paris in 1919, but it is clear that he did not seriously envisage the future course of Arab–Jewish relations as the zionist movement gathered strength, and that his only interest was the tactical one of securing another source of support against the French.[3]

The existence of Arab antagonism to Jewish settlement was notorious enough to cause anxiety in England: 'If we are placed in the position of having approved of zionism, and not being able to get it carried out we shall quarrel with everybody besides producing something like chaos in the country concerned'.[4] Balfour himself was unmoved by claims that all the populations freed from Turkish rule were entitled at once to democratic self-government, and made it plain that he set the importance of zionism well above that of the Palestinian Arabs.[5] And there were still voices who believed that British and Jewish interests were identical and that if it was difficult to provide the required military forces, the solution was to arm the Jewish colonists for their own defence.[6] Needless to say, this method of relieving the defence burden was unacceptable and British policy remained at the mercy of the rival

[1] Memorandum by Mark Sykes, 22 January 1919. Since it is often assumed that the British government did not anticipate Jewish immigration to the extent of creating a Jewish majority, it is worth quoting one sentence from this document: 'As regards the Zionists I think it is only fair and reasonable that if the Zionists are protected so long as they are a minority that the Palestinian population should enjoy equal protection when the Zionists become a majority.'
[2] Kedourie, op. cit., pp. 153–5.
[3] Ibid., pp. 151–2.
[4] Cecil to Milner, 8 August 1919. Lothian Papers, Box 142.
[5] Memorandum by Balfour, 11 August 1919. B.D.F.P., series 1, vol. IV, pp. 340 ff. What Balfour did admit was the impossibility of reconciling all the several undertakings given with the covenant.
[6] Lewis Namier to Kerr, 6 September 1919. Lothian Papers, Box 187. Sir Lewis Namier (1888–1960), a friend and confidant of Weizmann's, had served in the propaganda department and the department of information during the war; from 1918 to 1920 he was in the political department of the Foreign Office, specializing on the affairs of the Habsburg lands; from 1929 to 1931, he was to be political secretary of the Jewish Agency for Palestine.

pressures. The ideal would be Arab–Jewish agreement within the framework of a British-oriented Middle East,[1] but there was no agreement on how this end was to be achieved. Meanwhile, the mandate having been accepted, military rule ended and on 1 July 1920, Sir Herbert Samuel assumed office as high commissioner. Samuel, as has been seen, was the first British statesmen to bring the zionist claims to the attention of the British government; but he was himself a zionist sympathizer rather than a zionist, and strove manfully to keep the balance even between Arab and Jew without impeding the growth of Jewish settlement and the development of the country's resources.

The fall of Faisal in Syria raised, however, the question of the future of what came to be known as Trans-Jordan, which had formed part of Faisal's dominions but had now (unlike Syria) been allotted to the British.[2] An expedition mounted from the Hedjaz under Faisal's brother Abdullah and nominally directed against Damascus, now advanced into the area and Abdullah was acclaimed ruler in Amman. The issue was one of those presented to the Cairo conference which was Churchill's first important intervention in Middle East affairs after his transfer from the War Office to the Colonial Office in February 1921. Once the decision on Iraq had been reached something had to be done for Abdullah who had been a claimant to the Iraq throne, and it was therefore decided to accept him as emir of Trans-Jordan. This decision amounted to a separation of Palestine east of the Jordan from the rest of the country though it remained under the same high commissioner, and resulted in killing a plan which had apparently been under consideration for resettling there such Arabs as might choose to sell their lands for Jewish settlement. While Trans-Jordan was not within the area claimed for the national home by the zionists, the limitation of zionist endeavour permanently to cis-Jordanian Palestine did have the effect of giving it less opportunity of manoeuvre, and so weakened whatever chance may have existed for a reconciliation of Arab and Jew under British auspices.

The first outbreak of Arab violence in May 1921 led to assurances

[1] A prominent member of the Round Table group argued that Jewish immigration to Palestine could only benefit the indigenous population, provided that Palestine could be fitted into some wider Arab federation throughout which there could be opportunities for Jewish enterprise: 'The only kind of partition that is indefensible is one that aims at a real and final parting of the ways for the different parts of the Arab world', John Dove to R. H. Brand (from Iraq 1920). R. H. Brand (ed.), *Letters of John Dove* (1938), p. 156.
[2] Sykes, op. cit., pp. 58 ff.

from the high commissioner that Jewish immigration would be controlled, and thus set the pattern for subsequent events in which the British authorities, whose prime concern was peace and security, found that whatever measures they took alienated one or more often both of the communities.

The debate in the House of Commons of 14 June, at which Churchill reported on the Cairo conference, and subsequent events revealed the uncertainties and difficulties under which British opinion laboured.[1] The possibility of fulfilling Britain's obligations to both parties to the dispute in Palestine was again assumed by the government. Some zionist sympathizers called attention to the strategic value of a British military base created as a result of the building up of the Jewish role in Palestine. Others preferred to concentrate on the general responsibilities of the mandate, and to assimilate Palestine to Iraq and Trans-Jordan. This implied progress towards the creation of self-governing institutions, despite the fact that in the current temper of the Arabs such institutions would scarcely be compatible with the Balfour declaration which both government and opposition regarded as fixed British policy. Confronted with the realities of rival nationalisms, the British liberal tradition seemed to have no answer to offer; and Palestine was only a microcosm among the new problems of empire.

It was not only nationalism that presented problems in the Middle East. The British gained the exclusion of other great powers from the Arabian Peninsula,[2] but the problem of which local source of authority to back was not easy to resolve. The Indian government favoured the ruler of Nejd, Ibn Saud; the Foreign Office, as has been seen, Hussein of the Hedjaz. And their rivalries were to prove insoluble except by force.[3] Later troubles with minor rulers on the Gulf and along the coast also suggested that indirect rule on Indian-inspired lines was not itself an answer to all the problems of the latest and final phase of British imperial expansion.

But for the time being the problems of this area lay in the future. It was over Turkey itself that the relations between Britain and the

---

[1] For what follows, see Sykes, op. cit., pp. 62 ff. The league council in September 1922 accepted a British proposal exempting Trans-Jordan from the obligations of the Mandate respecting a special régime for the Holy Places and the development of the Jewish National Home.

[2] Memorandum on Arabia by Sir Erle Richards, January 1919. PRO. CAB. 29. 2.

[3] In 1924–5 Ibn Saud conquered the Hedjaz and elevated himself to the position of king of Saudi Arabia.

Islamic world first came to a critical point, and that the breach with France first made itself fully apparent.[1]

The degree to which Turkey could be made to suffer outside her Arab provinces for her role as Germany's ally was still open at the end of the war. Much British opinion favoured turning the Turks out of Constantinople.[2] The Indian Office, which had never been fully reconciled to the alienation of Turkey, now argued against depriving it of its capital.[3] If it was not to remain with Turkey, then to whom was it to go? The service departments were strongly opposed to the idea of an American mandate, which would have given the Americans an 'opportunity and pretext for basing a strong American fleet in the Mediterranean' which they regarded as a danger from the strategical point of view, and one to be avoided at all costs.[4]

But an international régime had little chance of general acceptance, and Lloyd George seems to have been reconciled to the idea of an American mandate for both Constantinople and Armenia. By the autumn of 1919 this prospect too was fading fast, and the position was complicated in May by the landing of Greek forces at Smyrna with the approval of the Supreme Allied Council, and by the creation in central Anatolia, under Mustapha Kemal, of a new nationalist movement equally hostile to the allied claims and to the now helpless government of the sultan-caliph at Constantinople.

Despite the dwindling of allied military power, the British and French governments still talked as though they were in a position to impose solutions; but inter-allied talks in December 1919 revealed a considerable gulf between British and French opinion.[5] The British still wished to turn the Turks out of Constantinople, and to make territorial concessions to the Greeks, the French preferred to see the sultan remain at Constantinople where he could be subject to allied pressure and control. It was, however, the pressure of the India Office and the War Office rather than of the French, that brought Lloyd George round to this point of view, and he gave way reluctantly at the

[1] See Northedge, op. cit., pp. 133 ff.
[2] Memorandum by Curzon, 3 January 1919. PRO. CAB. 29. 2.
[3] Memorandum by Montagu, 8 January 1919. Ibid.
[4] 'The Future of Constantinople and the Straits'; recommendations of a conference between representatives of the departmental missions of the British delegation, 30 January 1919. PRO. CAB. 29. 8.
[5] Note of Anglo-French conversations in London on 11 December 1919. PRO. CAB. 29. 81. The Foreign Office documents on the Turkish question at this time are in *D.B.F.P.*, series 1, vol. IV, ch. 3; vol. VII; vol. XIII.

London conference of the supreme council in February 1920, though he secured agreement for some form of international control of the Straits.

During the London conference at which these decisions were arrived at, nationalist Turks inflicted a defeat on the French in Cilicia which confirmed both them and the Italians in their reluctance to get further embroiled in Asia Minor. The peace treaty with Turkey drawn up at the San Remo conference, and presented to the Turkish government on 24 April, took, however, no account of the rise of Kemalism. Nor did it meet the full realities of the military situation, with its demand for an independent Armenia and confirmation of the Greek position in Smyrna (subject to a later plebiscite) as well as concessions to Greece in European Turkey and the islands. The allies, it is true, had taken action to forestall Turkish resistance by occupying Constantinople in March and by insisting upon the formation of a pliable cabinet, but the result was to shift all real authority outside the range of allied military power to the Kemalists in central Anatolia. A Greek advance during the summer did, it was true, appear to justify hopes that the Turkish resistance might be overcome; and in August the sultan's government signed the treaty of Sèvres, as the instrument was known. But thereafter events decisively turned against Lloyd George's hopes and plans.[1]

In the renewed fighting in the summer of 1921, the Greek cause suffered severely, and on 20 October the French signed an agreement with the Turks which separated them finally from the British phil-Hellenic commitment. The full tragedy of the Graeco-Turkish conflict still lay in the future, but by the time of the meeting of the imperial conference in June 1921, the importance of the Kemalist movement could not be gainsaid. It was not, however, clear how far the emergence of a purely secular nationalism of this kind would change the role that Turkey was assumed to hold as the centre of the Moslem world. In 1914 Hussein had already been tempted by the thought that the war might lead not merely to the aggrandizement of his territorial status but to his replacing the Turkish sultan as caliph of Islam.[2] These hopes had faded and the settlement of Arab affairs had been of a different kind. But on 1 November 1922 the sultanate was abolished by the victorious Kemalists – and, indeed, declared retrospectively in abey-

[1] The fall of Venizelos and the return to his throne after the accidental death of King Alexander of the ex-King Constantine who had been deposed by the Allies and was a brother-in-law of the Kaiser, did not help the Greek cause in British eyes.
[2] Kedourie, op. cit., pp. 50 ff.

ance since the allied occupation of Constantinople in March 1922.[1] On 3 March 1924 the caliphate was likewise declared at an end. For Britain as the major political power in the Moslem world the effect of these changes on Moslem sentiment elsewhere was bound to be an important one. Would a sense of Moslem unity survive the disappearance of the only trans-national Moslem institution, however shadowy its authority might long since have become?

The new role of Greece in British foreign policy, and the advent of a Turkish nationalist state, were both significant for Britain's possession of Cyprus. The subject of its possible cession to Greece had been raised as early as August 1915,[2] but the idea was not well received. After the end of the war Curzon declared himself strongly opposed to the cession for strategic reasons; it was a possible base for an attack on the Suez Canal and Greece would be too weak to hold it. His views on this were supported by the chiefs of staff,[3] and by Long.[4] In June 1919 Curzon and Milner both expressed anxiety lest the subject be raised again, but received categorical reassurances from Balfour.[5] Thus Lloyd George's phil-Hellenism was curbed in the case of Britain's one possession in the Greek-speaking world, and Britain was left to deal with the frustrations of Greek sentiment on the island and the fears of the Turkish minority, whose presence was the memorial to the period of Ottoman rule there from the sixteenth century until Disraeli acquired it for Britain.

During the period of reconstruction in the Middle East, Cairo remained the centre from which British authority radiated. But Egyptian nationalism was also stimulated by the events or the period. Immediately it was over the Egyptian nationalists presented their demands for independence,[6] and as a result of the British refusal to negotiate with them a period of political strain, confusion, and violence set in. Allenby, sent out in March 1919 as the new high commissioner, determined almost at once to seek accommodation with the new forces of nationalism. A mission under Milner was sent out to examine the ways in which this policy might be put into effect, but by the time it reached Egypt in December nationalist sentiment had reached the level of total non-cooperation, and the mission left in March 1920 without

[1] Lord Kinross, *Ataturk* (1964), pp. 346 ff.
[2] Cecil to Balfour, 14 August 1915. Balfour Papers, B.M. Add. 49737.
[3] Memorandum: 'The Future of Cyprus', by Curzon, 3 January 1919. PRO. CAB. 29. 2.
[4] Memorandum: 'The Future of Cyprus', by Walter Long, 9 January 1919. Ibid.
[5] Correspondence between Balfour, Curzon, and Milner. Balfour Papers, B.M. Add. 49734.
[6] Marlowe, *Anglo-Egyptian Relations*, pp. 212 ff.

making contact with the nationalist leaders. Negotiations followed in London between Milner and the nationalist (Wafd) leader Zaghlul and agreement was reached on Egyptian independence which was coupled with a treaty giving Britain the right to retain British forces in Egypt to secure imperial communications, and a role in Egypt's financial institutions and in the regulation of the position of foreigners under Egyptian law. But Zaghlul's followers in Egypt, no doubt with his acquiescence, demanded further concessions which were refused, and in November 1920 Milner broke off the negotiations.

Attempts were now made to negotiate a somewhat similar settlement with the sultan of Egypt's government, but it was clear that the freedom permitted to the nationalists to agitate against any treaty gave the negotiators little scope; and although the ostensible reason for the failure of the talks was Britain's insistence on maintaining a garrison, the real reason was the certainty of nationalist opposition to any terms at all.

Egypt provided yet a further example of the difficulties inherent in attempting to distinguish between Britain's imperial requirements in a territory, and control of the local situation. So long as a nationalist movement was given scope to agitate, the tenure and indeed lives of any government willing to compromise with the imperial power were at risk. But to suppress the nationalist movement was out of keeping with the basically liberal philosophy that now dominated British opinion at home and affected the advice of Britain's proconsuls overseas. In the Egyptian case there was, however, another important issue involved. If one were to accept the right of countries such as Egypt to self-governing institutions along the lines proposed by the Milner committee, then one could not stop at Egypt just because of the anomalous basis of British control there. Why, people asked, were the conclusions of the Milner committee 'not applicable to India as well as Egypt; and to all other territory of the same kind', though not, it was added, to territory where the aborigines 'were in a state of savagery'.[1]

Constitutional Advance in India

One reason why the degree of independence that even conservative Englishmen were prepared to see given to Egypt seemed inappropriate

[1] Edward Grey to Gilbert Murray, 1 September 1920. Gilbert Murray Papers, Grey correspondence. Grey probably had a wider definition of 'a state of savagery' than was to be in the minds of a later generation of decolonizers.

to India, was the curious social gulf that had been allowed to grow up in India itself between the resident British community and British officialdom on the one side, and even the most educated and enlightened sections of Indian society on the other. It was this difference which struck Montagu when he wrote, after visiting Egypt, to point out that Egyptians were freely admitted to English clubs in Cairo on equal terms, whereas this did not happen in India. It was this 'social soreness' that in his view lay at the bottom of much of the political unrest in India,[1] but it was not something which could be remedied by the expression of liberal sentiments in London and there seems little doubt that the gulf between the two peoples was if anything widening.[2] It is for historians of India to establish how and whether Montagu was correct in his view. It was certainly widely held among British intellectuals,[3] though the absence of such discrimination did not prevent the growth of violent anti-British feeling in Egypt and elsewhere in the Middle East.

Progress had in any event to be made in two other directions, the recognition of India's international role, and constitutional advance along the lines of the Montagu–Chelmsford report. Montagu not only insisted that India, like the dominions, be independently represented at the peace conference, but also that its representatives could put forward views not identical with those of the British Empire delegation, despite the fact that the secretary of state, the ultimate authority, was a member of the British government and responsible to parliament.[4]

The reasons for this insistence did not derive merely from the abstract question of India's status in the Empire; the Indian government continued to cherish views of its own.[5] The Indian delegation consistently opposed the imposition of severe terms on Turkey, and any idea of taking Constantinople from her, as an anti-Moslem policy.[6]

---

[1] Report by Montagu from Egypt, 28 October (?) 1918. Lothian Papers, Box 141.
[2] It was noted that the number of officers in Indian regiments who knew their men well and could speak their language was declining. Sir William Birdwood to Milner, 19 January 1921. Milner Papers, Letters 1921, Box V [Bodl. 207]. Field-Marshal Lord Birdwood who had first served in India in 1902 was from 1920 to 1924 commander-in-chief of the Northern army in India.
[3] E. M. Forster's *A Passage to India* (1925) is only the most famous of literary treatments of the problem of personal relations between the British and Indian peoples.
[4] Waley, *Edwin Montagu*, pp. 193–7.
[5] Montagu to Hankey, 14 January 1919. PRO. CAB. 21. 140.
[6] British Empire Delegation: 'Report of Committee on Greek Territorial Claims'; memorandum by Indian Delegation, 1 April 1919. PRO. CAB. 29. 11. Cf, Waley, op. cit., pp. 198, 209, 239 ff. Montagu was repeatedly warned by Chelmsford, and by Reading who succeeded

On 17 May the Aga Khan was allowed to plead the case of the Indian Moslems before the Council of Four. On this occasion he claimed that the principal victories over the Turks had been won through the efforts of the Indian Empire, and that Hindus as well as Moslems would be outraged if the Turks were deprived of any part of their Anatolian homeland, of Constantinople, or of Thrace.[1] The pressure on this score from India continued even after the San Remo conference.[2] In the event, it is hard to see that the Indian representations made much difference to the main aspects of the Turkish settlement, though Indian interests in the Persian Gulf and the Arabian peninsula were as we have seen fully recognized.[3] It was clear, however, that the more Indian opinion was allowed to influence the policies of the Indian government, the more room there would be for divergent interpretations of India's role in the new imperial structure.

The main principles of the Montagu–Chelmsford report – 'dyarchy' in the provinces and an elected majority in the central legislature – were enacted in the government of India act of 1919.[4] Elections were held in 1920 and the new constitution came into operation in 1921,[5] but meanwhile the breach had been widening both between the administration and congress, and between congress and those Indian liberals who were prepared to co-operate in working the new constitution.[6] The 'Rowlatt' sedition bill, extending for three years the Indian government's wartime powers, provoked violent counter-agitation which in turn led to the imposition of martial law in the Punjab. In the course of enforcing the regulations against political gatherings, there occurred on 13 April 1920 the Amritsar massacre in which 379

---

him as viceroy in April 1921, that anxiety among Indian Moslems about the Turkish peace terms was a most serious element in the Indian situation. Ibid., pp. 240, 246.
[1] P. Mantoux (ed.), *Les Délibérations du Conseil des Quatre* (Paris 1955), vol. 2, pp. 98–9. Lloyd George in bringing the Aga Khan's views before the committee on 13 May gave a somewhat exotic account of him, stating that he could only be compared to the Count of Monte Cristo, and that his great fortune had been made by selling places in Paradise in advance. Ibid., p. 55.
[2] On 19 March 1920 an Indian delegation saw Lloyd George to argue the case on religious grounds for the retention by the caliph (i.e. the sultan of Turkey) of a sufficient territorial dominion which should in their view include the Arab lands. Philips, op. cit., pp. 219–20. On 8 June 1920 the Aga Khan wrote to Montagu that the British government's pro-Greek policy would inevitably compromise his constitutional reforms. Aga Khan to Montagu, 8 June 1920. Lothian Papers, Box 186.
[3] Clement Jones calls attention to some resemblances between some features of the treaty of Sèvres and the memorandum of the Indian delegation. 'The Dominions and the Peace Treaty', ch. IX. PRO. CAB. 29. 80.
[4] Extracts in Philips, op. cit., pp. 273 ff.
[5] Coupland, op. cit., pp. 61 ff.
[6] Moore, op. cit., pp. 116 ff.

Indians were killed and 1,200 more wounded. General Dyer, who had ordered the firing, was supported by his superior officer and by the governor of the Punjab, Sir Michael O'Dwyer.

Montagu, shocked by the episode, secured the appointment of a committee of investigation upon whose report Dyer was asked to resign his commission.[1] But Dyer received the sympathy of a strong element in the House of Commons, and of a majority in the House of Lords, and was the beneficiary of a large public subscription. These indications of a basic lack of sympathy with India's national aspirations did as much as the original event to prevent the development of the co-operation necessary between the government and the national movement if there were to be real prospects of a peaceful and orderly transfer of power.[2] Congress moved from working for progress towards full responsible government through strictly constitutional means, and towards the non-cooperation advocated by Gandhi and launched under his leadership in August 1920. The Moslem league, alienated by the treaty of Sèvres, joined with them. By the end of the year, there was for the first time a powerful section of opinion in India contemplating full independence outside the Empire and taking its cue from the nationalist movements in Ireland and Egypt; but since this goal was rejected by Gandhi its adherents failed to capture congress.[3]

It was obvious to those who believed in the possibility of applying to India the pattern of constitutional advance set by the old dominions that the difficulties lay deep in the ideas governing the administration. Indian civil servants would now have the additional task of training their successors, and some people doubted whether the new purpose would be so attractive to potential recruits for the service.[4] The old-style official in the India Office itself was seen as one obstacle to progress.[5] And what was needed, it was thought, was a new version of the Milner Kindergarten seeking 'to create an Indian people and an

---

[1] Report of the committee appointed to investigate disturbances in the Punjab, Cmd. 681. Extracts in Philips, op. cit., pp. 210 ff.
[2] Mehrotra, op. cit., p. 112. Chamberlain commented sympathetically on Montagu's problem as a Jew in lecturing a hostile House of Commons on the iniquity of the ideas of racial ascendancy which he believed to underlie the actions of Dyer and his friends. Moore, op. cit., p. 119.
[3] Mehrotra, op. cit., pp. 110 ff.
[4] John Dove to R. H. Brand, 28 November 1919. *Letters of John Dove*, p. 113. The general anti-imperial climate discouraged I.C.S. recruiting, anyhow.
[5] E. ff. W. Lascelles to Kerr, 24 November 1920. Lascelles (1880–1959), a New Zealander by birth had served on the Indian General Staff and was trying to build up something like a Round Table group in India. Lothian Papers, Box 187.

Indian nation'.[1] But the Round Table ideology would hardly seem appropriate to Indians who regarded themselves already as a people and a nation; and the more so at this time since common opposition to the administration had temporarily stilled the Hindu-Moslem rivalry. But even if the Indians had been prepared to delay their assumption of power until their administrative apprenticeship was complete, the mood of the British did not seem encouraging. Clemenceau, who visited India at the end of December 1920, was surprised to find so many Englishmen saying there was nothing left to do but to get out and (a great many Englishmen were in fact taking this line) being unprepared to envisage working as a team or on terms of equality with Indians.[2] Indeed, there was a period in which the majority of new recruits to the I.C.S. was Indian, and it was not until the pendulum swung back in the mid-1920s to a position of half-and-half recruitment that a generation came in who fully accepted the need for full co-operation.[3] By then the movement for independence had gathered further strength.

Meanwhile the Viceroy and his government remained in charge of India's external interests and of internal security, which had become more closely connected as a result of the bolshevik revolution. Montagu added to his criticisms of British policy his claim that it had enabled the Russians to exploit Moslem grievances.[4] And the bolsheviks' propaganda among 'the disorderly elements in India', their promises to the frontier tribes, and supplies of arms and money to the Afghans, were seen as important reasons by the Indian General Staff for not reducing the number of British troops. Bolshevik activity in Turkey, the Arab countries, Persia, and Afghanistan was all seen as preparation for the final objective of creating a revolution in India itself.[5]

[1] Lascelles to Kerr, 20 January 1921. Ibid.
[2] Lascelles to Kerr, 13 February 1921. Lothian Papers, Box 187.
[3] P. Woodruff, *The Men Who Ruled India*, vol. 2 (edn, 1963), pp. 254-6.
[4] Montagu to Chelmsford, 9 September 1960. Waley, op. cit., p. 236.
[5] 'Defence of India', memorandum by the General Staff in India, 10 May 1921. PRO. CAB. 16. 38. For soviet activity in Asia at this time, see E. H. Carr, *The Bolshevik Revolution, 1917-1923*, vol. 3 (1953), pp. 229 ff. The Russians gave public approval to the emir of Afghanistan, Amanullah, when he denounced the treaty with Britain and encouraged armed incursions into India in May 1919. In February 1921 the Russians signed a treaty with Afghanistan, recognizing the country as fully independent in violation of the Anglo-Russian accord of 1907 by which Russia agreed that all its dealings with Afghanistan should be through the British government. In Persia, after the Russian military collapse, British troops advanced into the northern zone allocated as the Russians' sphere of influence in the 1907 agreement and were thus in occupation of the whole country at the time of the armistice, and in a position to assist anti-bolshevik forces in the Caucasus. On 9 August 1919 an Anglo-Persian treaty was signed, giving Britain a virtual monopoly in the provision of financial and other assistance and in military supplies. With Russian encouragement the Persians failed to ratify

It was also, as the India Office had already pointed out, increasingly difficult to get from India troops for garrisoning places that had been historically or were now regarded as important to her security: Aden, Palestine, and the Black Sea, for instance.[1] No opportunity was being given for Indian settlement in Mesopotamia, and Indian opinion was hostile both to zionism and to the Anglo-Persian agreement.

The viceroy reported a few weeks later that there were strong objections in India to further calls for troops to serve overseas, and that the objections were sustained by many British residents. No similar demands were being made on the dominions; British troops had been rapidly demobilized after the war and in case of internal trouble in India any military requirements would have to be met from its own resources. While India like Britain was an original member of the league, it was Britain not India which had received the mandate for Mesopotamia; why should Indian (and largely Moslem) troops be expected to provide the garrison?[2] The Round Table group in India took the view that no coherent British policy could be found in the area between the Mediterranean and the eastern borders of Persia, and that India (like the dominions) would insist on her defence obligations being limited to her own borders. Indian opinion would always take the view, even if unjustifiably, that any defence contribution outside them would fall upon the Indian taxpayer. There must therefore be a general consultation with Australia and New Zealand as well as with India so as to arrive at a joint Commonwealth policy that could be implemented: 'My view in a nutshell is that if the back of the Commonwealth breaks it will break over questions "East of Suez".'[3]

Official eyes did not regard India's situation as similar to that of the dominions. The Esher committee, set up in 1919 to look at the position

---

the treaty and after the withdrawal of British troops from the north of the country, Russian troops landed on the southern shore of the Caspian and set up a soviet-type régime in the adjacent provinces which lasted until October 1921. After the nationalist coup by Riza Khan in February 1921, an agreement was made with the Russians giving them far-reaching rights of action against any power using Persia as a base for intervention against them.

[1] 'Naval, Military and Air Obligations Devolving on India': memorandum prepared in the India Office. 13 July 1920. PRO. CAB. 4. 7. It was noted that troops were also required for Egypt, the Malay States, Hong Kong, Colombo, and North China. The British garrison at Batum on the Black Sea had actually been withdrawn on 7 July.

[2] Viceroy (army department) to secretary of state, 3 September 1920. PRO. CAB. 6. 4. With regard to a possible naval contribution by India, Montagu pointed out at the imperial conference in 1921 that this must necessarily involve recruiting Indian naval officers. Montagu to Hankey, 21 July 1921. PRO. CAB. 21. 187.

[3] Lascelles to Kerr, 30 December 1920. Lothian Papers, Box 187.

of the army in India, reported along traditional lines that "the military resources of India should be developed in a manner suited to imperial necessities'.[1] But the Indian Legislative assembly, now more representative of Indian opinion, defined the role of the army in India as 'the defence of India against external aggression and the maintenance of internal peace and tranquillity' and declared that for any other purpose the obligations resting on India were to be optional and self-imposed as in the case of the dominions.[2]

Although this proposition was not formally disputed by the government of the United Kingdom, it did not in fact guide practice. Just as the defence of India itself against any major aggression would clearly call for reinforcements from Britain, so in ordinary times Indian troops were required for garrison duties in imperial outposts outside the subcontinent. As the constitutional position was also unaffected by the Montagu–Chelmsford reforms, and the disposition of India's forces was still under the control of the home government, the parallel with the dominions was not, and could not be, exact.

Co-operation between India and the dominions, to which the Round Table looked forward, was rendered as difficult as ever by attitudes to Indian settlers and immigrants. At a meeting during the 1921 imperial conference, Smuts refused to contemplate any equality of treatment between Indians and white citizens. Hughes and Massey, while refusing to accept Smuts's basic principle of racial discrimination as compatible with the declared ideals of the Empire, both defended the exclusion of Asian immigrants on economic grounds but argued that once they were accepted as residents they could not be excluded from full rights on grounds of colour alone.[3]

India's position was also asserted in the case of the new mandates. As well as Mesopotamia whose government was actually represented at the peace conference by the Indian delegation, German East Africa was an area of interest to Indians.[4] There were strong protests against

---

[1] *Report of the Committee Appointed to Inquire into the Administration and Organisation of the Army in India* (Cmd. 943, 1920).
[2] Sir Nandan Prasad, *Expansion of the Armed Forces and Defence Organisation, 1939–1945* (Official History of the Indian Armed Forces in the Second World War, ed. Bisheshswar Prasad) (Calcutta, 1956), p. 8. Admiral Jellicoe's suggestion in 1919 that a Royal Indian navy should be created did not come to fruition till 1934. S. Roskill, *Naval Policy between the Wars*, vol. 1 pp. 276–8.
[3] Meeting at the Colonial Office, 15 July 1921. PRO. CAB. 32. 3.
[4] British Empire delegation; memorandum by Montagu: 'Mandates', 10 March 1919. PRO. CAB. 29. 9.

South African and Australian measures to exclude Asians from German colonies, where this policy had not previously been in force,[1] but neither the Indian nor the British government could hope to change the policies of the dominions in any matter upon which they felt at all strongly.

It was still with South Africa that India's relations were the most difficult, and despite the Smuts–Gandhi agreement new discriminatory legislation had been passed and more was being advocated. At the 1921 imperial conference the Indian representative moved a resolution claiming for Indians in the dominions all the rights of citizenship. The other prime ministers received it sympathetically; Smuts was adamant that no South African government could agree. The resolution that was passed declared the recognition of the Indians' rights to citizenship to be in the interests of the British Commonwealth. For the first time the rule of unanimity was waived; South Africa's dissent was recorded, and India's protest against that dissent. And South African support was given to the claims of white supremacy in Kenya also.[2] India might still gain from its relationship with Britain itself as liberal opinion in both Britain and India believed; it was much harder to see what if anything she gained from membership in the Commonwealth system.

MacDonald, the labour leader with the greatest interest in India, did indeed argue that it was as a self-governing dominion that India would best be placed to fight the case for its overseas immigrants, and would have been prepared to see India exercise the mandate for Tanganyika. The labour position on India at this time was not indeed notably radical. Most socialists still thought that large multinational units would act as barriers to international conflict, and that the possibility of influencing India's progress in a socialistic direction was more important than any abstract Indian claim for total independence; they were also most at home in India with the more moderate wing of congress. Many of labour's working-class supporters were concerned about India's role as a market for British goods and were generally somewhat imperialistic in their thinking. Even the British communist party was conscious that the idea of a total dissolution of the Empire was not something upon which they could rely for support. The influx of former liberal intellectuals into the labour party, though it brought

[1] Conference of British Empire delegation at Foreign Office, 8 November 1920. PRO. CAB. 29. 28/2.
[2] Hancock, Smuts (Cambridge, 1968), vol. 2, pp. 141–5.

with it a number of men basically sympathetic to Indian aspirations, did not much alter the picture. Although this group was more concerned with foreign affairs than with domestic policy its general orientation was a European one, and it was the alleged iniquities of the treaty of Versailles in generating future conflicts rather than imperial or colonial questions that excited their attention. The pressure of labour as the official opposition was directed towards speeding up the process of democratizing and Indianizing India's institutions and thus helped to provide a balance to die-hard pressure in the other direction. But labour's spokesmen did not take up positions conspicuously irreconcilable with the proclaimed purposes of Montagu himself. The goal of what was coming to be called 'dominion status' seemed adequate enough.[1]

Dominion Status: India and Ireland

The phrase dominion status itself, which was to pay so large a role in the subsequent debate over India's future, received its first official recognition as a result of the statement in the Anglo-Irish treaty of December 1921 that Ireland should have the same 'constitutional status in the community of nations known as the British Empire' as Canada, Australia, New Zealand, and South Africa. And when Lloyd George asked himself in the debate on the treaty a week later what 'dominion status' meant he could only define it by reference to 'the measure of freedom' enjoyed by the existing dominions.[2] Once again we find this curious interlock between the Irish and the Indian roles in the ultimate dislocation of the imperial structure. Yet during the post-war period the actual course of events in the two countries had been very different. Committed to hold India undivided, the British government's ability to do so was not seriously in question; seeking to deal with Irish claims for independence, Britain became committed to partition.[3] In this sense Ireland's fortunes from 1919 to 1921 were paralleled by India's between 1945 and 1947. But in Ireland an attempt was first made to circumvent the dilemma and the dangers which Irish independence was

[1] See on this whole subject the fully documented analysis in Georges Fischer, *Le Parti Travailliste et la Décolonization de l'Inde* (Paris, François Maspero, 1966).
[2] K. C. Wheare, *The Constitutional Structure of the Commonwealth* (Oxford, 1960), pp. 10 ff. For the negotiation of the Irish Treaty itself, see the account in F. Pakenham (the Earl of Longford), *Peace by Ordeal* (1935).
[3] On this phase of the Irish question and its significance in the development of the Commonwealth, see Hancock, *Survey of British Commonwealth Affairs*, vol. 1, ch. III, 'Saorstat Eireann'.

thought to present by the use of force; in India, a memory of that previous experience was no doubt among the factors that made the use of force for holding the imperial position generally unacceptable.

Indeed, from the very beginning of the struggle which began in Ireland with the declaration of a republic in Dublin on 21 January 1919 by 37 of the 73 Sinn Fein members elected to the British parliament in the previous month, the parallel with India and the likely impact of what was done on Indian opinion were never far from people's minds.[1] Bryce, holding a view of labour's position on India which was as we have seen hardly in accordance with the facts, was deeply critical of both government and opposition: 'It looks to me as if between the reckless ignorance of the Labour Party and the cowardly folly of such a Minister as Montagu India will be lost within a generation. And it will not be strange if the Dominions should follow. The Labour Party are quite capable of letting Sinn Fein cut the painter.'[2]

After the treaty had been signed, Carson argued that the surrender to force would make it impossible to hold on anywhere:

When we are told that the reason why they had to pass the terms of the Treaty, and the reason why they could not put down crime in Ireland, was because they had neither the men, nor the money, nor the backing, let me say that this is an awful confession to make to the British Empire. If you tell your Empire in India, in Egypt, and all over the world that you have not got the men, the money, the pluck, the inclination, and the backing to restore order in a country within twenty miles of your own shore, you may as well begin to abandon the attempt to make British rule prevail throughout the Empire at all.[3]

But if Irish experience could be used to support the diehard position – and it was so used in the 1930s again – it could also be used as an argument for coming to terms with Indian nationalism:

Unless we find room for the national sentiment [wrote Kerr in the critical year 1929] we shall start non-cooperation once more in an

[1] The Easter Rising and subsequent events killed the old home rule party. In the election of December 1918, Sinn Fein fighting on a Republican and abstentionist ticket won every seat but one in three-quarters of the country. Many of the victors were in prison in January 1919.
[2] Bryce to Dicey, 9 July 1920. Bryce Papers, English Correspondence, vol. 4. Bryce still believed it possible to give Southern Ireland home rule, with defence and foreign affairs wholly reserved to the imperial government. H. A. L. Fisher, *James Bryce* (1927), vol. 2, pp. 256–8.
[3] H. L. Deb., 14 December 1921.

intensely aggravated form and suffused with the theory and practice of Leninite revolution. We shall be gradually driven towards the position which we finally had to adopt in Ireland of governing the country by a species of Black and Tannery and we shall eventually be defeated, as we were defeated in Ireland.[1]

But if Ireland was an imperial problem it was, like other British imperial problems, one which Britain had to solve for itself. In a secret session of the House of Commons on 10 May 1917 Asquith had urged that the dominions should be brought in to help enforce a settlement. But Lloyd George had rightly pointed out that the dominion statesmen were not going to burn their fingers in the matter; Borden was dependent on the Orangemen, Hughes was absent (precisely because of his troubles with the Irish at home), and Smuts declined to go it alone.[2] Nor by now was there much hope of solving the Irish problem through drowning it in the wider imperial one. The idea of a federal scheme for the whole United Kingdom as a stepping-stone to some new imperial system, still canvassed by Austen Chamberlain in 1918, was hardly a starter.[3] Nor was Hewins's view, that Ireland's demands could be settled by economic action within a system of imperial preference, any more attuned to the new realities of Irish nationalism.[4]

The Irish attempt to internationalize the question by appealing to the peace conference was, however, equally unsuccessful. President Wilson was, of course, under strong pressure at home to secure a hearing for representatives of the Republic of Ireland at the peace conference, but he was able to use the provocative behaviour of a group of representatives of Irish-American societies on a visit to Ireland as an excuse for his unwillingness to press the matter. He was not ready to break with Britain on the Irish issue and so jeopardize the things he cared more about and he thought the league would solve such problems in the future.[5] The issue was thus left to be decided by whether the Irish would tire of terrorism before English dislike of the counter-terrorism of the supplementary forces, the 'Black and Tans', became

[1] Kerr to Marris, 23 October 1929. Lothian Papers, Box 190.
[2] Waley, *Edwin Montagu*, p. 125.
[3] 'The Irish Question and Federalism': memorandum by Chamberlain, 17 June 1918. Austen Chamberlain Papers, Box AC. 31/101.
[4] Hewins, op. cit., vol. 2, p. 207.
[5] Tillman, op. cit., pp. 197–200. But the issue continued to bedevil Anglo-American relations. See the report on American opinion by Sir William Wiseman, 1 July 1919. *D.B.F.P.*, series 1, vol. V, pp. 981 ff., and for Wilson's proclaimed view that it could come before the league. Lindsay to Curzon, 22 September 1919. Ibid., p. 1000.

too strong for the government to ignore. In the end indeed, as has been well said, 'both sides had surrendered to force'.[1] The Irish got 'dominion status' and Ulster its exclusion. Britain appeared to retain the minimum prerequisites for her own security.[2]

The British interest in Ireland had been largely a strategic one and this aspect of it had been threatened by Germany's effort to exploit Irish discontent during the war. Nevertheless, an Ireland reluctant to remain in the Empire was not an asset. In 1917 the General Staff had pointed out that Ireland was a net loss from the manpower point of view; more troops were needed to keep order in Ireland than Ireland had raised for service abroad.[3] A contented Ireland would have its advantages even from a narrow security point of view. The really essential point was the control of the Irish ports, whose significance had been demonstrated in the struggle against the submarine: 'The Irish ports are as essential to the protection of the British coast and communications as the ports of Scotland or the English Channel, and I do not think that under any circumstances we could let naval bases in Ireland be under divided military control.'[4] By the 1921 treaty coastal defence was left in British hands – though with the provision that the Free State might take it over after a lapse of five years; certain harbours and other facilities were to be at the navy's disposal in peacetime and their use could be extended at the British government's request in times of crisis.[5]

British satisfaction with the treaty – shared by all but the diehards – was as illusory as the satisfaction felt at the time of the treaty of Vereeniging. On both occasions it was believed that national movements could somehow be channelled and contained by constitutional and treaty limitations. What for the British seemed an honourable settlement with concessions on both sides seemed to the Irish, as to the Afrikaners before them, a mere halt on the road to total independence in external as well as internal relationships. The fact was disguised for a time by the struggle against the treaty waged by the more extreme

[1] Medlicott, *Contemporary England*, p. 164.
[2] For Smuts's role in helping to bring about negotiations in 1921, see Hancock, *Smuts* (Cambridge, 1968), vol. 2, pp. 49–59.
[3] Milner Papers, Thornton's Diary, January 1917 [Bodl. 299].
[4] Edward Grey to Spender, 20 October 1920. Spender Papers, B.M. Add. 46389.
[5] Roskill, op. cit., pp. 110–12. In view of its importance it is surprising to find how little attention is paid in accounts of the treaty and its preliminaries to the naval aspect. Churchill's own account does not deal with it, and the appended map does not even include the relevant place-names. W. S. Churchill, *The Aftermath* (1929), chs. XIV–XVI.

faction in the Irish civil war of 1922. But the victory of the 'free staters' over the republicans merely postponed the challenge to the treaty itself. For Australians, New Zealanders, or English-speaking Canadians who felt themselves to be British (though British with a difference) dominion status gave them the substance of their national demands. For Irishmen with a vision of a united Ireland partition, not to mention the boundary settlement and the commitment to co-operation in defence and foreign policy which was implicit in the treaty, was ultimately intolerable. The Irish treaty was the final achievement of, and in its fate the final commentary on, the ideal of a liberal empire.

The 1921 Imperial Conference

In fact, the liberal empire had had its final apotheosis in the conference of prime ministers in the summer of 1921, while the struggle in Ireland was still continuing on its weary and bloodstained course. There were multiple reasons for this conclave which brought together for the last time the nucleus of the Empire's wartime leadership – Lloyd George, Chamberlain, Balfour, Curzon, and Churchill, Hughes, Massey, Smuts, with Arthur Meighen, Borden's successor as conservative leader in Canada, the only newcomer.[1] Some British figures still hoped that some economic contribution to the strength of the system might be forthcoming; there had been elements of imperial preference in the budget of 1919.[2] And there was some discussion of assisted migration, a subject of renewed interest in the light of the post-war problems of unemployment.[3]

In the dominions there was some uneasiness at the extent to which their governments had committed them to a new and more active role in imperial affairs. In Canada, opinion was split between those who feared this new role and those who feared on the contrary a further involvement in Britain's foreign and defence policies.[4] In South Africa Smuts's political position, as against the nationalist's demand for an overt recognition of the right of secession, had been weakened by the

[1] The account of this period in Hancock, *Survey of Commonwealth Affairs*, vol. 1, pp. 68–91, was, of course, written before much of the documentation became available but has not been superseded.
[2] Hewins, op. cit., vol. 2, pp. 183–4; Amery, op. cit., vol. 2, p. 187.
[3] Milner presiding over an empire conference on the subject in January 1921, emphasized the long-term benefits to the whole empire rather than the immediate alleviation of Britain's difficulties. Ibid., p. 206.
[4] Dawson, *Mackenzie King*, pp. 284, 328–9, 333–5.

election of March 1920.[1] In addition, the old question of the dominion contribution to imperial naval defence was revived. And finally, at least some of the dominion governments showed discontent about the extent to which they were being kept informed about British foreign policy and the direction which it was taking.[2] But here again there was the familiar problem that, while the dominions might urge a particular course of policy, they were not necessarily willing to supply the resources to carry it out.[3]

The formal position was that the imperial conference of 1917 had called for a constitutional conference to meet after the war, and by January 1920 inquiries as to what was proposed were already coming in. In April 1920 Milner reminded the dominion governments of the undertaking and suggested that the conference should be held in Ottawa in 1921, but Meighen, unlike his predecessor, was averse to a meeting which should concern itself with a further definition of the constitutional position.[4]

Instead of a formal conference the British government, with the dominions following its lead, accepted a suggestion (apparently put forward by Hughes) that a less formal meeting should be held of the prime ministers and other representatives of the empire governments, including India. The agenda would include the problems of defence, arrangements for securing a common foreign policy, the question of the renewal of the Anglo-Japanese alliance and the composition of the proposed constitutional conference as well as minor matters of common interest.[5]

There was indeed a considerable amount of attention given to foreign policy questions, Meighen in particular insisting on the need for continuous consultation between the United Kingdom government and

---

[1] At a time when the American government, so as to defeat congressional opposition to the covenant, was seeking assurances that the empire members of the League would not vote when one of them was a party to the dispute, Smuts and Hughes had intervened to prevent it. See the correspondence with Grey during his Washington mission in the autumn of 1919. *D.B.F.P.*, series 1, vol. V, pp. 1007 ff.

[2] Loring Christie (Canadian department of external relations) to Kerr, 5 April 1920. Lothian Papers, Box 186.

[3] Canadian anxiety over the fate of the Armenians was a case in point. Kerr to Grigg, 15 April 1920. Ibid.

[4] Christie to Kerr, 12 January 1920. Ibid.

[5] Notes by Hankey on 'the forthcoming imperial meetings', 16 June 1921. Austen Chamberlain Papers, Box AC. 26. Cf. Milner to Lloyd George, 8 October 1920. Gollin, op. cit., pp. 596–7. In a debate in the Canadian House of Commons on 27 April 1921 Mackenzie King challenged Meighen's view that defence would not form a principal topic and demanded that Canada enter into no new obligations.

the dominions – whose advice should prevail in matters where they had a paramount interest. The Empire should shun the balance of power principle and work for the success of the league, but it was made clear that final responsibility must still rest with the United Kingdom government and could not be shared.[1] The other prime ministers also did not show themselves backward in dealing with the major current issues of British policy.[2] The conference seems to have expected that this meeting would provide the model for similar 'peace cabinets' in the future.[3]

The question of the control of foreign policy depended on whether the ideas of a special constitutional conference were implemented.[4] Hughes opposed the proposal, denying that one part of the Empire could be at war while the others were not, or could make separate treaties. Important questions, however, should be decided by discussion between those responsible, and not according to a fixed legal code. There was no need for any extension of the constitutional rights of the dominions; it was only necessary to improve the machinery for consultation. If no special conference were held, Smuts favoured proclaiming some new formula to embody the now recognized equality between the governments and parliaments of the Empire. Because Canada was, like Australia, opposed to a special constitutional conference the chances of its being held were obviously minimal and Lloyd George accepted its rejection, even arguing that it was the degree of definition introduced into international relationships that was the weakness of the league compared with the more flexible structure of the Empire. The only dissentient voice was that of Massey, who deplored the notion of distinct foreign policies and separate membership of the league which could drive a wedge between the dominions; but his argument for a cabinet of prime ministers, to give joint advice to the monarch, had by now a wholly anachronistic ring.

In the sphere of naval defence the conference consolidated the defeat of any hopes still cherished by the Admiralty of a single imperial navy and of any expectations that the dominions would be prepared to make much greater contributions to their own naval defence.[5] The Admiralty

[1] Graham, op. cit., pp. 85–9.
[2] W. Farmer Whyte, *William Morris Hughes*, pp. 423 ff.
[3] Dawson, op. cit., p. 406.
[4] Notes of meetings of the prime ministers and others, 24 June, 11, 12, 22, 27 July 1921. PRO. CAB. 32. 2 & 4.
[5] B. B. Schofield, *British Sea Power* (1967), pp. 80 ff.

had kept its faith in a single fleet with the dominions supplying vessels under naval boards to be responsible to their own individual parliaments,[1] but the dominion prime ministers had turned this down as impracticable before the end of the war.[2] Further probing showed that the dominions maintained their position and the idea of separate dominion navies found some sympathy even in London.[3] By February 1921 the Admiralty was more interested in finding machinery to control policy and co-ordinate training and tactics, the ultimate objective being that the British and dominion navies together should be superior to that of any other power or combination of powers with which the Empire might find itself in conflict.[4] Although the Admiralty's preference for a single fleet was not abandoned, much emphasis was now laid on imperial co-ordination, the importance of reserves of fuel oil to the dominions, and dominion co-operation in developing the proposed base at Singapore.[5]

Thus when the prime ministers met in the summer of 1921 the Admiralty's accent was on sharing financial responsibility for the Singapore base with India and Australia to whom it was of intimate concern. It was argued that the heavy British expenditure on Malta should be regarded as a contribution to imperial defence, because a fleet at Malta would be much nearer Singapore than if it were in home waters.[6] When the ministers came to discuss these problems, Hughes argued for a sharing of naval expenditure within the Empire on a *per capita* basis adjusted for the white population of each dominion. Meighen was joined by Smuts and Montagu in his opposition to this proposal, though it was pointed out that it would be hard to expect Australia and New Zealand to assume further burdens when the exist-

---

[1] 'Naval Defence of the British Empire': Admiralty memorandum for the war cabinet, 17 May 1918. PRO. CAB. 1. 188.
[2] Memorandum from dominion prime ministers sent by Borden to first lord of the admiralty, 15 August 1918. Ibid.
[3] 'Imperial Naval Defence': Admiralty memorandum, October (?) 1919. Ibid.
[4] 'Empire Naval Policy and Co-operation', February 1921. PRO. CAB. 21. 187.
[5] Comments on the previous paper by the standing defence sub-committee of the C.I.D., 1921. Austen Chamberlain Papers, Box AC. 26. Imperial cabinet.
[6] 'Empire Naval Policy': Admiralty memorandum of 11 July 1921. PRO. CAB. 21. 187. There was no enthusiasm for Smuts's suggestion that naval expenditure should be a first charge against German reparations, since on a proportion of reparations due, the burden on Britain would be disproportionately large while the principal beneficiaries of naval defence, Canada, Australia, and New Zealand, would pay too small a share. Treasury memoranda, 13 and 23 July. Ibid. It was eventually dropped since there was no agreement between the prime ministers of the dominions themselves. Hankey to Churchill, 22 July 1921. Ibid.

ing arrangements were so unequal.[1] Meighen was suspicious of any proposal that looked like a financial contribution to imperial defence, despite the argument of Lloyd George that the British fleet had rid itself of its pre-war objective of protecting the British Isles against attack and was now primarily required for empire defence and to maintain the Empire's position in the world.[2]

In the end the dominion premiers agreed subject to the approval of their respective parliaments, and the Indian representative subject to the approval of the government of India, that the 'minimum standard of naval ship construction necessary for the maintenance of the position of the British Empire among the nations of the world' was 'an equality of fighting strength with any other naval Power'. But consideration of methods of co-operation in carrying out this policy was to be deferred until after the Washington conference on disarmament that had by now been agreed upon.[3]

Coming to Terms with Europe

The discussions in London merely served to show how far the dominions were from contemplating a major naval effort on their own part, and how localized were their own interests and anxieties.[4] In other respects too their influence, where cast into the balance at all, was essentially a negative one. Indeed, with the disappearance of the German challenge to Britain's world power the main emphasis of British policy had shifted to Europe where dominion interest in the details was relatively small. It is true that in the various discussions of the reparations settlement it was necessary to keep the dominions' claim in mind. Some forms of priority, it was pointed out by British ministers, would have the effect of satisfying all Belgium's claims before those of the dominions could be taken into account, despite the fact that the dominions' losses in men were eight times as great as those of the Belgians', and Australia's alone were three times as great. If an injustice were done, it would make the dominions less ready to play their part in a future war.[5]

[1] Note of meeting of 19 July 1921. PRO. CAB. 32. 4.
[2] Roskill. op. cit. pp. 296-8.
[3] 'Revised draft resolution on naval defence' circulated on 23 July 1921. PRO. CAB. 21. 187. Cf. notes of a meeting of the conference on 5 August. Ibid.
[4] Cf. Roskill, op. cit., ch. VII, 'Problems of Overseas Defence, 1918-1921'.
[5] Notes of Anglo-French conference at 10 Downing Street, 13 December 1919. D.B.F.P., series

But the real issue lay elsewhere. In the long-drawn-out British attempt to modify the peace terms over reparations; in the friction which occurred between Britain and France over the issue of war criminals; and in British attempts to prevent the occupation of further zones of German territory as a sanction for the payment of reparations or the fulfilment of the disarmament clauses, there was present a basic dilemma in British policy which outlived the Lloyd George coalition.[1] While the French feared that the British, having got their way on the colonial issue and on the naval terms (the German fleet had scuttled itself after surrender), were indifferent to the security of their allies, the British by and large suspected that the French were determined to impose a rigid military hegemony on the continent and to use their occupation rights for this ulterior purpose, treating the British and (while they remained there) the American forces as simple adjuncts of their own national policy.[2] British policy, on the other hand, was mainly concerned with Germany's recovery and return to the comity of nations. In the beginning, at any rate, the reasons for this did not lie primarily in the conviction urged upon the government by left-wing and other critics that the peace treaty itself was basically unjust and misdirected.[3] Nor was it simply that British colour prejudice was aroused by France's use of colonial troops for occupation purposes.[4] More relevant was Britain's need to resuscitate the European economy as an outlet for British exports and a cure for the country's mounting unemployment. There was also the fear that to press Germany too hard might lower her guard against bolshevism. In some cases, the opposition which the French put up produced an access of anti-French feeling and support for bringing Germany into the League of Nations even at the expense of a French withdrawal.[5]

In the government, however, opinions did not develop solely along

---

1, vol. II, p. 763. Notes of conversation between British and French governments at Lympne, 15 May 1920. Ibid., vol. VIII, pp. 261 ff.
[1] See M. Gilbert, *The Roots of Appeasement* (1966), chs. VII, VIII. Northedge, op. cit., ch. VII.
[2] See, e.g., Churchill to Balfour, 23 August 1919. Balfour Papers, B.M. Add. 49694.
[3] On the development of hostility to the treaty in British opinion and the role of Keynes's intemperate criticisms, see Gilbert, op. cit., chs. V and VI. Cf. R. B. McCallum, *Public Opinion and the Last Peace* (1944); E. Mantoux, *The Carthaginian Peace* (1946).
[4] The great spreader of atrocity stories about the French colonial troops' treatment of German women was E. D. Morel who had made his reputation as a defender of the Congolese. The so-called 'black' troops were mainly North African Moslems – but accuracy was unimportant to the anti-French Left. See C. A. Cline, *Recruits to Labour: The British Labour Party, 1914–1931* (Syracuse University Press, 1963), pp. 78–9.
[5] Cecil to H. A. L. Fisher, 24 September 1920. Gilbert Murray Papers, Cecil Correspondence.

this line. For one thing, people felt that the Germans were deliberately stalling on the allies' legitimate demands, and that Britain would be unwise to press her allies too far into making concessions to them; it was (rightly) suspected that Germany's disarmament should not be taken at its face value and that German nationalism had by no means disappeared as a factor in German politics. And if these fears turned out to be justified, then there seemed little alternative but to return to the pre-war alignment with France. By the summer of 1920 a proposal for military talks with the French and Belgians was before the government, and Chamberlain was arguing that if military undertakings were to be given again it would be far better that Britain's determination to defend the independence of the Low Countries should be incorporated in a public treaty, so that parliament and the people could not claim that commitments had been entered into unawares.[1] It was also argued, notably by Lord Derby from his vantage point in the Paris embassy, that the most useful measure of all would be a formal alliance with France. This would both remove from the French the haunting sense of insecurity which explained the intransigence of their policy, and show Germany the futility of a renewal of aggression.[2] The American rejection of the original guarantee treaty would effectively be remedied, and Britain would accept its obligation in the hope of getting at least America's moral support.

Such counsels had, however, to compete with the strong distaste both at home and in the dominions for a direct commitment on the continent. At the meetings of the Empire prime ministers in the summer of 1921, Curzon found himself compelled to defend the government against Smuts's charge of subservience to France, by pointing to the number of issues since the peace conference over which Britain had pursued an independent policy.[3]

[1] Note by Chamberlain, 'Our Future Relations with Belgium', 28 June 1920. PRO. CAB. 4. 7. On the other hand, Chamberlain was strongly opposed to facilitating contact with France and Belgium by building a channel tunnel. If all the requirements for one were fulfilled, 'England would exist for the defence of the tunnel rather than the tunnel for the defence of England'. Note of 26 February 1920. Austen Chamberlain Papers, Box AC. 34/105.
[2] Randolph Churchill, *Lord Derby* (1959), pp. 385, 397-8.
[3] Meeting of representatives of United Kingdom, dominions, and India, 27 June 1921. PRO. CAB. 32. 2.

Britain and the bolsheviks

The attitude to be adopted towards Russia and her neighbours was but one example. France was more affected than the British by the bolshevik revolution, partly because of the greater significance to France of the new government's repudiation of the financial obligations of its predecessors; she hoped for a time to make up for this by carving out some sphere of economic influence in the wake of the anti-bolshevik armies in the civil war. Later, in the belief that a resuscitated Poland could replace Russia as the counterweight to German power in the east, France's main concern was to make Poland as strong as possible, and, if the soviet government could not be overthrown, at least to see that it inherited as small a part as possible of the old Russian Empire.[1]

British, like American policy, was more complex. The defence of India and the impact there of bolshevik propaganda had helped to determine the direction of British intervention and to justify its perpetuation after the original reason – the re-establishment of an eastern front – had been rendered out of date by the defeat of Germany in the west.[2] Lloyd George, however, always felt that in the last resort Russia's form of government could not be dictated from outside, and that the military pressure exerted against her would consolidate rather than destroy the new system. He was fond of reflecting on the similarity between Britain's problem over the Russian revolution, and that facing Pitt in revolutionary France; to limit the forcible imposition of the new doctrine upon other countries was clearly legitimate, but support for overt counter-revolution had proved unproductive before and would be so again.[3] But such reflections had not prevented Britain from sending forces to Russia, nor did Lloyd George during the peace conference find it possible to suggest an alternative to hoping for the success of one

[1] See on the general western attitudes to the soviet régime, George Kennan, *Russia and the West under Lenin and Stalin* (Boston, 1960); Max Beloff, 'L'URSS et l'Europe', in M. Beloff, P. Renouvin, F. Schnabel, and F. Valsecchi (eds), *L'Europe du XIX et XX Siècle* (Milan, 1964), vol. III.

[2] In the summer of 1919 after the high point of Admiral Kolchak's success as leader of the anti-bolshevik forces in Siberia, it was pointed out by a member of the British delegation in Paris that Kolchak, even in his 'defeated condition', was defending the Indian Empire 'by the presence of his troops between Turkistan and European Russia'. Col. J. H. Kisch to Kerr, 29 July 1919. Lothian Papers, Box 186. As a result of British intervention in the south 'there was a period during 1919 during which travellers from Teheran to Constantinople via the Caucasus could sleep in a British mess every night'. Monroe, *Britain's Moment in the Middle East*, p. 46.

[3] There is a long comparison between Lloyd George and Pitt in a letter from Grigg to Godfrey Thomas, 30 March 1922. Grigg Papers, 1921 file, Godfrey Thomas Letters.

or other of the 'White' armies. The British government did not subscribe to the view that the permanent destruction of Russia as a great
power was either feasible or desirable. The Germans had to be prevented from exploiting the power vacuum, and securing their withdrawal from the Baltic provinces was one of the problems that intermittently preoccupied the peacemakers. Nor was it certain that Pan-
Turanianism would be a better neighbour in central Asia than a loose-
knit federal Russia.[1] Finally, British policy towards Russia became
much affected by the priority attached to economic revival in Europe
and by the desire to reopen the channels of trade with Russia, irrespective of all political differences. Trade as an emollient of international differences was an old Cobdenite view; what was interesting
was to find it espoused by a powerful section of the labour party.
For while in France the existence of a pro-soviet wing of the socialist
movement and the schism to which it led tended to harden the government's position, in Britain there was something of the reverse effect.
And labour pressure – from the unions as well as the political wing of
the movement – served as a balance to the pressures for vigorous
action exercised upon Lloyd George from his more activist colleagues,
Curzon and Churchill.[2]

In view of the diversity of the impulses by which it was governed, the
extraordinary difficulty of discovering what was going on in Russia
whether under bolshevik or anti-bolshevik rule, and the clashes of
opinion both inside and outside the government as to what should be
done, it is not surprising that British policy towards Russia should seem
largely incoherent in both conception and execution. Policy framing in
1918 was mainly the affair of the Eastern committee set up by the
cabinet on 21 March, and though its origin seems to have been a letter
from Milner to Lloyd George, neither of them was a member.[3] Subsequently the prime minister's office, the Board of Trade, the Foreign
Office, and the War Office exercised confused and overlapping respon-

---

[1] Lawrence seems to have advanced a scheme for winning over Kemal to accepting the loss
of Constantinople to the Turks by backing his Pan-Turanian ambitions. See the (undated)
letter from Eric Forbes Adam to Kerr. Lothian Papers, Box 186.
[2] 'The ruin of Lenin and Trotsky and the system they embody is indispensable to the peace
and revival of the world': Churchill to Balfour, 23 August 1919. Balfour Papers, B.M. Add.
49694. Another original supporter of intervention was Cecil but by March 1919 he had
swung round to regretting its calls on ships and men. See his correspondence with Lloyd
George. Cecil Papers, B.M. Add. 57076.
[3] Ullman, op. cit., p. 307 fn. For the later story, see R. H. Ullman, *Britain and the Russian
Civil War* (Princeton, 1968) and Roskill, op. cit. Chap. III.

sibilities.[1] Ultimately, as with so many other aspects of policy, it was the means – or rather lack of them – that determined the ends.[2]

The build-up of intervention in 1918 had brought British forces to Siberia, Archangel and Murmansk, the Caucasus and Transcaspia. When the peace conference met it was clear both that the supreme council could not provide the additional troops needed to make intervention a success, and that the anti-bolshevik forces ought to stand on their own with only arms and money to help them from outside. The dominion representatives were certainly unwilling to contribute forces to the Russian morass and the idea of fighting there made no appeal to England except in the narrowest circles. Ireland would need all the troops Britain had to spare. Equally, the attempt to hasten peace in Russia by diplomatic means proved abortive during the period of the peace conference; French influence on the anti-bolshevik groups was exerted to prevent the proposed all-Russian conference. By the end of February 1919 the prime minister's mind was moving in the direction of withdrawal, and a month later he was even contemplating accepting the likelihood of the soviet government's survival and entering into negotiations with it.

But such expectations were premature. It might be difficult to see how Britain could raise the forces needed to make intervention effective but much parliamentary and press opinion was still adamantly opposed to abandoning the attempt to secure a non-bolshevik Russia; and they were encouraged both by the activity of communists in central Europe (notably in the setting-up of the Bela Kun régime in Hungary) and by the apparent success of Kolchak in Siberia. Had these successes proved the forerunners of ultimate triumph there would have been new problems in store for the allies, as no right-wing government in Russia would have accepted the self-determination of the minority peoples on her western borders. In fact they were short-lived and attention was again switched to what could be built up in the west as a barrier to communist expansion in this direction, but this in turn created difficulties because of the conflicts between the border nationalities themselves, stimulated in particular by the effort of Poland to signalize its

[1] See the correspondence from Brigadier Terence Keyes about the course of events in Southern Russia in 1920 and particularly his letter to Kerr of 31 May. Lothian Papers, Box 186. The account by Louis Fischer in *The Soviets in World Affairs* (2 vols, 1930), though dated in attitude and needing revision in the light of the greater documentation now becoming available, remains indispensable for British policy in this period.
[2] See the summary of events in Northedge, op. cit., pp. 70 ff., which is based on the British and American official documents.

renewed independence by returning to its pre-partition great power frontiers and status.

By the end of July 1919, despite anxious self-questioning among ministers, the decision was reached to end the northern intervention and to limit participation in Siberian affairs to small military missions. In the autumn British backing was given to the attempt by General Yudenich to capture Petrograd by an expedition from the Baltic states; but his forces were driven back into Estonia in the second half of October. Denikin's southern armies thus remained the last recipients of British and French support. But here too disaster struck and by early in 1920 Denikin's cause was lost. The last 'White' forces under Wrangel held on in the Crimea until their evacuation in November – the virtual end of the civil war.

The independence of Finland and the Baltic states had been more or less accepted as definite by the summer of 1919; in the Caucasus, Britain, as we have seen, was more directly involved. In January 1920 she recognized the independence of Georgia and Azerbaijan, and in March all British forces, except for two battalions at Batum, were withdrawn. But after the soviet conquest of Azerbaijan it was decided that Batum also should be evacuated.

Meanwhile the Russo-Polish conflict had become a major source of trouble and confusion. It was neither safe to allow Poland to fall under communist domination nor prudent to let the Poles establish themselves so deeply inside the Ukraine that all their strength would be engaged in holding on to their position. British policy itself fluctuated with the fortunes of the war. By the summer of 1920 the Poles were in retreat, and at the Spa conference on 10 July Lloyd George promised British support should Polish independence be threatened; on 11 July the Russians were warned not to cross the provisional Polish frontier – which thus acquired its later appellation, the 'Curzon line'. A British mission as well as one from France went to Poland at the end of July to assist in planning the defence of Warsaw. Lloyd George now came closer to the French view of the importance of halting the Red Army, and on 8 August agreed with the French to provide help for the Poles if their peace talks with the Russians were to fail. Fortunately the British government was not called upon to honour this pledge. A Polish counter-offensive proved successful – the battle of Warsaw, as it came to be called, was won; and by the end of August, the Russians had been driven back out of all ethnically Polish territory. Russo-Polish talks were resumed on 20 September, an armistice and a preliminary peace treaty were signed on 12 October, and the final peace of Riga on 18 March 1921.

It was during the Russo-Polish conflict that the inherent contradictions in British policy were most clearly revealed. In the first place, from the end of May 1920, the British government was engaged in discussions with the Russians which despite their formal limitation to trade matters went from the beginning to the heart of the political issues between the two countries. In the second place, the reaction of trade union and Labour circles to the reports that Britain would go to the help of the Poles, and the actual obstruction offered to the dispatch of munitions, indicated that a whole-hearted acceptance of the French line might have the most far-reaching effects on social peace at home. The Polish victory was thus a great relief, since it was now possible, particularly in view of the ebb of the Red tide in Central Europe, to contemplate a normalization of relations with the soviet régime.

On 16 March 1921 the Anglo-Russian commercial agreement was signed officially as a preliminary to a formal treaty for peace. On paper the British government achieved its principal objective, since by the treaty the soviet government promised to refrain 'from any attempt by military or diplomatic or any other form of action or propaganda to encourage any of the peoples of Asia in any form of hostile action against British interests or the British Empire, especially in India and in the independent State of Afghanistan'.[1] But in giving this pledge, the soviet government, as events were to show, sacrificed nothing. The creation in 1919 of the Communist (Third) International, whose separation from the soviet state was treated as axiomatic by the soviet government, despite the fact that the International (like the soviet government) was an instrument of the Russian communist party, made it possible for that government to disclaim as irrelevant to its own functioning any subsequent accusations of subversive or propagandist activities outside Russia. Whether the hollowness of the undertaking was fully appreciated on the British side, or whether the decision was taken to accept the pledge at its face-value rather than jettison the hoped-for benefits of the treaty itself, is a more open question.

What the treaty did was to insert a new and unhealthy source of division into the British body-politic. The right continued to distrust the Russians and to assess developments elsewhere in the light of the en-

[1] Fischer, op. cit., vol. 1, p. 294.

couragement or impediment they offered to the progress of communism; the left found itself committed to the view that the soviet government was exclusively concerned with internal welfare, shared their devotion to peace and disarmament, and was a wholly benign influence in world affairs. To call attention to any evidence to the contrary was to be guilty of base reactionary sentiments. Not all the left shared these views all the time, not all the right magnified the soviet peril to the length of denying the existence of any other. But the initial confusion was never fully resolved, and indeed, in some quarters, has not been resolved yet.

The Anglo-American Understanding

The United States had played a much less important part in the latter stages of the conflict in and on the borders of Russia. American intervention in Siberia in August–September 1918 had been wholly directed towards extricating the Czech ex-prisoners of war who were trying to make their way to western Europe, and was based on the mistaken belief that they were likely to have to face hostile German and Austrian contingents of ex-prisoners. American forces were not intended to help overthrow the bolshevik régime, and in fact hardly came into hostile contact with the communists.[1] Originally the Americans were unwilling to intervene at all without Japanese co-operation, but they subsequently discovered that the Japanese were sending large forces and using the confused situation to install themselves as an occupying power in northern Manchuria and eastern Siberia. It was therefore decided that American troops could not be withdrawn after the German armistice; but by the end of 1919 it was clear they served no useful purpose by remaining, and the last of them left in April 1920. The American diplomatic pressure on Japan to follow suit continued, and was a further source of American–Japanese friction until the Japanese finally left the Siberian mainland in the autumn of 1922.

While Britain was therefore principally concerned with the impact of the Russian revolution on the balance of power in Europe and on the defence of the Indian Empire, the Americans were primarily interested in the effect on the balance of power in the Far East brought about by the Japanese gains at the expense of Germany and by the temporary collapse of Russian strength. This helped to bring into the foreground

[1] Kennan, op. cit., pp. 91 ff.

once more the future of the Anglo-Japanese alliance and of British naval policy.

It has been suggested that the failure to establish closer relations of confidence with the American government in the post-war period was due to Britain's failure to follow President Wilson's lead and to push boldly forward during the war along a common political path.[1] But as has been seen already, the United States was in some ways just as committed to its own ideas of a peace settlement as was Britain, and with the question of the 'freedom of the seas' unresolved, Britain was bound to be agitated by the new American naval building programme of 1918 which (if completed) would have given the United States definite naval preponderance.[2] British anxieties were not allayed by the fact that American admirals made no secret of their traditional jealousies of British naval power.[3] It was not easy to understand why the growth of isolationist and even pacifist sentiment in the United States should be accompanied by an apparent determination to achieve naval supremacy.[4]

The American attitude towards the problem was indeed a dual one.[5] As presented by the naval experts, the programme put before congress in December 1918 was based on the classic Mahan theory of the importance of sea-power to a great trading nation with world-wide interests, and on the conviction that Britain with or without her Japanese ally, must not be in a position to challenge American policies. Wilson's purpose was to use the threat of outbuilding Britain in naval armaments as 'a club to hold over the European Allies in general and over Great Britain in particular pending their adherence to President Wilson's comprehensive plans for the reduction of armaments and the creation of a new world order'.[6] The bill therefore included a provision

[1] A. Link, *President Wilson and His English Critics* (Oxford, 1959).
[2] In the three years between the armistice and the Washington conference of 1921–2, the United States did in fact build more warships than the rest of the world put together. N. J. Spykman, *America's Strategy in World Politics* (New York, 1942), p. 169.
[3] When Admiral Sims who was responsible for naval co-ordination with the British left for London in April 1917, the sole instruction given him by the Chief of Naval Operations was: 'Don't let the British pull the wool over your eyes. Its none of our business pulling their chestnuts out of the fire. We would as soon fight the British as the Germans.' P. Goodhart, *Fifty Ships that Saved the World* (1965), p. 65.
[4] A. A. Ekirch, jnr., 'The Popular Desire for Peace as a Factor in Military Policy', in H. L. Coles (ed.), *Total War and Cold War* (Ohio State University Press, 1962).
[5] The problem is fully treated from the American side in H. and M. Sprout, *Towards a New Order of Sea Power* (Princeton University Press; 2nd edn, 1945), pp. 55 ff., and from the British side in Roskill, op. cit.
[6] Ibid., p. 59. The brief account of the naval crisis in H. C. Allen, *Great Britain and the United*

to enable the president to suspend its operation in the event of an adequate agreement on arbitration and disarmament.[1]

Some British quarters realized that Wilson was genuinely concerned about where the naval rivalry might lead, and genuinely fearful about the exposure of America's eastern seaboard to Britain now that the disappearance of the German navy had given her complete maritime supremacy. He was, therefore, believed to be interested in securing an agreement for the joint policing of the world by the two navies acting together.[2] Some exponents of Anglo-American friendship also urged that British naval building should never take the size of the American fleet into consideration; though it was realized that Britain's position would be weakened if she confessed her inability for financial reasons to build competitively.[3]

But elsewhere and especially in naval circles there was ample indication of a desire to meet the American challenge. After Wilson's visit to London produced no naval agreement, the first lord of the admiralty argued that an attempt must be made to get the Americans to limit their programme since otherwise Britain would have no option but to go all out to maintain her traditional supremacy.[4] The issue came to a head when the American secretary of the navy, Josephus Daniels, came to Paris, and with his naval advisers met the first sea lord, Admiral Lord Wester Wemyss, and subsequently Long as well. Long now told the Americans that Lloyd George would not support the league unless he was assured that Wilson would promise not to attempt to outbuild Britain at sea,[5] and by now it seemed accepted by the British Empire delegation that signature of the covenant should be conditional upon a naval agreement.[6] Cecil opposed this kind of bargaining, largely because he felt that on other issues the British need of American support

States (1954), pp. 700–5, minimizes the importance of the issues involved to the future of Britain's world position.
[1] Wilson's opponents even among the 'big navy' men saw this provision as a main objection to the naval bill; the navy should be built for its own sake not as a bargaining weapon against Britain who should be allowed to judge of her own naval needs. Henry Cabot Lodge to Bryce, 4 March 1919. Bryce Papers, U.S.A. Correspondence, vol. 7.
[2] Derby to Balfour, 20 December 1918. Balfour Papers, B.M. Add. 49774.
[3] Curtis to Kerr, 1 December 1918. Lothian Papers, Box 139.
[4] Long to Lloyd George, 16 February 1919. Austen Chamberlain Papers, AC. 25.
[5] Sprout, op. cit., pp. 64–5. 'I was told yesterday that Long and Wemyss had informed the Americans that the British Government would not sign the League unless America agreed never to build a fleet as large as Britain.' Cecil to Lloyd George, 4 April 1919. Cecil Papers, B.M. Add. 51076.
[6] 'British Empire Interests': memorandum of British Empire delegation, sent by Sylvester to Kerr, 1 April 1919. Lothian Papers, Box 141.

was so great that the Americans were in the stronger position.[1] Yet within a few days of his voicing his misgivings, he was himself the instrument of a bargain along these lines, which took the form of a memorandum of a conversation with Colonel House on 10 April 1919.[2] Its essence was an understanding that the president would consider postponing the construction of ships authorized but not yet laid down, and would not press for the 1918 bill still before congress. The British would accept the covenant of the league, including the American reservation in favour of the Monroe Doctrine to which the French strongly objected.[3] Although this agreement was not of course made public, it was followed by a withdrawal of the American naval bill in May.

Wilson, however, proceeded to use the threat of a renewed naval armaments race in order to frighten the American public into accepting the League of Nations; and his remarks on this score further alienated British opinion.[4] From September 1919 he was of course out of action, but the administration allowed the navy to bring forward a new programme at the end of the year which violated the spirit of the Cecil–House agreement, and still further proposals were put forward in 1920. Throughout the debate in the United States Britain was depicted as a jealous and dangerous rival, who must either be kept under control by the proposed league system or decisively outbuilt at sea.[5] It is not surprising, therefore, that despite the continuous financial pressure for cuts the British Admiralty put up a stiff resistance, and on 17 March 1920 the first lord, Long, restated to the House of Commons the classical British position: 'I believe it is a fact that the naval policies of all past governments, whichever party they have represented, have at least included the common principle that our Navy should not be inferior in strength to the Navy of any other power, and to this principle the present Government firmly adheres.'[6] But his reference to the

[1] Cecil to Balfour, 5 April 1919. Cecil Papers, B.M. Add. 51094.
[2] C. Seymour, *The Intimate Papers of Colonel House* (1928), vol. IV, pp. 431–9.
[3] House apparently told Cecil off the record that the contemplated American fleet would be only two-thirds the size of the British navy. Cecil to Lloyd George, 10 April 1919. Cecil Papers, B.M. Add. 51706.
[4] The British position in September 1919 as noted in Curzon's instructions for Lord Grey's special mission to Washington was still one of not taking the strength of the U.S. navy into account when framing the naval estimates. Curzon to Grey, 9 September 1919. *D.B.F.P.*, 1st series, vol. V, p. 998.
[5] Sprout, op. cit., pp. 72–8. By November the British government was seeking to learn what the plans of the Americans' administration actually were. Curzon to Grey, 25 November 1919. Ibid., p. 1037.
[6] B. B. Schofield, *British Sea Power* (1967), pp. 72–4.

strength conferred by Britain's control of the world's major oil resources was additional material for the use of Britain's critics in the United States; and the opponents of any form of naval holiday pointed out that an agreement of this kind would leave Britain with twice as big a navy as the United States, irrespective of the strength she might gain through the Japanese alliance.[1]

In fact, the British position was much less firm than Long's speech indicated. In July the Admiralty, listing a number of precise naval commitments, concluded its account of them with the statement: 'The strength of the Navy is determined, however, not by the commitments referred to above, but by the necessity to maintain our supremacy at sea, which has long been recognized as the basis of our system of imperial defence.'[2] But given the persistent drive for economy this doctrine was unlikely to remain unchallenged. At a meeting of the C.I.D. in December 1920 the prime minister pointed out that the naval situation had changed.[3] Russia and Germany had been eliminated, and France was hardly a potential enemy. But there were two new and formidable powers, the United States and Japan, busy building against each other; and the fleet of either could be used against Britain. Nevertheless, the possibility of a rupture with the United States was no more to be considered now than before the war. The old arguments applied; the Canadian frontier was indefensible, and a naval race with the United States would bankrupt Britain and might induce the United States to insist upon the repayment of the war debt. His suggested division of naval spheres of influence with Britain conceded superiority in the North Sea, the Mediterranean, and the English Channel.

Churchill did not think this suggestion practicable. He believed that Britain must remain the strongest naval power and did not see why the United States should object, except for Britain's tie with Japan which was also a source of irritation to Canada, Australia, and New Zealand who already regarded the United States fleet in the Pacific as a safeguard for themselves. There should be no general review of naval policy until the whole question of naval armaments could be discussed with the new American administration. In the ensuing discussion Curzon stressed the importance and popularity of the Japanese alliance, and Bonar Law the need to avoid antagonizing American opinion.

[1] Sprout, op. cit., p. 79.
[2] 'Naval Commitments': Admiralty memorandum, 19 July 1920. PRO. CAB. 4. 7.
[3] PRO. CAB. 2/3. C.I.D. minutes, 14 December 1920.

Austen Chamberlain thought that to embark upon a policy of competition with the United States made little sense if the country could not afford it, and this would be the case unless there was unprecedented help from the dominions. The imperial angle was stressed by Field-Marshal Wilson who felt that the Empire could not be kept together unless Britain could freely move troops to all parts of it. But since competition with the United States was impracticable one must rely on the League of Nations, or preferably enter into alliances by which the balance of power would be adjusted. Churchill's final word was that there could be no more fatal policy than for Britain to combine with Japan against the United States. In Lloyd George's view there was one even more fatal policy, by which Britain would be at the mercy of the United States.

Despite the fact that Harding's incoming administration indicated its allegiance to the 'big navy' doctrine, it was still Britain's announced intention in March 1921 to build to at least a one-power standard. There was, however, an element of unreality on both sides. In Britain the financial pressure continued to make itself felt, and the discussions at the imperial conference in the summer showed that not much help was to be expected from the dominions.[1] On the American side, the opponents of major armaments gained ground in congress from December 1920, and by July 1921 they had defeated large appropriations and forced the acceptance in principle of the idea of naval limitation.[2] The appointment of so americanophil a first lord as Lord Lee of Fareham – who replaced Long on 14 February 1921 – had paved the way for informal soundings, so that President Harding's suggestion of a naval disarmament conference made on 8 July fell on prepared soil.[3] In August Amery as under-secretary was already explaining to the House of Commons why the government had decided not to try to maintain the one-power standard.[4]

By the summer of 1921 the issue debated at the C.I.D. in December had been settled in favour of Churchill and against Lloyd George, for it was clear that a naval agreement would not be obtainable without the abrogation of the Japanese alliance, and that without the alliance the

[1] Schofield, op. cit., pp. 74–9, 82–3.
[2] Sprout, op. cit., pp. 84–5, 117–28. The senate had attached a rider to the naval appropriation bill in March 1921 inviting the president to call Britain and Japan to discussions on naval disarmament. Schofield, op. cit., p. 92.
[3] Sprout, op. cit., p. 128.
[4] Debate on supplementary naval estimates, 3 August 1921. Schofield, op. cit., p. 78.

dependence of Britain on the United States, at least in the Far East and the Pacific, would be an accomplished fact. With a fleet inadequate to guard both the Atlantic and Mediterranean approaches and the Far East, Britain true to her European priority decided to concentrate her naval strength in European waters. It was believed, however, that if necessary the Far East could be reinforced if Britain possessed a major naval base in that part of the world, and after the C.I.D. had examined alternative possibilities, the cabinet accepted its recommendation on 16 June 1921, that the base in question should be Singapore.[1]

By these decisions the British government was in fact replacing a formal alliance with Japan by a mere understanding with the United States, and assuming that the latter's interests would be served by defending the security of the Pacific dominions, and Britain's own territorial and commercial interests in the Far East. Given the acute sensitivity of American opinion to the idea of 'special interests', its anti-imperial bias and its current phase of isolationism, the risks inherent in this decision were obvious and they were not assumed light-heartedly. The fact that the Pacific dominions, whose interests were so largely involved, were themselves won over to this solution no doubt helped to resolve the real doubts of British diplomats and statesmen.[2]

The Far East

Three new factors entered into a consideration of British policy in the Far East at the end of the war; the elimination of Germany; the Russian revolution and its effects, both inside and outside the territory of the old Russian Empire; and the series of upheavals in China that heralded the growth of a new nationalist movement without giving any clear indication of the lines that the country's future might follow. Japan, Britain's ally, appeared to be using these circumstances in order to

[1] S. Woodburn Kirby, *The War Against Japan* (H.M.S.O., 1957), vol. 1, pp. 2–3. Cf. Roskill, op. cit., pp. 290 ff. For the C.I.D. discussion of the issue, see the minutes of its meeting of 10 June 1921. PRO. CAB. 2/3. 29.
[2] The British documents relating to the abrogation of the Japanese Alliance (*B.D.F.P.* series 1, vol. XIV) did not appear till 1966. Most accounts are therefore based on dominion materials. See especially, J. B. Brebner, 'Canada, The Anglo-Japanese Alliance and the Washington Conference', *Political Science Quarterly*, vol. L (March 1935); J. S. Galbraith, 'The Imperial Conference of 1921 and the Washington Conference', *Canadian Historical Review*, vol. XXIX (June 1948); M. Tate and F. Foy, 'More Light on the Abrogation of the Anglo-Japanese Alliance', *Political Quarterly*, vol. LXXIV (December 1959); J. C. Vinson, 'The Imperial Conference of 1921 and the Anglo-Japanese Alliance', *Pacific Historical Review*, vol. XXXI (August 1962).

carve out for itself on the Asian mainland something in the nature of a closed commercial and financial empire – a move which, while possibly capable of reconciliation with Britain's material interests in the region, was already meeting with strong American opposition. This arose partly from the general American objection to exclusive spheres of influence, and partly from the degree of protection that America felt obliged, for reasons largely of sentiment, to afford to her particular protégé in the Far East, the Republic of China. For Britain the dilemma was whether to try to maintain the alliance hoping it would act as a restraining influence on Japan, or to cast her lot in with China and the United States in a common anti-Japanese front.[1]

By the autumn of 1919 it was already appreciated that a mere renewal of the alliance was not possible, and that the best arrangement to succeed it would be 'a union embracing the United States, Japan, and Great Britain, pledged to rehabilitate China, and to ensure the peaceful development' of the Far East, but it was conceded that American–Japanese hostility would make such an arrangement difficult if not impossible to maintain.[2] There was the further problem that if the alliance was given up, Japan might 'quickly drop into the arms of Germany and Russia'.[3] Despite the apparent incongruity of this combination while Russia remained under her bolshevik rulers, the possibility was not dismissed out of hand by observers on the spot,[4] and it was connected with rumours of the infiltration into Japan of German military and industrial personnel.[5] Bolshevik attempts to come to terms with Japan were also anxiously watched,[6] and it was also realized that even the alliance itself would not prevent the Japanese following policies disadvantageous to Britain if it suited them. Press discussions in Japan and Japanese encouragement to Indian sedition showed 'how grudging and undependable would be the help' to be expected from Japan 'in any complications affecting India'.[7]

---

[1] The formal position of British–Japanese relations as it stood in 1919 is set out in the introductory note to chapter II of *B.D.F.P.*, series 1, vol. VI. It covers British Far Eastern policy from June 1919 to April 1920.
[2] B. Alston, Tokyo, to Sir J. Tilley, Foreign Office, 7 October 1919. Ibid., pp. 761–5. Cf. the enclosed memorandum by C. Wingfield, ibid., pp. 765–9.
[3] Tilley to Alston, 11 December 1919. Ibid., p. 880.
[4] Alston to Tilley, 30 December 1919. Ibid., pp. 912–12. The Tokyo embassy repeated this warning on 17 June 1920. *D.B.F.P.*, series 1, vol. XIV, pp. 42–8.
[5] Alston to Curzon, 7 January 1920. *D.B.F.P.*, series 1, vol. VI, pp. 919–22.
[6] Alston to Curzon, 7 March 1920. Ibid., pp. 1025–6.
[7] See Wingfield's memorandum. Ibid., p. 767. The Indian government was subsequently to make it plain that while it hoped that friendly relations with Japan would be maintained it

The situation was fully examined in a Foreign Office memorandum in February 1920, in which the advantages of renewing the alliance were set out in some detail. Nevertheless, it was admitted that the dominant factor in considering the terms of a renewal would have to be the attitude of the United States, whose friendship was of the prime importance 'both from the point of view of material interests and racial affinity.[1] A tripartite arrangement was the ideal solution; short of this Britain must content herself with the next best arrangement – alliance with Japan, intimate co-operation and friendship with the United States of America and France.'[2] Unfortunately, the state of American opinion was to make this latter alternative as difficult to attain as the former.[3] Further consideration of the problem went on in Whitehall in the next two months, and the naval and army authorities were found to be at one with the Foreign Office in the priority they attached to avoiding any breach with the United States.[4]

If she abandoned the alliance, to satisfy dominion and American sentiment, Britain had to rely on the Americans to defend both her Far Eastern possessions and China against any future Japanese aggression.[5] It was hard to see how this could be achieved. Certainly the Americans tried to get British co-operation when it suited their immediate purposes, as for instance in trying to put pressure on the Japanese to get their troops out of Siberia, claiming they were in some sense trustees for the Russia of the future;[6] but it was also felt that the Americans had repeatedly let down the Chinese who had depended on them. Even so, there seemed to be no alternative to an Anglo-American

---

did not wish the defence of India to figure in any revised treaty. *D.B.F.P.*, series 1, vol. XIV, pp. 334, 338.

[1] For U.S. pressure on Britain to abandon the alliance., see ibid., pp. 19, 38.

[2] Foreign Office memorandum, 28 July 1920. *B.D.F.P.*, series 1, vol. VI, pp. 1016–23.

[3] The case for a tripartite agreement was set out in a Foreign Office memorandum by V. Wellesley on 1 June 1920. *B.D.F.P.*, series 1, vol. XIV, pp. 32–6.

[4] *B.D.F.P.*, series 1, vol. VI, pp. 1049–55. The Foreign Office was also concerned about the congruity of the treaty with the League of Nations covenant and secured Japanese assent to a joint note to the league on 8 July 1920, saying that it was recognized that the treaty could not continue in its existing form after July 1921. *B.D.F.P.*, series 1, vol. XIV, p. 38. There was a difference of opinion as to whether the treaty continued unless denounced or expired automatically unless renewed. For this reason the Japanese opposed the British suggestions in the spring of 1921 for a three-month temporary renewal to give time for negotiations. The Japanese position was upheld by the Lord Chancellor. I. H. Nish, 'Japan and the Ending of the Anglo-Japanese Alliance', in K. Bourne and D. C. Watt (eds), *Studies in International History* (1967), pp. 376–7. Cf. *B.D.F.P.*, series 1, vol. XIV, pp. 287 ff.

[5] Kerr to Dove, 13 July 1920. Lothian Papers, Box 186.

[6] *B.D.F.P.*, series 1, vol. XIV, p. 70.

combination to contain Japan,[1] though hopes of modifying the agreement so as to make it more acceptable and a prelude to a wider agreement including the United States were not abandoned.[2] A Foreign Office committee which re-examined the problem in October–November 1920 reported on 21 January 1921 with a renewed emphasis on the cardinal importance of Anglo-American relations, and once more advocated a tripartite *entente* as the best solution. The second-best alternative was to renew the agreement in a modified form allowing for the eventual adhesion of the United States.[3]

It was therefore not in dominion eyes alone that relations with the United States had become the decisive factor. The same thing was recognized inside the British government, and there was considerable parliamentary pressure also against renewing the alliance. Yet this is not to say that dominion pressure was unimportant.[4] In commenting on correspondence with Canada on this subject it was pointed out in the Foreign Office that, unless satisfaction was given to the Dominions, it was by no means impossible that Britain would come to see 'a gravitation of Canada, perhaps also of Australia and New Zealand, towards America for a union of Pacific Nations of the Anglo-Saxon stock'.[5]

Canadian opinion was, then as later, sensitive to what was actually said south of the border, and there is some evidence that pressure was brought to bear on Meighen to express his objections to the alliance; but the main arguments put forward by Canada were based on her own assessment of the situation.[6] The basis of Canadian policy can be found in a memorandum by the legal adviser to the department of external affairs, Loring Christie, who wrote it after discussions in London with Curzon and Lloyd George in January 1921. Christie dismissed the need for the alliance on the ground that both the Russian and German threats were things of the past, and suggested that Canada take the initiative in proposing to the Americans the calling of a conference on naval and Far Eastern affairs.[7] The actual proposal along

---

[1] Memorandum by Sir B. Alston, 1 August 1920. On it Sir Eyre Crowe minuted: 'I wish I could share Sir B. Alston's robust faith in American "co-operation" in China or elsewhere.' *B.D.F.P.*, series 1, vol. XIV, pp. 81–6.

[2] Memorandum by Wellesley, 1 September 1920. Ibid., pp. 106–11.

[3] Ibid., pp. 154, 224–6.　　　　　　　　　　　　　　[4] Nish, loc. cit.

[5] Memorandum by Mr Lampson on correspondence with the Canadian government relating to the Anglo-Japanese Alliance, 8 April 1921. *D.B.F.P.*, series 1, vol. XIV, pp. 271–6.

[6] Graham, *Meighen*, vol. 2, pp. 75–6.

[7] The memorandum dated 1 February 1921 is printed in A. R. M. Lower, 'Loring Christie

these lines was made by Meighen to Lloyd George in a telegram of 15 February, but the British government held out against taking any decision before the imperial conference met and although not averse to discussing the idea of a Pacific powers conference at the meeting, could not assent to it in advance because of the position taken up by Australia.[1]

Public pronouncements by the Australian prime minister indicated indeed that Australia still regarded the Anglo-Japanese alliance as useful provided it could be made acceptable to American opinion. New Zealand opinion was even more unequivocal on its favour, and Canada was therefore somewhat isolated in the extent of both governmental and public condemnation of the alliance.[2]

On 30 May 1921 the British cabinet decided that it should ask the imperial conference to support renewing the alliance and to look to the United States to call a conference to deal with the wider issues.[3] It is probable that this decision was in part the result of a frosty reception given to Willert when he sounded out the State department on the proposed replacement of the alliance by a tripartite pact,[4] but there could be no doubt that any decision for renewal would meet with strong American hostility.[5]

At the first discussion of the subject at the imperial conference on 21 June, Hughes suggested a conference with the United States and Japan to find out a mutually acceptable basis for a renewal of the alliance, and Massey also defended its renewal as against Smuts's assertion that alliances were no longer needed.[6] On 25 June a telegram arrived from the British ambassador at Washington describing a con-

and the Genesis of the Washington Conference of 1921–2', *Canadian Historical Review*, vol. XLVII (1966). 'Christie as the trusted adviser and confidant of both Sir Robert Borden and Arthur Meighen' was 'largely responsible for whatever intellectual coherence Canadian external policy possessed during the period 1918–1921'. Eayrs, op. cit., p. 23 fn.

[1] Secretary of state for the colonies to governor-general of Canada, (draft), 26 April 1921. *B.D.F.P.*, series 1, vol. XIV, p. 276.

[2] Tate and Foy, loc. cit., pp. 535–8.

[3] M. G. Fry, 'Anglo-American Canadian Relations with Special Reference to Far Eastern and Naval Issues, 1918–1922', *Bull. Inst. Hist. Research*, vol. XXXIX (1966).

[4] Vinson, loc. cit., p. 257.

[5] For an account of agitation against the treaty in the United States, see the despatches from Sir Auckland Geddes of 6 and 24 June 1922. *B.D.F.P.*, series 1, vol. XIV, pp. 300, 310. Sir Auckland Geddes (1879–1952) (first baron, 1942) held a number of ministerial posts between 1917 and 1920. He was ambassador to the United States March 1920–February 1924. For previous American representations about the Alliance, see *U.S. Foreign Relations, 1920*, vol. 2 (1936), pp. 679–85.

[6] Meeting of representatives of United Kingdom, dominions and India, 21 June 1921. PRO. CAB. 32. 2.

versation he had had with the secretary of state, Hughes, on the previous day in which the latter had shown strong disquiet at the suggested renewal of the Anglo-Japanese alliance but had favoured some declaration of policy by all three powers in the form of identical notes.[1] The conference was thus aware of the basic American position when, on 29 June, Meighen made his speech demanding the abrogation of the treaty.[2]

Meighen received Smuts's support, but Balfour's report of the C.I.D.'s contention that Britain's naval weakness in the Pacific area made the alliance essential, fortified Curzon's earlier defence of the instrument. And Hughes (with support from Massey) pointed out how difficult it was to ascertain American opinion, or to assess the American naval programme. If she had the choice, Australia would prefer the United States as an ally to Japan; but the choice was not on offer. Nothing but full assurances by the United States of Australia's security would lead him to vote for abrogation.

On 1 July, however, Lloyd George agreed to a suggestion by Meighen that the foreign secretary should hold discussions with representatives of Japan, China, and the U.S.A. to prepare the ground for a Pacific conference. Hughes felt the decision to renew the alliance should be taken at once and that conference discussion should be limited to the form of the renewal.[3] It must be assumed that the British government's marked change of front indicated an awareness of American pressures rather than conversion through Meighen's pleadings, and in any event the programme more or less agreed upon by the Empire prime ministers was overtaken by an American initiative. It was made plain that (whatever false impressions may have been created by an inadequately instructed American ambassador in London) the American government would not approve of the prolongation of the Anglo-Japanese alliance in any form, and it was strongly hinted that the prospects of a naval agreement were bound up with this issue.[4] On 8 July, the day on which an agreement on the United States naval programme was reached (and on which a truce was declared in Ireland) the American government sent its note calling for a conference on armaments; on July 9 the scope of the proposed gathering was widened to include the whole

[1] Geddes to Curzon, 24 June 1921, *D.B.F.P.*, series 1, vol. XIV, pp. 311–12.
[2] Meetings of 28 and 29 June. PRO. CAB. 32. 2.
[3] Notes of meeting on 1 July 1921. PRO. CAB. 32. 2. Balfour's oral report is in PRO. CAB. 21. 187.
[4] Geddes to Curzon, 6 July 1921. *B.D.F.P.*, series 1, vol. XIV, p. 326; 7 July, ibid., pp. 328–9.

range of Far Eastern questions. On the following day President Harding agreed to make these initiatives public.[1]

It is clear that the expansion of the proposed conference was due to the interlocking of the British and American initiatives. Curzon had suggested to the American ambassador on 5 July that the American president call a conference to deal with the Far Eastern question.[2] The prime minister was now under pressure to make a statement of his intentions, and would thus be obliged to indicate that this inquiry had been sent and that a reply was awaited. Politically it was highly un-desirable that the president should appear to be responding to a British initiative and the ambassador in London urged the secretary of state to forestall it.[3]

But the American initiative went further. It had been Curzon's intention that the meeting of the Pacific powers should be held in London before and separately from, the Washington meeting on dis-armament.[4] There were two strong reasons for this. It did not seem to Curzon that there was any hope of an agreement on naval disarmament unless there had been a prior agreement on some system of security to replace the Anglo-Japanese alliance, and London was far better situated for the full representation of the dominion governments. A conference in Washington trying to take all these questions together would result in confusion.[5] But President Harding and secretary of state Hughes were not going to be deprived of their glory, and after struggling along for a few more days, Curzon was obliged on 1 August to call a halt and accept the American plan as it stood.[6]

It is possible that Curzon underestimated the difficulties for the United States government, at a time when anti-Japanese and to some extent anti-British feeling ran so high, in accepting London as the scene for a conference dealing with an area where the United States had come to claim a preponderant interest. In the reaction against the results of the peace conference any excursion by an American presi-dent or secretary of state into the European area was bound to be politically harmful, and this was even more obviously true if London were the capital in question. Flanked by the dominions, whose new

[1] Sprout, op. cit., pp. 131 ff.
[2] Curzon to Geddes, 9 July 1921. *D.B.F.P.*, series 1, vol. XIV, pp. 336.
[3] G. Harvey to Hughes, 8 July 1921. *U.S. Foreign Relations*, 1921, vol. I (1936), pp. 19–21.
[4] Curzon to Geddes, 14 July 1921. *D.B.F.P.* series 1, vol. XIV, pp. 342–3.
[5] Memorandum by Curzon, 24 July 1921. Ibid., pp. 345–51.
[6] Curzon to Geddes, 1 August 1921. Ibid., p. 363.

status the Americans neither understood nor approved of, Britain might appear to retain the leading position that it was essential to deny to her if any agreements reached were to have a chance of securing congressional approval.

Nevertheless, in retrospect it is clear that the agreement to leave Pacific and naval questions to the outcome of a conference held in Washington marked a turning-point in Britain's affairs. The great international congresses of the past had indicated by their venues the balance of forces prevailing at the time: Vienna, Berlin, Paris. As these dealt with the affairs of the European continent, Britain as a semi-detached member of the European system could afford to accept these arrangements, but she could not so easily dismiss the implications of a conference dealing with global matters. Instead of the Anglo-Japanese alliance, based on a nice calculation of mutual interests and relative capacities, Britain was to enter into a new system whose functioning would principally depend upon the incalculable shifts and whims of the American democracy. No one looking at the Wilsonian record could have much confidence in the outcome.

From the point of view of all the governments concerned the decision to give absolute priority to the American relationship could easily be defended; bitter experience had shown that Britain could no longer maintain a European balance without being certain of ultimate American backing; Canada, Australia, and New Zealand, all determined to defend policies of racial exclusiveness against pressure from Asia, found in the United States a power closer to their own way of thinking and better placed to assist them than the distant mother-country. South Africa was mainly concerned with the negative desire to keep out of European affairs so as to preserve her own uneasy political balance and believed that British alignment with the United States was the best guarantee of Britain pursuing an isolationist policy. But what was true of the parts was not necessarily true of the whole. The Americans might find it in their interests to give support to each of the several English-speaking democracies, but to the Empire as a system – political or economic – they remained either indifferent or actually hostile. To place the defence of empire in the hands of the Americans was to accept its ultimate demise. In this sense, the instincts of Curzon, as of Milner, were perfectly valid. But the working out of the consequence of abandoning the claim to maritime supremacy were not to be visible for some time yet.

Chapter 7

APOGEE OF EMPIRE

When the prime ministers of the British Empire conferred in London in the late summer of 1921 they represented an empire that had reached its maximum territorial extent. Although the allocation of mandates by the League of Nations was still unconfirmed, Britain and the dominions had added to their island possessions in the Pacific, acquired very large areas in Africa, and extended their hold over Egypt to a large part of the eastern Mediterranean littoral and to the valley of the Tigris and Euphrates. The patriotic schoolboy could rejoice in maps of the world in which more was coloured red than had ever been coloured red before, and was ever to be coloured red again. But to the schoolboy, as indeed to most of the public at large both in Britain and abroad, the precise distinctions between dominions, colonies, protectorates, and the various classes of mandate were not of any great significance. The unity of the crown concealed the diversity of status of the ruled.

Yet the problems confronting the Empire–Commonwealth as a whole and those of Britain, its heart, in particular, had by no means been resolved by wartime victory or the largely successful diplomacy of the peace. For almost a century Britain had faced two principal rivals. The first of them, Russia, weakened by revolution and civil war, was for the time being incapable of renewing her attack upon Britain's world position except through the weapons of propaganda and sedition. Germany, its fleet destroyed and its army severely limited by treaty, was likewise in no immediate position to resume the contest. France, lately Britain's ally, might appear to many people to be pursuing a course in Europe that had little long-term prospect of success; but despite the unresolved friction between the two powers in the Middle East, there could be no serious expectation that relations between them would deteriorate to the point, last reached in the 1890s, when an Anglo-French conflict had to be reckoned as a serious possibility. This was even truer of Britain's principal new rival at sea, the United States. Serious strains might be felt from time to time, but neither British nor dominion opinion could imagine their settlement through recourse to arms.[1]

There remained, then, only Japan as a power with possibly conflicting aims, against whom in the last resort armed resistance might become necessary; and this explains the reluctance of British statesmen to whittle away the ties that had linked the fortunes of the two island empires for the past two decades. But there was another reason, too, for trying to avoid a direct clash with Japan. The competition between the European imperial powers that had provided the main stuff of international politics for centuries was clearly no longer the sole danger. The combined strength of European technology, European social and military organization, and European self-confidence, that had made Asia and Africa, like the Americas before them, an arena of conflict rather than an active element in world politics, no longer appeared supreme. Stimulated by the spectacle of the internecine warfare in which European civilization appeared to be destroying itself, and offered in communism and related revolutionary doctrines which were more powerful stimulants to resistance than their traditional creeds, the non-European peoples were claiming the right to be heard. It is true that the process was a gradual and an uneven one, and even where the new nationalisms were most vocal only the minority, mainly western-educated, were directly involved. But this minority might appeal outside its own ranks, if only because of the violent reactions which could be elicited by evidence of European and North American colour prejudice.

In such a perspective Japan's claim to racial equality, spurned by Wilson and the makers of the covenant but now insistent throughout the Pacific area, gave a new and sinister aspect to any possible conflict. Would not the subject peoples of the Empire heed the call to throw off white domination and would this not result in civil war within the Empire between its white and coloured peoples?[2] The fact that such questions could be asked at all suggested that the imperial problem was no longer one of satisfying the aspirations to self-government of peoples of broadly similar background and racial stock to the British – the

[1] Hankey in 1920 was still arguing that in defence planning it was necessary to consider the possibility of war with the United States being forced upon Britain. 'Survey of the Naval, Military and Air Obligations of the British Empire', prepared by the secretary for the C.I.D., 27 September 1920. PRO. CAB. 4. 7.
[2] See Admiral Sir P. Grant to Edward Grigg, 2 July 1921, and Grigg's reply: Grigg Papers, Unclassified box (1921).

Irish, the French-Canadians, the Boers – but of finding a *modus vivendi* with non-European peoples of a bewildering variety of colours, creeds, and cultural patterns. Superimposed upon Britain's conflicts with her old and new rivals was this new conflict between all the nations which had for some four centuries been carrying European civilization across the oceans and the peoples whose own development had been, for good or ill, violently wrenched out of course.

One must not imagine that things presented themselves in this neat and schematic way as early as the aftermath of the first world war; least of all did most statesmen perceive them in these terms. It was rather that the duality of the problem complicated their tasks and gave a certain ambiguity to their professions. It was not the Japanese (nor for that matter the Russians) alone who were willing to meddle for profit in the nationalist stirrings within other people's empires.

We have already seen how complex were the emotions with which the British faced the demand for constitutional progress in India, and how hard it was to decide at what point the need for a wider degree of consent should be given priority over the demands of efficiency which usually counselled a slower degree of change than the nationalist leaders were willing to accept. But in the post-war years the Egyptian situation provided even clearer examples of the problem. At the imperial conference Smuts had argued that Britain should limit herself as far as possible to holding on to such of her gains as were strategically essential; attempts to govern oriental communities on western lines were bound to fail. Massey replied that this in effect meant abandoning all such countries and this in turn would mean the end of the British Empire. No country was as important to the Empire as Egypt, except Britain herself. Australia and New Zealand might be parted with and the Empire continue; but it could not survive without its main artery.[1]

What was difficult for the British to realize was that the leaders of these countries, even the so-called moderates, would not be prepared to fit into a system created for quite different purposes at an earlier time: 'Lloyd George,' we are told, 'saw nothing amiss in taking Adli Pasha ... into the room in which the Imperial Conference had sat and pointing to a chair which he said was being reserved for Egypt's entry into the British Commonwealth of Nations.'[2] Any attempt to assert the British vision of the future by force would expose Britain to the taunt of

[1] Meeting of 6 July 1921. PRO. CAB. 32. 2.
[2] Monroe, op. cit., p. 71.

346

aggressive imperialism, and she was the more exposed to such taunts because of the disappearance of the old autocratic and military empires of the continent.[1] Could Britain stay in Egypt or elsewhere unless she could defend her action in terms of benefits conferred upon the peoples concerned? 'My own feeling is that in Egypt, as in India, we have now to face the ultimate question whether we regard ourselves as having any moral basis of our own or merely a diplomatic position which must be progressively weakened by pressure and agitation along nationalist lines. If we do not proclaim our own belief in our moral basis and act up to it in every way there will be very serious trouble in store.'[2]

But it was precisely this sense of a moral basis for imperial rule that was lacking in Britain itself. Anti-imperialism in Britain had once more to be taken into account, particularly, of course, when questions arose of actually adding to Britain's overseas commitments. The Mesopotamian imbroglio gave this feeling its most obvious opportunity of influencing policy.

> You are going to have an Arab state [wrote the permanent secretary of the India Office] whether you like it or not, whether Mesopotamia wants it or not . . . All these things are going to be contrary to our most cherished hopes, and nothing you or I can say or do will alter them . . . the idea of Mesopotamia as the model of an efficiently administered British dependency or protectorate is dead (the same thing is dying in India and decomposing in Egypt) and . . . an entirely new order of ideas reigns.[3]

Military and financial weakness made direct rule impossible; the only hope was to set up some 'modicum of Arab institutions' which could safely be left while the strings were pulled from Britain, something which would not cost very much, that labour could swallow consistently with its principles (since labour was bound to come into office soon), but which would preserve essential British interests.[4] However, concealed imperialism was to prove as hard to defend and not all that much cheaper than the open imperialism that was thought to be on the way out.

The reasons why anti-imperialism had made these new strides were

[1] Chirol to Grigg, 26 December 1921. Grigg Papers, ibid.
[2] Grigg to Godfrey Thomas, 26 January 1922. Grigg Papers, 1921 file, Godfrey Thomas letters.
[3] Arthur Hirtzel to Arnold Wilson, 16 July 1919. John Marlowe, *Late Victorian* (1967), p. 165.
[4] Hirtzel to Wilson, 2 February 1920. Ibid., pp. 182–3.

347

not always easy to disentangle. Hirtzel may have exaggerated the purely economy aspect. The effect of the war in confirming the prognostications of earlier exponents of the anti-imperialist argument may have been more important.[1] While there was an ideology of the new Empire-Commonwealth, its principal protagonists were less influential intellectually than their opponents. 'Bloomsbury' and other literary circles were more likely to be strongly anti-imperialist and sceptical or derisive where traditional views of Britain's rights and duties overseas were concerned.[2]

One aspect of this attitude was a renewed sensitivity to the use of force to safeguard what were presumed to be narrowly British interests and with it went a tendency to deride the authority and expertise of the man on the spot. This was not unimportant. The most able young men were unlikely to want to pursue careers which, whatever their intrinsic attractions, carried diminishing prestige at home; and those already serving acquired a sense of grievance because their predicament was not understood and the dilemmas they often faced ignored. Just as the sympathy expressed for General Dyer after his dismissal exacerbated Indian opinion, so the fact that his action had been disowned by the politicians at home exasperated many of the British serving overseas.

The state of British opinion was the more important in that it became clear between the end of the war and 1921 that whatever new forms might be devised for the Empire, the notion that it could function as a single unit was untenable in the light of all the evidence to the contrary. Some people might profess to ignore the extent to which the growth in strength and self-reliance of the dominions tended to make them emphasize their own national aspirations at the expense of common objectives, but the Smuts–Botha concept of the Commonwealth was in tune with the basic line of development. If a conservative Canadian premier like Arthur Meighen could take so doggedly independent a line, his likely liberal successor, Mackenzie King would hardly be more amenable to imperial persuasions.[3] Hughes's imperial talk did not con-

---

[1] The impact of the war on British society and British opinion generally is far from having received a definitive treatment. See the provocative survey of some of the writing on the subject in Arthur Marwick, 'The Impact of the First World War on British Society', *Journal of Contemporary History*, vol. 3 (1968).

[2] Indications of the outlook of fashionable intellectuals can be gathered, for instance, from the autobiographies of Leonard Woolf and David Garnett, and from Michael Holroyd's *Life of Lytton Strachey*.

[3] W. L. Mackenzie King (1874–1950), a former liberal minister and specialist on labour relations, was elected as Laurier's successor in August 1919. He became prime minister after

ceal a very precisely Australian view of the world. Only New Zealand, as Massey's pronouncements showed, was compelled by its remoteness, weakness, and orientation towards the British market to beat the imperial drum for want of any other instrument.

Imperial federation was a dead duck; so too was Chamberlain's idea of an Empire united into a single economic system by the magic of preference. The idea that meetings such as that of the summer of 1921 indicated the continued existence of some form of 'imperial cabinet' totally disregarded the power of the centrifugal forces. In consequence it was Britain, and Britain almost alone, that bore the burden of maintaining the imperial system, ruling the dependent territories, providing for their defence, assisting in their economic and political development and representing their interests in and to the world at large. And however the social and intellectual consequences of the war may be assessed, there can be no doubt of the material difficulties that Britain faced in fulfilling these tasks.

To assess the war's impact on the British economy in quantitative terms is not easy.[1] In many respects it merely accelerated certain trends which were already perceptible before 1914 and may indeed have been important largely as an excuse for ignoring them and for believing that the problems themselves would disappear when the effects of the war had been overcome. The loss in overseas investments, the setbacks in overseas markets where American and Japanese competition had been favoured by Britain's need to concentrate upon war production, and the slow recovery of Britain's former customers in Europe, the tangle of war debts and reparations – all these helped to weaken Britain's ability to maintain and extend political and military commitments abroad. Furthermore, pent-up home demand and a shift towards higher standards of personal consumption helped to give force to demands for reduced taxation and to explain the zeal with which economy in public spending was pursued.

Once the peace conference was over it was possible to try to assess the new situation and to see how far it was possible to assist in recovery by keeping levels of armaments as low as possible.[2] We have seen the

the election of December 1921 and held office until 1930 (except for the period June–September 1926). He became prime minister once more in 1935 and held office until 1948; for all but the last two years of this premiership he also held the office of secretary of state for external affairs.

[1] For a summary view of the question, see W. Ashworth, *An Economic History of England, 1870–1939* (1960), ch. XII, 'The Economic Consequences of the War'.

[2] 'Towards a National Policy': memorandum by Hankey, 17 July 1919. PRO. CAB. 21. 159.

impact of these considerations upon naval affairs. Where the army was concerned, a return to the voluntary system was treated as inevitable, though attempts were made to reshape the forces to the new views of the demands likely to be made upon them. In the view of the military the principal change from the pre-1914 period was the disappearance of the dangers of invasion or of a great European war. There was thus no need to be in a position to contemplate a sudden expansion of the forces or to have troops specifically allotted to home defence. Elsewhere in 1919 the state of Ireland seemed as bad as in 1914, and the dangers of trouble in Egypt, Mesopotamia, and India much greater. One would therefore require forces not only for garrison duty but also as reserves capable of providing reinforcements at short notice.[1]

Nevertheless the concentration of military advice upon the problems of internal security in the Empire and its opinion that there was no prospect of a full-scale war in the near future justified the cabinet's decision on 15 August 1919 that planning in the services should be based on the assumption that there would be no major war for ten years ahead; and the 'ten-year rule' thus began its career; it was later several times extended and in 1929 made self-perpetuating.[2]

The general staff was not happy about the extent of its commitments. In a new survey of the position in the summer of 1920, it pointed out that although the cabinet had ruled out the possibility of a new war on the continent for from five to ten years ahead – the 'ten-year' rule was obviously still not a hard and fast one – there was the question of the guarantee to France and of the tasks allotted to British forces under the peace treaty or by the League of Nations. While the existence of the latter organization might just possibly reduce the likelihood of war against 'civilized powers', in the Middle East it would have just the reverse effect since it would provide a forum for complaints against British rule. The existing forces were fully stretched, and there were no reserves to meet emergencies. Only the strength of the air force prevented the position from being even more serious.[3]

In a further survey of the situation prepared by Hankey in the autumn, it was argued that the development of the forces of the self-governing dominions made it unlikely that the obligations on the imperial government to come to their aid would be greater or even as

[1] Note by Sir Henry Wilson on the strength and functions of the post-war army, 7 August 1919, Austen Chamberlain Papers, Box AC. 24/99c.
[2] Johnson, *Government by Committee*, p. 199. Roskill, op. cit., p. 215.
[3] 'Military Liabilities of the Empire': General Staff papers, 27 July 1920. PRO. CAB. 4. 7.

great as before the war. Meanwhile it was not possible to dismiss the European scene altogether. The failure of the United States to ratify the treaty of Versailles had technically invalidated the guarantee to France, but it seemed incredible that Britain would stand idly by if France were the victim of German aggression, and she could certainly not afford to see the Low Countries dominated by Germany, or France over-run. Guidance must be given before military plans could be made; and there was also the question as to what might be implied by Article X of the league covenant, though so far the league council had given no indication of what members were supposed to do in order to be in a position to uphold it.[1]

British defence policy was thus in a not unfamiliar predicament. While the planners wanted a firm indication of the commitments they were supposed to meet,[2] the government could not be certain of how the situation would develop in different parts of the world, nor was it willing to insure against all possible trouble through heavier defence expenditure. By the summer of 1921 the dominance of the financial factor could be taken for granted. It would still be helpful if dominion troops could be relied upon in an emergency, for instance in the Middle East, should the necessary British forces not be available.[3] But the dominions could hardly be expected to concur.

The only relief for Britain was that she no longer needed to retain an imperial garrison in South Africa. In principle that country's responsibility for its own defence had been accepted at the time of the Union and by 1916, all British forces had been withdrawn. In 1921 the imperial command in South Africa was finally wound up and the naval contribution first paid by Cape Colony and Natal in 1898 also ceased to be paid. All that remained was the naval dockyard at Simonstown,

[1] 'Survey of the Naval Military and Air Obligations of the British Empire', prepared for the C.I.D. by the secretary, 27 September 1920. PRO. CAB. 4. 7. Article X: 'The Members of the League undertake to respect and preserve as against external aggression the territorial integrity and existing political independence of all Members of the League. In case of any such aggression or in case of any threat or danger of such aggression the Council shall advise upon the means by which this obligation shall be fulfilled.'
[2] A Foreign Office memorandum contained a formidable list of British commitments under six headings: 'Treaty obligations of a nature to involve H.M.G. in war or military action; treaty obligations of a less specific character; treaty obligations of a local and limited character; obligations not yet undertaken but which may shortly be embodied in a treaty; obligations incurred not by signed treaty but by a public or written assurance; moral responsibilities.' 'British Commitments Abroad': Foreign Office for C.I.D., 10 July 1920. PRO. CAB. 4. 7.
[3] Standing defence sub-committee of the C.I.D.: 'Revised summary of Military Agenda for Imperial Cabinet' [sic]. Austen Chamberlain Papers, Box AC. 26. Cabinet file.

whose use was guaranteed to the British government in perpetuity though its own defences were henceforth a matter for the Union.[1]

For these reasons the hope of permanent high level dominion representation on a revived committee of imperial defence was not to be fulfilled,[2] and the machinery of defence became an almost entirely United Kingdom affair.[3] Even so, its appropriate form was again a matter of some doubt.

The problems arose in part, of course, from the existence of the new air arm. After much discussion, the Air Ministry had been set up as a separate service department in January 1918 and the Royal Air Force had taken on its independent identity in April.[4] Efficiency and economy both seemed to argue for a single ministry of defence with a single supply agency, but the Haldane Report on the machinery of government, published in January 1919, rejected the proposal and advocated a return to the pre-war C.I.D. system.[5] The suggestion was also strongly resisted by Hankey when the problem was considered by the standing defence sub-committee of the cabinet, under Balfour's chairmanship in 1920–21.[6] It was, however, commended on grounds of economy in the Geddes' report in February 1922.[7] The C.I.D. itself as a committee under the prime minister did not resume its activities until February 1921 but the system of sub-committees which was its characteristic method of functioning was once more in full swing soon after the end of the war.[8]

It was not in defence matters only that the swing back towards the pre-war methods of handling government business was pronounced. The war cabinet system itself lasted only until November 1919, when the old-style cabinet of departmental chiefs was restored with, initially, a cabinet numbering twenty. Most of the new ministries set up during the war were abolished: Information in November 1918, National Service in March 1919, Reconstruction in June 1919, Munitions,

---

[1] *C.H.B.E.*, vol. VIII (2nd edn, 1963), pp. 669–70.
[2] Johnson, op. cit., p. 213.
[3] The need for dominion representation was stressed in proposals put forward by the House of Commons army committee to the prime minister on 14 June 1920. PRO. CAB. 4. 7. Cf. Johnson, op. cit., p. 170.
[4] In January 1919 Churchill became both secretary of state for air and secretary of state for war. The air ministry was given a separate head again in April 1921.
[5] *Report of the Machinery of Government Committee.* Cd. 9230. 1918.
[6] 'The Standing Defence Sub-Committee was for two years or more' – 1920–1922 – 'the virtual replacement of the C.I.D.' Johnson, op. cit., p. 170.
[7] *First Interim Report of the Committee on National expenditure.* Cmd. 1581, 1922.
[8] See papers on proposed ministry of defence. PRO. CAB. 4. 8; Roskill, op. cit., p. 37.

Shipping and Food in 1921. Only Transport and Pensions survived – and in a rather subordinate status.[1]

All that remained from the wartime was an increasing use of cabinet committees and, despite strong parliamentary attacks, the cabinet secretariat.[2] Even so, the growth in the functions of the state had been accelerated and this helped to fortify the claims of the Treasury to pre-eminence in the governing machine, and the unification of government service (except for the foreign office and diplomatic service) under its aegis. Before 1914 there had been a great degree of autonomy in the departments on staff matters and interchange of staff was unusual. But immediately after the war, the tripartite system of the administrative, executive and clerical classes was introduced into all ministries – the executive grade itself had existed since 1875. In 1919, the permanent secretary to the Treasury was given the title of head of the civil service and the task of advising the prime minister about civil service appointments. In the same year a group of establishment divisions was established in the Treasury, and in 1920 it was laid down that the consent of the prime minister (advised of course by the head of the civil service) was to be sought for the appointment or removal of permanent heads of departments, their deputies and the principal finance and establishment officers.

The impetus which this gave to unification and centralization in the civil service machine and the problems aroused by the ambition of the first holder of the office of head of the civil service to bring the Foreign Office within the scope of his responsibilities belong to a later period.[3] But the origins of the later clash were already visible, and the Foreign Office itself and the diplomatic service were somewhat under a cloud when the war ended, as a result of wartime criticism of their alleged failings.

Some of the criticism was the inevitable outcome of specific failures, notably in the Balkans for which other and deeper reasons may well be advanced. But it could also be argued that in a newer and fiercer world some of the characteristics of the old system were an obstacle.[4] Britain,

---

[1] H. Daalder, *Cabinet Reform in Britain, 1914–1963* (Stanford University Press, 1964), p. 56.
[2] J. P. Mackintosh, *The British Cabinet* (1962), pp. 355 ff.
[3] The first holder of the new post was Sir Warren Fisher (1879–1948) who was permanent secretary to the Treasury from August 1919 to September 1939 after a civil service career on the revenue and social service side. It is clear that he was to be second only to Hankey, if that, in his influence on affairs, for instance on the defence side, but the extent of his influence is difficult to document and no adequate study of his career exists.
[4] 'Give yourself the pleasure of an interview with any of our moth-eaten Ambassadors who

it was argued, was now a democracy and this should be felt in its diplomacy as well.[1] In the immediate post-war period, one important change was made. Between 1919 and 1920, effect was given to the recommendations of the royal commission of 1911–14 in the amalgamation of the staff of the Foreign Office in London with that of the diplomatic service abroad. It was hoped that, as a result of this change, the office in London would contain men whose experience in missions abroad would make them more effective interpreters of incoming dispatches, while those who went to serve in foreign capitals would do so in fuller awareness of the trends of thought in Whitehall. For the time being the consular service remained separate, as did the new commercial diplomatic service created to develop the work of the former commercial attachés and working under the aegis of the department of overseas trade which had been set up in 1917 as the joint responsibility of the Foreign Office and Board of Trade. The promotion of British business was therefore not given the priority that some people would have wished to see in the new competitive world; and although the abolition of the old requirement of an independent income for entrants into the diplomatic service and the prescribed two years initial service as an attaché without pay were clearly moves in the direction of widening the area of recruitment, the foreign service continued to be considered, and not wholly without reason, as one of the principal remaining aristocratic elements in the body-politic.[2]

Nevertheless, it would be wrong to make too much of this fact. There is no reason to believe that the foreign service as inherited from the pre-1914 world, or as now modified, was in itself less realistic than other sections of British government, or than the broad mass of politicians themselves, in its perceptions of the country's dangers and opportunities in the new era. The real difference remained between those for

have returned from the belligerent countries: and I do not even yet despair of getting you to agree with me that the diplomatic service, with its predilection for promotion by seniority, its method of recruitment, its concomitant of divorcing the ambassadors from everything that the Home Government is thinking, its practise of refusing to speak English but of communicating among themselves or at home in the language of diplomatic telegrams – all these have robbed our diplomacy of life.' Montagu to Eric Drummond, 26 February 1916. Waley, op. cit., p. 92.

[1] 'At the root of this failure' (to establish tighter bonds with France and effective British leadership in the alliance) 'lies the inability of our people to understand that Democracies cannot manipulate successfully an old-fashioned oligarchic instrument such as the Foreign Offices of Europe and its diplomatic service provide.' Esher to Sir William Robertson, 20 June 1917. Balfour Papers, B.M. Add. 49719.

[2] D. C. Bishop, *The Administration of British Foreign Relations* (Syracuse University Press, 1961), p. 206.

whom foreign policy was a matter of securing the requirements of the nation at the minimal cost and recognizing the increasingly severe limitations that Britain had to accept, and those who were prone to believe that the incantations of the proper formulae would make foreign policy in the old sense a thing of the past.

The temptation to rely upon the League of Nations as a method of avoiding effort and expense was an ever-present one. Dislike of the way in which it appeared to have become a substitute for action by the British Empire was expressed by Massey at the imperial conference. Hughes, who was also suspicious, took comfort from the fact that Curzon had suggested (he denied this!) that the league could be ignored and the dominions could act directly through the Foreign Office when it was in the Empire's interests that they should do so.[1] But, as we have seen, of the two forms of possible collective action it was the league, as the less demanding, that was gaining ground.

Indeed much that has rightly been criticized in post-war Britain — the intense conservatism of the restored peacetime regular army, and its apparent unwillingness to take account of the lessons of the war itself, must in part be ascribed to the very modest role that armed force was now allotted in the eyes of the country's political leadership.

Nor finally was the inchoate state of party politics in the concluding years of the Lloyd George régime and his intensely personal methods of conducting affairs conducive to a full appraisal of Britain's position in the world. Britain at the apogee of its empire lacked a doctrinal basis for that empire's defence. Indeed, the defeat of doctrinaire conceptions was treated as a net gain; empiricism was in the ascendant.

In the atmosphere of the immediately post-war years with their violent economic fluctuations, it was not easy to see what might be the long-term effects of the war upon the argument that Britain's best hopes of maintaining her world position lay in the development of empire trade, as it was still called. Between 1909 and 1913 British possessions had accounted on average for 24·7 per cent of Britain's imports; in the war years, the figure had risen to 28·8 per cent and in 1919 to 32 per cent. A drop to 25·3 per cent in 1920 was followed by a rise in 1921 to 27·8 per cent. Exports had followed a rather different course: 35·4 per cent in 1909–13; 34·1 per cent in 1914–18; 23·3 per cent in 1919, and up again to 34·3 per cent in 1920, and 39·9 per cent in 1921. Re-exports went from 12·3 per cent in 1909–13, to 12·8 per cent in 1914–18, down

[1] Meeting of 7 July 1921. PRO. CAB. 32. 2.

to 5·3 per cent in 1919, and then back up to 10·9 per cent in 1920, and 11·8 per cent in 1921. On the other hand, Europe which had taken 34·7 per cent of British exports in 1913 and whose diminished purchasing capacity could not be regarded as permanent remained no less important as a market. Its share had indeed risen during the war and was 55 per cent in 1919; it fell to 37·8 per cent in 1920, and to what proved a low point, 31·7 per cent in 1921. Imports by contrast sank very low during the war but began to rise again and accounted for 23·6 per cent in 1920, and 28·6 per cent in 1921.[1] (See Chart.)

It was too soon to see what the new patterns of migration and investment might be; but it could not be overlooked that by 1913, 78 per cent of British migrants were remaining within the Empire and that it accounted for 47 per cent of all overseas investment. By the provisions of the 1919 finance act, investment within the Empire was made more attractive by tax concessions.[2]

The fact remained, however, that no possibility of choice existed. However much the pattern of trade might alter, and however large the share of the Empire might continue to be, Britain could not dispense with her European markets nor fail to respond economically as well as politically to the changing face of the continent. A foreign observer of the British scene was to put the matter succinctly a couple of years later: 'In spite of the temptation to retire from the affairs of the Old World and devote all her energies to her Empire, Britain whether she wishes it or not, is always brought back to her European preoccupations. The very fundamental conditions of her existence force an international outlook upon her.'[3]

The economic factor is also relevant when considering the importance attached to the different parts of the Empire–Commonwealth. Of the total of British trade with the Empire in 1909–13, the dominions had accounted for 54·6, per cent, India for 26 per cent, Britain's other Asian possessions for 13·1 per cent and tropical Africa for only 3·4 per cent. The African empire was now enlarged, but it is worth noting surely how small a role was played by the main area of the new imperialism, by Joseph Chamberlain's 'undeveloped estates', in the general economic scene.

What is most difficult of all is to relate these and other statistics to

[1] W. Schlote, *British Overseas Trade from 1700 to the 1930's* (Oxford, Blackwell, 1952), statistical tables.
[2] S. Pollard, *The Development of the British Economy 1914–1920* (London, 1962), pp. 20, 196.
[3] A. Siegfried, *Post-War Britain* (London, Jonathan Cape, 1924), p. 67.

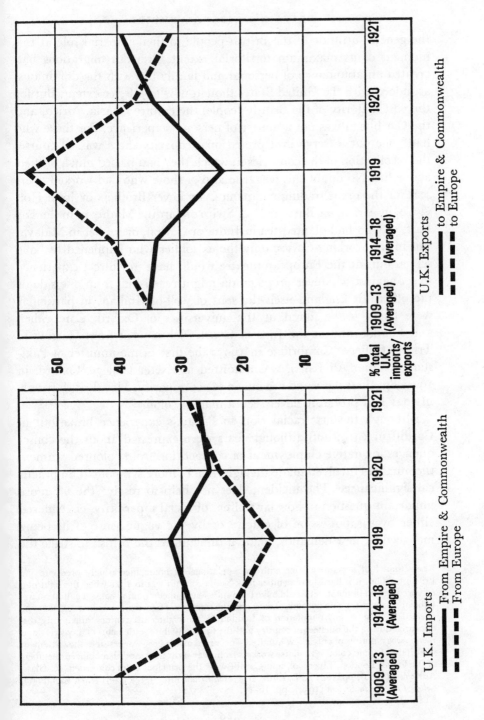

% total U.K. imports/exports

50
40
30
20
10
0

U.K. Exports

1909–13 (Averaged) 1914–18 (Averaged) 1919 1920 1921

—— to Empire & Commonwealth
---- to Europe

U.K. Imports

1909–13 (Averaged) 1914–18 (Averaged) 1919 1920 1921

—— From Empire & Commonwealth
---- From Europe

N

the general attitude of the British people to their imperial role at this moment of its maximum territorial extent. Previous migrations had created an abundance of personal and family ties with the dominions, as indeed with the United States though now to a lesser extent. But for the vast majority of the British people, the empire in Asia, Africa, and the Caribbean was not a matter of personal experience. For those who had gone out to serve in a professional capacity there was, of course, the recollection of the countries in which they had passed much of their active life. No doubt this was true also of those who had worked overseas for the great trading companies, for Lever Brothers or John Holt & Co. in Africa, for Butterfield & Swire or Jardine Matheson in the Far East, or who had planted tea in India or Ceylon, or rubber in Malaya. But in the working-classes, only the ex-soldier who happened to have served outside the European theatre would have any direct experience to set against whatever propaganda might reach him from one side or the other. In England itself the sons of well-off Indians in particular were likely to be found at the universities of Oxford, Cambridge, and London and at the Inns of Court. Nehru went from Harrow to Trinity College, Cambridge in 1907; the first prime minister of Pakistan, Liaquat Ali Khan, was admitted to Exeter College, Oxford, in 1921. But these were and are only a select minority. Most British people in 1921 had probably never seen a man of colour.[1]

Although the first racial riots in Britain's experience broke out in Cardiff in 1919, and although fears were expressed about the consequences for native employment of competition from coloured seamen, the numbers involved made the agitation of more symbolic than practical significance.[2] The incident does not help to resolve the far more important question of how far feelings of racial superiority, engendered either by the possession of empire or by the vague sense of its being menaced by new demands, made it difficult for the British to strike the

[1] Less than half a century later with 'race-relations' at home increasingly preoccupying British opinion, it is hard to remember how 'white' Britain was in 1921 when the sight of a coloured person in the street would have been sufficiently uncommon to cause a child to stare. Official statistics took no account of race and the number of non-white residents can only be guessed at. The Negro population of London in the eighteenth century apparently disappeared during the nineteenth century and the first non-white settlements of any size – and then it was a matter of only a few hundred – occurred as the post-war result of the settlement in Britain of some coloured sailors, workers from war industries, and demobilized members of the forces. London, Liverpool, and Cardiff were the principal cities concerned. R. Glass, *Newcomers* (1960), pp. 1–2; K. L. Little, *Negroes in Britain* (1947), pp. 56–7; A. H. Richmond, *Colour Prejudice in Britain* (1954), pp. 16–17.
[2] Little, op. cit., pp. 57 ff.

proper balance between concession and firmness of rule in the new and more explosive situation that now existed overseas. It has been said that the years 1880–1920 were, in respect of India, those in which British feelings of racial superiority were most pronounced, and that a less rigid attitude was just beginning to make itself felt at this time.[1] If the straightforward paternalism of previous decades and the sentiments that inspired it seemed difficult to accept for a more sophisticated and introspective generation, what was to take its place during what was generally seen as a very long process of devolving power and responsibility to the country's wards? Any change would mean a very great degree of adaptation of British social custom and of attitude; and with no new guiding philosophy, this was going to be difficult to achieve. Preoccupation with constitutional and economic issues – understandable in the case of the old dominions – helped to prevent a full realization of the fact that the new problems of empire were largely psychological.

Despite the confidence that the peace-makers seemed to show in their willingness to see Britain assume yet further imperial burdens, one has the feeling that there was an underlying readiness to share them and that this explains the degree of concern for American opinion even at a time when the American government was at its least helpful. But by now there was hardly any evidence on the American side of a similar appreciation of the world scene. The death of Theodore Roosevelt removed the only important American statesman for whom the British Empire possessed even an equivocal appeal.

The United States had its own views of where its interests lay; it was determined to pursue them, preferably on its own; it had not rejected Wilsonianism in order to replace it by an intimacy with Great Britain alone. A historian of Anglo-American relations at the time of the Spanish war and the 'Open Door' notes about China has summarized his conclusions as follows:

> At the turn of the century, as so often in the future, there were two basic conditions for Anglo-American co-operation in international affairs. The first was that Britain should wait upon the slow development of United States opinion and policy and then endeavour to accommodate to America's unilateral decisions British interna-

[1] P. Mason, *Prospero's Magic* (1962), p. 29. This little book does make a beginning but only a beginning with the task of trying to put British attitudes to race into the general context of the country's social and cultural development during the period of empire and its decline.

tional commitments made during this waiting period. The second
was that Britain should resign from any attempt to maintain in the
American hemisphere those policies which the United States regarded as being in any way inimical to her national interests.[1]

Two decades later, the second of these desiderata was fully accepted.
The Washington conference was to find Britain equally prepared to
meet the first.

The relationship with the United States which had assumed such
importance in British eyes was to exercise an important restraining influence on British diplomacy without providing any alleviation of
Britain's burdens by precise American commitments. Isolationism
towards Europe, and anti-imperialism of a vague and unconstructive
kind in respect of the rest of the world, provided no foundations for
joint action. In the financial field – in which the alteration in the respective status of the two countries was the most marked – a measure
of co-operation was easier to achieve at any event at the central bank
level.[2] But the general tenor of United States economic policy with its
emphasis on protectionism was not well designed to enable New York
to fulfil London's old role as a regulating factor in world finance. With
Britain's war debts and the doubtful prospect of recovering what was
due to Britain from others, and with the need to make structural
changes in the economy at home, Britain was not in a position to resume her old sway.

The position of Britain in 1921 was for these and other reasons quite
different in fact from what it appeared to be outwardly. Despite the
severe labour troubles of the deflationary period that followed the immediate post-war boom, Britain might seem to much of the tortured
continent a haven of solidity. For its combination of energy, experience,
and sheer ability, Lloyd George's coalition government had few equals
among preceding British governments and certainly none among its
peacetime successors, but it had little luck.

The British position in the Victorian high noon had rested upon a
combination of circumstances now fast disappearing. To be at the
centre of a world-wide network of trade and finance and at the same

[1] R. G. Neale, *Great Britain and United States Expansion, 1898–1900* (Michigan State University Press, 1966), p. 215.
[2] Lester V. Chandler, *Benjamin Strong, Central Banker* (Washington, D.C., 1958), ch. VII. The British scene was dominated by the figure of Montagu Norman who became governor of the Bank of England in 1920 and held the post until 1944. See Andrew Boyle, *Montagu Norman* (1967).

time close to the great concentration of wealth in Europe, with the more developed markets that this represented, was to have a situation at once rewarding and precarious. Given stability and prosperity in Europe and conditions overseas encouraging to investment and trade, it might be possible to concentrate upon the essential process of adapting the country to a high rate of technological change. But if commercial opportunities were reduced by war, revolution, or policies of autarky whether adopted for economic or ideological reasons, the prospects would be dimmer. Nor as we have seen could Britain hope to create out of her Empire a closed economic system that could enable her to ignore developments in the rest of the world. It was thus right that Lloyd George should attempt to undo the damage that the war and the Russian revolution had done to the fabric of European commerce and finance, and to an imperial policy designed to elicit the maximum of consent and so make the minimum demands on British resources for merely security purposes.

But both in Europe and overseas this involved effort and risk, and Britain in 1921 was understandably not in the mood for either. The Victorian high noon of prosperity had not spread its benefits evenly; there were now voices at home as well as overseas pressing for a more equitable distribution of wealth and opportunity. Britain was indeed entering upon a period in which questions of internal reform and of the balance of classes at home would form the major theme of politics and dominate the issues between the parties. There was neither a doctrine to justify a more active external policy nor a will to pursue one had it been enunciated. It might seem that in 1921 the British role in the world had been triumphantly reasserted. But despite the illusion conveyed by the maps and tables the meridian had been passed; the final liquidation of Britain's world power – the Imperial Sunset – lay only fifty years ahead.[1]

---

[1] In 1921 Major Clement Attlee was mayor of Stepney, Captain Harold Macmillan was working in the family business, and Harold Wilson was five years old.

GREENLAND

C A N A D A

Vancouver I.

BRITISH
ISLES

NEWFOUNDLAND

UNITED STATES

.Bermuda

Gibralt

Bahamas

ATLANTIC

PACIFIC

Br.
Honduras

Jamaica

Trinidad
Br. GUIANA

GAMBIA

SIERRA
LEONE

OCEA

SOUTH
AMERICA

Ascension

St. Hel

OCEAN

Pitcairn I.

Tristan da Cunha

Falkland Is.

St. Georgia

G R E A T   S O U

British E

The

ARCTIC OCEAN

ASIA

Cyprus

PACIFIC

OCEAN

INDIA   BURMA
Hong Kong

ADEN
Socotra   CEYLON
BR. SOMALILAND   BORNEO   NEW
BRITISH   MALAYA   GUINEA
EAST AFRICA
Zanzibar Seychelles

INDIAN   Fiji Is.

Mauritius

TRANSVAAL   AUSTRALIA
NATAL   OCEAN
ORANGE FREE STATE

NY   NEW
                                  ZEALAND
            TASMANIA

ERN   OCEAN

connecting Empire countries   ///// Boer Republics

e 1897

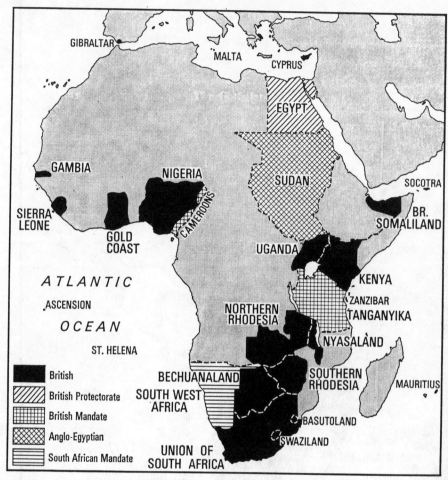

GIBRALTAR

MALTA

CYPRUS

EGYPT

GAMBIA

NIGERIA

SOCOTRA

SIERRA
LEONE

GOLD
COAST

CAMEROONS

SUDAN

BR.
SOMALILAND

UGANDA

KENYA

ATLANTIC

ASCENSION

OCEAN

ST. HELENA

NORTHERN
RHODESIA

ZANZIBAR
TANGANYIKA

NYASALAND

MAURITIUS

British

British Protectorate

British Mandate

Anglo-Egyptian

South African Mandate

BECHUANALAND

SOUTH WEST
AFRICA

SOUTHERN
RHODESIA

UNION OF
SOUTH AFRICA

BASUTOLAND

SWAZILAND

The peace settlement in Africa

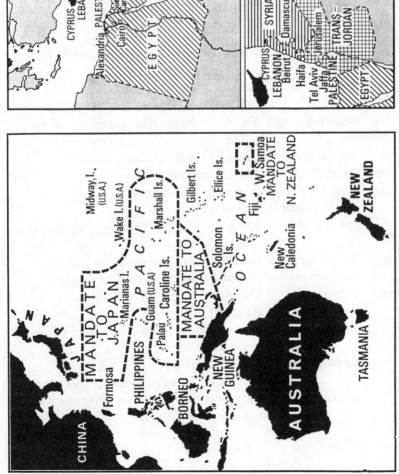

The peace settlement in the Middle East

The peace settlement in the Pacific

CHRONOLOGY 1897–1921

1897	March	Milner appointed high commissioner in South Africa
	June	Queen Victoria's Diamond Jubilee
		Colonial conference
1898	July	Minto appointed governor-general of Canada
	August	Curzon appointed viceroy of India
	September	Fashoda crisis
1899	October	Outbreak of Boer war
	February 5	First Hay–Pauncefote treaty
1900	June	Boxer rising
	September–October	General election
1901	January 1	Inauguration of Commonwealth of Australia
	January 22	Death of Queen Victoria. Accession of Edward VII
	September 14	Theodore Roosevelt, president of the U.S.A.
	November 18	Second Hay–Pauncefote treaty
1902	January 30	Anglo-Japanese alliance
	May 31	Treaty of Vereeniging
	June–August	Colonial conference
	July 12	Balfour succeeds Salisbury as prime minister
1903	September 18	Resignation of Joseph Chamberlain
	October 20	Alaska boundary arbitration award
1904	February	Outbreak of Russo-Japanese war
	April 8	Anglo-French *entente*
	May 4	Treasury minute on committee of imperial defence
	October	Dogger Bank affair
		Fisher becomes first sea lord (till 1910)
	December	Earl Grey becomes governor-general of Canada (till 1911)

1905	March 31	William II lands at Tangier
	April	Milner leaves South Africa; succeeded by Selborne
	August 12	Anglo-Japanese alliance renewed
	September 5	Peace of Portsmouth
	October	First dreadnought laid down
	November	Curzon succeeded as viceroy by Minto
	December 5	Sir Henry Campbell-Bannerman, liberal prime minister
1906	January–March	Algeciras conference
	January 31	Grey authorizes Anglo-French staff talks
	January–February	General election, liberal landslide
	December 6	Transvaal gets self-government
1907	April–May	Colonial conference
	June 5	Orange Free State gets self-government
	August 31	Anglo-Russian *entente*
1908	April 5	Asquith, prime minister
	March 4	Taft, president of the U.S.A.
	October 5	Austria annexes Bosnia-Herzegovina
1909	April 29	Lloyd George's 'People's Budget'
	May 25	Indian Councils act. (Morley–Minto reforms)
	September 20	South Africa act
1910	January–February	General election, liberal majority cut
	April	Parliament bill introduced
	May 6	Death of Edward VII. Accession of George V
	May 31	Union of South Africa inaugurated; Botha, prime minister
	November 23	Minto succeeded as viceroy by Hardinge
	December	General election, no change
1911	May–June	Imperial conference
	July 1	*Panther* at Agadir
	July 21	Lloyd George's Mansion House speech

1911	August 10	Parliament act
	September	Canadian general election; Laurier defeated; Borden, prime minister
		Italian war with Turkey (to October 1912)
	October 23	Churchill, first lord of the admiralty
	November	Balfour resigns as conservative leader; Bonar Law succeeds November 13
	December 12	George V at Delhi durbar
1912	February	Haldane mission to Berlin
	April 11	Third Home Rule bill introduced
	October–December	First Balkan war
1913	March 4	Woodrow Wilson, president of the U.S.A.
	June–August	Second Balkan war
1914	March	Curragh 'mutiny'
	June 28	Assassination of Francis Ferdinand
	July 21–24	Buckingham Palace conference
	August 4	Britain declares war on Germany
	August 5	Kitchener, secretary of state for war
	September 18	Home Rule act
	October–November	First battle of Ypres
1915	March 18	Allied agreement on Constantinople
		Dardanelles campaign begins
	April 25	Treaty of London (Italy)
		Landings at Gallipoli
	May 23	Italy enters the war
	May 25	Asquith forms coalition government
	October 27	Hughes becomes prime minister of Australia
	December 15	Haig, commander-in-chief
	December 23	Robertson, C.I.G.S.
1916	January	Final withdrawals from Gallipoli
	April 4	Hardinge succeeded as viceroy by Chelmsford
	April–May	Second battle of Ypres
	April 24	Easter rising begins in Dublin

1916	May 16	Sykes–Picot agreement
	May 31	Battle of Jutland
	June 5	Death of Kitchener
	July–November	Battle of the Somme
	November 14	Hughes forms coalition government
	December 16	Lloyd George becomes prime minister; war cabinet formed
	December	Indian National congress demands full self-government for India
1917	March 15	Russian Czar Nicholas II abdicates
	March–May	Imperial war conference
	April 2	United States declares war on Germany Crisis of submarine war
	April–May	Nivelle offensive
	July–November	Passchendaele
	August 20	British government accepts responsible government as goal of constitutional development in India
	October 31	Balfour declaration (Palestine)
	November 7	Bolshevik revolution
	December 9	Allenby takes Jerusalem
1918	January 8	President Wilson's 'fourteen points'
	February 16	Sir Henry Wilson, C.I.G.S.
	March 3	Treaty of Brest-Litovsk
	March–July	Final German offensive
	March 26	Foch appointed to co-ordinate allied armies
	June–August	Imperial war conference
	July 6	Montagu–Chelmsford report Intervention in Russia begins
	August	Final allied offensive begins
	November 11	Armistice
	December 14	General election, coalition victory
1919	January 10	Full cabinet restored
	January 12	Informal opening of peace conference at Paris
	January 21	Irish Republic proclaimed

1919	March 21	Bela Kun takes power in Hungary (till August 1)
	April 13	Amritsar incident
	May 1	Text of peace treaty handed to Germans
	May 26	Allied note to Kolchak
	May 29	German counter-proposals
	June 16	Allied reply to Germans
	June 28	Treaty of Versailles
	July	Kolchak's retreat begins
	August–September	British troops withdrawn from northern Russia
	August 27	Death of Botha; Smuts, prime minister
	September 10	Treaty of St Germain (Austria)
	November 19	Treaty of Trianon (Hungary)
		U.S. senate rejects treaty of Versailles
	December 23	Government of India act
1920	January 10	Ratification of Versailles treaty
	January 16	First meeting of League of Nations council
	January 21	End of peace conference
	April 19–26	San Remo conference
		Britain gets mandate for Palestine
	July 7	Borden retires; Meighen, prime minister
	August 1	Non-cooperation begins in India
	August 10	Treaty of Sèvres (Turkey)
		Battle of Warsaw
	November	End of allied intervention in Russia
	December 23	Government of Ireland act
1921	February 9	Government of India act comes into operation
	March 4	Harding, president of the U.S.A.
	March 16	Anglo-Russian trade treaty
	March 18	Treaty of Riga
	April 2	Chelmsford succeeded as viceroy by Reading
	June–August	Imperial conference

1921 June 24   Lloyd George invites de Valera to
                    negotiate

     July 9   Anglo-Irish truce announced

     July 11   President Harding summons Washington conference

     December 6 Anglo-Irish treaty signed

INDEX

Page and footnote numbers printed in italics refer to biographical details of the subject of the entry.

INDEX

Sylvester, A. J., 287 n., 332 n.
Syria, 242, 258, 261, 264, 297–8, 299, 301

Tanganyika, *see* German East Africa
Tangier, 25
Tardieu, A., 288
Tariff reform, 16, 47 n., 93–100, 126–7,
129, 137, 138, 144, 166–7
Tashkent–Orenburg Railway, 72 n.
Temperley, Harold, 59 n.
Teheran, 165, 325 n.
'Ten Year Rule', 350
The American Commonwealth (Lord Bryce),
43 n., 54
The Commonwealth of Nations (Lionel Curtis),
122 n.
The Expansion of England (Sir John Seeley), 41
The League of Nations: a Practical Suggestion
(Smuts), 292 n.
The New Machiavelli (H. G. Wells), 111, 160 n.
The Problem of the Commonwealth (Lionel
Curtis), 122 n., 215
The Round Table, 132–3
The State, 132, 133 n.
The Times, 21 n., 57 n., 84, 246, 276 n.
Thrace, 308
Tibet, 90, 108, 197, 284
Tigris–Euphrates valley, 344
Tilley, Sir J., 337 n.
Toronto, anti-home rule association in, 29
Toulon, 74
Toynbee, Arnold J., 294 n.
Transcaspia, 197, 327
Transcaspian Railway, 25 n.
Transjordan, 301, 302
Transvaal, *see* South Africa
Treaties:
Anglo-Portuguese Treaty, 1661, 70 n.
Clayton–Bulwer Treaty, 1850, 87
Mediterranean Agreements, 1887, 25 n.,
74
Anglo-Portuguese Agreement, 1899, 70 n.
Anglo-German Treaty *re* Partition of
Portuguese Empire (secret), 1898, 70 n.,
125
Anglo-German Agreement over China,
16 October 1900, 101
Hay–Pauncefote Treaty, 18 November
1901, 87, 106
Treaty of Vereeniging, 31 May 1902, 123,
128 n., 317
Anglo-Japanese Alliance: treaties signed,
30 January 1902 and 12 August 1905,
16, 18, 70, 71, 75, 100–4, 106, 108, 136,
148, 149, 158, 170, 278, 319, 331,
334–43
Anglo-French Entente, 8 April 1904, 53,
61, 70, 71, 108, 125, 172
Anglo-Russian Agreement, 31 August
1907, 61, 70, 71, 73 n., 74, 108, 119,
125, 141, 163, 164, 178, 196, 310 n.
Anglo-French Agreement, 1912, 70 n.,
159

Anglo-French Agreement on Naval Co-
operation, February 1913, 153–4
Agreement of 12 March 1915 (France,
Russia and Britain), 204
Treaty of London, 28 April 1915, (secret)
between Allies and Italy, 204
Sykes–Picot Agreement, 1916, 260, 261,
262, 277, 280, 297, 298
Agreement of 12 February 1916 on
Belgian independence (France, Russia,
Britain), 206 n.
'Secret Treaties' (during First World
War), 182
Treaty of Brest-Litovsk, 1918, 269 n.
Treaty of Versailles, 28 June 1919,
278–9, 281, 285, 286, 288 n., 289, 290,
291, 295, 314, 323, 351
Anglo-Persian Treaty, 9 August 1919,
310–11 n.
Treaty of St Germain (Allies and
Austria), 10 September 1919, 285
Guarantee Treaties, 9 October 1919,
288, 324
Treaty of Neuilly (Allies and Bulgaria),
27 November 1919, 285
Treaty of San Remo, April 1920, 298
Treaty of the Trianon (Allies and
Hungary), 4 June 1920, 285
Treaty of Sèvres (Allies and Turkey),
10 August 1920, 286, 304, 308 n., 309
Treaty between Russia and Afghanistan,
February 1921, 310 n.
Anglo-Russian Commercial Agreement,
16 March 1921, 329
Peace of Riga, 18 March 1921, 329
Anglo-Irish Treaty, December 1921,
314, 315, 317, 318
Locarno Treaties, 1925, 117
Treaty of Rome, 25 March 1957, 1
Treitschke, 113
Trevelyan, Sir George, 231 n.
Trevelyan, Charles, 140 n.
Triple Alliance (Germany, Austria, Italy),
75
Tripoli, 153
Trotsky L., 275 n., 326 n.
Turkish Empire (Ottoman Empire), 18,
73, 141, 163, 165, 182, 194, 198, 204,
205, 207, 240, 242, 254–60, 265 n., 266,
274, 286, 295, 296, 298, 300, 302–5, 307,
308, 310
Turkistan, 325 n.
Tyrrell, Lord (William Tyrrell), *81 n.*, 206

Ukraine, 328
Ulster, 114, 131, 166, 167, 168, 176, 218,
317; *see also* Ireland
Union of Democratic Control, 125 n., 276 n.
United Europe, 3, 5, 13
United Kingdom:
Army, 22–3, 34, 39, 66–9, 72, 79, 80, 85,
88–90, 103, 108, 120, 128 n., 129, 142,
146, 150, 153–4, 159, 167, 174, 179,

A